The Beginnings of Capitalism in Central Europe

This book is part of the Peter Lang Humanities list.
Every volume is peer reviewed and meets
the highest quality standards for content and production.

PETER LANG
New York • Bern • Berlin
Brussels • Vienna • Oxford • Warsaw

Lawrence Krader

The Beginnings of Capitalism in Central Europe

Edited and translated by Cyril Levitt

PETER LANG
New York • Bern • Berlin
Brussels • Vienna • Oxford • Warsaw

Library of Congress Cataloging-in-Publication Data

Names: Krader, Lawrence, author. | Levitt, Cyril, editor. | Levitt, Cyril, translator.
Title: The beginnings of capitalism in Central Europe / Lawrence Krader;
Cyril Levitt, [editor and translator].
Other titles: Anfänge des Kapitalismus in Mitteleuropa. English
Description: New York: Peter Lang, 2020.
Includes bibliographical references and index.
Identifiers: LCCN 2020016058 (print) | LCCN 2020016059 (ebook)
ISBN 978-1-4331-7210-6 (hardback) | ISBN 978-1-4331-7207-6 (ebook pdf)
ISBN 978-1-4331-7208-3 (epub) | ISBN 978-1-4331-7209-0 (mobi)
Subjects: LCSH: ABC | DEF | XYZ.
Classification: LCC HC290.795.C3 K7313 2020 (print) | LCC HC290.795.C3 (ebook) |
DDC 330.9430009/03—dc23
LC record available at https://lccn.loc.gov/2020016058
LC ebook record available at https://lccn.loc.gov/2020016059
DOI 10.3726/b15916

Bibliographic information published by **Die Deutsche Nationalbibliothek.**
Die Deutsche Nationalbibliothek lists this publication in the "Deutsche Nationalbibliografie"; detailed bibliographic data are available on the Internet at http://dnb.d-nb.de/.

80 Broad Street, 5th floor, New York, NY 10004
www.peterlang.com

Table of Contents

Illustrations

Eight illustrations from the "Ständebuch" by Hans Sachs and Jost Amman

Illustrations are found on pages 292-309

Tables

About the Author and This Book

Cyril Levitt

Lawrence Krader (1920–1998) was an American philosopher and anthropologist whose fields of interest included ethnographic and ethnological studies of Central Asia including those of the Altaic-speaking peoples of the Steppes. He was the world's leading expert on the ethnological notebooks of Karl Marx, which he transcribed from the original notes and published under the same title in 1972. As a philosopher he studied with Morris Raphael Cohen at the City College of New York (CCNY) and at the University of Chicago, served as a research assistant to Alfred Tarski at CCNY and, while in Chicago, studied for a year with Rudolf Carnap. Before his enlistment in the US Merchant Marine during World War II he was influenced by Franz Boas and his students at Columbia University and developed an interest in anthropology. He received his doctorate in that discipline from Harvard University in 1954. From 1972 to 1982 he was the Director of the *Institut für Ethnologie* at the *Freie Universität zu Berlin*.[1]

The focus of this book concerns an aspect of the question of periodization in human history. There have been many attempts to classify stages, epochs, cultures and civilizations from the time of the ancient Greeks down to the present in Western thought and in many indigenous non-Western traditions as well. Krader's interest in this issue can be traced back at least to the time in which he worked as an assistant to Karl August Wittfogel at the Far Eastern and Russian Institute at the University of Washington in the late 1940s.[2] Wittfogel had been concerned with the specific configuration of ancient Chinese society as an Oriental despotism which he argued was centred around the state control and management of hydraulics, irrigation and the supply of water. Wittfogel also believed the concept of Oriental Despotism applied to Ancient Egypt, Mesopotamia, classical Greece and Rome, the Moghul Empire and the Incas in Peru before the Spanish conquest. And he argued that contemporary Soviet and Chinese communist regimes conformed in many ways to the paradigm of Oriental despotism. Krader preferred to follow a line different from both that of Wittfogel and of orthodox Marxism with its fixed stages of human development. Through his empirical work on the Altaic-speaking peoples of the Central Asian Steppes and his prodigious efforts in transcribing, editing and introducing Marx's ethnological notebooks, Krader counterposed the concept of the Asiatic mode of production (to which Marx had turned his attention in the 5 or 6 years prior to his death) to Wittfogel's notion of Oriental or hydraulic despotism.[3] It can be argued that Krader was no less critical of Marxist orthodoxy than Wittfogel but he used Marx as the basis for his critique of Marxism, not unlike Karl Korsch, another one of his senior colleagues whose work, *Marxism and Philosophy*, employed the same critical approach. But Krader's use of the concept of the Asiatic mode of production was more developed and nuanced than that of Marx as it was informed by a century of empirical work, including his own. He was able to apply the concept to most of the societies which Wittfogel had seen as hydraulic despotisms. But his focus was not primarily on the state's totalitarian control and management of vital resources but rather on the movement from the communal to the civil condition, which includes the formation of a division of the community into social classes, the very beginnings of a parcelling out of the private and public spheres and of the formation of the state. In doing this he called attention to the question of the form and substance of labour as a key element in the transitional communal-social form of production, a label which removes the ethnocentric and geocentric focus of Marx's original concept.[4]

Krader's extensive work on the Asiatic mode of production was related to the problem of the periodization in human history in an important way, for it represented the transition from a communally organized mode of life without systematic class distinctions, with the means of production in common, with a rudimentary division of labour based on age and sex, without a state and hence without a separation of a private and public sector. In other words, it was not a civil condition of society.[5]

Having spent several decades elucidating features of the Asiatic mode of production, in this current book he addressed the beginnings of capitalism in Central Europe. If the transition from the communal to the communal-social formation of society represented a major break in human history for Krader, the development of capitalism in Europe represented a transition from feudalism, arguably a uniquely European phenomenon (with the possible exception of Japan), to capitalism with its beginnings in Europe but its ultimate extension to the international economic order. Krader knew his Marx and he appreciated Marx's work even as he recognized deep contradictions, false steps and incomplete thoughts, which Krader increasingly took up in his various publications. His first posthumously published book *Labor and Value* (Krader, 2003) was an ambitious attempt to reconcile objective theories of value from Aristotle to Marx, with the subjective theories of the British and Austrian schools. The reader of this current work will appreciate Krader's recognition and critique of Marx's understanding of the beginnings of capitalism in Europe, as indeed he also recognized and criticized the contribution of the other great writers on the origins of capitalism. And here and there Krader ventures into the territory of those who looked more broadly at the origins of capitalism from the 14th to the 16th century in Europe. But his true focus was narrower than all of Europe.

In writing this book he was primarily interested in the beginnings of capitalist development in the mostly German-speaking areas of Central Europe. The argument that he has made in the pages that follow is based on the writings, illustrations, drawings, engravings and other evidence from that early time. Furthermore, he provides a substantial review of most of the leading 19th and 20th century thinkers who occupied themselves with the question of the beginnings of capitalism in Europe. Krader was also careful to distinguish sporadic appearances of capitalist elements from their later systematization from the 14th to the 16th century. With regard to his primary focus, that is, the beginnings of capitalism in *Central Europe*, he elaborated in some detail on specific areas of economic life—mining, metallurgy, metal working and smelting, coinage, clock-making, shipbuilding and maritime navigation, printing and publishing, as well as trade, commerce and credit. These branches of industry and commerce were strongly influential in German-speaking Central Europe in the beginnings of capitalism, at first sporadically, and then systematically. But even in these few industries and in trade and commerce, the development and systematization of capitalist forms and relations were complicated and mediated. No one individual, no one theory, no one element can encompass the beginnings of development of which Krader writes: "We consider the historical course of this development as complicated and take a position against those who have tried to simplify it." At the same time, the thinkers whom Krader extensively cites contributed something to our understanding of the complexity of the beginnings of capitalist development and systematization.

There is an odd symmetry between this work on the beginnings of capitalism in Central Europe and his numerous books and articles on the Asiatic mode of production. The development of the Asiatic mode of production, or the communal-social form of economic formation, constituted the foundation for civil society almost everywhere. In this sense it was a series of indigenous developments among indigenous peoples in different parts of the world largely unconnected with one another in time and space. The beginning of the development of capitalism in Central Europe was part of what was later to become a global phenomenon, originating first in Europe.[6]

In the Festschrift in honour of his 75th birthday, Krader (1995) denied that he had ever been a Marxist. His criticisms of Marx, especially in his first two posthumously published works, *Labor and Value* (2003) and *Noetics* (2010) are more sharply critical of Marx in different ways. In *Noetics* especially, his reconsideration of the theory of nature in relation to the human order, represents a break with materialism, or rather a reformulation of the relation of the material order to other orders of nature.[7] In this current book, reference is made to the advancement of Krader's thinking regarding nature and materialism in his 2010 posthumously published work in comparison to the position taken in this volume.

In addition to the problem of periodization in human history to which this book is a contribution, it has also taken up the matter of the form and substance of freedom from the tradition of Goethe, Hegel, Marx, and other classical thinkers. For Krader, as for these other thinkers, the advance of capitalism as a system related to the development of formal freedom, concretely with political freedom and equality in law, in the freedom of the individual and the class of social labour to contract with the agents of capital for the sale of their labour power, in the freedom to move from location to location, from one employer to another. In the development of these formal freedoms, the forces pushing for their realization encountered resistance not only from the feudal authorities, the Church and other institutions tied to the old order, but from the organizations of labour themselves—the guilds in their various forms and constellations. But Krader refers to the question of the substance of freedom which had not been realized in the course of capitalist development but does not speculate further about it. He simply follows Goethe who lamented that it had not been attained in the new order and allowed himself to dream about its realization by millions at the conclusion of *Faust*. One of Krader's achievements in this volume is to have clearly distinguished between form and substance with regard to the freedom of social labour. It is a book that can be appreciated and enjoyed as a clarification of our understanding of the complexity of the beginnings of capitalism in Central Europe, by extension to Europe as a whole and ultimately to the contemporary international order.

Notes

1. For further biographical information on Krader please consult: D. Schorkowitz (1995, pp. xi–xxiv) L. Krader (2010, pp. xi–xxiii); S. Sander, C. Levitt, and N. McLaughlin. 2017; C. Levitt and S. Sander (eds.) (2017, pp. 3–53); and 'Reply to Krader in Context' in this volume.
2. Although his interest in evolution in general can be traced back to his many trips in his youth to the Museum of Natural History in the City of New York.
3. "The history of the formation of the civil society and the state among the ancient Aztecs and Incas, the Yoruba and Asanti, the ancient Greek, Slavic and Germanic peoples, Mongols and Turks, follows the same course, which at first led to the development of the Asiatic mode of production among them. The opposition of the interests of the individual and the collectivity is the means of dissolution of the latter. Civil society and the state issue forth not from the dissolution of the ancient gentes, clans and village communities, but from the opposition between the class-individuals and the communal forms, which continue to exist long after civil society and the state have been formed." L. Krader (1979), *A Treatise of Social Labor*, p. 184. On the notion of class-individuality see Marx's interpolation to Henry Sumner Maine's 'Lectures on the Early History of Institutions' in Krader (1972, p. 329).
4. In his book, *The Asiatic Mode of Production*, Krader (1975, p. 114) explicitly criticized Wittfogel's identification of the Oriental society with modern communist states on account of the state's ownership of the land as follows: "The argument is based upon the identification of the relation of ownership and the mode of production. This is the error of taking *pars pro toto*, the part for the whole. The fact that the State owned all the land in the Oriental society and in modern socialist countries is a superficial analogy; the modes of production of the two systems are totally different: in particular, the relations between labor and capital." He continued his critique of Wittfogel in a long footnote on the following page of that same book: "K. A. Wittfogel, *Oriental Despotism*, made the hydraulic interpretation of the Oriental society into the central one; thereby he focused his attention on the category of the despotism, the political side of the problem, as opposed to the category of the society as a whole ... He further made the categories of despotism and totalitarianism into economic structures ... He proceeds from the State to the society and thence to the political economy." (op. cit., p. 115n)
5. It should be noted that the Asiatic mode of production is an economic formation and not a society. For Krader, a large variety of different societies have been identified with this organization of production. Nevertheless, those societies in which the Asiatic mode of production prevails are those in which we can discover the beginnings of the parceling out of social classes, the formation of the state and the first appearances of the elaboration of a public and private sphere, however weak the latter development might be. For Krader, it has to be emphasized, the focus on the so-called Asiatic mode is justified insofar as it represents the transitional form of economic organization in those societies which are in the process of development from the primitive communal to the civil condition of the humankind.
6. Max Weber's thesis developed out of a concern with regard to capitalism's geographical home in Europe rather than in China which in the 16th century was more advanced in science and technology than Europe. This led Weber to look for a 'spiritual' impetus for capitalist development in the Protestant Reformation, more narrowly, in the psychological impact of Calvinist theology on its followers which in turn greatly impacted their economic behavior. Krader did not

gainsay Weber's thesis but he did not consider it the major force in the beginning of capitalist development.

7. For further discussions of these matters please see: C. Levitt and S. Sander (eds.). *Beyond the Juxtaposition of Nature and Culture: Lawrence Krader, Interdisciplinarity, and the Concept of the Human Being*. Peter Lang Publishers New York 2017.

Preface

Krader in Context

David Levine

Historians—and their historical studies—are products of their own time. This is, of course, a truth universally acknowledged. Lawrence Krader's study of the beginnings of capitalism in Central Europe is very much a work of mid-century scholarship even though it was first published in German in the 1990s. Readers of Krader's essay will come to appreciate what has been gained as a result of academic scholarship concerned with early-modern German capitalism and industrialization. What they will mostly learn is that the results of archival research "in the field"—provide us with a complicated understanding of the uneven development of early-modern capitalism and industrialization. But, perhaps most significantly, the results of this new research shift the focus away from formal documentation and towards the wider context of social relations.

Reading this manuscript gave me a sense of déjà vu—it was eerily reminiscent of Maurice Dobb's *Studies in the Development of Capitalism*.[1] Both works concentrate on the origins of capitalism in the formal relations between capital and labour; neither work gives much credence to the agricultural origins of industry, consumer demand, urbanization, historical demography, transportation, technology, and, in particular, energy sources. Indeed, Krader's essay—like Dobb's—is remarkable for the way in which a 21st century student of "the transition" recognizes the absence of the gigantic historiography which is pertinent to this subject. It could be said that contemporary studies render Krader's vision almost unrecognizable or, at the very least, anachronistic.

At the heart of this difference is the way in which the "transition debate" spawned an almost entirely new subject—social history. Nowhere, perhaps, is this difference made clearer than in a simple comparison between the sources and references in Krader's essay and those provided by the more than three dozen authors whose essays have been collected in the three volumes of *Germany: A New Social and Economic History.*[2] Each of these essays is buttressed by dozens and dozens of footnotes, almost-all of which refer to studies published in the 1960s, 1970s, 1980s, and 1990s when the series itself was published. One can only imagine how much denser, wide-ranging, and intensive the bibliography would be in a revised publication.

Capitalism—buying low and selling high—was hardly a novel invention of the post-feudal, early-modern period. What was new about early-modern capitalism was the ability to harness labour-power in a systematic fashion to the production of both goods and services. Of course, there were precursors to the factory system—the famous (and perhaps apocryphal) workshop organized by Jack of Newbury or the Venice Arsenal (and its English, Spanish, French and Dutch contemporary competitors) are pertinent examples of pre-modern, large-scale, integrated works—but what was new and revolutionary was the way in which inanimate energy made it possible to replicate these methods spreading across the economy into new sites of production, from brewing to publishing.

Moreover, the very nature of the questions asked by the "post-Krader" generations of scholars has changed. Perhaps the foremost difference can be neatly summarized as follows: a modern industrial economy required not only abundant supplies of cheap energy but also a method of transporting coal from its point-of-production to its point-of-use. The key to this issue is that the substitution of inanimate energy for other sources—wind and waterpower as well as human- and animal-power—opened vast new horizons for production.[3]

Bulk commodities were liable to extra-ordinary transportation surcharges. In the South Tyneside coal industry, for example, there were radical and revolutionary technological innovations before the Industrial Revolution—first, in place of carriages, wooden waggon ways and then iron-flanged wheels and rails criss-crossed Whickham parish, the centre of production; next came the advent of steam-powered engines—used for draining pits from the 1690s.[4] These early machines were built according to the design of Thomas Newcomen. Then, in the third quarter of the 18th-century, the internal combustion models vastly increased efficiency while constant tinkering with the Boulton/Watt design led to massive increases in efficiency—three-fold in the next thirty years. Yet, it was only in the 1820s that these transportation and energy systems were married in the most characteristic technology of the Industrial Revolution—the railways.[5]

From the 1500s onwards, the north-eastern English coal-economy grew largely as a result of innovations which were built upon factor endowments of cheap, water-based transportation from the mines to their primary markets. Statistics portray a stark difference between English and German experiences of substituting inanimate energy from coal. In the early 19th-century, the English mined 30,000,000 tons of coal; German mines produced 1,700,000 tons. German mines did not reach the English 1830s-level until the last quarter of the 19th century. It was only around 1900 that German production equalled the output of English mines. What began as a gigantic divergence which was crucial in the beginning decades in the third quarter of the 18th century converged—but only after more than a century into the Industrial Revolution.

The key point here is that Germany—like China, today's largest coal-producer—had vast supplies of coal but lacked the wherewithal to move that resource to market. The result was that in early-modern Germany—just as in Imperial China and, more generally, continental Europe and the USA—production was not modernized or, to put it more succinctly, "revolutionized". The Industrial Revolution came to Germany in response to English competition that threatened local, proto-industrial producers with technological obsolescence—this threat was altogether modern because these traditional entrepreneurs had to innovate or die. And the Germans did innovate—and, in comparison to the English, their primary innovation was to apply engineering studies (largely based in new educational institutions) to production routines.

In the earlier "proto-industrial" economy of the early-modern period, capitalists had access to an almost-unlimited supply of under-employed labour which could be used to undertake repetitive processes. There is now a vast literature on this subject which began with the publication of Franklin Mendels' pioneering, 1971 essay.[6] While his original argument has been repeatedly contested, the relevant point in relation to Krader's essay is that Mendels drew attention to the linkages between the labour supply of under-employed cottagers—men and women, girls and boys—and the demands of urban producers who "put-out" materials to cottagers in the "Verlagssystem". Mendels argued that "proto-industry" (perhaps more accurately described as "cottage industry") was the first phase of industrialization but critics of his thesis have cited numerous examples that this was not the usual route—in fact, a great many rural industries rose and fell in the unredeemed time of "the transition".[7] With regard to Krader's arguments, Mendels' thesis is significant because it points to a blind-spot—Krader relied heavily on urban, guild documentation whereas cottage industries were usually set up to side-step the conservative labour regulations of these institutions.

Krader's reliance on formal, urban documentation—as opposed to the informal and largely unregulated evasions of their surveillance mechanisms—significantly narrows the scope of his vision of capitalist enterprise in early-modern Germany. Even in the evidence he has consulted regarding mining—gold, silver and copper—in the south-eastern Saxon Erzgebirge borderland with Bohemia, his primary source of documentation comes from formal sources and, of course, the famous contemporary writings of Georgius Agricola [Georg Bauer] (*De re Metallica*) or the business dealings of the Fugger Bank. Yet in the thirty years before its publication in 1993, there were numerous scholarly works which delved into the particularities of the social history of mining but none of these found their way into Krader's essay. Indeed, the comparison with English economic historiography on this subject is quite notable by its absence.

The significance of these omissions is that for a 21st century reader, this essay is incomplete. Whether it's labour organization or, even more significantly, labour supply, the micro-variations in experience are largely outside the scope of Krader's research. In a sense, this narrow scope gives his work its anachronistic flavour. But it also gives the reader a sense of what an earlier generation of library-based scholarship overlooked because it did not attend to the particularities of early-modern capitalist industries. Learning about these particularities and exceptions has been the province of social historians whose scholarly output can be likened to a tsunami which has overwhelmed the earlier historiography that privileged progress over regression or industrial involution. To be sure, some local success-stories provided the lineage of later developments—especially in regard to capital accumulation and marketing. What better example of this point are the family histories of Max Weber and Friedrich Engels? In Weber's family there were connections with proto-industry, their wealth had been based on putting-out thread to the cottagers in the Westphalian textile industry while Engels was the child of a Barmen/Wuppertal industrialist who was a partner in a Manchester spinning factory. Did the Engels' factory-spun yarn supply raw materials for the Weber's cottage weavers? Of course, neither Weber nor Engels is remembered today for these connections but their ascent into the upper bourgeoisie was founded upon wealth accumulated in the transition from early-modern to modern capitalist industrialization. Yet for every Weber or Engels who successfully benefitted from the inheritance of cultural capital in this way, there were countless others whose experiences were less remarkable—many (most?) experienced downwards mobility as their businesses were overwhelmed by the revolutionary changes of the transition from localized production to international competition.

Notes

1. M. Dobb, *Studies in the Development of Capitalism*. Routledge London 1946.
2. B. Scribner, ed., *Germany: A New Social and Economic History*. Volume 1, 1450–1630. London Arnold 1996. S. Ogilvie, ed., *Germany: A New Social and Economic History*. Volume 2, 1630–1800. London Arnold 1996. S. Ogilvie and R. Overy, eds., *Germany: A New Social and Economic History*. Volume 3, Since 1800. London Arnold 1996.
3. E. A. Wrigley, *Energy and the English Industrial Revolution*. Cambridge University Press Cambridge 2010.
4. D. Levine and K. Wrightson, *Wickham: An Industrial Society in the Pre-Industrial World*. Oxford University Press Oxford 1991.
5. M. W. Flinn and D. Stoker, *The History of the British Coal Industry*. Volume 2, 1700–1830. Oxford University Press Oxford 1985.
6. F. Mendels, "'Proto-industrialization': the first phase of the industrialization process", *Journal of Economic History*, 31, 1971, 241–261.
7. J. Schlumbohm, "Proto-industrialization' as a research strategy and a historical period—a balance sheet", in S. C. Ogilvie and M. Cerman, (eds.) *European Proto-Industrialization*. Cambridge University Press Cambridge 1996, 12–22.

Reply to Krader in Context

Cyril Levitt

In the Author's Foreword to *The Beginnings of Capitalism in Central Europe* Lawrence Krader describes the focus of his work as follows: "The present work concerns the beginning of the capitalist system and of modern bourgeois society in Central Europe, primarily in the German-speaking region and is presented as a contribution to the solution of an essential part of the question of periodization in human history. Yet, this book is not offered as a history text." In spite of this specific focus, I thought it would be interesting to ask a scholar of late medieval and early-modern Europe for his views on Krader's work. Since Dr. Levine and I have been colleagues and friends for decades now and share similar views on freedom of expression and attempts within the academy to limit the same, and, recognizing his pre-eminence as a historian in this field of work, I offered him a platform to assess Krader's work in English translation, a first draft of which he read and extensively commented upon. I am grateful for his input. I did not expect his work, or the work of any single historian, to present a full picture of this narrow field of history and it may be that his comments may not in fact be representative of this area of the discipline. And yet in the spirit of debate and principled criticism which he and I both respect and encourage, I will take this opportunity to respond to some of his comments in relation to the present work.

Palaeontology, Anthropology, Archaeology and related disciplines have been concerned with the question of periodization of human history and over the course of the last several centuries have proposed various schemata regarding such classification. Some of these classificatory systems are based primarily on the use of materials in tools and have entered into popular consciousness in expressions such as the Old Stone Age, the New Stone Age, the Iron Age, etc. Other classifications, especially those created by late 19th century evolutionists used broad cultural markers for the designation of periods, such as that of the American lawyer and amateur anthropologist Lewis Henry Morgan's tripartite division of Savagery, Barbarism and Civilization, the British jurist and leader of the Historical School of Law, Henry Sumner Maine's phrase 'from status to contract', Emile Durkheim's contrast of mechanical and organic solidarity, Ferdinand Tönnies *Gemeinschaft und Gesellschaft*, and many others.

As an anthropologist, Krader outlined his theory of development which he distinguished from the theory of evolution, the former limited specifically to the human order, the latter to the material-biotic order of nature. The major discontinuity within the over-arching continuity of human development is the division between communal and civil society, the latter distinguished by the division into social classes, the presence of a public and a private sector, and the formation of the state. Within civil society, there are various organizations of economic and social life, distinguished among other factors by the specific relations to material nature (tools, technics, raw materials, means of production, intellectual achievements in mathematics, philosophy and the sciences, etc.) and the relations between the classes of the labouring population and the classes of non-producers (state officials, priests, healers, landowners, etc.). In this book Krader wrote of capitalism that it is the form of organization of the economy in modern civil society.

One of the important, although not the only way of distinguishing among the various economic formations of civil society concerns the form and substance of social labour. In all forms of civil society labour is bound in substance. In the so-called Asiatic mode of production, the substance of labour is social, the form, communal. The communal-social form of labour is bound to the village by custom, habit and tradition; it is thus a transitional form from communal to civil society, with a state, a weak division into a private and a public sphere and nascent social class divisions. A surplus is made over to the state in the form of rent-tax (for the separation of the private—rent and the public—tax had not been systematically elaborated). In classical antiquity the predominant form of labour is slavery by which the slave is bound as the property of the master who is invested with the *ius utendi et abutendi*. In feudalism, which Krader, following Marx in this matter, believed was a phenomenon limited to European history (with the possible exception of Japan), the serf was bound to the land *glebae adscripti*. The advance of the capitalist organization of the economy and along with it the development of the ideology of freedom is given expression in both the organizations of the class of wage labour in the towns and among the peasants in their rebellions and uprisings in the countryside. Along with the growth of wage labour and as a necessary aspect of it the formal freedom of wage labour, came the right to contract for the sale of its labour power as juridically equal to the owners of capital (some of whom in the earlier period of mining, for example, were also wage labourers), the right to mobility, the freedom of movement, etc.

Philosophically, Krader has taken up and employed a number of categories found in the writings of Hegel, that of form and substance having already been mentioned. Other categories prominently employed by Krader from this source include mediate and immediate relations, subjective and objective aspects of human development, the notion of moments in the theory of development and of mediation in the theory of labour. No reference is made at all in Levine's critical assessment of this book to any of these important concerns given Krader's focus on the problem of periodization in writing it. And the definition of capitalism that Levine presents in his review—buying cheap and selling dear—is lacking in historical specificity and is overly simplistic. Buying cheap and selling dear would apply to almost any society in which commodities are produced, which as Engels pointed out in his introduction to Volume III of *Capital*, is something like 5,000 to 7,000 years old and is not specifically related to any form of capitalism let alone to its modern system. If one were unkind one might refer to it as a kind of Fred Flintstone view of contemporary capitalism. Perhaps it is a watered-down version of C.B. Macpherson's notion of possessive individualism.

One gets the feeling that in ignoring Krader's specific intentions and objectives in writing this book that Levine has set up a straw man. Not only does he not take note of the fact that Krader's main concern is with the question of periodization—even if historians don't consider it worthy of their attention—leaving it out of mention altogether sets up the argument for criticism by a misrepresentation of its concerns. The same can be said of the book's very title: *The Beginnings* of Capitalism *in Central Europe* (emphasis added). Almost all of Levine's references are related to the English data and most of these are from the 17th, 18th and 19th century, whereas Krader's overwhelming concerns are related to the 15th and 16th centuries. Krader does, on occasion, refer to comparative data with England, Italy, France, Turkey, etc., but his primary concern is with Central Europe in the 15th and 16th century. Krader explicitly states that England had overtaken Germany in the production of coal for use in mining by the middle of the 16th century: "Yet, in the second half of the 16th century, England had taken over the leading position in the production of iron in Europe and maintained it during the subsequent industrial revolution till the 19th century." And, "Hard coal was used as industrial fuel in

England earlier than in Central Europe." If Krader did not develop a comparative treatment of capitalist development in England with that in Central Europe, it was on account of the fact that it was not his intention to write such an account.

Furthermore, Levine's linking Krader's approach with that of Maurice Dobb ignores Krader's explicit critique of Dobb (and Sweezy and Hilton) in this book (pp. 49, 78, 79, 94, 126n) and a much more extensive criticism of Dobb and other apologists of Marx, and indeed of official communist versions of the theory of value in his book *Labor and Value*. Additionally, along with an appreciation of some of Marx's insights regarding the origins of capitalism in Europe, Krader is critical of Marx's oversights (pp. 50, 53, 65, 77, 96, 103, 109, 119, 130, 324). A further point of contention is Levine's criticism of what he refers to as mid-century methods and data sources which he suggests were outmoded before the 1990s when Krader published this book in the German original. But again, this is a straw man, since the question concerning periodization is ignored by Levine who takes up the book as a history text which Krader explicitly denied at the outset of the work.

Consider the following statements by Levine regarding Dobb and Krader: "Both works [Dobbs' and Krader's] concentrate on the origins of capitalism in the formal relations between capital and labour; neither work gives much credence to the agricultural origins of industry, consumer demand, urbanization, historical demography, transportation, technology, and, in particular, energy sources. Indeed, Krader's essay—like Dobb's—is remarkable for the way in which a 21st century student of "the transition" recognizes the absence of the gigantic historiography which is pertinent to this subject. It could be said that contemporary studies render Krader's vision almost unrecognizable or, at the very least, anachronistic." One of the explicit themes of the book concerns the relations of form *and substance* with regard to labour, to rights and freedoms in the modern condition of civil society under developing capitalism. But the achievement of formal freedom by wage labour—for the first time systematically in human history—first by the town proletariat and somewhat later and at a slower pace by the peasants in the countryside—stands in contrast to the lack of the substance of freedom, a condition acknowledged poetically by Goethe at the end of *Faust*. And I leave it to the reader of this work to judge the fairness of Prof. Levine's criticism that Krader has ignored everything but the formal relations of capital and labour. See for example, with regard to the peasants' important role in the beginnings of capitalist development in Central Europe: "The peasants and the working class remained separate from one another; only sporadically did they take up contact. However, they did not behave passively to each other, as Karl Marx believes, when he speaks about the expulsion of the peasants from the countryside; they were in no way the mere recipients of the initiatives of others, but rather an active moment in history." And

"In substance, the peasants had participated in the world market already in the 15th to the 17th century and they had already contributed in an essential way to money revenue at first west of the Elbe, thereafter in the territory east of the Elbe as well." And again: "Capitalism was established by the total activities of the peasants, the town working class and the entrepreneurs. These activities were carried out not through the common consciousness, but rather separated in the various social classes in the different countries. Thus, one cannot speak of a unitary revolution but rather of several waves of activity independent of one another." The charge that Krader ignored changes in technics and technology is incomprehensible to the translator of this book who spent hours trying to find English language equivalents for developments in technics and technology from the 14th to the 16th century in mining, metallurgy and smelting, and in other trades over the course of that time. Transportation and the role of different fuels were also extensively covered in the book, as even the casual reader will easily see. Demographic changes are presented in a number of different tables as well as in the text.

And in conclusion, one can only wonder that for all of the anachronism with which Levine charges mid-20th century scholarship not one single example of how the new historiography has shown that any of Krader's main points concerning the *beginnings* of capitalism in *Central Europe* has been significantly challenged by its discoveries.

History students of the late Charles Tilly were rumoured to have given a clever twist to the title of their professor's collection of essays *As Sociology Meets History,* referring to it "As Sociology Eats History." We might, with some justification, suggest Levine's treatment of this book is an example of contemporary historiography's self-congratulation in ignoring both anthropology and philosophy.

Translator's Foreword

Translation from one current living language to another is a daunting task. A translation of this sort can be considered a true art form if it can transmit the aesthetic sense, mood, connotation, etc. from the originating to the target language in addition to rendering an adequate meaning of the original. The task is even more challenging when one translates historical terms and notions that were in use 500 years ago, especially if those elements were specialized at the time of their use. In the case of the book at hand, Krader's German is contemporaneous with the English translation. Not so his sources, many of which are cited from 15th and 16th century German or Middle High German. Krader frequently referred to sources in which certain terms, particularly those concerning late medieval and early-modern professions, were expressed in their local dialectical variants resulting in different words for one and the same type of work. Sometimes these words referred to professions that were so finely differentiated that it is not clear if they were a local variant of the term or a reference to an entirely different position (see, e.g. *Steiger* and *Hutmann, Huntezieher oder Karrenläufer,* etc. in the text). I am grateful to Dr. Sabine Sander, a native German speaker, for her assistance in helping me locate sources which enabled me to render many of these today obscure concepts into intelligible English. I bear sole responsibility for any inaccuracies in translation of these and other concepts.

Another persistent problem of translation had to do with the names for organizations of merchants, trades, occupations and the like—*Zunft, Gilde, Innung, Amt, Verband, Bruderschaft*, etc. One of the most vexing issues had to do with the fact that *Zunft* and *Gilde* are both rendered in English as *guild* in all dictionaries consulted. There is a specialist literature which treats the subtle distinctions among these words as they developed over time. We cite some of this literature but do not follow the intricacies in this translation. I do not vouch for the accuracy of the English words I've used to translate these terms, but I have always included the German originals in the text. Nor are the specifics centrally relevant to Krader's main arguments regarding the beginnings of capitalism in Central Europe.

I deem it necessary to point out several further difficulties in translation which were encountered in this book. For example, the noun *Bürger* in the German-speaking world today is equivalent to the English noun *citizen*, but in relation to the period of the 14th to 16th century, it generally applied to town dwellers as opposed to the peasantry, the aristocracy, the clerics and others more closely tied to the feudal order. Yet the adjectival form *bürgerlich* is more complicated still and can be used with different English words: *civil*, *bourgeois*, *middle class*, *pertaining to towns and cities*. The concept of *bürgerliche Gesellschaft* which frequently appears in this book can be translated as bourgeois society or civil society. The word bourgeois, of course, has entered English via the French which brings with it the 18th century imagery associated with the French revolution and the political writings which both preceded it, and which accompanied and followed it. It also brings with it a flavour of radical politics from Europe and is associated with socialist, communist and anarchist critiques of capitalist societies. In his earlier works following the publication of *The Ethnological Notebooks* (1972) Krader drew a clear distinction between civil society, a category which arches over the Asiatic or communal-social organization of economy and society, classical antiquity and feudalism in Europe and the beginnings of capitalism in Europe and its later spread worldwide. It also encompasses socialist and communist states in which the formal relations of capital and labour are managed differently. In these latter states the formal freedoms of bourgeois society are attenuated and compromised. All of these modes of production lie at the heart of different formations in the history of civil society. According to Krader, they are all to be distinguished from the primitive pre-civil communal organizations without a state, without the separation of public and private spheres and differentiations between social classes. When Krader refers to *bürgerliche Gesellschaft* in relation to Europe in the 15th and 16th century, the appropriate translation is bourgeois society, the form of modern civil society organized along capitalist lines. In Appendix III of Krader's (1979) *Treatise on Social Labor* 'On the

Relations of Civil Society in the Modern Period' he distinguished between bourgeois society and civil-socialist society.

Another issue with regard to translation concerns the German word *Stadt* which can be rendered as city or town in English. Since the cities of Europe in the 15th and 16th century were rather small in terms of geography and population in comparison to their size under high capitalism (Naples, as Krader points out, was the largest city in Europe at the time), I have for the most part translated the word *Stadt* with *town*. On occasion, especially when contrasting *Stadt* with *Land*, I've used the term city as contrasted with countryside or when referring to cities in the period of high capitalism.

Mining and metallurgy are one of the most important elements of the beginnings of capitalism in Central Europe and the terms *Knappe* and *Bergknappe* appear frequently in the text. When used alone or in an earlier context, the term *Knappe* refers to a younger labourer who is new to the job. When used in the composite word *Bergknappe* the reference is to a miner and is translated as such.

With regard to the Hegelian concepts *Aufhebung* and *Momente* I have used the somewhat awkward term *sublation* in English for the former which is meant to capture the simultaneous sense of cancellation and elevation in the German original. I have used non-Hegelian terms to translate *Momente* which removes the concept from the Hegelian reference in which Krader was deeply versed. Moments, elements, aspects and other such words do not do justice to the Hegelian *Momente* which implies members of an organic whole that are taken up singly and then in their significance within a growing process that gives it new significance in relation to the developing whole without losing their sense as something particular. This plays an important role in Krader's distinction between sporadic appearances of capitalism and their systematic development as well as between the elements of capitalism and its system.

The word *Kunst* and the plural *Künste* have in some instances proved difficult to translate. In modern parlance they fit nicely with the English words—art and the arts. And in some cases, these are appropriate translations. But when they are used, for example, to refer to classifications of labourers in mining in the 15th and 16th century they can't be so easily rendered. In this usage *Kunst* and *Künste* refer to a kind of expertise, knowledge, specialty with a practical component. Practical art or practical arts might fit in some instances. But in the examples of *Kunstmeister, Kunstknechte, Kunstschmied, Kunstjunge*, an English translation is difficult to find. It implies know-how and can relate to various sports, hobbies, activities of the body. All kinds of craftmanship are referred to as *Künste* although Grimm points to the distinction between the free and unfree arts. [For a complete survey of the word *Kunst*, see Grimm, *Wörterbuch*, volume 11, columns 2666–2684]. The

Kunstmeister, for example, would be a knowledgeable master in some trade or craft. The *Kunstknechte* would be those servants involved in specialized crafts or occupations.

The words *Genossenschaft*, *genossenschaftlich* have been rendered corporative association, corporative. The word *Genossen* in modern German is the word for comrade and has been used by members of Communist parties and their sympathizers as a means of address to one another. The Nazis used the term *Volksgenossen* to refer to a party member or a member of the 'Aryan' or Nordic race, who was racially 'pure'.

The *Genossenschaft* has played an important role in the history of law in both Germany and England. In Germany, it was the subject of a prodigious four volume work in the late 19th century by Otto von Gierke (1868). Entitled *Das Deutsche Genossenschaftsrecht*, it challenged the notion of corporate personality as a fictive person first clearly enunciated by Pope Innocent IV, with a realist theory of the living organicity of corporate groups. In the former theory, the legal personality of the group was seen as a fictitious creation of the law to treat cases of such matters as group ownership, group liability, group inheritance, etc. Frederic William Maitland, an English translator of von Gierke, suggested in the translator's introduction to a section of Volume III of Gierke's work, that the notion of corporate personality had been associated with the image of the joint-stock company, linked to the notion of society or *Gesellschaft* in German. Accordingly, the only way to deal with corporate entities in the law was by means of a legal fiction, that is, by treating the group as a whole as having a legal persona as a legal fiction. Maitland, following Gierke, however, championed a notion that those groups which had a traditional, living, communal foundation ought to be recognized as an organic, living entity in the law because they are real. Hence, the term *Genossenschaft* ought not to be translated into English by words that were derived from notions of *societas*, with its individualistic connotations but rather by notions that emphasize the collective, communal character of traditional, non-voluntary group life. As Maitland (Gierke, 1900 xxv–xxvi) explained it: "It was in a Germany that was full of new ideas and new hopes that a theory was launched which styled itself 'the German Genossenschaftstheorie.' Even the hastiest sketch of its environment, if it notices the appearance of the joint-stock company, should give one word to the persistence in Germany of agrarian communities with world-old histories, to the intricate problems that their dissolution presented, and to the current complaint that Roman law had no equitable solution for these questions and had done scant justice to the peasant … A name was wanted which would unite many groups of men, simple and complex, modern and archaic; and *Genossenschaft* was chosen. The English translator must carefully avoid Partnership; perhaps in our modern usage Company has become too specific and technical; Society also is dangerous; Fellowship with its slight flavour of an old England may be our least inadequate word … our German Fellowship is no fiction, no symbol, no piece of the State's machinery, no collective name for individuals, but a living organism and a real person, with body and members and a will of its own. Itself can will, itself can act; it wills and acts by the men who are its organs as a man wills and acts by brain, mouth and hand. It is not a fictitious person; it is a *Gesammtperson*, and its will is a *Gesammtwille*; it is a group-person, and its will is a group-will." The reader of this translation of Krader's work will understand that my use of 'corporative' is but an inadequate contrivance to render the sense of the German *Genossenschaft*.

Acknowledgements

This is the third posthumously published work by Lawrence Krader. The first such volume appeared in 2003 bearing the title: *Labor and Value*; it was edited and introduced by me and my late friend and colleague, the economic historian, Rod Hay. It treated the forms and substance of both labour and value and their interrelations. As a focus in this work, Krader attempted to bring the development of objective value theory into line with subjective value theory.

The second such publication was *Noetics: The Science of Thinking and Knowing* which appeared in 2010. When I met with Krader last in August 1998, he referred to the manuscript of *Noetics* as his *magnum opus*, a work which he had been writing on and off since his days as a student at CCNY in the late 1930s. This ambitious book represented nothing less than a reconsideration of the human order within the manifold of nature. Krader had reconceptualised our understanding of nature. There is, indeed, a material order of nature, but it is not congruent with nature as a whole, for the quantum order is different from the material order existing as it does in a different configuration of space-time. The human order represents yet again a different order of nature, for only in the human order do we find the objective and subjective as opposed to the 'thingly' in the material universe. *Pace* Marx, there is teleology in nature, but only in the human order of the manifold. The link between *Labor and Value* and *Noetics* lies in the attention to the dimensions of objectivity and subjectivity in both labour and value theory.

This current work represents another formidable contribution by Krader to the problem of periodization of human history. With the central importance Krader gives to the form and substance of the freedom of human labour in the beginnings of capitalism in Central Europe, he argues against an evolutionary understanding of this phenomenon of history and instead looks at the far more complicated *development* of the societies in which this mode of production prevails.

Unlike evolution in the material-biotic order of nature, human development is in part teleological, in part serendipitous, in part accidental, in part interactive with the material order and to a lesser degree with the quantum order, in part beneficial, in part malicious, etc. It is both subjective and objective, abstract and concrete, scientific and ideological. Machiavelli's bipartite categories of fortuna and virtù are too simple. It is with this understanding of development in the human order that Krader approaches the beginnings of capitalism in Central Europe and this links the book to the two earlier publications.

I want to acknowledge the earlier work with Rod Hay, whose counsel would have been warmly welcome on this project. The late Dr. Barbara Krader (1922–2006), Lawrence's widow, herself an internationally renowned scholar of ethnomusicology and folklore, was most supportive of my work in establishing the Lawrence Krader Research Project.

With regard to the present work I want to acknowledge the important help of Dr. Sabine Sander, adjunct assistant professor at the Krader Project, McMaster University. Elsewhere in this volume I have thanked her for her help with the translations of obscure German words and phrases. But her involvement in the project went beyond matters of translation. She read the book in German and made many valuable suggestions with regard to substantial matters beyond the technical issues of rendering a thought from one language to another. I would also like to acknowledge the contributions of Michelle Goldenberg, a research assistant at the Krader Project for the last two years and a senior doctoral candidate in the department of sociology at McMaster University. She read an earlier draft of the translation and commented on several passages which needed to be reworked in English for clarity. She also located the illustration appended to this book and prepared them and their texts for publication.

I would also like to thank my colleagues and former fellow students of Lawrence Krader, Drs. Brígida von Mentz and Rainer Winkelmann who worked with Prof. Krader on the original German text and whose advice and support with regard to this English translation has been invaluable.

I want to acknowledge as well the work of Janell Harris who served as copyeditor for (Levitt & Sander, eds. 2017) *Beyond the Juxtaposition of Nature and Culture*, the manuscript of our collection of papers from a conference on Krader's work at

McMaster University and at the Workers' Heritage Centre in Hamilton, Ontario on May 5th and 6th of 2016. She did a brilliant job. I thank her again for preparing the final manuscript of this book for submission to Peter Lang. I also want to take this opportunity to thank Meagan Simpson, editor at Peter Lang publishers, New York, for her ongoing support in helping bring Krader's works to the interested public.

Finally, I thank my family, Corinne, our children and grandchildren, for the time the preparation of this translation took away from them.

Cyril Levitt
Toronto, Canada
March 2020

Author's Foreword

The present work concerns the beginning of the capitalist system and of modern bourgeois society in Central Europe, primarily in the German-speaking region and is presented as a contribution to the solution of an essential part of the question of periodization in human history. Yet, this book is not offered as a history text. The various subjects and scholarly disciplines of political economy, sociology, ethnology, history, political science, philosophy and Marxism in the past have taken up the theme of this work and rendered significant contributions to it. Without these foundations and research activities our work would be unthinkable. The first and preeminent guide, which provided the orientation to our attempt at periodization, stems from Albrecht Dürer, the illustrator, painter, mathematician and world genius, who indeed grasped with precision the relationship of the modern rediscovery of the arts and sciences to antiquity. Agricola had also said something about this. The views, writings, assertions, activities and data of Dürer, of Agricola, Jakob Fugger, Hans Sachs, Jost Amman, Lazarus Ercker, Vannoccio Biringuccio, Ciriacus Schreittmann among others who were active in the 15th and 16th centuries in central Europe, constitute the materials of our work. The relations of the capitalist period to those of the preceding feudalism and antiquity as well as to other parts of the world will not in and for themselves be treated here; they will only then be included when they, as remnants of feudalism, form a component of the relationships within capitalist society. We mainly explore the conceptions of contemporaries such as Dürer, those of the rebellious peasants among others, in relation to their own experiences, as well as the views and ideas of researchers in this field in the 19th and 20th century. Karl Marx frequently returned to the problems of the beginnings of the capitalist system and the capitalist mode of production, and Max Weber concerned himself with an aspect of the same. Ernst Troeltsch asserted that both were materialists. Even though this was a fateful assessment, it is in this context neither final nor decisive. We shall see to what extent it is serviceable. In the post-war period, Schumpeter critically considered the views of Marx and Weber; in part his critique is on the mark, in part it is not. Our task is to present a unified system out of the differing practices, views, words and theories in the 15th, 16th, and 17th century and out of the conceptions of them in the 19th and 20th century.

The book published here is the product of our seminar in Berlin which, since 1972 has dealt with the thematic question of periodization in world history; the seminar has continued to the present day. Since 1977 we have also conducted the same seminar in the Centro de Investigaciones Superiores in Mexico, as well as in universities in Uppsala, Turin, Amsterdam, Leiden, Budapest, Utrecht, Milan, Leipzig, London, Delhi, Jalapa (Vera Cruz) and Morelia (Michoacan) in the form of lectures given there. For the interest, the intellectual support and the participation of the audience, of the students and the organizers who invited me, and for the collegiality on all sides, I am most deeply thankful. I acknowledge the contributions to our common theme of my late friends, Karl Korsch and Angel Palerm.

In immediate relation to the present work, I recognize the exchange of ideas with Dr. Brígida von Mentz and Dr. Rainer Winkelmann. Hildegard Dierks significantly contributed to the production of this work. I must especially express my thanks to Heinz-Peter Seidel for what he did in the elaboration of the book.

Author's Introduction

Modern bourgeois society is the most developed and most diverse organization of the process of production in world history. This appraisal of the capitalist system of production and of bourgeois society applies not only to its situation in the 19th century when Karl Marx composed it but to its contemporary situation as well. Success in the development of production and the diversity of its products contains opposing moments. It is social in its organization of labour as well as in the increase of its product, antisocial in the unequal distribution of its goods and in the exploitation of the labourers. The opponents of bourgeois society and their supporters proclaimed the demise of the capitalist system. Regarding the accuracy of such a forecast, we will remain silent; our primary task is to present the origin of this society in Central Europe. Some authors have questioned whether the origination process is a model for contemporary developing countries, so that they, if they were to follow the same path, might reproduce the diversity of current American, German or Japanese production. We shall return to this idea. The origin of modern bourgeois society presents itself as one of the most important problems of our era. It is notably important in content because we are better able to understand our society if we grasp and comprehend its origin. It is furthermore methodologically interesting since various thinkers have made the effort to solve the problem of origination. In a certain sense, there is a unified conception concerning the source and origin of our contemporary society. This conception, however, appears to be solely abstract, and, furthermore, it is a well-known platitude. If we were to conclude our investigation with it, it would thus be a pure simplification of the origination process. Nevertheless, we will begin with this agreed upon conception.

The epoch of modern bourgeois society coincides with the rise of the capitalist system. The unity of the two systems of economy and society is not based on a coincidence but rather on their inner connection. Thinkers in the past and present were conscious of the fact that there is a succession of historical periods, that our epoch configures a particular system in social history, that previously there had been another system of this kind and then its revolutionary transition to a new system had occurred. Concerning the general periodization and the ordering of historical events in the process of origination of the new epoch, there is unanimous agreement; concerning the presentation of dates and causes in relation to these events, there is, on the contrary, no such agreement. The disputes and conflicts are first related to the question regarding when and where the radical change of the old and the rise of modern society had taken place. Some researchers assume that its beginnings are to be found in Italy in the 13th and 14th century. Other researchers have discovered the same transition in the 16th century namely in Central Europe. There is a certain school of research that considers the appearance of modern bourgeois society and that of the capitalist system as a European exceptionality. Another school assumes that the historical categories and their laws are universally applicable and ought to be applied worldwide.

The lawfulness of the historical process is hereby presumed. There is a connection between European feudalism in the Middle Ages and the feudal system not only in one country but rather in several countries. We will not, however, inquire into world history, but rather only the history of Central Europe and, in particular, the history of Germany. We proceed on the basis that modern bourgeois society and the capitalist system follow the medieval system of feudalism and arose in Europe. The origination process quickly prevailed first in the region of the Mediterranean and then in Central and Western Europe. The feudal and the capitalist system are European historical phenomena. The representatives of both of those conceptions concerning the beginnings of modernity, whether the latter had developed in the 13th or alternatively in the 16th century, have made their contribution to the problem of origination. Through their investigations it can be ascertained that there is a capitalist system which dominates modern European life. Europeans early and late have always demarcated their era from the previous one; sometimes they did this with regret, in other cases with scorn. Such a poetic conception of history is not ours. Society in Europe is to be grasped in various ways. The Germans in Central Europe structure society in the following way. They have a common language and at times political unity. In another sense, Europeans frame a society now not on language but rather through the economy, art, science, politics and the system of law. We shall see that some occurrences in the history of modernity began in the region of the Mediterranean and then moved northward, that is towards Central Europe; others, on the other hand, begin in the north and subsequently move towards the south, into the region of the Mediterranean. In the second half of the 20th century a European community originated out of economic and social moments not ex nihilo but rather presented as resting on a historical foundation. Brisk traffic in the 14th, 15th and 16th centuries between the Italian cities of Venice, Genoa, Pisa, on the one hand, and Constantinople, and the cities of North Africa and of the Far East on the other, led to the development of trade practices, of the arts, of the sciences of geometry, arithmetic and of medicine in Europe. Conversely, economic practices in mining, in metallurgy, in assaying, and in scientific developments in Copernican astronomy and in chemistry arose in Central Europe and were exchanged with the countries of the Mediterranean.

These historical events are not superficial, but rather profound and they revolutionized the life of many European peoples. The movements, the displacement and massive changes, occur in a specific epoch. And yet, cultural events do not happen by themselves. They are disseminated and propagated by the emigration of people, by inner and outer exchange and imitation. Once there was a peculiar idea that culture is carried on the shoulders of men, who left on voyages, and their culture would settle in with them at an appropriate opportunity. We do not share this idea. Culture shapes an internal component of man and is inseparable from him. It is not carried on the shoulders of men like an eternal burden.

Capitalism and bourgeois society, neither separately nor taken together, constitute a European exceptionality. Japan, Singapore, Taiwan and South Korea have completely mastered the processes of the capitalist system. Thus, the fully developed capitalist system is not a particularly European phenomenon. The Europeans had only propagated it further in America, and it was developed further there. Yet, in its origin, the capitalist system is a particularly European occurrence. Those who are of the opinion that the capitalist system is a model for underdeveloped countries today, confound two different matters. Evidently it is not only possible but rather current and actual, that the capitalist system was and will be propagated beyond the European continent as has already occurred in America and Asia. But we are not talking about this. The question rather is whether the original conditions in the capitalist and modern bourgeois process of origination are repeated, or whether they are capable of being repeated. We take a stand against this notion. The conditions of the original capitalist system belong to the past. We will mention only one matter in relation to it. Modern civil society and the capitalist system were formed in Germany, England, northern Italy, the Netherlands and France. In the 15th and 16th century there was no country that stood higher in the development of the economy and society than they did. These countries in Western, Central and Southern Europe conquered and exploited other continents and by these means insured their further economic development and political superiority at the cost of others. Now their former colonies, which are called the Third World, are attempting to trail behind on the same path. However, it is difficult for the Third World to reproduce this process in development, for the possibility to exploit other countries and for treating them as colonies, is precluded. Hence, one of the fundamental conditions for the origin of capitalism as an internal process is lacking. The developing countries in the present have borrowed the processes of capitalism and of modern society in a purely external manner.

We shall only concern ourselves with the internal processes in the emergence of the capitalist system. We confirm that the exploitation of Mexico and Peru, Africa and Asia, by the Spanish among others, constitutes an essential part in the development of Europe. However, regarding this process of exploitation in relation to Germany and to the other parts of Central Europe, colonialism was mediated and not immediate. Fugger and other capitalists in Central Europe exploited the Spanish in turn; thereafter bankers in other countries of Europe did the same. There was a bellum omnium contra omnes, a war of all against all.

The systematic development of the economic processes arose through the stratification, differentiation, and interconnection of the means of production, of the increasing qualification of the labour force and the increasing interweaving of commercial relations. This development overcame the local confines of economic relationships. In this regard, war signifies an obstacle in part, but in part it brings about an advantage for further economic development. The peoples of Central Europe in the 15th and 16th century proceeded on the assumption that Italy—mainly the North Italian cities there—formed the centre of the merchant class, of art and science, which then radiated out over Europe. In this sense of the economic and intellectual [*geistigen*] movements Europe is to be regarded a social unity.

The break with the past was never completely and absolutely carried out. In the transformation period from the 15th to the 17th century, the German and the other Central European peoples had taken over and modified their principles of structuring and hierarchical organization from the Middle Ages. The members of this society, or some of the astute among them, considered themselves leaders of a process of transformation. They were conscious of the fact that they introduced a new epoch, but they did not consider themselves world-shattering revolutionaries. The rebelling peasants did not want to destroy authority, nor to threaten it. They appeared devout and obedient. They did not want to be as their fathers were; they wanted to be free. Like their contemporaries they wanted to free themselves from feudal domination. Neither did the path-breaking artists want to disrupt the political system; they only wanted to become wealthier in the sense of the new market economy and merchant class.

The social hierarchy was shaped by the estates and guild system, but this system had no explicit constitution. In one context, the word estate meant a calling (*Beruf*), in another, status, in a third, social class. The estates asserted themselves officially, hierarchically as a component [*Gliederung*] in the legal system and in the system of domination and servitude, whereby they both fought against the secular and clerical-political orders as well as supported them.

The hierarchical subdivisions of society and of the guild system reciprocally influenced one another, and through this, the organization of labour was hierarchically determined. Not everything in the organization of labour, its structuration and division is determined by the system of guilds, but in broad outline social labour of that time was organized hierarchically and in line with the guilds. We shall present and analyse the general characteristics of the organization of labour in mining, its structuration and division as well as some aspects of technics and their arrangements found outside the guild system. Some estates—secular and clerical—asserted their privileges; the majority of estates and the population, on the other hand, were poor and without privileges. Noble families ruled in the countryside, at the royal court and in the Church; and in the cities, the patrician families dominated. Their provenience was not from Roman history although the rich and influential families in the cities called themselves Patricians. They were not aristocrats, but it was the custom at that time under humanistic auspices to be qualified with a title from antiquity. The periodization in the history of a society, of a people or an alliance of peoples, poses the question of the demarcation of the historical trajectory of a society from other societies and from other periods in history. We conceive the relations between the periods as an interruption or discontinuity and at the same time as an extension or continuity in relation to the past. The beginning of modern society is based on the transformation of the systems in the preceding epochs, of which something still survives, in a new context.

The upheaval in this connection is to be understood with nuance. In some respects, it proceeds very quickly, yet some historical moments from the past are drawn out and continue into the 20th century, such as monarchies which sprout from millennial roots. To be sure, the kings and queens of our century are only monarchs pro forma, yet the autocrats, the aristocrats and the clerics in the Middle Ages and at the beginning of the capitalist era formed an actual ruling class in substance.

In the question posed here the matter concerns the continuation and revolution in the course of history in the period of modern bourgeois society of the peoples of Central Europe in tandem with the same processes in other parts of Europe, mainly in the Mediterranean region, but also on the Atlantic coast—above all among the Italians, the Germans, Dutch, English and French. Periodization as a question was treated by several representatives of the social sciences, by historians, sociologists, economists, political scientists, ethnologists as well as by philosophers of history and social philosophers. Those who have hitherto conceived this problematic not only argued about the chronological development of the system but presented the meaning of the words in this schema in different ways as well, even though they were in agreement about the general outlines. In the main, the key words capitalism and bourgeois society were understood differently.

Capitalism as a system is based on the two processes of the expansion of wage labour and of capital in the modern era. The medieval natural economy is driven back under these circumstances and on that account the circulation of money is required. Freedom and equality in society are propagated and intensified as forms of the bourgeois system of law. In this way, the moments of wage labour, the money economy, capital, formal freedom and equality of burgesses are closely tied to one another, as we shall see.

On the grounds presented in this work, we share the view that capitalism as a system only exists in modern times and not, by contrast, in antiquity or in the Middle Ages. Some people who can already be designated correctly as wage labourers and capitalists existed in antiquity; wage labour and capital appear sporadically, here and there, but they were not systematically propagated before the modern era. We shall extensively discuss the difference between sporadic and systematic historical phenomena.

We confine ourselves to categories and periods of European and not world history. It has been asserted that the system of fiefdom and feudalism are to be found worldwide as historical categories and periods. This view can only be taken up concretely in relation to the particular history of India, China, Africa, etc. and for that reason they are excluded from this current work. To apply the categories of European history to those of peoples in other parts of the world, would be a case of ethnocentrism by means of which the world is looked at through falsely polarised glasses.

We will not struggle everywhere against ethnocentrism. Those who call the current epoch "modern times" speak ethnocentrically in this context. Only from our standpoint does our time appear to be modern. Modern times as a concept was invented by Heinrich Heine and Ferdinand Freiligrath in the 19th century. In another sense, we can in fact only think, feel and speak ethnocentrically. We fashion our world out of pre-existing, given, and traditional means. It is not newly invented in each generation. To be sure, we can critically treat the given and traditional means of our life, the practices, concepts and words and we do that and endeavour to vary and to transform the old ways of treating them. The old guilds, on the contrary, endeavoured to hold fast to and enshrine the old ways and modes.

Our main theme is related to the formation of the capitalist system in the period of modern bourgeois society, which we submit as a contribution to the question of periodization in human history. This problematic on the world stage or the *theatrum mundi*, was emphasized by economists, historians and philosophers of the Enlightenment in the 18th century and later by Hegel and the Hegelians and by Marx and the Marxists in the 19th and 20th century. Those who considered this question in the 19th century, such as Lewis Henry Morgan, Friedrich Engels and Lord Avebury (John Lubbock—trans.), treated it at the level of world history. However, we do not accentuate the problematic of the world history of humanity nor the perspective for Europe as a whole.

Capitalism originated in Europe, after which it was disseminated worldwide through colonialism, colonization, trade and conquest. Capitalism in its origin as a system is an internal matter of modern European history, an external matter in relation to other parts of the world. Social research implicitly and explicitly concerned itself with classes and class oppositions. Werner Sombart, Lujo Brentano, Max Weber, Josef Kulischer, Jakob Strieder, Joseph Schumpeter among others ascribe the origin of the capitalist economic and social system to the practices and the ethic of entrepreneurship and begin with the establishment of modern society through the activity of the economically wealthy class. Otto Johannsen and F. M. Feldhaus put the class struggle into the foreground of their historical writings on technology. Karl Marx and Friedrich Engels had in 1848 presented all hitherto existing history as the history of class struggles. Johannsen and Feldhaus represented the view that the history of class struggles begins with the modern period; the history of the Middle Ages was supposed to have been peaceful as it were;

this view is found in J. Janssen, Vilfredo Pareto and O. Brunner, who look at the Middle Ages through rose coloured glasses, as we shall see. We will assess these views and introduce an ordered picture of the transition to the modern period.

The writings of Georg Agricola, Vannoccio Biringuccio, Lazarus Ercker, Johannes Kunckel, Adam Ries, Hans Sachs, Ciriacus Schreittman, Hartmann Schopper as well as those of Albrecht Dürer and the twelve articles of the rebellious peasants, and further, the drawings, wood cuts and copper etchings of Dürer and the images of Jost Amman, B. Weffringer among others, which accompanied the writings of Sachs and Agricola, serve as our main sources. Archival research is important, and we are dependent on its results. Yet, it is a science in and for itself, which we will not use further beyond our purpose.

The most recent research has investigated the transition from feudalism to capitalism and the beginnings of the modern bourgeois world. Some researchers in this field have selected a single determining cause as a *causa efficiens* in the establishment of the capitalist system. The overwhelming majority of these studies, for example, by Max Weber and Ernst Troeltsch, Henri Pirenne and Paul Sweezy, Werner Sombart and Josef Kulischer, Jakob Strieder and Joseph Schumpeter, gave prominence to the activities of entrepreneurs in the establishment of the capitalist system. Their suggestions appear to be reasonable and well-founded. They are not complete, but they complement one another. However, they appear insufficient and not balanced, even when taken together. They all assume that the beginning of modern bourgeois society and of capitalism is the matter of a social class. However, this class analysis is one-sided. It is not about one single social class, which caused the upheaval of the feudal system and the establishment of modern bourgeois society, but rather has to do with a number of social classes.

The concepts are artful [*listig*], and the corresponding words for capital, capitalism, capitalists, for the capitalist system and the capitalist mode of production, which are presented as *characteristica specifica* of the modern period in Europe, are not balanced, for they draw our attention from the start to entrepreneurship and the class of the wealthy. Other historical moments are thereby excluded from determining the process of transition. Wage labour and money wages for labour of this kind, the contract between the entrepreneurs and the labourers for recompense, the freedom and equality in the formal sense of both sides in the contract relation, become on the side of capital into determining moments in the transition from the feudal to the capitalist system. We will show that the people of the 15th and 16th century were conscious of these processes and relations.

The entrepreneurs provided a great contribution to the transformation of the old society and made money from it. If the answer to the question about the transition to capitalism were simple, then we could advise many countries of the Third

World of today to reproduce asceticism, or to buy up stocks, to set up stock markets, and to introduce double-entry bookkeeping.

Of course, the majority of the European population were bound by feudal bonds in the Middle Ages; nevertheless, the peasants in the 15th and 16th century in Italy, England, Germany, Bohemia, Moravia, France, Hungary and Austria tried to free themselves from these bonds and, in the end, they did free themselves from feudal domination. What some authors intend with the assertion that there was feudalism in non-European countries like India or China, is incomprehensible. Perhaps they mean these peoples are unfree, non-capitalistic, not primitive and not slaves—but feudalism is based on serfdom, which does not exist in a definitive way in Asia or Africa.

The movement of liberation of the peasants as a cause for the establishment of the modern period is just as important, fateful and significant as the activities of the class of entrepreneurs. The working class in the city and in mining had conducted their struggles in the Middle Ages and in modern times and became thereby class conscious and numerous. They developed their skill and their training differently, quickly in some branches of industry, slowly in others.

The importation of new weaving and ribbon looms not only led to the increasing skill of the labourers, since most workers in weaving and cloth production were unskilled children under those conditions in the 18th and 19th century. But in other branches of industry, such as in the metal industry, in steam machinery and in chemistry, later in the electrical power industry, there came into being a well-founded and expanded education and training of the working class, and that meant practically and concretely, that reading, writing and arithmetic were learned.

Our task is to present the origin of the capitalist system in Central Europe, that is, in Germany and its bordering countries. This question was already treated by Karl Marx, Max Weber, Joseph Schumpeter, Jakob Strieder, Fernand Braudel, Josef Kulischer, and other researchers whom we will mention. Without their labours this present work would be unthinkable. Nevertheless, our methodology is other than those of our predecessors. We begin with mining and other industries or industrial branches, such as the metal industry, the system of coinage, the art of clock-making, and the printing industry, which are closely related to mining, as they are to mines and smelting works. Expanded circulation of money, the banking system, credit institutes and monetary transactions presuppose the development of industries pertaining to mining and metal. This quantitative expansion of the process of production and commerce in the 15th and 16th century in southern, central and western Europe are related to the simultaneous concentration of the labour force and of the means of production. The liberation of the peasants led to a showdown with the landowners at the same time and in the same social context.

The industries mentioned not only contain the germ of capitalism; they are operated capitalistically. Labourers worked for money wages, enterprises sought after capital, for the accumulation of the same, and for profit. Both classes are distinguished purely quantitatively from the economic process in the 18th and 19th century, on the other hand, quantitatively and qualitatively from the economic practices in the Middle Ages. The housing, clothing and food industries were not transformed in the 15th to the 17th century and only in the period of the Industrial Revolution, were they operated according to later capitalist ways and means. The mining and metal industries had attained this level of development in the earlier period of the capitalist era without the introduction of steam driven machinery and of electrical power. Until the 19th century weaving and house construction were run mainly by the guilds in the German cities. The working class in the mining, metal and clock-making industries, the printing press and system of coinage together with the merchant class had already established the training and organizational forms of industrial capitalism, the necessary skill and productivity in relation to their era. Later inventions extensively expanded the creation processes in mining, in the metal branches and in the merchant class, but not, in contrast, qualitatively. The movement of the liberation of the peasants affiliated itself with the general striving for liberation, equality, wage labour and capital. Events in mining, in the hammer and smelting works, in printing, in the art of clock-making, in the merchant class and in commerce are, in this context, decisive and determinant.

Capitalism is founded not only on the systematic development of a two-fold process of wage labour and capital, but also on the concentration of the labour force and of the means of production. The labourers endeavour to activate themselves as wage labourers and to liberate themselves from compulsory labour [*Frondienst*] and compulsory collective labour [*Scharwerk*]. These efforts and strivings were sporadically developed in the Middle Ages, systematically in the capitalist period. The capitalists are engaged with the accumulation of profit. Their means to accumulate capital are related to the expansion of the market and money economy. For this reason, they extorted the working class, established the truck system, and saved their gains at first through asceticism. Savings and asceticism, inner-worldly and outer-worldly, were intertwined in the early period of capitalism. The workers attempt to increase their wages and to develop their skill. In this way, their productivity in the labour process is enhanced. The more they earn, the better the preparations and conditions of labour, the more they produce, the more the capitalist class profits.

The historical process in this context, is transformed from sporadic to systematic, a transformation, which is to be understood in two respects; first, from a regional to a widespread historical phenomenon; second, from one branch of industry to another. Regional can be understood as inter-city, or between countries, thus inter-regional, inter-urban and international. The printing press spread from Mainz, Frankfurt, Strasbourg, Nuremberg to Antwerp and Venice and thereafter across the Atlantic Ocean to Mexico and beyond.

The overcoming of local demarcations manifests a systematic development of the capitalist system in the 15th century in the incunable era [early period of book production—trans.]. The linkage of the various branches of industry indicates a systematic development of capitalism in the 15th and 16th century, in so far as it was regionalized, and in this sense, it is not to be considered sporadic. Neither is it sporadic in a second sense, in that it is not limited to a single industry, industrial branch or field of economic activity in this period. Transportation and communication were developed in various directions.

From this point of view Europe shapes a tradition with several unities fractured by language, by classes, by wars, and by cultural traditions. Thus, the European peninsula appears in modern history as a shaky social unity, which only now and after many scenes of horror is trying to broaden and smooth its path.

Economic development didn't continue at the same pace everywhere. The model of mining and of the metal industry, the amalgamation of pits, the freedom of the miners, the liberation of the peasants, the skill training of the working class, the development of technics, the accumulation of capital, and the expansion of the circulation of money, encountered resistance in several branches of industry. Hard coal and iron were used already in the 15th and 16th century in the process of production of mine, steel, and hammer mills and in the remaining metal workshops; but only in the 18th and 19th century were they industrialized through the invention and employment of steam machinery and the requisite organization of labour.

We have little to do with Church history and less with political-military events. The national states in the German-speaking regions were established towards the end of the early period and were expanded in the second half of the 17th and in the 18th century. The figure of the Grand Elector Frederick William is interesting, because during his reign fundamental changes in the regulation of the guilds, in the liberation of the peasants, in the merchant class and in civil liberty were decreed.

The different social classes are together but not in common, rather in struggle with one another they advanced in the same direction, disunited, antagonistic and opposed. The feudal masters offered resistance, so that the old forms of nobility, of the monarchy, and of the Church were preserved into the 20th century, while the substantial moments of the organization of the workers, peasant and capitalist movements go back to the 15th century in some branches of industry. These industries, like mining, shipbuilding, metal processing, also trade and commerce, the credit and printing business, served as models for further capitalist development in general. We consider the historical course of this development as complicated and take a position against those who have tried to simplify it.

The peasants and the working class remained separate from one another; only sporadically did they take up contact. However, they did not behave passively to each other, as Karl Marx believes, when he speaks about the expulsion of the peasants from the countryside; they were in no way the mere recipients of the initiatives of others, but rather an active moment in history.

The enhancement of the required skill of the working class through training is closely tied to the accumulation of capital in the first centuries of the modern period. Nevertheless, this linkage was not uniform, but exhibited differences. In the countryside, the methods and techniques of labour were newly configured only in later centuries, that is, in the 18th century new plant species, new instruments of labour, and new agricultural practices were introduced. It was only in the 18th century that weaving looms and ribbon looms, discovered two hundred years earlier, were spread in the production of cloth in Central Europe. In contrast, we shall see how mining was transformed through the new methods of labour and the arts, techniques, discoveries and machines in the 15th and 16th century. Commercial practices in the 15th and 16th century in Central Europe as well as the treatment of instruments of credit and securities were changed through new methods from the Mediterranean region. German salespeople, traders and representatives of credit and money institutes went to Italy, to learn how to master the new practices of entrepreneurship.

A trained and disciplined working class was developed in Germany *pari passu* with the accumulation of capital. The two events should be handled in a balanced fashion, not one side at the expense of the other. The development of agriculture, extensive and intensive, was first carried out in the 18th and 19th century, that is, after the liberation of the peasants in the period of Cameralism-Mercantilism, of the industrial revolution and of high capitalism. The spread of the money economy in connection with the upheaval of society from the 15th to the 19th century determined life on the land as it did in the city. The market, commodity relations, the buying and selling of labour time and its products dominated daily life. The natural economy was pushed back. In the formation of the capitalist system and of modern bourgeois society these processes and events are related to one another and are developed together. It would be a vain attempt to give prominence to and discern a single and particular moment that explains everything, claiming then here the mystery would be revealed. Martin Luther is of interest to us because he gave objective expression to the consciousness of his time, namely in the context of the measurement of labour time. We proceed from the fact that Albrecht Dürer is a great painter, nevertheless, the presentation of the aesthetic moment in his art is not the main objective of our investigation. Instead, what is important for us are his utterances on mechanics and geometry as well as his astute apprehension of history. Thus, he appears as a draughtsman, painter, educator and scientist, as one of the greatest Renaissance people in history. The spirit of Albrecht Dürer, whose wood cuts, copper etchings, and drawings pointed to the new ways in art and in science, hovers everywhere. His work belongs in the aesthetic sense to the new age, and he gave expression to thoughts which were later developed by Isaac Newton and C. F. Gauss. Our view of the periodization of history is to be found in his prior conception. The activities of individual personalities are in and for themselves not important for us, however, these people worked and recorded their ideas. They serve as our sources, and it is with their activities and writings with which we grapple.

The science of human society is objective, and therewith objective problems can be solved. The provenance of the capitalist mode of production, which dominates our age, presents an important problem of this kind. Many sciences have offered their contribution to the solution of this problem, which we acknowledge, whereas the very last word has not been spoken. We have emphasized the two moments at the centre of the capitalist process of origination, the development of the labour process in mining as well as in the metal industry and, the movement of liberation of the peasants. The development in mining and in the iron, copper and precious metals industry does not stand alone, but is tightly linked with the art of printing, the system of coinage, the circulation of money and of trade. The liberties of the mines were more or less known to the peasantry; the peasants served as transportation workers in the Harz Mountains and elsewhere, and afterwards aspired to become wage labourers. Their aspiration was imprinted by the social, economic, political and religious conditions of the 15th and 16th century. In the 15th century religion was certainly not the opium of the people but rather a way to self-determination, to self-consciousness and to self-control of the peasantry. The practices in the mining and metal systems were broadened, not only to include the peasants but rather to cover various branches of industry, although here resistance was offered. The weavers' guild, for example, on many occasions rejected the acquisition of the new modes of labour into the 18th century.

The mining business is only a centre of movement in the origin of the capitalist system. The metal industry as a whole can also be taken up in this context. For purely practical reasons we've begun with the mining business, because the writings of Agricola, Biringuccio, Ercker, Schreitmann and Kunkel are so prominent. Their works are not only prominent, but rather above all scientific, factual, strikingly objective and anti-mystical.

Equally important is the print industry, which is likewise to be considered a centre of movement like mining in the origin of the capitalist system. The printing press which came into being and was disseminated in the 15th century, stands in close relation with the development of the metal industry and of the publishing system, and the current book industry is in fact determined by the further progress of this system. The printing plant, in its early origin and development, had exerted an impact on industrialization, on the liberation of the peasants, on political consciousness and on the qualification of the working class. Merchants learned new trading practices and the art of calculation [*Rechenkunst*] from the new books. Science mastered the mathematics of Euclid and Archimedes from printed books. The peasants spread their calls to action, articles and reports through printed leaflets. The religious denominations printed not only indulgences, but articles, disputations and instructions as well. Books of antiquity and of modern times were printed and disseminated. The education of humanism and of the workers, writing and arithmetic were prepared through books. The new school system in its origin and development as well as the university system were bound up with the art of printing.

New navigation, shipbuilding and long-distance trade associations formed a specific centre in the process of capitalist origination and development. The new shipping industry from the Mediterranean region shaped the overseas trade of the neighbouring states of Spain and Portugal, England, Holland, Germany and France. The voyages of discovery to America and Asia were determined by developments in the art of shipbuilding and in the shipping industry in general and presupposed them. The armament and war industries were closely related to the new metal and shipping arts.

We begin with the business of mining on the above-mentioned foundation. The miners initially secured their liberties and propagated them to the greatest degree and were the earliest to do so. The freedoms of bourgeois life were abstracted from the model of the liberties of the towns of the early capitalist system. The freedoms we enjoy today are based on the old liberties of the past. They form the contrast to agrarian practices and feudalism. The liberties of modern bourgeois society are not abstract, but rather are to be understood concretely in the free movement of the labourers, in the freedom of contract, and in the liberation of the peasants from compulsory labour. We sing no songs of glory to the capitalist system, which is based on the exploitation of the indigenous peasants and labourers and on their oppression, later on the exploitation and oppression of the world outside Europe, of Africa, Asia and Latin America. The freedom of modern bourgeois society and of the capitalist system is a formal and not substantial freedom.

It is not about a single historical moment that led to the transformation of the feudal system and the establishment of the capitalist system. Some thinkers in the 19th and 20th century who investigated the problem of transformation and establishment came to the conclusion that there was a specific factor in the transition from the old to the new social and economic system. Now they have given emphasis to different factors and historical moments, such as the new ethic, new securities, new capitalist forms of organization, new bookkeeping practices, the discovery of America, etc. The search for such a single *causa efficiens* has its advantages and disadvantages. And important economic and social processes were explained by this quest for a singular and predominating historical moment. However, it appears to be the same quest as with the alchemists of old for the philosophers' stone, which transforms everything into gold. There is no simple way to understand the processes of history. Euclid said 2300 years ago there is no royal road to geometry; we stand on the side of Euclid, Agricola, Biringuccio and Ercker. The entire society in the 15th, 16th, and 17th century participated in the process of transition from the Middle Ages to the modern era. Some classes and interest groups were set in opposition to the new social order and wanted to maintain the good old times. Other classes and groups fought for the new social order. We treat the social and economic systems as totalities, which are linked and formed by the struggle between the opposed parts.

The historians of technique have made great achievements, and, in this way, they have earned our thanks for their researches. They have listed the sequence of inventions and discoveries. But, as a result, we only hold the parts in our hand, and the social bond is, alas, missing. To usefully apply the new inventions and discoveries, the workers employed the new methods in economic practice. Without their practical application, the discoveries and inventions remain like ghostly things in the air. The qualitative training and the quantitative expansion of the working class, the manipulation of the earth, of the air and water, and the formation of the entrepreneurial class, of technics and of science together prepare the foundation of the capitalist era. Traditionally, the past is investigated on three grounds: first as an object in and for itself, which we love, hate, marvel at or attack; second, in order to come to grips with historical process of the past down to yesterday or today; third, and what is most significant, to better understand the world today and, if possible, to master it. The first reason was represented by the neo-Kantians of the Wilhelmine period, to showcase history ideographically. Everything in human history is presented according to this method as a coincidental matter occurring by accident without lawfulness. Treating history pictorially as a beautiful or hateful form would require the spirit [*Geist*] and pen of Lessing, Schiller or Goethe, not ours. We take up the last two reasons, which are closely bound up with the question of periodization and of the lawfulness of history.

PART I

CHAPTER ONE

The Beginnings of Modern Bourgeois Society in Central Europe

The Bourgeois Revolution from the 15th–17th Centuries

A thousand years ago in large areas of Central and Western Europe, the feudal system, feudalism, serfdom, estates and the unfreedom of the peasantry dominated; now in the same region there is modern bourgeois society and the freedom of all citizens. A transformation of the old system occurred in the 15th to the 17th century, which was accomplished so quickly and so fundamentally that one could refer to it as revolution. The concept of a bourgeois revolution in the 15th to the 17th century is related to the introduction of the capitalist system, the expanded market and money economy, the liberation of the peasants, the development of urban industry and the founding of the nation state system of the modern era. The different estates, strata and classes of peasants, of merchants and of the urban working class have taken part in this transformation. Nevertheless, this revolution was in no way unitary; the aristocracy, the royal court and the Church together constituted the leading stratum in the European society of the Middle Ages and at the beginning of the modern era. The dominant role of this stratum in politics was not immediately refashioned.

Five hundred years ago many people were conscious of the fact that in their era it was not about the continuation of the past conditions of life, but rather that it was a new era in which new conditions of life occasionally surfaced not as isolated phenomena in this or that aspect of social relations, but rather everywhere, in the systems of economy and law, in religion, in the arts and sciences. In the south and in the north of Europe one spoke of a Renaissance.

Feudalism lasted for some time; it differed from antiquity. But in opposition to the transition to the modern era people in the Middle Ages did not delve into their distinction from the previous period of classical antiquity. They were not conscious of the transitional period, as were the painters, thinkers, poets and philologists of the modern era who distinguished their era from the previous one and separated the Middle Ages from classical antiquity. The notions of a succession of periods and of a periodization in human history are not new. Already in antiquity Hesiod sang of an earlier golden and beautiful period and of a later iron and ugly age. Aristotle repeated this idea in an altered form, and in fact did this in connection with his theory of myth, which he brought out in his *Metaphysics*. The period is the hallmark of a demeanour of people in the world; the end of a period is the indicator of the dissolution of that demeanour, of its upheaval and of the demarcation of the present from the past. However, a historical epoch is not a living being; it is not born, and it does not die. It disappears when the conditions which formed it are essentially changed.

What is called bourgeois society came about in several countries of Europe, first in the Mediterranean region, then in Upper Germany, on the Atlantic coast and on the Rhein. Communication of the north with the countries of the Mediterranean was driven by trade, the arts and the sciences. Scientists and artists went to Italy and studied there, and German traders were active in Venice, where they learnt the mercantile experience [*Praxis*] of practical calculation [*Rechenkunst*] and bookkeeping.

The new men were not entirely new, the medieval relations of domination not entirely superseded. These had been reproduced in urban patrician lineages and in the aristocracy of modern times. As one of the resplendent figures of the modern era, the printer Johann Gensfleisch zum Gutenberg, the son of a patrician family in Mainz, made his mark. The 16th century was commonly portrayed as the epoch of new beginnings. We, however, set the origin of capitalist system in Central Europe in the 15th century; it began still earlier in Northern Italy. It depends on what kind of a model is sought out for identifying the beginning. The focal point of this work is the idea and justification of the periodization and of the model which it assumes. If one begins with the Mediterranean region the process of origination appears to have begun earlier, in Central Europe later. The process of trade and production appeared in Northern Italy in the 13th and 14th century, a century later in Upper Germany. Weavers and merchants served as pathfinders of progress in the Mediterranean region. The weavers' guilds were not progressive in Germany; on the contrary, they reacted rather negatively to progress in production. Miners and merchants were progressive north of the Alps. These assertions are related to urban life. Equally important, perhaps even more important, is the origin of the peasant movement in Central Europe in the 15th and 16th century, somewhat earlier in Northern Italy and in England.

It is essential to know where and when one investigates the beginnings of the capitalist system. If the history of capitalism is set in the Mediterranean region, an entirely different model of the originating process than in Central Europe is obtained. The historical dynamic in the transition to capitalism in Italy and Spain appears bound up with the development of seafaring and shipbuilding more closely than in Germany; the same dynamic in Central Europe, on the other hand, appears to be more closely linked with mining, with the metal industry and printing than in the Mediterranean countries. The difference in the historical dynamic is huge not only regionally but also in terms of time. Transformations in the merchant class and in the practices of trade and banking begin earlier in Italy than in Germany; the Germans went to Venice to appropriate new processes and modes of commerce. One gets a completely different view of the origin of the capitalist system if the beginnings of it are examined in England and Holland, and this in turn changes if the origin of capitalism in France and Spain is the object of research, where mercantilism played an especially important role.

If one begins with the periodization of the capitalist era in Central Europe, the epoch of the 15th and 16th century thus appears to be the most influential in this process. Nevertheless, the capitalist system arises in specific countries under different conditions. The emergence of the capitalist system does not occur simultaneously in all parts of Germany, England, Italy or Holland. In Italy, it appears earlier in the north than in central and southern Italy, in Central Europe earlier in Upper Germany, in the coastal cities of the North and Baltic Sea; it appears on the Rhein and Main sooner than in the districts east of the Elbe. The weavers' guilds were opposed to manufacturing and the establishment of textile factories, although they instituted a putting-out system early in the capitalist historical process; house-building, too, remained medieval in that period.

The systematic development of trade, of capital, of wage labour, of the commodities market, of credit institutes and of the circulation of money occurred in the 15th and 16th century based on a sporadic appearance of the same process in the late Middle Ages. We will attempt to specify the definition of the system more precisely in this work. The capitalist system changed from one epoch to another and from one country to the other, but the system of wage labour and capital remained approximately the same in its economic relations. The transition from the Middle Ages to modern times has been traced back to the discovery of America, to the invention of the printing press and of the hand casting of type, to the Reformation, to the principles and practices of mechanics, to the establishment of the great trading companies, to the mercantile activities of the Jews, to the liberation of the peasants or the expansion of money circulation at the cost of the natural economy.

Each period has its own particularities and amazements. One talks about inventions and voyages of discovery, because they are palpable and worthy of wonder. Nevertheless, sensations are not the determining moments in the period or in the question of periodization. The purely military-political writings of history dealt with the conquest of Constantinople by the Turks in the year 1453 and its impact on intercourse between Europe and the Near East. We will consider these events not simply as a cause, but rather as an effect of further factors in the history of Eurasia.

Originally the new economic, social and artistic practices were judged positively and negatively. The peasants sought to become wage labourers; of course, not all, but many in Central, Southern and Western Germany took part in the process of transformation. Martin Luther selected and cursed the monopoly companies [*Gesellschaft Monopolia*] and the peasants' revolt, that is the two historical moments which were important in initiating the modern age. The monopoly company [*Gesellschaft Monopolia*] is not to be considered a joint-stock company, but rather the capitalist form of organization originating from medieval monopoly. Adam Smith opposed the organization of guilds, monopolies, slavery, and championed free trade, free labour, and the open market. This has to do with a market monopoly in the late Middle Ages and the beginnings of the modern era, so that the burgesses were only able to buy their cloth from one guild, their knives only from another. Conversely, the domestic workers who created their cloth and knives, needles and thread found the demand for their products only with one merchant, not with any other. This practice is called the monopoly company [*Gesellschaft Monopolia*]. The critique of the monopolistic practices of the 16th century was started by Luther; opinions of this kind had already arisen in the Middle Ages. The merchant class and manufacture in the 18th century attenuated the activities of the guild monopolies; the industrial revolution unfurled a bond with free trade and set itself against the mercantilism of the 17th and 18th century. This referred to the politics of insertion by men of state into the economic system. Adam Smith exercised a sharp critique of the intervention by the men of state into the healthy affairs of the industrialists, of the capitalists and of the private enterprises; the state was supposed to interfere as little as possible in the private sphere. *In hoc signo*, that is in this symbol of Lutheran condemnation of monopolies and of Smith's praise of private enterprise and interests, Marx portrayed modern bourgeois society as the most developed and complex organization of production in history, as we have seen above.

The peasant war and the Reformation are the great events of the 16th century in the history of Central Europe and it is thus no wonder that according to the theories of Karl Marx and Max Weber, this period is presented as the decisive one in the process of development of the modern bourgeois social formation. What both thinkers have said holds true for some aspects of the history of Central Europe, for others, on the other hand, it does not; nor does it apply in the case of the capitalist economic and social system in general. If the enquiry begins in Italy, then the same process of transition and of the new beginning could be regarded differently. The peasant liberation movements had their beginning at the close of the 14th century in Northern Italy and in England.

So as not to give a complete explanation for the process of transformation but rather to designate it as a problem, let us take as an example the figure of Jacques Coeur, who was a wealthy man in Bourges, a copper king. He was not an aristocrat but rather a man of the common people, who had risen up; then, in 1453, he was charged and arrested by the authorities in France. Jakob Fugger, the wealthy man, was also a copper king; he was not a nobleman but was born in the year 1459 into a guild family in Augsburg. If one situates the new era in the 16th century, then Jacques Coeur and Jakob Fugger would be considered capitalists and the large firm of Thurzo and Fugger as a capitalistic enterprise without capitalism. Marx asserted that modern bourgeois society appeared sporadically before, and systematically in the 16th century. This view can prevail if one highlights the period of the Reformation as the standard for the beginning of the capitalist historical process.

The question of periodization is not a matter of persons or of singular appearances such as inventions, but rather one of social moments and movements, personified in the above-named individuals. During the 15th century peasants in the different countries of Europe had attempted to free themselves. Shipbuilding and the arts of seafaring linked with it were developed in the area of the Mediterranean; the sea passages to America and India were discovered; the printing industry was founded in Mainz and Frankfurt. Trade between Upper Italy, Upper Germany, Brabant, Spain, Flanders, France, England, Holland and Portugal was expanded. Mechanical clocks, paper, cannons and gunpowder were produced in several countries of Western Europe. Mining was transformed and then the mine share certificates for the same were sold. We will relativize the above-mentioned views. What was valued as an innovation namely from the standpoint of Central European practice, is to be considered as an already systematically developed matter from the standpoint of Northern Italy. Nevertheless, taken as a whole, the capitalist moments of the 16th century were more fully developed than in the 15th in Europe overall.

The history of that epoch is not determined by the military or political events of the 15th century such as the conquest of Byzantium by the Turks and the Reconquista of Spain by the Spanish, but rather only delimited by them. Islam, which had spread over the Iberian Peninsula and Sicily in the early Middle Ages, was pushed back; in Southeast Europe it was propagated in the 15th and 16th century. The Middle Ages as a period and as a historical category, is related to European, not to Islamic peoples. For Islam, the epoch of new beginning and awakening is the 7th century. Finally, the extension of the Russian Empire beyond Siberia took place in the 16th, 17th, and 18th century, the liberation of the peasants in that country only in the 19th.

It was clear to the Europeans during the transition from the Middle Ages to the modern era that they were living in a period of radical transformation, as Petrarca, Alberti, Erasmus and Dürer attested. Further, they were aware of the duration and the extent of the process of transformation, as they were of its depth. Thus, Albrecht Dürer wrote in relation to painting in 1525: "In what honour and worthiness these arts were held by the Greeks and Romans, is demonstrated by the ancient books well enough. Even though they were subsequently lost altogether and even hidden for a thousand years and only two hundred years ago once again brought to light of day by the Italians [*die Wahlen*]."[1] In his opinion the Italians brought about the renaissance of art in the 14th century. His book relates not only to art but to Euclidean geometry as well. Giorgio Vasari in his book which appeared shortly thereafter held the same view concerning the painters, sculptors and architects. Tizian, according to Vasari's assertion, could be counted among the greatest painters through his mastery of colour, even though, as Fra Bastiano del Piombo declared, Tizian never visited Rome to view the statues there. The creative force of antiquity had an impact on the modern arts through its statues and its architecture.[2]

The recognition of change by the Italian scholars Petrarch and Alberti was discussed after them by Dürer and Vasari. The consciousness of the process of transformation was thus given expression, only with them the technical terms were missing such that the abstract *termini technici feudal* and *medieval* came into use only in the 17th century. The history of the concrete expression is other than that of the concrete word. *Feodum, fief* in the concrete meaning are both already mentioned in the medieval epoch. The general term and word for the feudal Middle Ages was related to the past in the linguistic usage of the 17th century.

There are multiple moments which led to the transition from the Middle Ages to modern bourgeois society. The contacts of the various parts of Europe to one another and to the external world in Asia, Africa and America in the 15th and 16th century, further the intercourse which this contact occasioned and the movements of people from the country to the city as well as from one country to another extended this transition or new beginning; in the qualitative sense they deepened and further developed it. This concerns externally free movements and inner compulsion. Copernicus, Dürer, Agricola freely emigrated to Italy and freely returned home. The religious views of that time, too, show the striving for a new beginning, not only out of free choice, but rather out of inner compulsion and necessity, as Luther's well-known expression: *I can do nothing other* declares. The concepts of new beginning and of restauration are not new. In their religions, the Hebrews, the early Christians and the Muslims spoke of a new beginning through the prophets and the Messiah and thereby heralded world renewal.

According to Dürer's understanding, the arts of his period had entered into a process of a new beginning. From our standpoint, the Renaissance is a form, an epoch of completion, an idiographic whole, not a part of something larger but rather the being in-and-for-itself of enormous creative human activity. The economic moments of that epoch, on the contrary, present themselves as a preparation and as a transition. The contemporary consciousness of it is the reverse. We shall concretize this assertion. Petrarch and Dürer believed they lived in a period of dawning, of spiritual *re-awakening*, on the doorstep of further development. Jakob Fugger, on the other hand, was not conscious that this had to do with something new, a new beginning in his time; in his view mercantile activity was in full bloom and he only wanted to continue what he and his fellow merchants had already set in motion, and to continue to drive what had already been undertaken. The scope of our survey ends in the 17th century. The epoch of early capitalism and beginnings of modern bourgeois society have their system which forms the object of the present work. This epoch gave way to the imposition of the free market, of the industrial revolution, of the nation state system and of the Enlightenment of the 18th century. The German Hansa, the Patrician system in Augsburg, Nuremburg, Mainz, and elsewhere, and the Holy Roman Empire of the German Nation did not survive the new moments. Neither the beginning stage nor the later industrial stage were introduced simultaneously everywhere. Thus, Dürer portrayed his historical perspective which appears to us to be so decisive. Capitalism in the 15th and 16th century is part of a larger system. John Winchcombe ("Jack of Newbury") Jacques Coeur, Fugger, Thurzo, Gutenberg, Erasmus, Petrarch, Dürer, Leonardo da Vinci, Fibonacci, Pacioli, Adam Ries, Luther, Calvin, Columbus, Vasco da Gama, Magellan, Agricola and Biringuccio were people and at the same time symbols which pointed to a changed human activity.

From 1347 to 1506 26 universities were established in Central Europe. At that time, students went to Italy for training in medicine, mathematics, arithmetic, astronomy, and classical philology; The universities of Salerno, Bologna, and Padua served as important reference points for higher education. The early universities in Central Europe, England and France were not centres for the natural sciences, but rather for the four disciplines of philosophy, law, medicine and theology as well, as Goethe had enumerated them. The Central European universities were endowed by various means, by papal bulls as well as by imperial or other noble authorization. In the 16th and 17th century 20 additional universities were established; some did not survive for long, 8 of them were abandoned shortly after their establishment. The universities were small in comparison with those of today. In 1588 there were 13 professors and 588 students in Heidelberg; they were for the most part, although not all, registered at the University of Heidelberg.[3] On average the number of students in a university at that time amounted to between 300 and 500.

The Italian, Giovanni Botero took a critical position against the universities. He believed it would be better if they had less to do with the conflicts of the tongue and of the dagger. Yet, he took note of the contribution of the university to the *grandezza* of the city.[4]

The establishment of the system of nation states in Central Europe took place at the end of the early period of capitalism. Development did not proceed in a straight line. When the nation state appeared in the 17th and 18th century in Central Europe, it disappeared again straightaway. Hegel complained in 1802 that Germany was no longer a state.[5] The beginnings of the mercantilist-cameralist system, manufacturing and the establishment of the German nation state signified the end of the early epoch of modern bourgeois society.

Our undertaking in this part of the book is to investigate the theories concerning the beginning and the first stages of the capitalist period in Central Europe. It is therefore a problem of periodization that was repeatedly taken up by historians, philosophers, political scientists, economists, sociologists, and ethnologists. All of these disciplines provided their contribution to our problem. Our task becomes complicated by the fact that the words change their meanings, as can be understood by means of the following examples. Books concerning the democracy of antiquity and of the modern period were published *en masse*. The word is derived from classical Greek; the practice, the theory and the meaning of the word in the present have nevertheless little to do with that of Socrates' times. We speak now only of formal democracy. In antiquity one already had the right to vote, but only a small part of the population—5 or 10%—could exercise it. In the Athens of antiquity slaves, women and foreigners constituted the majority of the population.

They were excluded from the political process of the city. Democracy and freedom in this sense signify political, formal democracy and freedom.

The peasants of Central Europe in the 15th and 16th century were, for the most part, serfs. They were not slaves as in antiquity, but they lacked formal freedom in the political sense. The theory of freedom was traced back to the Jubilee year in the Old Testament according to which the slaves were freed with a cry of jubilation; further expressions concerning human freedom are then to be found in the Institutes of the Roman Emperor Justinian. Hegel linked the concepts of freedom and political practice. In the East only the head of state was free, in his hands alone was political power united. In classical Greece some citizens were free; only they could vote, have a say, decide; slaves, on the contrary, could not. Afterwards, only those who were citizens availed themselves of freedom and the right to vote; the serfs could not.[6] As we shall see, Hegel brought together 350 years of Central European liberation movements and gave expression to them. *חרות*, *חור* (*Chor*, *Cherut*) in the Old Testament, *liber* in Justinian had at once the same and other meanings than *frei* (free) in modern times. There is a philological relationship between democracy in antiquity and in modern bourgeois society. We will return to this question.

The category of bourgeois society—societé civile, political and civil society—extends across Antiquity and the modern era, and thus we speak of the difference of modern bourgeois society from the civil society of Antiquity or of the Middle Ages. Democracy is also found outside of civil society, namely among the non-literate peoples or so-called primitives. Finally, we mention the words *natio* and nationality, which played a large role in the 15th and 16th up to the 20th century. Without our getting involved with the question of the nationality of Copernicus, Dürer or Agricola, we take note of the circumstance that in their age students in Italy were registered as members of this or that *natio*. The concept of German nation had a different meaning then than it does today.

The focal point of our investigation will not be the word *natio*, but rather the labour process in the 15th and 16th century in the Central European region, mainly in its German-speaking part.

The events, with which we are dealing, exist in space and in time. The delimitations and designations of the spatial details are not fixed and constant, but rather variable. Central Europe is not seen today the way it was in the 15th and 16th century. Hence, we will take up in a loose way the territorial concept in the sense understood then in that part of the world which lies between the Hansa cities of Hamburg, Lübeck, Danzig as well as Emden, the Calvinist Centre in the north, and Basel, Strasbourg, Vienna and Budapest in the south. Such a delimitation by city is still only partly accurate, because the population was mainly rural. Agrarian relations in the 15th to the 17th century were, moreover, not unitary. Agriculture in the eastern part of Central Europe was operated fundamentally differently than in the western part.

History can be treated as a continuous or as a discontinuous process. In the first case, the same relations, life conditions and ideas are encountered in the past and in the present, if not entirely, then nevertheless in a variation of the same. In the second case, however, there is an abyss which lies between the past and present in the historical process, or even several such discontinuities are noticeable. In the 17th century Leibniz asserted in relation to the first continuous mode of treatment, nature makes no leap: *natura non facit saltum*.

Another adumbration of the same idea emerges in the myth of the eternal return of the past, as well as in the assertion there is nothing new in the world. Human history is thus conceived as a recurring cycle. In opposition to this idea, we proceed from the notion that there are discontinuities in history, hence, periods in relation to which a discontinuity can be objectively indicated. The indices for this are manifested in two ways: in the idiographies of the fine arts and in the nomotheses of the labour processes. The idiographies are the peculiarities, the nomotheses are the laws, the positing of laws and the lawful aspects of nature and of the process of labour.

To be sure, the creation of a painting or of a poem includes both the objective as well as the subjective moments in itself. The objective moments in art were shown by Leonardo, Michelangelo, Raphael, and Dürer through the mastering of the theory of colour, of Euclidean geometry and through the laws of perspective according to Brunelleschi and Alberti. Dante and Petrarch mastered the objectively existing laws of Latin and Italian grammar. The nomothetic in the labour process constitutes the major theme of the present work. It is therefore true that the labourers and labour in the form of compulsory labour [*Frondienst*] were unfree and that wage labourers are free in the formal sense.

These research categories will be treated empirically and concretely. Two questions are to be distinguished, empirical research and the quest for universals. The first leads to scientific laws and conceptions, but not to universal, absolute principles. The attempts of the metaphysicians are abstract *sub specie aeternitatis*. Neither they nor Leibniz distinguished the universalisations, which were empirically conceived, from absolute universals. We have considered nature and human history as lawlike, because they display rule-like appearances under concrete conditions. They cannot be regulated under all conditions by the humankind.

The fine arts of poetry and of painting consciously introduced a new epoch in their history. The peasants consciously and deliberately fought for their freedom, and this struggle led to a new historical epoch. These two epoch-making phenomena are related to the beginning of modern bourgeois society; they determine the transition from the feudal period and delimit it from the modern bourgeois. The artists and the peasants were conscious of their activities. We have cited Dürer not as an embellisher, but rather as a self-conscious interpreter, one of the first, who mastered the concept of the New as a painter in Central Europe and discussed it theoretically as a thinker.

A brisk intercourse arose in the 15th and 16th century between the various parts of Europe, further, across and beyond the Mediterranean among the European, Asiatic and African countries, and finally across the Atlantic, Indian and Pacific oceans with America and the Far East. This intercourse was not only extensively, but rather also qualitatively and intensively developed and, in this way, was driven in peacetime by trade and by education differently than in times of war. In the state of war neither law nor intercourse are silent.[7] Agricola wrote a book about the war with the Turks; in mining and coinage Turkish coins came to Europe as did *darbhane* [mint, coinage]. In the Middle Ages one seldom had immediate access to the Greek texts of Aristotle, Euclid, Archimedes, among others, but after the Turkish conquest of Constantinople a number of Greek scholars went to Rome. The Italians, the Germans and others took advantage of this opportunity to study the Greek language and the ancient texts. Let's take an example: When the Greek Cardinal Bessarion went to Rome, the German mathematician Regiomontan came to him and studied the Greek language and the texts of Archimedes. After his return, Regiomontan had these texts printed and published.

Transport links became varied and multiplied in this regard: Italy—Byzantium, Upper Germany—Italy; Ancient Greek philology and the interchange between mathematicians and philologists; the connection between Archimedean geometry, book printing and instruction was advanced by Regiomontan in the 15th century. These activities are related to the field of mathematical theory, of book publishing and the book trade, of pedagogy, of linguistics and of the rising class of entrepreneurs. One could also add other fields of activity. The entrepreneurial activities of Regiomontan found favour with the public and the Church as well. His undertakings were crowned with success in mathematics, in the ecclesiastical hierarchy as well as in the book trade. Transportation links between Byzantium and Rome, between Italy and Germany were developed in both directions in the 15th century. In the 16th century Dürer had mastered the theoretical writings of Euclidean geometry and applied them in a practical way in painting, architecture and city planning and, in this way, contributed to pedagogy.[8]

Notes

1. A. Dürer, *Unterweisung der Messung*, Nürnberg, 1525. [In this and in later citations the writing is largely brought closer to current orthography].
2. G. Vasari, *Le Vite de' più Eccelenti Pittori, Scultori e Architettori* (1550), 2nd edition 1568.
3. F. Eulenberg, Städtische Berufs- und Gewerbestatistik (Heidelbergs) im 16. Jahrhundert, *Zeitschrift für die Geschichte des Oberrheins*, N.F. Bd. 11, 1896.
4. G. Botero, *Delle Cause della Grandezza delle Citta*, 1596.
5. G. W. F. Hegel, *Die Verfassung Deutschlands*, 1802. Hegel believed the state as well as other human institutions were not eternal things, but rather transient. They would disappear in order to re-appear in a new and almost unthinkable form. Hegel later changed his opinion concerning the state. Hegel's view, that Germany was no longer a state, is related to the year 1801/02. Prior to that, Germany was a state. Frederick the Great was the sole master of his state in the middle of the 18th century [*Vorlesungen über die Philosophie der Weltgeschichte*, J. Hoffmeister (ed.) Bd. 4 Hamburg 1968]. Hegel considered Frederick the Great the philosophical king. Heinrich von Treitschke took up Hegel's idea and saw Frederick the Great as a true head of state. This view was not universally held in the Wilhemine period. Hugo Preuss, *Die Entstehung des deutschen Städtewesens*, Leipzig 1906, wrote: "Germany was stateless for centuries—since the beginnings of the Reformation period."
6. G. W. F. Hegel, *Vorlesungen über die Philosophie der Weltgeschichte*, J. Hoffmeister (Ed.) 2nd edition (1839) Volume 1, Hamburg 1968.
7. The question concerning right and law in the state of war had an important meaning in the early epoch of modern bourgeois society. Hugo Grotius published his book *De Jure Belli ac Pacis* (*Concerning the Law of War and Peace*) in 1625. The laws correspond to right. Entirely to the contrary Thomas Hobbes asserted: Inter arma silent leges—in the state of war the laws are silent. He repeated Cicero (*Pro Milone*). Yet the interconnections were not interrupted by the state of war. Agricola composed a book against the Turks: *De Bello adversus Turcam*, Basel 1528 (In German: *Oration, Anrede und Vormanung … wieder den Türken*. L. Berman translator, Nürnberg 1530) But Turkish coins were described and disseminated in German mining and coinage.
8. Regiomontan: see J. Tropfke, *Geschichte der Elementarmathematik*, 4th edition, Vol. 1, K. Vogel et al. (eds.), Berlin, 1980. Albrecht Dürer, *Unterweisung der Messung*. Id. *Etliche Unterricht zu Befestigung der Städte, Schloss und Flechen*, Nürnberg, 1527.

CHAPTER TWO

Theoretical Conceptions of the Transition from Feudalism to the Modern Era in the History of Central Europe

Marx, Weber and Troeltsch, Sombart and Kulischer, Schumpeter

2.1 General Remarks

Central Europe in the epoch between the 15th and 17th century found itself in the process of configuring a new social formation. The region was not on its own in this process of transition and transformation, but rather stood enmeshed in contact with Italy, the Netherlands, England and the other neighbouring states on the Baltic and Atlantic. From today's standpoint one can consider the peoples of that time as developing, finding themselves in an imminent process which leads to high capitalism. On the other hand, the following should be noted: History has no railroad tracks and does not lead with necessity to contemporary conditions. In the past there were various forms of organization which appeared in the period of early capitalism. However, many of these paths of activity were abolished, such as the guild, the Hansa, the Fugger, and the putting-out [cottage industry] models. We shall see how these commercial organizations were not in keeping with their own time, nor adopted in a later time.

A teleological conception of history would have to assert that the capitalistic path leads with an inner necessity and independent logic from the earlier epoch to the later forms of enterprise. The system of guilds, of the town council, of the patrician lines of kinship, of those who provided the raw materials in the putting-out or domestic system [*Verlage*] in the city economy did not survive the

Reformation, the peasant rebellion and the Thirty Years' War. The English, Dutch, French, Spanish and Portuguese colonial systems, the mercantilist system, the system of free trade and of the Industrial Revolution pointed to other paths than that of capitalist development. The concept of *early capitalism* is in this respect deficient. Nevertheless, there are profound commonalities with the capitalist system in the 15th to the 20th century.

Neither Italy in the 14th nor Germany in the 15th century can be thought of as developing countries like Egypt or India are today. Hence the comparison between the developing countries of the 20th century and the countries in the 14th/15th century which we name here as examples, for short Italy or Germany would be futile, for Italy and Germany did not then exist. The Italians and the Germans were on the level of development of the other parts of Europe, and Europe was at the level of development of other parts of the world. In some cases, Central Europe was not so highly developed, in other cases, more highly so. In mining and metallurgy as well as in metal working, in the production of clocks and books, in commercial practices, in the banking and credit systems Central Europe was perhaps in advance of the other countries of Europe; however, the Germans adopted arithmetic and commercial practices to a large extent from the Italians. Around 1500 the Mediterranean countries were superior in seafaring and in shipbuilding in comparison to Central Europe. The concept of development was already at hand, but it was different than ours. Nicolas of Cuso used the word *explicatio* in the 15th century; *pli* has the meaning of *fold-*, hence, unfolding, development. The process of development was applied to nature, to the economy, to politics and to human beings. Today two developmental models for the Third World are presented; for the world of the 15th and 16th century in Asia and Europe there was no such thing. Thus, the theories and practices of development in the 15th/16th century are not comparable with those of the present. Development is conceivable in relation to the European past, but in another sense than in the present. A developmental model would be applicable in connection with the relations between parts of South Asia or West Africa (like Sri Lanka or Togo) and parts of Western Europe in the present, however, not between Central and Southern Europe in the 16th century and not at all for the Germans of the 16th century in relation to the 19th or 20th.

Economic development did not continue peacefully. Military events in Central Europe during the 16th/17th century constituted a historical, an active and at the same time a passive moment of development. Obstacles to economic growth which the wars of religion and of national states brought in their train, were later transformed into a progressive moment, because the old ruling class was weakened by the continuous warfare. They played a positive role insofar as the peasants were able to win their freedom under these conditions. The ancient chains of the peasant and proletarian estates were cast off in part in the 15th to the 17th century. But the absolutism of the 18th century was no heavenly kingdom of freedom for the peasants and the urban labourers. Lessing and Schiller portrayed the bondage of their epoch. It took centuries for the bonds of the past to loosen, in part through compulsion, in part through being forcefully removed, in part re-tightened. Historians have with reason separated the events of the year 1848 from previous years.

In the 16th and 17th century the authorities were constantly weakened on economic, political and military grounds. For these reasons the bourgeois class and the peasants could free themselves from the chains of the past.

2.2 The Transition from Feudalism to Modern Bourgeois Society According to Karl Marx

On a number of occasions, Karl Marx wrote about the transformation of European society in the process of transition to the modern era. Perhaps the best-known passage for explaining his view is in his book *Das Kapital* found in the chapter on so-called primitive accumulation, in which the events in Italy and England are paramount. "In England serfdom practically disappeared in the last part of the 14th century. The vast majority of the population then and even more in the 15th century consisted of free peasants engaged in subsistence farming ..." Earlier he noted: "In Italy, where capitalist production was developed earliest, the dissolution of servile relations also occurred earliest. The serf here was emancipated before he had secured any right of limitations on land and soil. His emancipation thus transformed him immediately into a completely free [*vogelfrei*][1] proletarian condemned to fend for himself as such ..."[2] Thereupon the labourers in the cities were driven onto the land as the peasants were previously driven from the farming village into the city.

Elsewhere Marx had assessed the participation of Central Europe in these developments from the technological standpoint. He mentioned Nuremberg as the main seat of craftsman-like and factory-based inventions of tools such as the clock (the *Nuremberg egg*), the jack for the fabrication and placement of the heads of pins; the thimble was also a Nuremberg invention. Manually operated paper mills, later water powered paper mills, were also produced in Nuremberg; further, the wholesale production of paper as well as the self-propelled carriages without a team of horses and with a gear train were products of Nuremberg in the 16th/17th century. The citizens of Nuremberg and Augsburg were at that time excellent cabinetmakers.[3]

Marx wrote about the transformation of the feudal system to the capitalist in Flanders, Holland, and Barcelona. The treatment of this transition was related to the process of production, trade and commerce: "The original historical forms in which capital appears at first sporadically or locally, beside the old modes of production, but gradually exploding them everywhere, is the actual *manufacture* (not yet the factory), on the one hand; this arises there where exports are mass produced for the foreign market—thus on the basis of large sea and land trade, in their large commercial centres, as in the Italian states, Constantinople, in the Flemish, Dutch cities, some of the Spanish, like Barcelona, etc. Manufacture includes at first not the so-called urban trade—but rather a secondary cottage industry based in the country, spinning and weaving, labour which demands the least genuine skill and artistic training. Outside of those large commercial centres, where they find the foundation of a foreign market, hence production so to speak geared *spontaneously* to exchange value—hence manufactures which belong together with seafaring, shipbuilding itself, etc.—establish their first home not in the cities but rather in the country, in villages without guilds, etc. The secondary trade in the countryside contains the broad basis of manufacture, while city trade requires highly advanced production, in order to be carried out at the factory level. Likewise, such branches of industry as glass factories, metal factories, sawmills, etc. which from the beginning require a greater concentration of manpower; from the start they utilize more natural forces, require mass production, as well as the concentration of means of production, etc. The same is the case with paper factories, etc. On the other hand, there was the rise of tenant farmers and the transformation of the agricultural population into free day labourers. Even though this transformation was achieved most recently in its ultimate consequences and in its purest form in the countryside, its earliest beginnings are also there. The old folks who never got beyond actual urban industrious artistry, could therefore never get to large industry. Its first requirement is the inclusion of the countryside in its entire range into the production not of use values but rather of exchange values. Glass factories, paper mills, iron works, etc. could not be operated in the way of the guilds. They require mass production; sales to a universal market; money wealth on the part of the entrepreneur—it's not as if he creates either the subjective or objective conditions; but under the old relations of property and production these conditions could not be brought together."[4]

Cloth as the product of secondary industry in the countryside comes into close connection with the great land and overseas trade of the port cities on the Mediterranean and on the coast of the North Sea. Seafaring and the shipbuilding arts bound up with sea trade require intensification of the labour force; this first happens within the guild organization. Rural enterprises in the countryside in cloth production as well were run by wage labour. Here wage labour was introduced earliest. The early capitalist putting-out system stands on the one hand in confrontation with medieval procedures in the same system, on the other hand in confrontation with the expanded circulation of money, with the tenant farmers, with manufacture and with the transformation of the peasants into piece and day wage workers linked to it. The guild system appears in this connection as something transitory and disappears in the course of development of the manufacturing process in the capitalist era. The natural forces of water, wind and gravity were applied through mechanisation in the labour process and in the products of the manufacturing period; natural energy itself is concentrated in the process of production and distribution and the products were produced as mass commodities.

The development of the capitalist system according to this conception of Marx was based in coastal cities like Genoa, Pisa, Venice, Antwerp, Constantinople, Barcelona and in their hinterland. Mining and the copper trade in Upper Germany as well as the printing industry were left out. The dynamic factors are manufacturing in the villages and barter trade with its products.

The movement of peasants in Northern Italy and in England were presented by Marx as the driving force in the dissolution of the feudal system. We distinguish the movement of liberation of the peasants from the setting in motion of the Italian and English peasants. The peasants were driven from the land and thereupon transferred back onto the land. In this way they were freed from the feudal burdens, but not as an active factor [*Moment*], but rather as recipients of the elements [*Momente*] of others. We assert to the contrary that in the 15th and 16th century the central European peasants structured their own movement of liberation and present themselves as an active historical moment. The class struggles were not treated by Marx in and for themselves in this context.

Prior to the 16th and 17th century, manufacturing was found in connection with mining, with metal processing and trade, and with money and mercantile capital in Constantinople, Italy, Spain and Flanders. Manufacturing is based on commerce, on the monopoly of mercantile capital, and it points to an artisanal process in the labour of mining. Free wage labour arose in antiquity, in the old Roman Republic—but not so the capitalist mode of production. Without slavery, it could have emerged. One condition among others of the capitalist system is that of wage labour, which is developed freely and systematically. The presence of slavery prevents the development of wage labour and thus the development of capitalism. Overseas trade, in relation to manufacturing, money trading, mercantile capital and the monopolization of it in the coastal cities, for example, in Constantinople in the 15th century, is a moment in the transition to the capitalist system. Barcelona is also mentioned (among others). Pauperization of the wage labourers and the accumulation of capital as well as the refutation of the ideas concerning so-called primitive accumulation of capital are also treated by Marx in this connection. The development of capital as something dominating the world and the entire economic formation of society first begins in the 16th and 17th century. "This is its childhood". The capitalist mode of production exists "first completely (if also only still sporadically developed) with large-scale industry, which dates therefore in its totality only from the last third of the 18th century."[5] Here the distinction between the capitalist system and the capitalist mode of production is introduced. Events in the last third of the 18th century are related to the economic formation of society which, according to Marx, constitutes the mode of production of the modern bourgeois period, and are not related to the capitalist system. The capitalist mode of production is developed mediately out of mercantile capitalism and mercantilism, immediately through the effects of the industrial revolution. Overseas trade as a moment in the dissolution of the feudal mode of production and in the transition to the capitalist, if only sporadically in its appearance, plays an important role according to Marx. Because this moment has become a point of contention among some Marxists in the 20th century, we will revisit it.

The historical moments which have led to the formation of modern bourgeois society, Marx considered as a dissolution, as an explosion, like the effect of an explosive. Feudal relations of serfdom in the countryside and the guild system in the towns, were from this point of view, obstacles in the advance of humanity. Thus, Marx said: "In great outline can the Asiatic, antique, feudal and modern bourgeois modes of production be designated as progressive epochs of the economic formation of society."[6] The succession of epochs from the antique to the feudal formation of society is progressive insofar as medieval serfdom appears progressive in comparison to antique slavery. Marx emphasized other historical moments in the dissolution process of feudalism, such as the transformation of the guild system, the expansion of the money economy and of trade as well as the development of manufacturing enterprises in the transition to modern bourgeois society.

The setting-in-motion of the peasants in the 15th and 16th century is related to Southern, Western and Central Europe. They are active and passive, moving and moved. They are not like smoke in the wind. The class struggles in the towns were not independent of the peasants' movement.

No isolated factor can be named as fundamental in the transition from the feudal to the modern bourgeois period. We call attention to the fact that Marx emphasizes among others the elements [*Momente*] of trade and traffic in money as well as manufacturing. The Marxists are divided into external and internal conflicting camps, the former represented by P. M. Sweezy, the latter by M. Dobb and R.H. Hilton. Sweezy traces the transition from feudalism to capitalism back to the role of external trade and its effect on the internal economy and society of medieval

Europe. The driving force of economic development in Italy during the feudal era was supposed to have been the activity of port cities like Venice, Genoa as well as Constantinople and Barcelona in their trade relationships with the Near East. This thesis points once again back to Henri Pirenne. Pirenne thought not that the invasion of the Germanic peoples or armies had constituted the historical dynamic in feudal Europe but rather events in the region of the Mediterranean, the expansion of Islam, military conflicts and in this connection trade and commerce in the Mediterranean region.[7] Sweezy had dropped the role of the invasions and emphasized the significance of foreign trade. The inner moments of development and dissolution of the feudal system can be traced back to the distribution of rural surplus in the form of annuities and to the struggle over the distribution of annuities by Dobb and Hilton.[8] The feudal system and the Middle Ages in general lie outside of our consideration, the question concerning the decline of the medieval system interests us rather for the reason that some authors whose thoughts relate to our matter, have also dealt with this question. The dispute around the assessment of the *inner* and *outer* factors in the development and dissolution appear rather to be a struggle over dogmas. Marx pointed to several historical moments in the decline of feudalism, such as the role of large-scale foreign trade (sea and overland trade) with regard to the Italian, Flemish, Dutch, Spanish and German cities, the mass production of commodities for export, the role of secondary enterprises in the countryside as well as the displacement of the peasants from the land into the city and from the city back onto the land. The discussion was simplified by the Marxists mentioned above insofar as they at times cited only one side of Marx's entire work. Our main task is to examine the Central European world from the 15th to the 17th century in which on the one hand the feudal elements of serfdom, compulsory labour [*Frondienst*], and the feudal system were continued, in which on the other hand, the new mining and metallurgy, seafaring and shipbuilding arts, mercantile practices, the credit and money system, wage labour and manufacturing were introduced. The peasant movements, the rebellions in the countryside and in the cities of Central Europe led substantially to the dissolution of the old system. Several feudal elements had continued into the new era not only pro forma but in substance, whose final elimination could be carried through only in the 18th/19th century.

The period of transition to modern bourgeois society arose in the countries of Southern, Central and Western Europe, earlier in the south, later in the north. Central European events in this context have their historical dynamic, which is not everywhere the same as in Italy, England, Holland, and so on. Some moments are indigenous, such as the social consciousness of the rebellious peasants, others on the other hand are common to the neighbouring peoples of Europe, such as the putting-out system, foreign trade and the seafaring arts. The factor of the spirit of capitalism, brought out by Max Weber, to whom we shall turn, appears to be an accompanying moment. It is not a cause of feudal decline or of the transition to capitalism, but rather a category of thought which concerns the capitalists and not the peasants or proletarians. If attention were confined to the spirit of capitalism, the peasants and the working class would disappear from the social stage, which would be difficult to understand. Our task in this connection is for one: to examine the historical dynamic of Central Europe in the transition to the capitalist era, second: to examine the social system within it in the given period. We proceed from the understanding that no people live in a chaotic condition, not even when their world finds itself in upheaval. People have their rules and laws even when it comes to a conflict between two systems, that of the old and the new or of the foreign and the indigenous. The spirit plays a role in the process of transformation, only the change in its orientation [*Verhalten*] is a phenomenologically late phenomenon, not an original one, and its significance can be exaggerated.

Several researchers have sought out a unique historical moment in this radical change at the expense of all others, which is unscientific, dogmatic and unrealistic. Some colleagues have asserted that Central Europe in the 16th century was a world of development, which says too much and too little,—too little, because each country and people develop. The specificity of development under given conditions and at the given time ought to be investigated. That assertion says too much, because development presents a powerful problem for the Third World in the second half of the 20th century. *Development* in relation to Central Europe in the 15th and 16th century appears to have little in common with the contemporary developmental problematic. In considering the specificity and unique character of the Central European historical dynamic it is not possible to simply generalize the process of development. Germany was not a colony; it sent out settlers and colonialists. The country found itself on the level of development which reached the entire continent.

We have treated capital and capitalism separately. Capitalism is a system, which appears in modern times and distinguishes itself from the previous epochs of history. Some character traits of the capitalist system appeared sporadically in the earlier epochs. Wage labour and capital, commodities, the market, exchange, the exchange value of commodities were developed in classical antiquity and in the Middle Ages, appeared, disappeared and resurfaced. Their appearance was not sufficient and not extensive, neither in Imperial Rome nor in the Middle Ages, and in this sense, they were sporadic and did not lead immediately to the development of capitalism. Capitalism concerns the relations of the wage labourers and the business enterprise. We know that the Spanish Queen had sold her jewels to pay the shipyard workers in Gades (Cádiz) when Columbus' fleet was built. The ships were assembled by wage labourers in 1490. Leonardo da Pisa was the son of a merchant family, whose father Bonacci was Secretary of the Republic of Pisa. Leonardo da Fibonacci or Fi(gli)bonacci, Bonacci's son's name, was sent to Algeria, to head a trading company. In the Algerian city of Bugia he practiced his commercial activity, and from 1192 to 1200 he learned to calculate with Indo-Arabic numerals.[9] Several of these events, which appear sporadically, can be mentioned, such as the merchant entrepreneurs in the putting-out system [*Verleger*] in Florence and the bankers in Genoa, who exchanged entrepreneurship in the North Italian cities, exchanged capital, credit and other commercial instruments. The merchant entrepreneurs in the putting-out system [*Verleger*] paid their wage labourers with money wages. Similar practices were expanded in the Upper German cities, in the cities on the Rhein and Main, in the Hansa cities, in the Netherlands, England and France. In the 15th century they were transformed into systematic phenomena. The stock exchanges of Barcelona and Naples were extended to Antwerp, Lyon and other places. We will not only deal with the entrepreneurs but with the wage labourers and the relations between the two as well.

Capital appears as the form of commerce of the means of production when and where wage labour appears; we speak here of the money wage and the money economy. Labour in this form and the corresponding exchange relations show themselves sporadically and temporarily, in this sense weakly, in the pre-capitalist epochs of civil society. Wage labour and capital were discovered in late feudalism. It is questionable whether this discovery relates only to the late Middle Ages and not to other epochs. The sporadic appearance of wage labour and of the circulation of money is also found in classical antiquity and in the later epochs of the Asiatic mode of production. Here we are dealing, to be sure, not with a single historical process but rather only with events and conditions, which surface, disappear again, repeat themselves, are strengthened and are made comparable. Capitalism on the contrary is the systematic form of appearance of the relations between capital and wage labour, which arise purely sporadically in an earlier form of society. There is not one single track in history, but rather several. The historical process of capital can be reasonably explained when the earlier appearances are examined in connection with money trade and money wages, not only as an exclusive event of late feudalism, but rather in classical antiquity as well. Both processes are systematized in capitalism and made into the foundation of the political system of the modern era. Marx's main point was the critique of the capitalist system, of political economy and—insofar as possible—of the destruction of this system in the 19th century. For this reason, he wrote little concerning the beginnings of the capitalist system and of the capitalist mode of production. However, there are a few excerpts concerning these matters in his works.

Manufacture in the early period of the capitalist system emerges from handicraft on a double path:

1. The simple cooperation of many craftsmen with their hand tools in one room, where they all perform the same labour and who introduce the first concentration into production. In the old weaving and cloth preparation manufacture, the division of labour appears hardly at all; there is only the joint use of the general conditions of labour such as buildings, firing; to that is added the ultimate supervision by the factory owners, hence the element which in general belongs specifically to capitalist production.
2. Unification of craftwork divided into many independent branches in a factory. The division of labour is found here, but each part is worked as independent handwork.[10]

To point 1: The demand, supply, transportation and import of raw materials such as wool, cotton, linen and so on, as well as the export of processed commodities should be added. Further the infrastructure, for example, the outward and inward bound routes belong to the joint use of the conditions of labour. The watermill is a further part of the process of production in this period.

To point 2: In the domestic system rolled wire is a commodity which is processed in the manufacture of needles; the needle is a second commodity. In the system of manufacture rolled iron is processed in the same workshop as the needle. The entrepreneur buys the rolled wire as a commodity, and it is distributed in the process of needle creation as a means of production. The rolled wire together with the means of heating, coal and so on, is not treated as a commodity within the manufacture of needles. The entrepreneur buys the raw material, the means of production and the labour time and sells the needles created in the commodity form. In this way, the capitalist system was developed from the putting-out workshop [*vom Verlag*] to manufacture; the middle stage of traders, of commercial capital and the buying and selling of commodities is set aside; the process of production is to this extent rationalized.

The putting-out system [*Verlagssystem*] is not the only component part of capitalism in the first centuries of modern civil society. The guild system, mining, agrarian economy, the banking and credit system and trade constituted the further elements of the economic system and economic social formation. The totality did not form a unitary system. Marx said: “As it is not incumbent upon one to believe in sudden sharply differentiated periods in the succession of different geological formations, so is it also not in the formation of the different economic formations of society. The beginnings of manufacture are developed in the lap of craftwork and are found here and there in individual spheres and for individual processes already with the use of machinery."[11] A social system like other systems, consists in recognizable parts which are ordered among themselves. The system is durable and does not immediately disappear. It consists of parts which are bound together as well as differentiated by inner and external relations of the parts and of those elements of the system in turn to other systems and parts of them. Human social systems are heterogeneous, disparate, but they reveal themselves as systems. The parts, like the agrarian economy, trade, urban trades, are once again systems with parts, non-uniform elements, oppositional. Nevertheless, they are bound up with one another and impact one another such that changes in one part can transform others.

The social system persisted and boasted a certain stability. The intentions of the participants were varied; the aristocrats and the guilds tried to maintain the old elements; the new capitalists and the poor, namely peasants and proletarians, wanted to change the old system. From the standpoint of high capitalism, the earlier periods appeared chaotic. Nevertheless, the main interests of the later system were already present here: The working class was a class of wage labourers or strove to become a class of wage labourers. The capitalists wanted to gain as much money as possible. The labourers demanded a higher wage, shorter work time and better working conditions. The peasants wanted in part to become wage labourers. The money economy was expanded. Some industries and branches of industries were already entirely or mostly organized according to the workshop system [*Verlagswesen*], like weaving or the printing industry; others, like mining, the system of coinage, seafaring and shipping companies, the banks and credit institutes were organized capitalistically in the same sense as is the case in high capitalism. The smelters and hammer mills were in part arranged like mining, in part like domestic workshops [*Verlage*] and guilds. If we give emphasis to mining as the typical or characteristic element for the further development of capitalism in Central Europe and in all of Europe, then we take note of wage labour, the accumulation of capital, the consolidation of the mines, the system of credit, the organization of labour, the rationalization of the labour process, the division of labour and the enhancement of technology in the 15th as in the 18th and 19th century. This branch of industry reveals the same ascending curve over five centuries and more. The same can be said for seafaring, shipbuilding and shipping companies. The development of weaving is viewed differently. Its great ascendancy takes place only in the 18th and 19th century.

The concentration of the work force and of the means of labour in glass and metal, wood and paper manufacture, was introduced in the capitalist system, not in the pre-capitalist mode of production. The concentration presumed the increase and training of the working class, the increasing role of trade, of the circulation of money, of the market economy and of credit instruments. Mastery of new means of production in mining, in the printing industry and in the branches of the manufacture of paper, of type casting and of the printing press in the branches belonging to it, in shipbuilding and in the glass, wood and metal industries, required the increase in training in the working class, the growth of qualified labour and the expansion of the organization and division of labour. To this end, the development of new technology in the branches of the economy was necessary. The concentration of means of labour was developed in the production as well as in the distribution process. New technology doesn't stand alone; it is rather operated and used by skilled workers. In the sea trade the new arts of shipbuilding and seafaring were introduced in the 15th and 16th century, first in the region of the Mediterranean, then on the coasts of the Baltic and North Sea.

At the same time, parts of the working class lost their skill in the production process. The new manufacture-machinery simplified labour in the process of production to a certain extent. The main developments in this area first arrive in the period of the industrial revolution and of high capitalism, that is, after the initial period, and they will therefore not be treated in our work. On the same grounds, the difference between the capitalist system and of the capitalist mode of production will not be further explored. Here the foundation of the capitalist period of history as an inwardly contradictory system will be treated.

Externally considered, the economic system that Smith, Ricardo and Marx analysed, is without a beginning, unlike a person who has a beginning at a certain point in space and in time. Treating the capitalist system in this way, would be an anthropomorphism. We will not derive this system from the activities of bankers in ancient Babylon, nor from the market in the high mountain valley of Mexico at the time of the Spanish conquest, stories of which conquistadors had described, nor from the speculative dealings of tax farmers in ancient Rome. Internally, the capitalist system of the 19th and 20th century is made up of the moments of the labour process, of industry, finance and credit institutes and of the market. The system was formed in southern, central and western Europe and determined the transition to modern bourgeois society.

Elements of the system, which appear sporadically in different countries, under different conditions, in different historical periods, have another history. They are not only concerns of late feudalism, but rather of ancient Rome, China, Egypt, India and of the Islamic cities of the Mediterranean as well, wherever and whenever wage labour and market relations can be historically established. Under these conditions the unsystematic and sporadic appearance of capital will be discussed. Capital is not an atom, but rather an object which can be analysed further into parts, and the same will be said here of wage labour. With wage labour time is valued and exchanged against money or money equivalent. Wages, labour, labour time and money will be analysed further later on. Capital is a commodity and has no independent activity; it has an objective presence [*Dasein*] but no self-valorisation, a formal, but not a substantial existence independent of human beings. Capital is analysed in the formal moments of economy and of law. In the capitalist system, as it appeared in the 15th to the 20th century, capital investment was generalized, expanded by credit institutes and formally democratised. Step by step with the expansion, generalization and formal democratisation of capital and of credit instruments, the civil rights of capital and the owners of credit were expanded and generalized. Civil rights were formally secured for human beings in the history of the capitalist era in this way.

The appearance of the capitalist system as a system occurred in the region of the Mediterranean in the 14th, in the Central European and Western European region in the 15th and 16th century. It is a capitalist system but only in the sense of preparing for the high capitalism of a later epoch. Fundamentally, everything that can be observed in the 16th century, can also be discovered in the 14th or 15th century in increasingly more branches of industry. The transition to steam machinery in the 18th and to electricity in the 19th century is a splendid accomplishment of the human spirit. The technology of the steam or electrical industry can be considered as a driving force in history, but only in connection with the adversarial process of labour related to production, distribution and consumption. Technics in the assembly of the mechanical clock is based on the labouring human being who masters metal processing, geometry, arithmetic, time measurement and mechanics. Nevertheless, he does not master time but rather appraises it.

2.3 Max Weber and the Spirit of Capitalism

Weber treated two main problems of capitalism, the place of capitalism in history and the connection between capitalism and its *spirit*. We will take up the first problem here, since the question concerning the position of capitalism in the ancient or modern meaning relates to our periodization problematic. In this connection Weber wrote: "'Capitalism' existed in China, India, Babylon, in classical antiquity and in the Middle Ages", a capitalism, which distinguishes itself from the modern through its lack of spirit. Weber defined capitalist activity in general as follows: "A 'capitalist' economic act we understand to be one which is based on the expectation of profit by making use of exchange-opportunities: on (formally) peaceful opportunities for gain." This capitalist economic act is found in China, India and Europe in traditional times and in modern capitalism. What distinguishes the investor of antiquity from the modern is supposedly the peaceful use of prospects for profit in the latter. The Occident in the modern era aside from war-oriented capitalism knows an entirely other kind of capitalism developed and nowhere else on earth: "the national-capitalistic [operational] organization of (formally) free labor."[12] We speak here only of Western European-American capitalism. What distinguishes it from the Babylonian, medieval and Fugger capitalism, is the *spirit* of modern capitalism, a unique ethos, characterized by the *ethically* coloured maxim for a way of life: "The human being is concerned with acquisition as the purpose of his life, no longer with gain as means to the end of satisfying his material wants and needs in life." The ethos of the capitalists is expressed in gainful employment as does ascetic Protestantism. The Calvinist capitalist feels an internal call to acquire capital and to asceticism. In this way Calvinist Protestants are distinguished from the Lutheran, Protestantism in general from Catholic and Jewish capitalism. Luther's notion of the calling is other than that of Calvinism. A student of Weber's demonstrated that there was statistically fewer Catholic than Protestant capitalists.

Weber remarks in his study on the Protestant ethic in the chapter *Confession and Social Stratification*—a look into occupational statistics—shows that the possession of capital and entrepreneurship is predominantly *Protestant* in character. The calling according to Luther was religious in character having nothing to do with capitalist acquisition and was *traditionally* oriented to medieval social practice. It stood in opposition to Calvinist practice. The opposition between the spirit of this capitalist enterprise and that of the Jews applies to a thesis of Werner Sombart's with which Weber quarrelled; it will be taken up in the following section.

Weber put Central Europe into the centre of the transition from the Middle Ages to the modern era. According to his conception, the transition takes place in the 16th century, not through Luther's Reformation, but rather through Calvinism. Modern capitalism appears in the Calvinist parts of Switzerland, Germany, the Netherlands, and Great Britain. The contributions of the Italians, of the Huguenots, the Cahorsins [Lombards or userers—trans.], the Catalonians, among others, are set aside in this transition. What was missing in them was inner-worldly asceticism. Marx came to the same conclusion, the capitalist system is a phenomenon of the modern era; it appears sporadically in the 14th and 15th century in Northern Italy, then as a system in the 16th century in Central Europe. To follow Weber, capitalism in antiquity in the Far East and in Europe reveals itself but not in its modern form. This assertion leads to a contradiction between Marx and Weber.

Ernst Troeltsch, following Weber's analysis of the relation between Protestantism and capitalism, emphasized the differences of the two confessions, Lutheranism and Calvinism. Lutheranism called forth a type of political passivity and an agrarian-conservative conception of human society (around 1910), which can still be felt in the German-Prussian way of dealing with matters. On the other hand, Calvinism inwardly merged itself with political-liberal-democratic and modern bourgeois capitalist society and thereby provided the Calvinist population down to the present with a religiously sanctioned and well-founded social attitude of an entirely unique kind.[13] Weber discussed the opposition between the *feeling* of Lutheranism and the *ratio* of Calvinism; Troeltsch expressed the opposition between Lutheran nationalism (German-Prussian) and Calvinist internationalism (Calvinist peoples in Geneva, the Netherlands, England).[14] Otto von Gierke examined Calvinism in Emden.

About Max Weber, Troeltsch said: "Weber brilliantly shed light on the origin of modern capitalism through investigations concerning the origin of the economic disposition necessary to it out of Calvinist Puritanism, without ignoring the fact that this Calvinist Puritanism was overrun by economic class stratification …" Weber as a neo-Kantian re-thought the ideas of Hegel and Marx.[15] Weber believes the Reformation was revolutionary not in relation to the secular world, but only within church history. The revolution of belief of Calvinist inner-worldly aesthetic rationalism is for Luther a reprobate matter [*eine verworfene Sache*].[16]

Concerning the comparison between the doctrines of Luther and Calvin, Troeltsch writes that Lutheranism shuns capitalist development and seeks to maintain economic life at the level of preferably agrarian-handicraft production, because capitalist speculation is against love and against the belief in prophecy. Out of this arises the duty to labour and of the calling, the growth of economic labour, the calling as a mandate from God as the individual-spiritual movement as well as the appraising capitalist spirit of Calvinism that values labour for labour's sake. Troeltsch finds a spiritual movement similar to Calvinism in Pietism and among the sects. Calvinism is politically liberal, economically free, Lutheranism on the contrary anti-democratic, its orientation to the state absolutist.[17] Even when Troeltsch and Weber meld the different historical epochs together, their juxtaposition of Lutheranism and Calvinism remains valid for us.

Marx spoke about the capitalist system, Weber on the contrary about the capitalist act, not the system; the modern system of such acts does not appear in economic relations, but rather—for Weber—in the Calvinist spirit. Neither Marx nor Weber allowed for a system of Italian capitalism in the 14th/15th. Even Fugger the capitalist was not recognized by Weber as such in the modern sense. The system of capitalism appears in modern times first in England, the Netherlands and Central Europe.

For Marx, there was only *one* system of capitalism, namely that of modern bourgeois society. Theodor Mommsen wrote about capital and annuities from the yield of capital, about the class of capitalists, money and the finance economy and the speculation in money[18]; but this conception was rejected by Marx. To be sure there was a different use of the concepts on the continent on the one hand and in England or America on the other. Marx considered the use of the word *capitalist* in relation to antiquity in just the same way as the popular idea, which carries forth an ancient tradition of past conditions.[19] He agreed with the use of the word in English.

Corresponding to these historical categories, Marx divides civil society into a modern period and an epoch which preceded it, while Weber, according to his historical categories, divides capitalism into two epochs, the modern and the antique. Marx describes civil society as flexible, dynamic in history, Weber, on the contrary describes capitalism as flexible and dynamic which in the past was something different than in the present. In Marx's notion capitalism exists as a system, or it doesn't exist at all. Capitalism in Weber's conception exists, on the contrary, in different forms, antique and modern; bourgeois society does not appear as a specific category in history in this connection.

In Max Weber's conception, capitalist enterprises in the money economy, in the systems of trade, finance and credit, in the commodities market as well as in the fabrication of commodities in the town workshops in the Far and Near East and in the region of the Mediterranean from antiquity down to the most recent epochs of European history, are being continued. This historical process is interrupted and divided into periods not through capitalist relations in the commodities market and in the workshop, but rather through the spiritual effect of the Calvinist ethos on the capitalist relationships of production and commerce. Weber's conception of history would be, as Troeltsch asserted, materialistic.[20] Weber speaks of social strata and classes.

In relation to the question of periodization, it is different in Marx than in Weber; not capitalist enterprise but rather civil society continues forth from classical times into the capitalist period. What is new is the capitalist system, whose processes transform the civil society of the past into the modern. Marx concerned himself with the capitalist system of the 16th to the 19th century, which determines the system of modern bourgeois society; Weber, on the contrary, occupied himself with the system of the Calvinist ethos, which determined the passage to the modern capitalist economic act. The question of periodization can be treated either in terms of classification, that is as a contribution to the social sciences

[*Geisteswissenschaften*] or as a contribution to the understanding of the moments, which have determined society in its system and history. The treatment of this question varies accordingly.

Weber returned several times to the problem of capitalism and to the problem of the spirit. In his book, *Economy and Society,* he occupied himself with the two-fold nature of that which is called the *capitalist spirit*: first with the spirit which seeks after booty, slaves and stolen goods, and second with the spirit, which seeks after inner-worldly asceticism. This two-fold nature, in the one meaning that of the pirate, and in the other, relating to the character trait of dependability, is also found, as we shall see, in Werner Sombart.

The threads which tie the European economic system of the modern era with that of classical antiquity cannot be simply tied together without further ado. Particularly in the area of law, which regulated economic practices in Roman antiquity, the links or parallels are hard to find. The institutions of modern private law are not derived from the old Roman system of law. An array of commercial practices of the modern era such as debentures, covered bonds and annuity certificates, the mortgage with land registry security can be highlighted. The history of the joint-stock company has no immediate roots in Roman antiquity. The consideration of a hiatus and new establishment of economic practices and of economic law of the modern era is related not only to the history of modern private law, but also to public law. Hence, for example, no precedent case for war debts, war bonds, war credits in antiquity will be found, whereas they are very common in modern times. These comments by Max Weber concern public as well as private economic life. They are apparently systematic, enduring and internally articulated and are closely related to the modern capitalist system. Modern capitalism exploded the old social structure by the decomposition of the economic foundations of the old estates. (The urban system of guilds and patricians could not survive this decomposition, but the landed aristocracy was able to resist, at least until the Wilhelmine period.[21]) According to Weber the inner discipline of the workers and the rationalization of technique are characteristics of capitalist enterprise, which only the Occident knows. The preconditions for modern capitalism are rational capital accounts, the rationalization and predictability and therefore the mechanization of technique. To these rational moments in the appearance of modern capitalism come the libertarian elements which are to be added: free ownership of autonomous private enterprises; the freedom of the market from irrational limits on trade; free labour, since only on the grounds of free labour is rational capital calculation possible. Only through the labourers, who offer themselves formally voluntarily—in fact forced by the whip of hunger—could the production costs of the products be rationally calculated. The liberties are bound up with the available capital and the rational organization of labour. Modern, specifically occidental capitalism is developed from the 16th to the 18th century in corporative [*ständischen*] Dutch and English political associations. The commercialization of the economy and the possibility of the exclusive focus on covering demand in relation to market opportunities and the return on investment lead to speculation.[22] Modern capitalism begins with the rationalization of enterprise, with the calculability of capital and of technique, of the predictability of law, and it ends with speculation, which constitutes an irrational moment in human life.

The contradiction does not lie in Weber's execution, but rather in the object of investigation. The freedom of the person is formed by the freedom of the market, of property and of commerce. The formally free labourers are driven by hunger to offer themselves on the free labour market. Through the offer by free labour the costs of production can be rationally calculated. Freedom according to Weber's conception is the freedom of the labour market, which is derived from the rationalizing moment in production and in commerce. This freedom is purely formal.

The pursuit of profit and of booty and asceticism do not lead to a contradiction. One and the same group or person can at one and the same time be addicted to profit, addicted to booty and behave as an ascetic. There is no struggle between those who are driven by the spirit of Calvinism and the spirit of booty. Thomas Hobbes and G.W.F. Hegel considered bourgeois society as the spiritual animal kingdom of individualities [*das geistige Tierreich der Individualitäten*], as a theatre of war of all against all, which is in and for itself real. But there was nevertheless a struggle between the old landed gentry and landowners on the one side and the new ascetic and frugal capitalists addicted to profit on the other, and this struggle is just as epoch making and characteristic for modern bourgeois society as the struggle for money wages. The struggle of the peasants for their freedom and struggles of all classes against one another are indispensable for the creation of the capitalist era.

2.4 Sombart, Kulischer, von Below, Strieder, Brentano, Janssen, Pareto, Braudel

Sombart was not a systematic thinker like Marx or Weber. Nevertheless, his accomplishments as an economic historian were highly esteemed after the First World War as were those of Josef Kulischer, and those of C. M. Cipolla in this field after the Second World War. When Joseph Schumpeter complains that Sombart had acquired everything second hand, it doesn't ring true, since he, Sombart, cites primary sources from the period of early Italian capitalism. The historical category *early capitalism* is used in this work not without hesitation because it is only from the standpoint of a later epoch that the previous one can be designated as *early*. Jakob Fugger certainly didn't consider himself an early capitalist yet this designation of him is widespread. Sombart does not appear to have been conscious of this anachronism.[23] We are going to make use of that designation *passim*, even though we are conscious of the inner anachronism of the term. Early capitalism begins in the modern era and is therefore neither a phenomenon of antiquity nor of the Middle Ages. It specifies the modern era and prefigures it. *Modern* [*neu*] will also be used from the standpoint of the period following it as a historical designation.

Weber and Sombart tried to solve not only the problem of periodization in history through the social concept of modern, that is to say, early capitalism, but also to discover the psychological or spiritual [*geistigen*] motivations of the capitalists. According to Weber, there is an irrational drive for profit, which is maintained through taming, through rational tempering. Capitalism, says Weber, *can* be identical with rational tempering. In any case, capitalism is identical with the pursuit of profit.[24] Weber found the same contradictions and moments in economic pursuit in all epochs and parts of the world in the history of capitalism. Sombart had examined capitalist motivations, but only in the context of the economic world of the modern era. Sombart found two features in the early capitalist spirit, one Romantic, and one bourgeois. The Romantic feature is adventurous, used to winning, brutal as with pirates, sea robbers and buccaneers and the crews of ships of discovery. The difference between merchant and adventurer, between warrior and businessman under these conditions is hardly worth noticing. The bourgeois trait in the spirit of capitalism has the cardinal virtues of the sanctity of contract, of honourable acquisition, of economic efficiency, of industriousness, of frugality, of moderation. The chief example of this type of entrepreneur is found first in Italy, then in England, Holland and America. Germany is not mentioned by Sombart in this genealogy of professional business ethics.[25] Josef Kulischer begins with the assumption that Sombart was the first to discover and explain the capitalist spirit. The bourgeois [*Bürgergeist*] spirit is rational, purposefully oriented, economic rationality appears in the calculability of all events, in double-entry bookkeeping, which maintains calculable information concerning the success and failure of every single measure, and generally guarantees foremost an orderliness of enterprise.[26] Obviously spirit is conceived of in different ways by economic historians and sociologists of religion. Weber examined the spirit in both fields, but in another sense than Sombart.

Weber also wrote about adventurers in the first years of the modern era, but his main point was to contribute something to universal cultural history. According to his conception, the decisive characteristic that distinguishes our period from the preceding one—hence the *conditio sine qua non* for the transition—is the capitalist economic act which arises in Calvinism. Weber sought for the cause of the transformation and found it in the Calvinist spirit, which appeared to him, literally, as epoch making. Sombart's work is related to economic history, which he divides into the epochs of early and high capitalism, not to universal cultural history and not to its causes.

In a specialized work Sombart gave expression to the role of Jewry in the formation of capitalism; in particular he had pointed to the fact that Jewish law was entirely congenial for the development of the modern forms of securities.[27] Sombart's opinion was widely criticized. Weber had noted that Jewish law didn't have much of anything in particular to do with trade in modern securities or with the contemporary system of credit.[28] Sombart's thesis was judged deficient by Max Weber: The Jews lacked those actions and legal practices which appeared specifically as modern-capitalistic. He thus limits himself to a negative justification for his assessment. Sombart's thesis is rejected as flawed also on positive grounds, that is, on grounds of what *was* practiced not only what *was not* practiced. The Jews and the Cahorsins [sometimes labelled "Lombards"—trans.], were regarded as usurers in the Middle Ages. The latter were originally businessmen and coiners from Cahors, a city mentioned in Dante's Inferno as the Hellish headquarters of usurers.[29] About the usurers in the Middle Ages the contemporary sources had said: "In the year 1236 King Louis IX of France wanted to put a stop to the usury of the Jews; but his barons explained that it would be better to tolerate Jewish rather than Christian usurers who would squeeze their debtors to a much greater degree."

And: "One of the best English patriots of that time [middle of the 13th century] the learned Bishop Grosseteste of Lincoln, explained in his last solemn addresses that the usury of the Cahorsins was worse than that of the Jews."[30] The social, legal and economic position was not sufficiently strong to introduce or enforce the stricter practices of usury and pawning by the Cahorsins themselves. This situation had not changed at all in the course of the following four centuries, that is down to the early capitalist period; Christian usurers, credit institutes, bankers and gold and copper kings of the 15th, 16th, and 17th century had not suffered under these social, legal and economic deficiencies. Fugger, Imhof, Welser and consorts were rich and powerful men, patricians, aristocrats and so on. If the talk is not about the social, but rather the economic condition of these rich bankers, so in this connection the same can be asserted as was maintained with regard to their social position. Their wealth, their power, and their influence neither caused nor guided the transition to the modern bourgeois and capitalist age, although their economic activities are tightly bound up with this transition.

A notion, which wants to confer a similar economic role to the Jews, appears to be exaggerated and unrealistic.

Kulischer shared Sombart's views that the capitalist mindset first evolved among the Jews, that they are responsible for economic rationality, free trade, and free competition.[31] But the activity or effectiveness of the Jews in the late Middle Ages and in the era of early capitalism was limited. The advantageous position of the Jews in the economy of Europe during the early Middle Ages was later lost to them. In the first centuries of the modern era, from the 15th to the 17th century, they were not doing well; the Jews represented the *good entrepreneurship*, such as free trade and rationalization, and the market in Central and Western Europe was closed by the monopolies and guild practices, that is by *bad* entrepreneurial practices. Luther had cursed the social monopolies [*Gesellschaft Monopolia*] from the medieval not from the capitalistic standpoint. Weber and Troeltsch already pointed out the difference between Lutheranism and Calvinism in this regard. They started from the point that Calvinism is associated with capitalism to a greater degree than is Lutheranism. We shall see that Luther had profound traits in common with the capitalism of his day. The virtues of the free market, of free trade, of civil rights for all was first championed in the 17th century by the political tolerance of the Great Elector Friedrich Wilhelm and by Oliver Cromwell in England, as well as by the poets and thinkers of the 18th century, G.E. Lessing and Adam Smith. These virtues correspond to the Industrial Revolution and the high capitalism of the 18th and 19th century and are projected back into the situation of the late Middle Ages by Sombart, hence treated anachronistically. He goes further in his work and it appears as if capitalist rationalism, free trade and civil law are purposefully directed from the beginning with necessity and teleologically. Sombart expressed his satisfaction with the state of affairs as he found them. He highlighted the model of social-economic peace in Central Europe during the 14th and 15th century, but he idealized all of it and treated it dogmatically. Sombart's views, which have recently been taken up by O. Brunner, could have been debunked already in his own day. Conflicts and quarrels between apprentices and masters were already well documented in the sources from the 14th and 15th century and earlier.[32]

Jakob Strieder gave prominence to the problem of the capitalist spirit; he derived it from the development of the individual, which in turn derives from economic individualism, from the acquisition of money as an end in itself. The spirit of capitalism was spread from Italy over all of Western Europe. Strieder positions the capitalist period earlier than Marx, Weber, Sombart and Kulischer.[33] It is always difficult to exactly delimit a historical epoch but in relation to the fact that in Italy capitalist commerce was taken up earlier than in Central Europe, we assume that capitalism as a system did not yet appear in Italy.

Those who begin with the system or the spirit of capitalism only in the 16th century, have excluded Italy from their consideration. Weber appears to argue, that the establishment of modern capitalism occurs only in Central Europe. Marx certainly named Italy as the birthplace of the capitalist system, but it appears there only sporadically; systematically on the contrary it first appears in Northern Europe; England and Holland are his prime examples.

Those who see the first appearance of capitalism in Southern Europe, do not necessarily begin with the 16th century. Fernand Braudel anchors the early epoch of capitalism in the 15th to the 18th century.[34] Now it depends on which standpoint one chooses for determining the beginning of the new era in space and in time and on this basis to delimit and to periodize the transition from one period to the next. Lujo Brentano presented modern capitalism as an event of the 13th to 15th century in Italy.[35] If one draws a distinction between the sporadic and systematic appearance of capitalism, it is conceivable that it developed sporadically in the 13th century and systematically only later.

Georg von Below sets the originating process of modern capitalism in Italy in the same epoch and illustrates this with the example of the cloth industry in Florence.[36] He grounds the process quantitatively on the expansion of economic activity and on the transition from the natural to the money economy. Production and commerce belong together in this process; commerce doesn't stand alone. Enterprise is led by individuals and not by communities (city, Church, and so on); it strives for profit and for the extension of its scope. Henri See and Henri Pirenne, Richard Ehrenberg and Jakob Strieder all proceeded on the basis that capitalism had been developed in the 15th century. The countries of the Mediterranean are according to them the place of its origin, not Central Europe.

Maurice Dobb specifies the beginning of capitalism in England as his prime example, namely in the second half of the 16th and early in the 17th century. According to his opinion, this process begins with the penetration of capital into production, whereby the quantum and the extent of capitalization constitutes the decisive factor. Capital either appears in the more mature relation between capitalist and wage labourer or else in the putting-out system. Nevertheless, he distinguishes merchant capitalism from production capitalism, which constitutes true capitalism. In this conception of history, peasants and proletarians play no role; the initiative in the transition process lies in the relation of capital and the capitalist to commerce and to production. Whether the transformation occurs in Italy, Flanders or in Central Europe, is unessential. The difference between merchant capital and production capital in the originating process of capitalism is emphasized by Below as well as by Dobb.[37] The transformation of peasants into proletarians is a complicated process, to which we shall return. In this connection, not only is the relation between merchant and production capital important, but also between entrepreneurship and capital and between entrepreneur and wage labourer as well. The role of the working class as the driving force of this process of development in the history of England was singled out by E. P. Thompson (1968).[38]

Johann Janssen, originating from the Catholic side, had described the transition from the Middle Ages to the modern era as follows: At the end of the Middle Ages agriculture was flourishing, commerce had undergone an extraordinary development, mining had created fabulous wealth. Prosperity in commerce and trade stood higher in Germany than in other Christian states, so that it was the wealthiest state in Europe. Labourers in the countryside and in the town workshops were mostly well off at the beginning of the 16th century. But little by little, the balance in the great branches of labour was disturbed; speculators had begun to smother value producing labour, prices were manipulated, monopolies were set up in spite of all governmental decisions, and the working class was exploited by capital. Large businesspeople and capitalists dominated the politics as well as the life of the people. The rich had openly flaunted their wealth in the face of the poor. Their material prosperity awakened the desire, the hot hunger for increased profits, for possessions and pleasure in all social classes without distinction.[39] In the Middle Ages this was not the case; secular and religious rulers had not flaunted their wealth before the poor, on the contrary, they veiled it and there was a difference between rich and poor.

2.5 Schumpeter

Schumpeter was of the opinion that the rise of capitalism in the 13th century destroyed the social world of Europe. There was an already earlier entrepreneurship of a capitalist kind, however, the institutions of capitalism, the great enterprises, the stock market, speculation in commodities and the financial system were developed between the 13th and 15th century. Schumpeter had difficulties with the concept of capitalism, which was vague for him (for Braudel the concept is shaky). Yet Schumpeter was able to discover the majority of capitalist phenomena at the end of the 15th century.[40] His explanations in this context have a different origin than those which have already been mentioned, thus his way of treating them offers a new perspective, which is just as important as those of the economic historians. He dealt critically with Marx and the sociologists as well. He recognized the close relationship between Central and Southern Europe in the given period; he awarded to Italy the beginning of capitalism not as something sporadic, but as a widely systematic phenomenon. He begins with the upheaval of the feudal world from the 13th to the 15th century, though on different grounds than L. Brentano. Schumpeter wrote as follows: "As a result of the significance of the expansion of capitalist production and of capitalist commerce through the monetary system, the development of law and of the practice of negotiable securities and of *created* deposits, offer perhaps the best indication of a temporal determination of the rise of capitalism. Both are developed in the course of the 14th century in the Mediterranean region; however, negotiability was definitively introduced only in the 16th century."[41]

Marx said, the beginning of the capitalist system appears sporadically in Italy prior to the 16th century, Schumpeter on the contrary, that capitalism arose in the 13th to the 15th century and that the negotiability of securities was only fully established in the 16th century. Both are agreed on the point that only in the 16th century do we have to do with capitalism as a system. Our object is only related to this system, insofar as it appears as part of a society in the aforementioned historical period. Marx begins with the physical movement of the peasants, Schumpeter with the negotiability of securities. The social relations, the problems, the system and dynamic are related to both historical appearances. Both moments are dynamic; yet there are other moments at that time in Central Europe and Italy, which are likewise systematic and dynamic, like the peasant uprisings and the development of mining, of the book industry and of the seafaring arts. People, like their society and their history, are so complicated that we cannot focus on one single process, no matter how important it might be. Marx and Schumpeter only treat economic processes and this kind of treatment also determines ours. Schumpeter focussed his attention primarily on the capitalists and their activities. In this way, he separated the sociological from the economic theories of Marx and only considered the former as correct.

Schumpeter discussed his theory of transition from feudalism to capitalism further in a critical disputation with Max Weber; although he rejected Weber's thesis of the capitalist spirit, he recognized his protagonist as an *authority*. Schumpeter had, nevertheless, proposed a distinction between entrepreneur and capitalist. We can conclude from this that the enterprise and not capital had existed in antiquity and that its transformation into a capitalist enterprise occurred only in modern times. The distinction is made on the basis of function. The enterprise is related to functions like profit and monopoly prices and not to the functions in production. Market strategy and acquiring inventions, patents, and so on, are the activities of the entrepreneur, not activities and functions of production.[42] Weber had asserted, as we have seen, that capitalism was not new; it had already made an appearance in antiquity, in Babylon, China, Rome and was only transformed through the Protestant Ethic (*Geist*) into a modern form. Schumpeter had expressed his basic rejection of Weber's views in this way: "Sociologists like Max Weber, who champion the method of *Verstehen* [interpretive understanding]—who thus believe our most important work consists in grasping which ideas people of that time link together with specific concepts—can easily come to the position that adducing ideas which were foreign to contemporary thought leads to the mistaken conclusion that their thinking is moved in the same orbit as our own." The danger of this way of thinking, to follow Schumpeter, would be to consider the history of economic science as a history of ideologies. Schumpeter believed that the construction of abstract pictures of social systems which we then equip with characteristics, is the method of (logical) ideal types of Max Weber and belongs to the pseudo-problems of science.[43]

Schumpeter separates *spirit* from religion: "The development of capitalist entrepreneurship created not only a new economic system and new problems, but also a new orientation to … all these problems." And: "There was no 'new spirit of capitalism' in the sense that people had to appropriate a new way of thinking, to be able to transform a feudal economic world into a … new capitalistic one."[44] Schumpeter asserts further that the categories of pure feudalism and capitalism are unrealistic creations of our minds. The Reformation brought forward no new spirit.

Schumpeter had considered history as continuous as well as discontinuous. According to his view Weber had subjectified the process of transition from feudalism to capitalism; it was related not only to the (logical) ideal types in this transition; Weber simplified the process as well; It had to do not only with the Protestant spirit [*Geist*], which distinguished modern from ancient capitalism. Although Schumpeter examined objective moments in history, he left some of them out. Hence, he simplified the process of transformation from the feudal Middle Ages to modern capitalism, when he says: "The development of capitalistic entrepreneurship created a new economic system." The active moment of this creation, however, does not consist only in the fact that capitalist entrepreneurship, but also that peasants, miners, metal workers, printers and seafarers were active in this transition and contributed to it, as we shall see.

2.6 The Capitalist System and Modern Bourgeois Society

Civil society existed in antiquity and in the modern era in each case in different class societies in the context of the origin of the state. Civil society reaches over the different forms of society which has founded the state, including the Greek polis, the Roman civitas and the city states of the Italian Rinacimento. Bourgeois society is that form of society which founded the national states of the modern world. Civil society is unknown in societies without a state, or social classes. Modern bourgeois society is a particular variant of civil society in general, and is different from it, insofar as economic, juridical and political relations were changed in modern times. The market, exchange of commodities, forces of production, wage labour, commerce are expanded and intensely developed in the modern era. The system of law is generalized within nation states; universal law dominates within a given state. In the political system of the state there are ministries, offices and chancelleries, responsible for the systems of education, of health and care, of the physically dependent; in earlier periods the Church and the family had taken over responsibility for these tasks. The systems of law and the state did not change their essence immediately; they were developed later but arose under the same conditions as the capitalist system of modern times. Productivity in the economy is related to profit, to the capacity of the labourer, to education and to health. This linkage of the various elements of the productive forces, is developed in the history of the modern era, in Europe and America, then in other parts of the world. There is no *causa efficiens* or simple explanation of this transformation of social forms. The different factors work upon one another. The rationalization of the system of labour, the structuration of productive forces, education and with it the spread of writing and arithmetic, of science and technic were expanded and consequently the irrational, opposing forces of modernity, namely, chauvinism, mysticism, anomy and alienation, genocide and ethnocide as well. We recognize these problems as decisive for modern times, however, not specific to them. The changed forms of the legal system in Europe have led to the condition that the administration of justice in the era of high capitalism was universal and in theory was valid for all. Universal equality in legislation as legal idealism had an impact on court proceedings. The evaluation of legal process in this sense was at first favoured by radicals and liberals, but it was validated as decisive in conservative circles in the 19th century as well. In any event, the universal principle in the legal system impacted the local traditional practices of law and went beyond the customary law of peoples. In the theory of the system of the state there should be only *one* legislation and *one* system of law for all and for the whole country. This effort had practical meaning in Central Europe where it was largely actualized, that the differences between the peasants in the east and in the west were abolished in the 19th century. All citizens of the state are legal persons and in this legal and statutory sense were equal before the law. That which was actualized in the period of high capitalism, arises as a potentiality, hence *in nuce* during the era of early capitalism. The regime of Archduke Frederick William had for it its expression: he who has money is recognized as a legal person. Democracy of those well-off stands in contradiction to the medieval feudal system. This struggle over universalism in the state under law lasted for several centuries, from the 15th to the 19th century, till the victory of the radical and liberal ideas of equality before the law and of legal freedom. What was implicit in the early-modern period, was brought to expression in the later epochs.

Not only in the formal domain of legal personality, of equality before the law and in legislation, but also in the substantial processes of education and further developments in high capitalism could be observed before its advent. Advances in arithmetic, in metallurgy, in the printing press, in mining, in chemistry, in geography and astronomy had led to the fact that more and more people could read, write and do arithmetic. Objectively it can be asserted that large industry required a qualified working class and productive force. However, this rationalization of training constitutes only a part of the entire process. Printed leaflets were distributed in the 16th century and played a large role in the peasant revolt of 1524/26. The movement towards freedom and equality during the 15th and 16th century is associated with the formal actualization of this movement in the 19th century, and both have an inner connection with the abolition of illiteracy in Central Europe. We will not pursue this line further, for it goes beyond our period of concern. It is however important to understand that the achievements in the struggle against illiteracy in the period of high capitalism depends on developments and potentialities of the previous epoch of early capitalism. Oppositions between formal and substantial freedom and formal and substantial equality of people as well reach across the two periods of early and late capitalism. They all relate to the epoch of modern bourgeois society and by means of this problematic unify the same oppositions, the same social legislation, the same system of law and the same social structures.

All these contrasts and structures are not actualized immediately and simultaneously. Only after the First World War were the formal inequalities of the monarchical system abolished in Central Europe. These developments can be traced back to the social and economic movements in the 15th and 16th century. At this time aristocracies of profit and money distinguished themselves, on the one hand, the *Bundschuh* movement, the *Arme Konrad* movement and peasant bands made their appearance, on the other. In the city enterprises it has to be stated as well, that a poor man, when he concludes a contract with a wealthy man, is his equal and both are free, otherwise the contract is invalid. The poor insisted that freedom and equality were to be recognized further, in social spheres outside of contracts, as, for example, in the political right to vote.

Capitalism, structurally considered, is related to the economic, juridical and political processes of the modern era. Capital in connection with the market system, with commodity exchange, with wage labour and the money economy was present in antiquity, but its scope was developed only sporadically, and its reach limited. The labour process in the countryside was conducted almost entirely or fully by self-sustaining family farms; production in the countryside as well as in the city was taken up to a large degree by the unfree workforce, slaves, serfs, predial labour, etc. The conditions of unfree labour and production were continued in the Middle Ages. In the first century of the modern era these bonds began to tear. Social differences in rank were relativized by the money economy, wage economy, market, trade and commercial politics. Confessional disputes underscored and radicalized these movements. On the one hand, early capitalists on the Upper and Lower Rhein and in the region of Ems found their expression and their spiritual support in Calvinism. On the other hand, rebellious peasants and federations of apprentices found their expression and their spiritual support in the followers of Wycliffism, among the Hussites, Taborites, definitively in the Reformation in general. The rebels joined the Reformation movements of all colours, Zwinglian, Lutheran, Müntzeran. To be sure, Luther rebuffed their efforts. However, the rebellious peasants remained true to their ideas, each belief community having the right to choose their own ministers. The freedom of the belief communities as well as the freedom and equality of people are closely tied to the freedoms of the market, of trade and of the freedom of movement as developments and expression of the modern era.

Capitalism is the expression of the superiority of capital in the economic, societal and thought process. Capital continues in connection with the system of money and credit; it presents itself in connection with the market—and wage labour process. Capital does not make or do anything. It is a form, it has no self-feeling, no existence in and for itself. It does not valorise or self-valorise; it is valorised or devalued by the activity of labour. It is personified in the capitalist. Capitalists have their money; labourers find themselves in the contradictory condition, of behaving like capitalists without money. The property of the working class is their labour quality and labour time, which they sell. Both sides, capitalist and labourer, are seated across from one another at the bargaining table as formally equal partners, for both are equal in the system of law. Both are equally entitled by law to sign a contract. The contract is the labour contract regarding the sale of labour time for a wage. Both sides are free in the formal sense. In the 15th and 16th century this was the case in the mining system, and in the 20th century it applies everywhere. The freedom of movement of the miners was associated with the freedom of the capitalist to dismiss the workers. The feudal-patriarchal behaviour disappeared. These relations and their changes constitute the main differences between the feudal and the capitalist system. *Nihil ex nihilo*—the capitalist system is not a new-born child in the 15th century. In the new era, processes and features from the past are continued, but to be sure the old characteristics are newly structured and assessed. The transition from the old to the new system is not continued out of necessity. In the head of human beings there is a guiding principle, in history and in nature there isn't one. The economic system of the modern era is not like a mathematical or logical system. The determinations of the system of economy, of law, of politics, are conditioned by many circumstancess and coincidences, which for the most part are not capable of being mastered or controlled. Nevertheless, the systematic processes of society and economy are closely linked with one another, hence their effects on other parts of the system either come to light immediately or after a delay, when some relations in the market, in production or in legal contract are developed. Capitalism is a complicated phenomenon, which is to be illuminated from many sides. Sombart, Weber, Ehrenberg, Strieder, Brentano, von Below, Schumpeter, Kulischer began in their considerations with the entrepreneurs, Marx, on the other hand, with the accumulation of capital, sea trade, technics and the physical movement of the peasants. We are sensitive to these points: the physical movement and the liberation movement of the peasants as well as the elements [*Momente*] of wage labour, of the circulation of money, of increasing productivity, of the spirit, of increasing revenue and commerce, of increasing capital accumulation and of the class struggle in the new era. The driving force in the process of development of capitalism is not only the entrepreneurial class or—in Schumpeter's sense—the capitalist class alone.

2.7 Social Form and Substance

Human society has formal and substantial processes within it. The social form is not an abstract, eternal being, but rather is empirical, concrete, changeable and variable in history according to given social conditions. We speak therefore of social forms, which are distinguished from human substance in that the former are external in their origin, the latter are internal. Social forms are expressions of human relations to one another out of which a social system is constructed. The social systems of law, of politics and of the cults are forms of human activity and creativity and of their relations. The human substance is in part formed out of the process of social reproduction in production, distribution and consumption. We will not define the human form and the human substance here, but rather will treat them by means of examples. The human individual has other formal and substantial processes than the society, corporeal and spiritual [*geistig*]. We stay focussed on social forms and the social substance in the labour process. The forms, which constitute the external side of social life, are the different systems of law under given conditions of civil society and the state. These forms, external in their process of origin, like the rules of social life, do not remain outside of our works but rather are internalized. The laws of normal life in society come from without and are assimilated, imitated, learned, mastered and by these means internalized. The substantial processes of reproduction of human life in society do not exist without a form, the forms do not exist apart from the substance. They can be considered figuratively as basis and superstructure; human being does not exist outside of society; human being is according to his nature a social being, and this has a formal process of regulations which is expressed in law as well as in the other social systems. Humans cannot exist or continue to exist without the social-economic processes of reproduction. The forms and human substance are changed in history; the history of forms is different from that of substance.[45]

Each country, in the course of its history, has suffered much. Gustav Freytag and J.A. Schumpeter, starting from the different viewpoints of belletristic and of economics, have remarked how the Thirty Years' War divided and crippled development in Germany. The invasion of foreign troops and the local bands of robbers had made large parts of Central Europe into a living hell 1618–1648. It was no different in Italy. With Francesco Guicciardini one gets the impression that 15th century Italy was a prosperous and peaceful country. It must be noted that Guicciardini was a wealthy man, highly learned and influential. The Italian peasants had a different fate and would have been able to report it differently. For both the poor and the rich an extended war ensued from 1494 to 1538. During the war, Italy as a battle zone was repeatedly laid waste by Spanish, German and French armies, and one recalls the Sacco di Roma. In the 16th century the Huguenots were driven out of France.

The suffering of the Dutch under the Spanish yoke in the 16th and 17th century was described by Friedrich Schiller. The transition to the modern era was also not peaceful in the other countries of Europe. In Russia, this same period from the end of the 16th century to the beginning of the 17th, was called Smutnoye Vremya, that is, the time of unrest. The systems of law and state of the Middle Ages were fragmented in the wake of war. The process of transformation following on its heels, was not accomplished in a simple fashion, but rather through various ways and means and affected several peoples and social classes. This had to do with the revolution of society in the West, which was dominated by clerical-Catholic and secular-aristocratic feudalism. The majority of the population in all parts of Europe were the peasants.

We distinguish the substantial process of the bourgeois revolution from the formal. It can thus be asserted that around 1700 the aristocratic social class in Germany, England and France had the power in their hands in the formal, political sense. The royal court, the noblesse d'épée, the noblesse de robe and the Church together constituted the leading stratum in the politics of France. Nevertheless, the ruling class in France at the same time accomplished the transition to the money economy. Minister Colbert had led the government politics of mercantilism in the second half of the 17th century. These policies and the money and credit institutes along with the creation of the stock markets of Lyon among others closely related to it, show that the bourgeois class of France was substantially victorious in the 16th and 17th century, not, however, pro forma.

At the time of the French Revolution the bourgeois class had already substantially won their revolution, but the poor in Paris, Marseille and in other cities and in the countryside had taken part late in this revolution; only at the end of the 18th century could they join with the bourgeois revolution. Through these two processes—with the bourgeois on the one side and the proletarians on the other—the French Republic was established. The formation of this republic is a formal-political process, which followed the substantial-economic and the substantial-societal transformation of France after several centuries. The French peasants had begun their uprising much earlier; the movement of the Jacquerie is an event of the 14th century. Formally the French peasants had gained their civil rights only after the citizen revolution of 1789.

In England the revolution did not occur differently, for peasants were rising in the 14th century as well. Through a drawn-out process a social revolution was ushered in, which occurred and was supressed several times. It was not about ten days that shook the world.

The transfer or expulsion of the peasants from the land into the city, which Marx emphasized, is related to the substantial relations of the cultivation of the land, of wage labour in the town and of the changes in agricultural enterprises and in the cities in Northern Italy and England. The corresponding transformations of the constitutions of Italy and England were not closely linked with these economic processes; on the contrary, they followed the economic revolutions only after a delay of some centuries. The constitutional changes are formal-political processes of these states. In the English civil war of the 17th century some formal rights for the common people were able to be introduced, others could be asserted only 200 years later in the period of the Chartists.

The contexts and disputes between the substantial and formal historical moments are shown likewise in Central Europe during the transition from medieval to modern bourgeois society. There arose a succession of peasant and town-proletarian uprisings and wars in the 15th and 16th century in Bohemia, Moravia, Saxony, Thuringia, Alsace, in Swabia, Baden, Frankfurt, Wurttemberg, Bavaria, in the Palatinate, in Westphalia, in Hesse, in Austria and Hungary as well as in many other parts of Central Europe.[46] The peasants had not immediately won the rights to land ownership, property in land and inheritability, to buying and selling, and later, their political and legal rights as well as personal rights and suffrage, but rather only little by little. In some cases, the formal process took until 1848; the substantial processes had begun in the 15th century. Except for the philosophical and psychological moments of human dignity on the one side and the political-legal process in the formal sense on the other, there is no immediate connection between the substantial process of general social relations, of the traditional culture of the people, of the daily struggle for bread and children's education, of the oppositions between town and countryside and of those between the classes. The confluence of the formal and substantial relations and the systems of the same could endure for centuries and then be destroyed by an opposing social movement.

The comparison of the Chinese with the European economy was undertaken by Leibniz in the 17th and Adam Smith in the 18th century. It was possible to justify a reason favouring the superiority of one as well as of the other. Marco Polo had described the wonders of the Orient, but in the Middle Ages it was believed that he had exaggerated the matter; one did not wish to believe him and had given him the mocking name *Marco Millions*. Yet he had not lied; Europe was not as highly developed then as were some of the countries of the Orient, and it could only overtake China through the expansion of modern bourgeois society.[47] Paul Kennedy has recently highlighted the following moments as foundational for the predominance of Europe from the 16th to the 20th century; Europe had been politically disunited. The centralized power in China impeded economic progress, which could not have been the case in Europe. In Europe the open market, the modernization of the economy, technological innovation, the laissez-faire system, political-military pluralism and intellectual freedom were developed.[48] This attempt to consider several factors is sensible, but in doing so, too many historical moments are dropped, as though Marx, Weber, Schumpeter, Kulischer and Strieder had never treated the matter.

Peasants in the different countries of Europe were not in communication with one another, the clerics, on the other hand, were. Wycliff had made an impact upon Hus through his teachings, the Reformation further developed this teaching of the individualization of conscience. The peasants in the south and west of Germany adopted and transformed this doctrine in their rebellious declarations.

The Industrial Revolution of the 18th century, which had defined the end of the early capitalist period, was identified as the separation of two civilizations and as the crossroad of the old to the new by A. Toynbee, T. M. Ashton and C. M Cipolla. F. Fraudel, J. U. Nef and S. Kurowski tried to concretize these generalizations. It was asserted that iron and the refinement of metal separated two civilizations. Nef added to this that the marriage of bituminous coal and iron heralded the beginning of the industrial age. The historians of technology F.M. Feldhaus and O. Johannsen had imagined that linkage rather as a polygamous marriage: several inventions, discoveries and enterprises and not only iron and its marriage with bituminous coal, but in addition seafaring and shipbuilding as well should also be considered epoch making. Feldhaus and Johannsen speak entirely openly about the exploitation of the labourers and of the class struggles in the systems of mining, hammer and iron works in the 15th and 16th century. These fashion not formal but rather substantial processes of bourgeois society.

Social form in human society is not like a husk, the substance not like the flesh, the nut, the pit or the fruit. Form is the outer side of events, of the institution or of the period in human history, that we see; substance is the system of inner relations of people in society. The political, juridical and ritual systems in society constitute the forms; the objectivity of social education, of labour, of social struggles and the subjectivity of friendly, loving, oppositional and hateful relations constitute the substantial side of human connectivity. The capitalist system appears in Central Europe during the 15th, 16th and 17th century. This is only a code word for the mass of peasant liberation declarations and rebellions, for the increasing number of wage labourers, liberal entrepreneurs, the circulation of money and credit institutes, for the cottage industries [*Verlage*] and manufactures in this period, which comprise all the substantial expansions and changes in social and economic life. The political forms of autarchy and of the aristocracy were easily shaken, but they were able to stabilize themselves and establish the absolute state in Germany during the end of the 17th and in the 18th century. Capitalism in Central Europe continued in the mercantilist-cameralist period of European history, while the feudal powers protected themselves from bourgeois foes. The absolute ruler and the aristocrats had circled the wagons around themselves in the face of the enemy. Subsequently the bourgeois had won the victory over the feudal forms in Germany, but the struggle lasted a long time into the following period from the 1790s to 1848 and even 1871.

The forms were changed or were transformed, while the social substance was changed in another way, by other means and at a different rate. It is clear that modern bourgeois society in Central Europe, in Germany, Austria, Switzerland had already been established at the time of the Reformation. Max Weber and Ernst Troeltsch had emphasized not the cause but rather the expression, that is the change in form in the religiosity of these events. Inner-worldly asceticism is linked with savings and with the accumulation of capital. We shall speak no further about relations among the Hussites, Tabarites and Anabaptists down to Lutherans and Calvinism. However, the societal forms are internalized by people, assimilated and eventually constitute an essential part of the social substance.

The uprisings of peasants, miners and apprentices as isolated movements did not cause the transition from feudalism to capitalism. Only in connection with the other elements [*Momente*] have they exerted their influence. All elements [*Momente*] affect one another, the Reformation emboldened and shaped the peasants in their uprising, however they were already rebellious in the 15th century and had nothing to do with the Reformation. In the 16th century, the peasants acted as Protestant reformers, but against Luther's will. The conflict between the Reformation and Counter-Reformation appears as an expression of unrest in the transition to the capitalist era; the Thirty Years' War was a further indication and cause of the unrest in the same process of transformation. In opposition to it, the feudal authorities were able to consolidate, they were able to retain the forms of their predominance and temporarily to continue them. The forms did not remain the same, the absolute state of the 18th century was not the Holy Roman Empire of the German Nation with a different name. But the ruling class in the period of absolutism was cobbled together by the same princes and aristocrats, while the bourgeois [*Bürger*] limped behind in their seizure of power. Only in the following century was the victory of the bourgeois Reichstag and of parliamentary democracy achieved. Nevertheless, from the 15th to the 19th century the economic activity of capitalism was extended, and the influence of the bourgeois was steadily rising. The capitalist system in the 15th and 16th century was shown in the economic-substantial and formal sense through the domination of political and juridical institutions in the period of high capitalism as a complete economic and social, as a formal and substantial system.

Form and substance in human history are not separated and later screwed, nailed or glued together in a mechanical system as it were. People developed the difference of form and substance and the relation of both to one another. They internalize the form and make it into an element [*Glied*] and part of the substance; they externalize the substantial relationships and make them into an aspect [*Glied*] of the forms.

The liberals, bourgeois and democrats despised the absolutism of the 18th century. The political and juridical form was not in alignment with their desire and experience. Already in the 18th century enlightened thinkers like C.A. Helvetius and the materialists like P.T. Holbach had taken up the struggle against absolutism. However, compared to the conditions of the Thirty Years' War, the absolutism of the 18th century was a blessing. The people had enough of the unrest; this was true for the poor as well as for the rich. They concerned themselves with the desire for peace and quiet and therefore transformed feudal forms into absolutism and internalized them. However, the economic substance became more bourgeois still. The state, too, transformed itself into a bourgeois enterprise.

The form is not simple or merely the superstructure; the substance is not only the base in history. The superstructure has a form and a substance, the base as well. The form and substance, the superstructure and base are actually existent. There is no further reality behind this actuality; it is not an appearance, which occludes another actuality. The state is a superstructure, but it has to do with the economic base as well; the form determines the substance and the substance the form. These relations represent a theoretical problem which we will not solve here. We remain with the concrete state in the transition to the period of high capitalism.

The role of the state in the transformation of society and economy is shown with increasing clarity in the 17th century. The state introduces an essential moment in the economic transformation. It organizes the complex [*Anlage*] of capital and its accumulation in the public treasury. Political power was centralized and personified in the figure of the head of state. The system of the national state carries the name of the absolute state. This designation is perhaps an exaggeration. However, the aristocrats, the bourgeois and the Church constituted no essential alternative to it, and the concentration of public power in the hands of the head of state could proceed in the 17th and 18th century. The state in Germany, Russia, England, France, Sweden, Spain, Portugal and the Netherlands played an important role in the development of shipbuilding, then of mining and of the war industry (that is saltpeter, gun powder, small arms, cannons) further of coinage, assaying and other parts of the metal industry. The state is also not only a formal matter but rather to be considered a substantial moment in history as well. Hence, the bourgeois class in the 19th and 20th century had a centralized state power which it had itself not established but rather took over and in part restructured.

Astute people in the 15th and 16th century who had experienced the transition from medieval times already knew that the old times had passed. Concepts like reawakening, antiquity, and in the 17th century the concept Middle Ages were employed for the interrelationship of these processes.

As late as in the 19th and 20th century, researchers published apposite explanations of the events of transition for us, which we present in the following:

1. It's a question of a transformation of an economic system and of human society and of the foundation of a new epoch.
2. There is no single factor which dissolved the old epoch and no single factor which introduced the new one. The historical process cannot be derived

from only one moment, neither from external trade nor from the struggle over annuities, neither from one invention nor from one discovery. There is no secret to the revolution.

3. It's a question of a social system, that brings with it several traits of the past and transforms them. Even though we shall treat several factors, our investigation however, will not be accomplished eclectically but rather uniformly.
4. The past is not continued; in historical studies there is a type of treatment which points out the roots of the new from the previous period. Society and its history consist in formal and substantial moments which describe different and opposed tendencies.
5. Human history is put together out of continuous and discontinuous moments. The history of the formal systems of law, of politics and of culture form traits, signs and delimitations of two periods. The formal systems do not determine the exit of the old and the rise of the new periods in history.
6. The period of transition to modern bourgeois society and the society from the 15th to the 19th century itself have their system, whose guiding threads, consisting of the opposed relations of the labour process, we shall consider more closely. This process is composed of the organization and division of social labour, of production, distribution and consumption of products and commodities. The labour relations of this period are in part unfree in compulsory labour and military service [*Fron- und Militärdienst*], in part in formally free piecework and daily wage labour. Further categories of labour and the freedom or unfreedom of the same will be presented in the following chapter.[49]
7. According to Marx it had to do with a dissolution, a demolition of the feudal bonds during the 16th century in large parts of Europe and simultaneously with the formation of a new, modern bourgeois society. Weber shared this view and asserted the spirit of the new age is shown in the Calvinist ethos, which constitutes an active moment in the historical process. The assertion that an ethos forms such a moment, is abhorrent to the Marxists. The moments of dissolution were present in the 16th century; the road to the dissolution of feudal society was prepared by the activities of peasants and merchants in the 14th and 15th century as well. The process of dissolution had lasted hundreds of years, and was formed not only out of the substantial moments of the peasants' movement, of the movement of liberation, of the movement of wage labourers, of the movement of merchants and of the movement of bankers, but rather also out of the formal moments of political disputes of the feudal and bourgeois parties, as well as out of the expression in the system of law and state. The processes of the

feudal past were continued and by means of their internalization during the transitional period they shaped an essential part of the moment of dissolution. Therefore, we speak of continuous as well as discontinuous processes of the period of transition.

8. Those who had taken part in this process of transition were able to internalize and give expression to their attempts at freedom, which they did. Peasants in the 14th to 16th century were rebellious and had externalized with increasing consciousness their program of social revolution, in the 14th century with lesser, in the 16th with greater clarity. In the 19th and 20th century ideological revolutions had begun; first came the thought, then came the deed. In the 14th and 16th century that was reversed. It would be false to project our current orientation in these matters onto the past.
9. The revolutions at the beginning of the modern era had their formal as well as their substantial sides, which encompass the whole of society, including the poor and the rich, those who were conscientious as well as opportunists. Bookkeeping took part in these revolutions, and thus it might have been self-flattery for a writer, a merchant or for a bookkeeper around 1902, when he could read that 400 years ago one of his kind, exactly like Coryphaeus in the ancient Greek dance, introduced the great bourgeois revolution through double-entry bookkeeping. Sombart and the others who shared this theory are not the only ones who simplified history and ascribed to one single historical moment an exaggerated significance.
   - 9.1. The transition from feudalism to the modern era was a complicated process. In relation to this complexity we note that Marx had conceived the model of the decline of the feudal system in his prediction of the end of the capitalist era and a breakthrough of modern bourgeois society. Schumpeter had made the same prediction, but on other grounds. Both views are to be taken seriously and not to be treated ludicrously like that of Sombart. But the matter of decline, rise and decline of the system was complicated by ideology. The treatment of the category of feudalism and capitalism as well as the prediction of a collapse of capitalism is in part an objective, in part an ideological, political and subjective matter, influenced by our wishes and desires.
   - 9.2. We will investigate the period of the 15th to 17th century in relation to the ideological disputes of the 20th century as little as possible. Of course, we cannot completely bracket these disputes; if we see through our own ideologies, we can then understand how they have influenced our conceptions of history. Only then can we grasp the process of origin of modern bourgeois society. Both tasks are important in themselves.

We can liberate ourselves in part from ideological bias if we understand the ideological context between the rise-and-fall analysis of capitalism. We forego a model for the collapse of feudalism which could serve as a paramount example for the collapse of capitalism.

9.3. In one sense feudalism and capitalism are not comparable: the one carries within itself the oppositions of unfree labour, the other not. The dream of a serf would be to be a wage labourer. The inner oppositions of the capitalist system are something different.

10. In relation to capitalist development in Central Europe in the period of the 15th to 17th century we can only now assert that at that time some false steps were made. The types of enterprise from Hansa and Fugger, which appeared as practically and theoretically pathbreaking in their time, were abandoned. The guild system and the putting-out system of the early capitalist period were at first expanded and afterwards abolished. All forms of unfree labour such as slavery and serfdom were considered illegal in the period of high capitalism.

The modern factory system in the period of high capitalism developed the production of commodities *en masse*, turnover in a general market and the money assets of the entrepreneurs. Marx (see above) asserted that that was all missing in the guild system with regard to the production of cloth, but it appears nevertheless, in early glass, paper and iron manufacture. To this the following is to be noted: The guild system was primarily related to private consumption; weaving, shoe and hat making, house construction and foodstuff enterprises were plied in guild-like fashion. The guilds and the council kept the monopoly on the creation and sale of commodities for themselves and they controlled it. They dominated the organization and delimitation of production of these commodities first through the regulation of quantity and quality of the products, second through price and market regulations, third through the regulation of the magnitude of undertakings and the number of labourers in them, fourth through the regulation of training, of the qualification and of the wages of the labourer, fifth through the regulation of the means of production and their employment. We will later return to the regulation and prohibitive system of the guilds. Outside of the guild system stood shipbuilding, the war industries, mining, assaying and coinage.

The first centuries of the capitalist period distinguish themselves through the restraint of the medieval corporations, of the guild system, through the blossoming and the delimitation of the putting-out system, the advance and the containment of the production process in Central Europe. Nonetheless, foreign and internal trade and foreign and domestic markets were extended across Europe. In this period some special areas of capital such as the German Hansa and the Upper German credit institutes were blossoming; they were later lost. The focus of capitalist trade in the 17th century was transferred to England and the Netherlands. Yet everywhere in Central and Western Europe the credit system, stock markets, the international market, joint-stock companies in private hands and state undertakings and capital investments were expanded.

The working class increased through the immigration of peasants and foreigners into the towns of Central Europe. Through the spread of mining, entire districts, which were previously agricultural, were transformed into mining towns in Upper Germany, Bohemia, Tirol and in the Harz. In part, the working class became poorer, wages sank, and especially so through the increasing labour of children and women. In part, the working class was better trained through the spread of literacy and numeracy. As a whole, the level of qualification of the working class increased.

The organization of labour through the increasing articulation and division of labour in the process of production and distribution was continued. Rationalization in manufacture and in distribution was partly and sporadically introduced. Only in the period of high capitalism could it be systematically and greatly utilized. Yet, in some industries, for example, in mining, production could be advanced with increasing rationalization and productivity. Enterprises were enlarged, the value of production rose, yet the number of labourers did not increase. Only later could the clothing industry, house construction, and the like be accomplished with the same degree of rationalization and expansion. The printing industry was hardly changed and remained static until the 17th century. Hard coal, steam machinery, the railroad network, and electricity were developed and employed in a practical way in the 18th, 19th, and 20th century.

The activities, tasks and contributions of the capitalist entrepreneurs were treated and praised by a number of authors and researchers. Some of them highlighted the spirit of entrepreneurship as the most significant moment and as the leading voice for capitalism. This view is accurate, yet one-sided and overly simplified. The liberation of the peasants, their uprisings and struggles essentially contributed to the rise and expansion of modern bourgeois society in southern, western and northern Germany. The spread of the wage system in the city and the circulation of money linked to it contributed just as much to the rise and advancement of the capitalist system.

The activities, tasks and contributions of discoveries and technics were also singled out in the rise of the capitalist system by many writers and researchers. However, the technological view of history is one sided and overly simplified as well. Technics, discoveries and science are elements of the labour process; manual labour is a further element of it. Discoveries constitute a part of the changes of the means of production. All these historical moments have led to the transition to the capitalist system and to its formation. The rationalization of the production process rests on improved training and the composition of the workforce.

The transition from medieval feudalism to modern bourgeois society can be considered as a revolution, yet in this respect one should free oneself from a model of the French or Russian revolution. Revolution is a radical transformation of the social and economic system of a people, of a state, an empire, etc. The French revolution of 1789 or the Russian revolution of 1917 occurred within a short period of time, during which new political systems came into being. A new social system arises in another sense, which does not occur moment to moment, but rather the conflicts and oppositions between the old and new continued for centuries. Only by looking back can the essence and the significance of what happened be understood. In the Middle Ages the feudal and estate system stalled, the economy was primarily a natural economy, productivity stagnated. In the modern era the feudal system disappeared, estates became outdated, classes are now talked about, the circulation of money and commodities comes to predominate in the economy, and the conflicts among the old aristocrats, Church leaders and wealthy men with regard to political domination increase. The uprisings, oppositions, conflicts between the peasants and their masters began in the 15th century, in fact already at the end of the 14th century in Europe. The very last vestiges of the clashes of the old aristocrats and the new money masters continued into the 19th and even into the first half of the 20th century. Trade and commerce increased, the first signs of the consumer society show themselves, as Janssen and Pareto tell it; wage labour and capital become the determining forms of economic and social life, formal freedom and equality are expanded, new forms in religion arise. The individualism of the modern era is related to the increased profit, to the spirit, to the psychic process, to the guilt and responsibility of the individual and finally to the ways and means of how contracts are concluded and maintained.

Labour in capitalism is not performed by communities, corporations and brotherhoods but rather undertaken individualistically. We say individualistically according to the way contracts are signed, individualistically not in the sense of great figures in history. Apprentices, miners [*Bergknappen*] and manual labourers in the cities of Central Europe found themselves together in guilds [*Zünfte*], mining guilds [*Gilden*], offices [*Ämte*], fraternities, guild halls [*Innungen*] and associations.[50] The council and authorities prohibited fraternities of apprentices; the guild masters in the 15th, 16th, and 17th century assumed leadership of the organizations, of the guilds, of the societies of share-holders [*Gewerksgesellschaften*] and fraternities. After an interruption of two or three centuries, new trade unions then began their activities in the 19th century. The means of labour are steam machinery; iron and hard coal dominate the technics of the industrial process. Capital, credit—and the money system arise and control the economic life of the cities in the 15th century and thereafter, but they have no control over the politics and the system of law in Central Europe. In England the bourgeois class shows itself in the 17th century, in the 18th, the American and French class of commercial traders. In Central Europe the bourgeois revolution is slowed, and only four hundred years after the first appearance of the money economy in Upper Germany was the process of transition completed. In the region of the Mediterranean the same process of transition takes just as long. It's also a question of grasping a new process and categories of thought and of a revolution of this sort, which is completed over centuries. Perhaps we can only now understand its scope, since the bourgeois revolution has been carried out over five hundred years. To begin with, it appears complicated and reveals itself differently in the region of the Mediterranean, in England, Germany, the Netherlands and so on. We see its beginning in Central Europe. Marx highlighted several moments in the first appearance of the capitalist system. Schumpeter some others. Now Germany is not the place of the primal beginning, but it was here that an important contribution to the origin of capitalism in the human and inhuman sense was achieved. In the German mining system, the first steps were made towards high capitalist industrialization, which were continued in England. We will neither attempt to simplify this complexity nor to trace a *causa efficiens*. Neither Jacques Coeur nor Jakob Fugger, neither Luther nor Calvin transformed the feudal world. Personality does not play a determining role in history. Literary figures are powerful; François Rabelais or Sebastian Brant, both men of the transition to modernity, both authors, have outlined the period of transition in a convincing fashion. *Der fressend Naar* by Hans Sachs makes its appearance—Hartmann Schopper called it Laemargus—like a figure out of the ship of fools. The fool, money fool, stock fool, appear in Hans Sachs and Hartmann Schopper as a figure of jest, not as a living human being. Such literary figures and forms we leave for the literary historians, who can better treat of them.[51]

2.7a. Form and Substance of Freedom: Faust's Last Words

Freedom has form and substance. Goethe brought the substance of freedom to expression in the second part of *Faust* (Scene VI Great Outer Court of the Palace) in the following:

A swamp lies there below the hill,

Infecting everything I've done:

My last and greatest act of will
Succeeds when that foul pool is gone.
Let me make room for many a million,
Not wholly secure, but free to work on …
… He only earns his Freedom and Existence,
Who's forced to win them freshly every day.
Childhood, manhood, age's vigorous years,
Surrounded by dangers, they'll spend here.
I wish to gaze again on such a land,
Free earth: where a free race, in freedom, stand.

(translation by A.S. Kline)

Freedom like labour is objectified and confirmed through the activity not of the single individual, but rather of the people, through the labour of many millions in the mastering of nature; external nature is dangerous and contaminated, the murky pool is sluggish and only through social labour will it be made fruitful. Freedom is not presented as the end result, also not as a unique event, but rather as a continuous process. Here the pure substance of freedom is presented, there is no talk of the form of freedom in the area of law. Freedom is offered as a human potentiality, which will be actualized in the future through the common activity of many. The active moment of this process of actualization is the oppositional relation between man and the external world.

In his *History of Florence*, Machiavelli asserted that Venice had been founded on a swamp, which was according to its nature, unhealthy, and only through the labour of a people was it made whole and fruitful. The founding of the city of Pisa originally situated on a contaminated swamp as well, is derived from the same common and wholesome process of labour. Both men share the view that the cultivation of the earth, the founding of the city and of the human struggle against an adverse nature constitutes one and the same process. In his work *Il Principe* Machiavelli referred to the formal conditions of freedom which lie exclusively in the hands of the people, in opposition to the princes and oligarchs. Goethe took a further step in that he emphasized common labour as the objective and substantial condition of freedom.

Around 1830 Goethe extended and deepened his concept of freedom. In relation to the form of freedom he expressed his disappointment and his pessimism in *Hermann and Dorothea* (*Sixth Canto, Klio*) 1797. Klio is not the muse of history here, but rather of the age, which lost its hope.

Nicht kurz sind unsere Leiden!
Denn wir haben das Bittre der sämtlichen Jahre getrunken,
Schrecklicher, weil auch uns die schönste Hoffnung zerstört ward.
Denn wer leugnet es wohl, daß hoch sich das Herz ihm erhaben,
Ihm die freiere Brust mit reineren Pulsen geschlagen,
Als sich der erste Glanz der neuen Sonne heranhob,
Als man hörte vom Rechte der Menschen, das allen gemein sei,
Von der geisternden Freiheit und von der löblichen Gleichheit!

Our suffering is not short!
For we have drunk the bitterness of poisoned years,
More frightening, because the most beautiful hope of ours was also destroyed.
For whosoever truly denies it, that his heart raised him high,
Beat in him the free breast of a pure pulse,
When the first light of the new sun raised itself up,

When one heard of the rights of men, that all are common,
Of inspirational freedom and of prized equality!

Freedom as the right that is common to all, was asserted by the peasant rebellions in the south and west of Central Europe as well as by the North Italian and English peasants at the beginning of the capitalist era and this assertion prevailed over the course of the 15th, 16th, 17th and 18th century. The French peasants won the right to freedom and equality in the revolution of 1789. These rights were confirmed by the miners of Central and Upper Germany as well as the organizations of apprentices and masters in the cities of Europe in the same epoch. In these cases, freedom appears as form. Only Goethe, and after him the people, had successfully asserted their formal freedom in the 15th to 18th century, did the expression of the substance of freedom achieve its expression, which first appeared as poetry and was taken over in the following centuries as the ideology of freedom.

Freedom and equality, which should be common to men by right, appear only as forms. The poor, the peasants, like the urban working class, experience to their disappointment, that they indeed won the right to free movement either in the city or from one city to another as well as the right to contract freely—but the right to freely relocate and of the free contract had no substance, when one looks in vain for a dwelling. All enjoy the same right to vote and are in fact politically and juridically equal, but the mastery of the system of state remains in the hands of the rich. Capital alone can guarantee employment. The poor are, therefore, forced to work for another, through which their substantial freedom disappears. The tone of the 90s of the 18th century follows, which Goethe brings to expression in the sixth canto of *Hermann and Dorothea*.

Goethe appears at the end of the initial period of modern bourgeois society and represents the transition from it to the high capitalist era in the 19th century. The peasants of West Germany, the miners and the working class in the cities of the entire country won the formal freedoms as a right. Big capital, modern trade unions and organizations begin their activity at this point in time.

Faust *in articulo mortis* had foreseen the conditions of substantial freedom, but like Moses, he could not enter the promised land. In other analogues to biblical history the people in *Faust* did not obtain the land, like the ancient Hebrews, as a free gift, but rather made it their own through its cultivation. The substance of freedom is not the result of the labour process, but rather a part of the process itself. Formal freedom, on the contrary, is the precondition of labour under modern social conditions. First comes liberation, then comes productive labour. Goethe grasped this series in the relation of formal freedom to the process of labour. Thus, he wrote in *Torquato Tasso* (*IV, 5 and IV, 2*):

Laßt mich in Freiheit, daß mein Glück sich finde.
Frei will ich sein im Denken und im Dichten.

Allow me in freedom my happiness to be found
Free, I want to be in thinking and versifying.

The fundamental condition for the human spirit is its freedom. Only thereafter can he think and write poetry. It is formal freedom that is meant here, for substantial freedom lies in writing and thinking itself. The poet is not someone in the past. The audience immediately grasped that Goethe was writing about the conditions of their and his present. Our concepts have actualized the poem. The poet represents working modalities of every kind, of the manual as of the intellectual labourer of modern society. Hence the poem is an actual theme for us.

The right to freedom and equality in bourgeois society is a formal one and in the hands of Goethe is conceived of as a formal matter. It is taken up by others as an object of exaltation and a song of praise, otherwise it has no qualities for them. Goethe's great discovery, which we call substantial freedom, follows at the end of a century's long struggle for liberation in broad parts of Europe. Formal freedom in and for itself is empty and without substance. However, with it a new epoch in the struggle for freedom begins, concerned with the substantial liberation of humanity. Goethe stands at the beginning of this new period. The freedom already achieved awakens our hope, yet when it is without substance, it arouses only our disappointment. Formal freedom has no qualities, because it is separated from the substance of freedom. Goethe first appeared as the poet of freedom, but then he was considered as its main ideologue, in this case in relation to its substance.

Nothing is said here about the right of people to freedom. A form, which inherits or can be inherited, comes not into question. Goethe's poetic style in the treatment of the substance of freedom changed. In relation to the form of freedom and equality he remains distant from this object: in 1797 one heard about the rights of man. Freedom and equality become the object of a mediation through hearsay for one, for another through legal action, which proceeds only in a convoluted manner, never straightforwardly. It is written in the Bible: Lord, don't go to court. Freedom and equality appear only as rumours, not in actuality, but rather as something from the distance and out of the past, when one only argues about the right to them. The struggle of the peasants for freedom in the 16th century is forgotten, and only in 1848, in the bourgeois struggle for freedom, is it reawakened. The single object of this struggle is now the form of freedom and equality. The connection between Goethe's struggle for freedom in *Faust* and the struggle of the rebellious peasants consists in the fact that both have freedom as their goal. The peasants did not want to disrupt the state and the Church, only abolish the unfreedom of the feudal system. The third article of the peasants of 1525 reads: "Third, the custom till now has been that we have been kept by them as their own people, which is pitiful … Therefore, it follows from scripture that we are free and want to be free. Not to be totally free and want to have no authority; God does not teach us that."

In *Faust* Goethe ascribed to substantial freedom some qualities and characteristics. Formal freedom, which the peasants demanded, is limited and relative; they do not demand the abolition of all authority. Goethe wanted humanity to become completely free. The poetry about freedom in *Faust* starts from the premise that people have conquered their formal freedom, now the struggle is about the conquest of external nature, about the winning of substantial freedom. In this case freedom is not empty and without content, rather palpable and objective. It is a matter of the whole of life, from childhood to adulthood and old age; it is the matter of the social whole, of the working people; it disappears when we do not renew it daily; it and we are surrounded by danger. It is beautiful, not like a statue, but rather like living beauty: It belongs not to the past, but rather to the present. The verses in the poem are not cool, embittered, distanced as in *Hermann and Dorothea,* but rather a freeing of the breast and pulsating: "*Eröffn' ich Räume vielen Millionen.*" [I open spaces for many millions]. And: "*Auf freiem Grund mit freiem Volke stehn.*" [To stand on free earth with free people.] Even the earth on which free people stand is free.

The peasants of 1525 are not the same as those of 1848, for the former were unfree in form and in substance and because they fought for their formal liberation and were victorious in that struggle. 1848 was about the expansion of formal bourgeois freedoms, mainly—but not exclusively—in the political sense. Almost all the peasants of South and West Germany were already nearly completely liberated in the formal sense.

2.8 On the Theory of Labour and Technique as Part of the Labour Process in the Period of Early Capitalism

Since humanity reproduces and sustains itself through labour, labour is defined under all conditions of the human order as self-reproductive activity. The human process of reproduction—in opposition to physiological reproduction—includes production, consumption as well as the mediation between the two sides of that process in itself. Mediation in the process of human reproduction is actualized as distribution in society. Distribution is further concretized in modern bourgeois society in the process of exchange and trade of commodities. The latter includes capital and money circulation as its essential and indispensable component.

Labour is organized and structured according to the organization and structuration of society. If society is organized collectively or communally, according to the principles of kinship and neighbourhoods in tribes, sibs or village communities, then labour is organized accordingly. If society is organized through the structuration of social classes, then labour is organized according to the structuration and division of classes, and labour is structured in classes of society, and thus corresponds to social organization. On the contrary, if labour is organized communally as in village communities, instead social whole is organized on this basis. Central Europe in the period of early capitalism and in the period of modern bourgeois society was a class society, structured into a ruling and a working class. The ruling class was composed of oppositional elements: Sole rulers, courtiers, nobles, patricians, councillors, merchants, bankers, manufacturers and guild masters. The interests of these elements were different and in part internally antagonistic. The organization of the working class was somewhat complicated. The peasants were in part landowners; agricultural labourers were paid daily wages, burdened with compulsory labour and feudal dues. A third element of the peasantry had maintained the communal arrangement from the time prior to written history. The resonance of all these elements and movements can be found in the distributed writings, articles and instructions of the peasant war. The workers in the city and in mining and metallurgy outside the city were basically free. The workers were principally wage labourers and were paid a daily or weekly wage, that is, by the piece or a piece work wage. The guild organization was not universal but yet quite widespread in Central Europe. The guild system was commonly organized into three groupings: into masters, journeymen, and apprentices. The masters were in part well off, busy in their own enterprises, in part however, they were poor and found themselves in the same condition as the journeymen. The putting-out system was developed in many kinds of enterprises, as secondary operations in the villages, as primary operations in the printing industry. The production of cloth, metallurgy and mining were in part systematically organized as putting-out systems in the villages. The textile, construction and metal-working guilds constituted the basis for the production of commodities in the city.

The individual comported himself practically with his needs in relation to external nature as a part of the external world, just as the external world constituted a part of the individual, namely as an immediate relation between man and nature from the standpoint of man. In nature, this relation is direct, practical and concrete. In order to satisfy his needs and to diminish them and in this way to dispose of them, man goes 'mediatingly' [*vermittelnd*] to work. This process is objective, in part simple, immediate, practical and concrete, in part it is complicated, mediate, theoretical and abstract. The work is the result, the labour by contrast is the means to obtain the result. The objects of labour and the things of nature offer various resistances to the efforts of men. In order to subjugate them, man interpolates other natural things, and turns nature against nature itself thereby, and invents instruments of labour to this purpose[52] iron against stone and stone against iron. The implements constitute a part of the mediation between body and mind, hand and head, man and nature. Since the use of tools is targeted and the labour has a purpose, teleology arises in the human world and through it in nature.

Man comports himself to external nature in a theoretical and a practical way. Perhaps human behaviour in relation to subjective artwork is practical but in relation to its effect and its creation labour is practical and theoretical, concrete and abstract. It is an ironic chapter in the theory of labour that Hegel, the idealist, emphasized the practical and concrete side of the labour process, whereas Marx, the materialist, the theoretical and abstract side. Marx took up the Hegelian analysis of the labour process and of the relation between man, needs/wants, tools and external nature and developed them. Labour, says Marx, is a process between man and nature, in that man mediates, regulates and controls[53] his metabolic interchange with nature through his own deeds. In this process, there is nothing but the material of nature and human labour activity. But suddenly and in a miraculous way mind, consciousness, planning, will, mentality, ideality and teleology appear in this natural process, are created, und introduced into matter. Nature, which till now had no purpose, no telos, no plan, no purposefulness within it and knew neither mind nor spectre [*Spuk*]—now all of these are made its own through human labour. Labour is the means to the elaboration of these new processes in nature. Humanity is reproduced in a human way through its labour so that labour is defined as human self-reproducing activity. The human process of reproduction is actualized through distribution. The mediating process of labour is the *differentia specifica* of the human being; it arises not only in the relation between man and nature, as Hegel says, but also in relation between production and consumption, distribution and the circulation of money, between labourer, means of labour and raw material. For the comprehension of technics, the understanding of the theory of labour is indispensable. Yet labour is not only a process between labour, means of labour and raw material.

Labour consists of a material element in which humanity processes the inner world and the external world of nature and transforms it, so that we may live and reproduce ourselves. Labour consists in a non-material element, in which humanity organizes its labour and work activity in the imagination. We conduct ourselves in a mediating way to external and internal nature and mediately to it. Labour is, however, more than the ensemble of these relations to nature. We objectify the human animal, subjectify and mediate it and transform it so that it becomes in part human. The organs of the hand and of the head are objects of labour, just as grain and meat, fur and wood. But labour is not only a process between man and animal; it is just as much a process between man and man who goes to work in a mediating way in the organization of labour, the combination of labour and the division of labour.

Man objectifies himself through labour in such a way that labour, tools and the relations of men to one another are transformed in the process of labour and are transfigured in the objects of human labour. When, in this process, man interpolates a natural thing and uses it against another, a complicated process thus arises. Hegel and Marx spoke about the practical and the theoretical process in this connection. The positing of a goal and the purposefulness of labour is not a natural phenomenon.[54] Man makes his labour activity into an object of his mental and corporeal labour and transforms them in the labour process itself. He selects new bodily movements, pounds stone with the hammer or cuts meat with the knife from the side and not, as before, from above. He makes the tool into an object of his mental and corporeal activity and creates the wedge for the processing of hard stone with the help of the hammer. He makes the process of labour into the object of his activity and develops the collaboration of many men in the hunt and in the damming up of a river. Meanwhile the organization of labour develops through the conjunction and differences of the sexes, of chronological age and of the physiological characteristics of weight, of muscle power, of visual acuity, of hearing and so on. Men develop the structuration of labour, the combination and division of labour in society and make this structuration into the object of the self-developing process of labour.[55] The labour process makes men, and man makes his creations through his labour in production, consumption distribution and reproduction into the object of his mental and corporeal labour. Labour is organized, structured, divided, consolidated and individuated. Through the fact that men work on their own labour process, simplify it and complicate, multiply, change, vary, improve, mediate and advance it, they make their labour, the external world and themselves into the object of labour. In this way, the world, labour in relation to the world and labour in relation to men is objectified. In the latter case labour is the self-objectification of man.

The natural thing in the labour process becomes transformed into a human object and with this, ceases to be a natural thing.[56] Man ceases to be a natural thing through labour. He makes himself into the object and subject of his activity, of his relations and powers.

Labour is not static but develops. It is changed through relations in nature and in society and changes the natural and social relations of men. Labour as a process of mediation between man and external nature becomes increasingly more complicated. The stages between man and nature multiply. The burghers of the towns of modern society do not eat what they have sowed but rather buy bread that is baked. The baker too has not planted the grain for his baked goods but rather bought them, and so on. Labour becomes more complicated through its structuration, organization, combination and division. The structuration of labour through the differences of the sexes, through the processes between adults and children, between the strong, the weak, the quick, the more talented, etc. become transformed. These details of the structuration of labour are on the one hand physiologically determined and on the other reorganized by membership in a tribe, a village or in a sib. An early reformation and restructuring of labour in the history of Central Europe was introduced by the guild system and labour cooperatives. The putting-out system and the rationalization of labour in manufacture are further stages in the history of the structuration of labour in the capitalist era.

Labour in bourgeois society is comprehended as labour time. Under more primitive conditions it is difficult if not impossible to distinguish between labour and labour time and to analyse the two categories independently of one another. Labour time in bourgeois society is apportioned into a preparatory and a working stage. Such a step-like apportionment would be difficult to detect in the more primitive conditions of the labour process. The preparatory stage of the labour process is for one the mediate process of instruction of the school child in which he is taught reading, writing and arithmetic as well as a general knowledge of geography, history among other subjects. The immediate process of learning by apprentices is the concrete and practical advancement of the preparatory stage of the labour process in society. The amount of time employed in the different stages of preparation can be calculated. These learning processes are to be distinguished from one another in that the preparation time for a schoolteacher takes longer than that of a cabinet maker or a metal worker in a factory; the training time for an electrician or a doctor takes longer than that of a schoolteacher and so on. The preparatory stage or the learning activity for a manual labourer in the metal industry, textile factory, etc. takes about ten to twelve years in modern bourgeois society, that is from the age of six to sixteen or eighteen on average. The preparatory stage for a schoolteacher takes four years longer, that is until the age of twenty or twenty-two on average, the preparatory stage for a doctor, a biochemist, a physicist, an electrician takes in turn three or four years longer still on average. These relations in training vary from country to country and as a tendency they become increasingly long in comparison to the past. The further investigation of the problem of time of training will be more precisely ascertained by those in various countries.

Labour time in the different branches of industry can also be enumerated and mathematically-algebraically evaluated in connection with the preparatory and training time. This mode of treatment is related to labour time in medicine, in chemistry, physics, in engineering, and so on.

Labour time is concretized in the product of labour shown as a means for consumption, for further production and for distribution. The means of labour are abstract in planning and in outlines, in mathematical, chemical and physical formulae for further labour in the process of reproduction (production, distribution, consumption process). The means of labour are concrete in the means of production and distribution, as are the tools of manual and intellectual labour in general. The means of production and distribution encompass an essential component of the means of labour, but not their totality.

Technology consists of material and non-material elements and constitutes a part of the labour process. Technics are in this sense the art of processing the means of production and distribution, of the concrete tools and abstract instruments of labour. Technics in a second sense is the creation of the means of labour, of the concrete and abstract means of production and distribution, of tools and the instruments of labour themselves.

Technics like the organization of labour in general is not static but rather dynamic, and it is carried forward in the opposition between what is handed down and renewing of what is handed down according to different social conditions and in the embedded relations of the given society in different epochs of its historical process. Invention is, as we see, to be considered part of the all-encompassing process of technics, just as technics shows itself as a component of something greater, that of social labour. In practice, invention is a part of the process of innovation, the innovation is a part of the opposition between what is handed down and its variation, reworking and transformation in the human process of reproduction.[57]

Everything is in a state of flux, nothing remains fixed, as Heraclitus of old said, yet technic is changed and varied, although subordinate to social labour, with a different rate and another historical tempo than in the process of human reproduction and hence does not simply go along with it. Technics and its transformation as material processes are without doubt more apparent than the abstract relations in the course of human history, but to be sure they are in no way the determining factor in this process. The transformations in technics are determined through the transformations and metamorphoses in the relations between men in the organization of labour, irrespective of whether communal or social; and in the latter case oppositional relations between the social classes constitute the determining factor and motor of history. Nonetheless, technics function as the immediate relation of the labourer to the means of labour and participate in the transformation in all the other processes. If the period of transformations of technics in the Palaeolithic period are to be measured in tens of thousands of years, then in the history of Chinese technics and science in antiquity the effective time of innovation, of a material discovery or invention stretches over thousands of years, which awakens the impression of stagnation. On the contrary, it is determined that human life in the archaic, primitive conditions or in the course of the history of the Asiatic mode of production developed in constant change and in no way stagnated, as the history of technics shows, even though these processes advance more slowly in their impact than those that appear in our immediate historical experience.

Those researchers who occupy themselves with the history of technics and of science in ancient China, endeavour to show that this country in practice had an advantage over the West, but these scholars in this area put the question imprecisely and have held appearance and the surface for the deep factor.

The transformations and metamorphoses in social labour are not determined through transformations in technics and science, but rather conversely: the transformations in the labour process determine the effects of a discovery or invention in the areas of technics and of science. In this context two things are to be noticed. First: the social labour process is as a category a complex of determining factors in human history, as signified above. Second: Technics and science are included in this determining process and are not to be overlooked. The ancient Chinese made great progress in science and technics; Aristotle had positively assessed the progress of the ancient Egyptians in mathematics. The greater progress of capitalist society of Europe in technics and science cannot be explained by the fact that the Europeans had overtaken the Chinese, which would be a simple vicious circle; it is rather to be explained by the fact that the Europeans of this period, in spite of a less progressive technical and scientific starting position, succeeded in actualizing the potentiality through the social development of an intensive as well as extensive linkage and impact of production, distribution and exchange relations, of setting in motion the linkages and impacts of the economic relations of the commodity and exploitation conditions of capital reproduction thereby appropriating the achievements of their Chinese contemporaries in technics and science, and to surpass them. The relatively increased acceleration of the linkages and effects of production and further relations of that time was determined by the changes in the then existing labour and reproduction process so that the philosopher Leibniz, who in the matter of intellectual development tended subjectively rather towards a "Chinese" model than to a European one, had already put into question the so-called Chinese advantage in those areas mentioned according to his objective estimation. At the beginning of the capitalist era and of the corresponding epoch of modern bourgeois society developments in technics and science were carried through with an increasing rate of acceleration, which in no way waned, as was reflected in the war industry ("defence industry") as well as in the petrochemical and electronics industries. At the time of Hans Sachs, Georg Agricola and Gerhard Mercator the process of innovation was relatively slowly advanced in comparison to our century, so that the impact of an invention or discovery is to be measured in centuries or decades. However, there were exceptions at that time, for example, in the printing industry.

Since technics constitutes a part of the labour process, tools and other means of production belong as parts of the total field of labour, and in fact as the accomplishment of the discoveries and inventions of the human kind over the course of centuries, in the transmission, continuation and variation of what is transmitted, in corporeal and intellectual labour. Tools are material, like the plow, spades and needles and they are ideal or—in another sense—immaterial. Ernst Kapp presented the tool as a projection of an organ and understood the practical, concrete-palpable tool in this way. Yet there are other kinds of tools in the process of production, consumption and distribution. Technics consists of a material and non-material element: hand and fist wedge on the one side, planning and formulas on the other. But not only what is used, say the corporeal organs and the concrete tools, but also the manner in how they are used, applied and practiced is important. Technics is *in abstracto* the total skilfulness of labour and the preparation for it, that is, technics in education, in the power of inventions and discoveries of social labour. In this sense the word technics can be traced back to the Greek techne, with the meaning: manual labour, art, industry.[58] Technology is the science of technics. According to its theoretical side technics is difficult to distinguish from technology, since the science of tools and its employment in the labour process is common to both spheres.

In technology as science the way in which the tool is fabricated and how it is employed, as well as the history of its processing and employment is investigated. This belongs to the theoretical side of technics as well.

In the present much has been written about the history of technics in relation to chimpanzees and other pongidae [pongids which include gorillas, gibbons, chimpanzees, and orangutans]. Thus, the question is posed about monkey tools and their employment. An attempt is made to destroy the equation homo sapiens = homo faber. Man is not the only being on earth that makes and uses tools. Wolfgang Köhler had already shown at the beginning of the 20th century that chimpanzees could solve puzzles, and that they could use one or two pieces of wood in order to bring food into their cages from the outside. In recent decades Jane Goodall observed that chimpanzees used tools which were prepared: the branch was bent in order to get ants from the sand hill. But these observers were only involved with chimpanzees who live in human society and who are acculturated as a result. The aforementioned experiments and observations are thus lacking scientific precision and control. Perhaps the chimpanzees are capable of bending and reshaping natural things. Today we only confirm that they prepare tools, bend branches, etc. in the human environment.

Monkeys are known for their ability to imitate. We call a person, for example, a child who imitates his parents, a monkey. Folk wisdom understands what scientists have forgotten or have not properly grasped. The labour of the latter is more likely infatuation with the cleverness of the monkey than it is science. Imitation is a component of the learning and teaching process among some animals. It is transformed in the presence of man. Closely bound to this is the imprinting in the case of domesticated animals which is different from that of the feral. We can further ascertain that the appropriation of tools among animals constitutes a component part of its learning process and is transfigured in its acculturation or its domestication. Technics is not only the physical or intellectual tool of man, his invention and discovery, but rather also his preparation, accommodation and organization in the labour process. Technics is then an essential component of the human reproduction process but not an autonomous factor in it or in human history in general. Those who consider technics as a specific and powerful driving force in the societal and historical process have thus exaggerated their cause and torn it out of its context.

Technics and technology are not to be separated from tool and implement of labour. We distinguish between tool and implement of labour in the following way: both take part on the technical side of the production process, however each in a different way. Tools in the process of production are practical, concrete, consumable and they are consumed in this process. The knife loses its edge in cutting wood or meat, the needle its point in sewing. Brakes and tires are worn down in passenger cars and trucks. Implements of labour on the contrary are practical and theoretical, concrete and abstract. Abstract implements as well as the concrete tools are necessary for production. Nevertheless, the abstract implements do not disappear in the production process but rather are carried forward and are further developed. Geometric formulae are just as important for the construction of a railroad line or a bridge as are shovel and hammer, coal, iron, sand and wood; yet while hammer and nail, coal and iron are used up and disappear in construction, mathematical formulae remain preserved and are even developed further. The process of labour is *in abstracto* uninterrupted and continuous, and the abstract implement of labour, like the formula in chemistry or the plan of a bridge construction is maintained and not consumed. The process of production *in concreto* is continuously interrupted in the tool and in the product; yet it is in both cases sublated [*aufgehoben*], renewed and again and again continued.

Notes

1. *Vogelfrei* in German usage denotes the status of a person on whom a legal penalty of outlawry has been imposed. However, the original meaning of the term referred to independence, being "free as a bird"; the current negative meaning developed only in the 16th century.
2. K. Marx, *Das Kapital*, Vol. 1, 2nd edition, Chapter 24.
3. Marx, Manucript 1861–1863, *Zur Kritik der politischen Ökonomie,* MEGA II, 3.6, Berlin, 1982. In the course of German history, the corporate and guild organizations fought "with the imperial and feudal power, constantly broken by it, yet constantly asserting itself anew." "But as soon as the material basis—the technological basis of the organization had ceased being the dominant one, hence as soon as it lost its revolutionary and ascending character, as soon as it ceased being relevant in its time and partly against manufacture, partly coming together with large-scale industry at a later time, it was sponsored as a reactionary element from reactionary governments and with the estates allied with them." (Marx, loc. cit., p. 1975).
4. Marx, *Grundrisse,* MEGA II, 1.2, Berlin 1981, p. 413.
5. Marx, MEGA II, 6., Berlin 1982, p. 2375f.
6. Marx, *Zur Kritik der politischen Ökonomie*, 1859, Preface.
7. H. Pirenne, *Mahomet et Charlemagne*, Paris, 1910. For an evaluation of it see: P. E. Hübinger (ed.) *Zur Bedeutung und Rolle des Islam*, Darmstadt, 1968.
8. P. M. Sweezy, in: R. H. Hilton (ed.) The Transition from Feudalism to Capitalism, 2nd edition, 1976 (German tr.: Frankfurt, 1984). M. Dobb, Studies in the Development of Capitalism, London, 1975 (Ger. *Entwicklung des Kapitalismus vom spätmittelalter bis zur Gegenwart*, 1979. R. H. Hilton, op. cit.: L. Kuchenbuch (ed.), *Feudalismus–Materialien zur Theorie und Geschichte*, 1977. Hilton traces the decline of the feudal system back to the struggle over land rent (see below, III § 2). A comparative dispute arose in the 1930s concerning the cause of the new period and its worldview. Then Franz Borkenau 'Zur Soziologie des mechanistischen Weltbildes,' *Zeitschrift für Sozialforschung*, Jahrgang I, 1932; idem, *Der Übergang vom feudalen zum bürgerlichen Weltbild*,

1934, Repr. Darmstadt 1971' and Henryk Grossmann 'Die gesellschaftlichen Grundlagen der mechanistischen Philosophie und die Manufaktur,' *Zeitschrift für Sozialforschung*, Jahrgang V, 1935 discussed this question. Borkenau traced the transition back to the period of manufacturing of the 17th century and quotes Marx for the justification of his historical conception. Marx (*Das Kapital*, 2. Edition, chapter 13, § 2) confirmed: "... Descartes with his definition of animals as simply machines sees with the eyes of the manufacturing period in distinction to the Middle Ages, for whom the animal only serves as a helper of men ...". Grossmann mentioned not Descartes but rather Leonardo da Vinci as the first man of the new age and the Renaissance in place of the 17th century as the determining period of the transition, for machinery began with it earlier than Borkenau thought; the period of manufacturing followed it. But Grossmann did not point out that Leonardo was a mechanical thinker, only that he built or sketched machines. The classification and division of labour begin in mining, in the refining of metal, in the printing industry, in shipbuilding, from the 15th century on, that is some 200 years earlier than Borkenau opined. Further, it took some centuries until the mechanical worldview succeeded to predominance. The transformation of the process of labour through its segmentation, mechanization and the continuously repetitve routine begins in the 15th century, perhaps earlier, and is continued in the following centuries. The thinking processes are developed in the mechanical worldview in connection with these transformations in the labour processes. See Kurd Lasswitz, *Geschichte der Atomistik vom Mittelalter bis Newton*, 1890, reprint Olms, 1984. E. T. Dijksterhuis, *Die Mechanisierung des Weltbildes*, Berlin 1983 researched the history of mechanization from antiquity to the modern period. In this he took notice of the completion of the mechanical worldview in the 17th century. Grossmann points to the passage where Marx writes: "Although the first beginnings of capitalist production confront us sporadically already in the 14th and 15th century in some cities on the Mediterranean, the capitalist era first dates from the 16th century. (See Marx, op. cit., *Kapital*, 24, §1; Grossmann, op. cit., page 17). This is not about a conflict over who can cite Marx better. Marx said in the passage cited by Grossmann: "The point of departure of development, which created both the wage laborer as well as the capitalists, was the bondage of the laborer." To this the following is to be noted:

1. The labourers in the 15th century in mining were free, not bound.
2. In this sector and in others, they were already wage labourers.
3. The development here signifies the free development of production and the free exploitation of man by man.
4. This development did not create the wage labourer and the capitalists, but rather conversely, the activity and the contradictions, the bringing together and setting apart the wage labourer and the capitalists created the free development of production and the free exploitation of man by man. In this way, human activity liberated and developed production.
5. Capitalism was first sporadically, and subsequently systematically developed. This difference between the two forms of appearance in the historical sequence according to Marx is important. Segmentation and division of labour in the weaving enterprises were sporadically introduced in early capitalism. Only in the 18th century, at the time of the Industrial Revolution and later in the period of high capitalism, were they systematically driven. The production of woven goods was rationalized at the time, child labour was introduced, labour activities were mechanized and simplified. The ribbon loom and weaving loom were systematically diffused in the 18th century and in fact officially; earlier they were secretly employed in the

manufacture of woven cloth. The rationalization and systematization of production in mining was introduced in the 15th and 16th century.

6. Hence, the course of the historical process is not as simple as Borkenau and Grossmann believed. The imprint of the mechanical system of manufacture in the thought process did not find its immediate expression in the mechanistic worldview of the 17th century; representing the world in this way was already brought out in classical antiquity and in the Middle Ages. The practical and concrete machines and drawings of machinery were built and printed by a line of mechanics in the 16th century. In relation to mining and assaying we pointed to the activities of Rühlein von von Calw, Biringuccio, Agricola, Ercker und Schreitmann. Guidobaldi dal Mante published his influential work *Mechanicorum liber* in 1577. Above all, we call attention to the book of Capitano Agostino Ramelli, *Le Diverse et Artificiose Machine*, 1588. (See also *Schatzkammer Mechanischer Künste des ... Herrn Augustini de Ramelli*, 1620). In the sub-title it is written: "In it there is to be found ... ingenious machines, which one can use in times of peace and war in and on fortifications ..." Ramelli was a military engineer in the service of the French and the Poles.

9. K. Vogel, Fibonacci. *Dictionary of Scientific Biography*. J. Tropfke, *Geschichte der Elementarmathematik*, 4th edition, Vol. 1, K. Vogel (ed.), Berlin 1980.
10. Marx, MEGA II, 3.6, Berlin 1982, p. 1965, 1972.
11. Marx, op. cit.
12. M. Weber, *Gesammelte Aufsätze zur Religionssoziologie*, Vol. II, 2nd edition, Tübingen 1922.
13. E. Troeltsch, *Die Kulturbedeutung des Calvinismus*, 1910. M. Weber, *Die protestantische Ethik II*, J. Winckelmann (ed.), Hamburg 1972.
14. Id. *Aufsätze zur Geistesgeschichte und Religionssoziologie*, III, §§ 4–5, Tübingen 1925.
15. Id. *Der Historismus und seine Probleme*, 1922, Chapter III, § 6 C, Tübingen 1922.
16. Weber, *Wirtschaft und Gesellschaft*, 5th edition, V, §II, Tübingen 1972. There seems to be a play on words here since the term 'verworfen' or reprobate in Calvinist theology refers to those souls who have been predestined to damnation by God and thus have no hope of salvation—trans.].
17. E. Troeltsch, *Die Kulturbedeutung des Calvinismus*; idem., *Aufsätze zur Geistesgeschichte und Religionssoziologie*, Tübingen 1925.
18. T. Mommsen, *Römische Geschichte*, 6th edition, Vol. 1, 3rd Book, Chapter 12, Berlin, 1874.
19. Marx, *Das Kapital*, Vol. III, Chapters 20 and 47.
20. E. Troeltsch, *Der Historismus und seine Probleme*, Chapter IV, § 3.
21. Weber, *Wirtschaft und Gesellschaft*, 5th edition, Tübingen, 1972, p. 74, 817.
22. Weber, loc. cit., p. 96, 139, 645f. idem., *Wirtschaftsgeschichte*, Berlin 1981, p. 239f.
23. W. Sombart, *Das Europäische Wirtschaftsleben im Zeitalter des Frühkapitalismus, vornehmlich im 16., 17. Und 18. Jahrhundert*, Berlin 1902, p. 1969.
24. Weber, *Religionssoziologie* 1, loc. cit.
25. Sombart, *Der Moderne Kapitalismus*, Vol. 1, 1. Halbd., Chapters 4 and 5.
26. J. Kulischer, *Allgemeine Wirtschaftsgeschichte*, Vol. 2, p. 407.
27. W. Sombart, *Die Juden und das Wirtschaftsleben*, Berlin 1911.
28. M. Weber, *Wirtschaft und Gesellschaft*, loc. cit., p. 721. Weber was right, but he tried to dispose of Sombart's conception on purely technical grounds. But it concerned itself not only with the technical side but with the sociological as well.
29. Accordingly, the usurers from Siena, Bologna, Rome and other places were called Cahorsins, Kawersens, Kawarzens, Kabartsens, Gawartzens. All these dialectical displacements of the word

Cahorsins had the meaning of usurer in the Middle Ages and in the early epochs of modern times. They were also identified as "Lombards".

30. R. Ehrenberg, *Das Zeitalter der Fugger*, Jena 1896, Vol. 1., p. 66. He cites Matthaeus Parisiensis, *De peste caursinorum* (concerning the plague of the Cahorsins). Matthaeus Parisiensis was a chronicler in the middle of the 13th century; according to him, Bishop Robert Grosseteste explained: "If one gives the Cahorsins a promisory note [*Verschreibung*] for 159 Marks for 100 Marks received, even so they take no partial payment , but rather insist on the repayment of the entire sum of the debt, while the Jews benevolently receive [*recipient benigne*] so much money at the given time as is proportionate [commensurate]." Cf. Simon Depping, *Les juifs au moyen age*, Paris 1834.
31. J. Kulischer, loc. cit., p. 412f.
32. Sombart, *Der moderne Kapitalismus*, Vol. 1.1. According to Sombart's view the communal family is the oldest bearer of the economic form of artisanal labour. The members of this community including the apprentices and trainees are the protected and commanded by the master. A similar idea of the "entire house" is found in O. Brunner, *Das "ganze Haus" und die alteuropäische „Ökonomik"*, in idem., *Neue Wege der Vefassungs- und Sozialgeschichte*, 2nd edition, Göttingen 1968. Against this view see Bruno Schoenlank, *Soziale Kämpfe vor 300 Jahren*, 2nd edition, Leipzig 1907. Schoenlank and G. Schanz sharply criticized the patriarchal conception of social conditions. B. Schoenlank, G. Schanz, 'Gesellenverbände.' *Handwörterbuch der Staatswissenschaften*, 4th edition 1909. W. Reininghaus 'Das "ganze Haus" und die Gesellengilden,' in *Deutsches Handwerk in Spätmittelalter and früher Neuzeit*, Göttingen 1983 (R. S. Elkar, ed.) writes: „Zwischen Meistern und Gesellen kam es zu Zerwürfnissen und Streitigkeiten."[Quarrels and conflicts arose between masters and journeymen.] See also W. Reininghaus (*Die Entstehung der Gesellengilden im Spätmittelalter*, Wiesbaden 1981) against the concept „Schutz und Schirm" [Protection and Screen] in relation to these forms of society. Karl Bücher, to whom we shall return, had also written about „Schutz und Schirm" in the 15th and 16th century.
33. J. Strieder, *Studien zur Geschichte kapitalistischer Organisationsformen*, 2nd edition, München 1925, p. 55ff.
34. F. Braudel, *Civilisation matérielle, économie et capitalisme; XVe–XVIIIe siècle*, Paris 1979 (Ger.: *Sozialgeschichte des 15–18. Jahrhunderts*, 3 volumes, 1985/86).
35. L. Brentano, *Die Anfänge des Kapitalismus*, 1913, in: *Der wirtschaftende Mensch in der Geschichte*, Leipzig (1923) 1967.
36. Georg von Below, *Probleme der Wirtschaftsgeschichte*, Tübingen 1926, p. 39ff.
37. M. Dobb, *Studies in the Development of Capitalism*, London 1975.
38. E. P. Thompson, *The Making of the English Working Class*, Pelican 1968.
39. J. Janssen, *Geschichte des deutschen Volkes seit dem Anfang des Mittelalters*, 19th edition, Vol. 1. Freiburg, p. 594. V. Pareto (*Trattato di sociologia generale*, 2nd edition, Florence, 1923, § 2384) fundamentally agrees with this conception and only adds that Janssen left Italy out of account.
40. J. A. Schumpeter, *History of Economic Analysis*, 1954 (Ger.: *Geschichte der ökonomischen Analyse*, Göttingen 1965). He investigates the periodization of feudalism and of capitalism in relation to his critique of the theories of Thomas Aquinas, Karl Marx, Max Weber among others. Schumpeter characterized the discussions of Sombart as "brilliance without substance" without "genuine research."
41. Schumpeter, loc. cit., p. 121f.
42. Schumpeter, loc. cit., IV, Chapter 6, § 2.

43. Schumpeter, loc. cit., p. 68 and 124.
44. Id. p. 122, 124; also part IV, Chapter 4, § 2 (d).
45. Aristotle, *Politics* I, wrote that the human is a social animal. Outside of society he is a god or a beast, he is not a man. These discussions of the great thinker are related to the human substance. The forms of society are the human organization of life, as it actualizes itself, as the family, the community or *Koinonia*, the Greek polis, etc. G. W. F. Hegel spoke of the form and the substance in his *Logic*. We can take from this that the form is actualized by the substance, the substance by the form. Karl Marx, *Das Kapital*, Book I, wrote about the value form and value substance. Value and human labour as well and human history have their form and substance in a structured, lasting, non-uniform, oppositional system. But the form is not the eternal form of things but rather the ephemeral, the substance is as well not eternal, but rather ephemeral. The forms of the value of labour and of human society exist in history, the substance of it likewise. History is grasped only empirically-concretely and in this way taken up so that it is not only unitary but multiple. The unitary and universal history of humanity is a utopia of the future. The history of social forms is other than that of the social substance. The form, the substance and the history are each related to a concrete society. Concerning the theory of forms and substance of labour, value and freedom relations and systems, see L. Krader, *Treatise of Social Labor*, Assen 1979; id. *Labor and Value*, Peter Lang New York 2003.
46. The movements of peasant liberation were presented through the investigations of Carl Grünberg, G. F. Knapp and G. Franz.
47. L. Krader, *Asiatic Mode of Production*, Assen 1975.
48. P. Kennedy, *Rise and Fall of the Great Powers. Economic Change and Military Conflict from 1500 to 2000*, New York 1988. R. S. Elkar, Umrisse einer Geschichte der Gesellenwanderungen, in: R. S. Elkar (ed.), *Neuzeit*, Göttingen 1983. The early-modern period is basically related to the period from the 16th to the 18th century; modernity is the epoch of industrialization. The apprentice guilds arose in the late Middle Ages. Cf. W. Reininghaus, *Die Entstehung der Gilden im Spätmittelalter*, 1981. Idem. *Die Migration der Handwerkergesellen in der Zeit der Entstehung ihrer Gilden (14. bis 15. Jahrhundert)*, 1981. Accordingly, the late Middle Ages continued in Central Europe until the 15th century. Brentano, Schumpeter, von Below among others highlight Italy as the country in which modernity begins, namely earlier than in Central Europe. It depends on which country or which part of Europe one chooses to identify as the beginning of modernity. It also depends on which class or estate one has chosen. Friedrich Lütge, *Deutsche Sozial—und Wirtschaftsgeschichte*, 3rd edition, Berlin 1966, concerns himself with a structural change of the social and economic culture of Germany in the 14th to 15th century, which continued to develop until the Thirty Years' War. The colonization of the East ended in the 14th century. On technical grounds he avoided the word 'capitalism,' which was done to death in common parlance. We don't find this common parlance so frightful that we must avoid it. What is meant here is not the talking of it to death, but rather a more-or-less ideological overuse. 'Capital' and 'capitalism' are good words, even if they are used under certain conditions as curse words. So too are the words 'Protestant' and 'Catholic' among others, used as epithets (as in Ireland). Without finally deciding the question of periodization, we call attention to the fact that opinions in this connection vary and are dependent on the sources, the raw material and the area of investigation. The economists have a different view, and the historians of Italy a third. As soon as one poses the question of periodization, one is inclined or determined scientifically-theoretically and scientifically-historically to assume an interruption in human history.

49. On the system of social labour and the abstract categories of freedom, see Lawrence Krader, *Treatise of Social Labor*, chapters 1 and 3. On labour form and substance and the relations of social labour, see Lawrence Krader, *Labor and Value*, Part I, pp. 23–71.
50. On the complexity of these terms in the 15th and 16th century in Central Europe See: F. Irsigler: 'Zur Problematik der Gilde und Zunftterminologie.' https://doi.org/10.11588/vuf.1985.0.15772; R. Schmidt-Wiegand: 'Die Bezeichnungen Zunft und Gilde in ihrem historischen und wortgeographischen Zusammenhang.' https://doi.org/10.11588/vuf.1985.0.15771.
51. The monk was no gorging fool, Jakob Fugger no money fool. The first was mentioned in Gerald Strauss, *Nürnberg in the Sixteenth Century*, 1966; however, he existed only in the imagination, not in actuality. Such a way of treatment is not our concern, for we have nothing to do with literary figures or species. Sebastian Brant lived in Straßburg around 1457–1521, Hans Sachs and Hartmann Schopper lived in Nuremberg in the 16th century.
52. In G. W. F. Hegel it reads differently: "Der Mensch verhält sich mit seinen Bedürfnissen zur äußerlichen Natur auf praktische Weise, und geht dabei, indem er sich durch dieselbe befriedigt und sie aufreibt, vermittelnd zu Werke. Die Naturgegenstände nämlich sind mächtig und leisten mannigfachen Widerstand. Um sie zu bezwingen schiebt der Mensch andere Naturdinge ein, kehrt somit die Natur gegen die Natur selbst und erfindet Werkzeuge zu diesem Zwecke. Diese menschlichen Erfindungen gehören dem Geiste an, und solches Werkzeug ist höher zu achten, als der Naturgegenstand." (*Vorlesungen über die Philosophie der Geschichte*, Sämtliche Werke, 11. Band, Stuttgart 1949, S. 316) ["Man comports himself with his needs/wants to external nature in a practical way and thus goes mediatingly to work in that he satisfies them and diminishes them. The natural objects are namely powerful and offer various resistance. In order to force them man inserts other natural things turning nature in this way against itself and invents tools to this end. These human inventions belong to the mind [*Geist*] and such an implement is to be regarded more highly than the natural object."] The bases of the labour theory as well as the theory of technics is found in this passage. We distinguish between natural things and objects of human activity. We make our world into objects of our labour and objectify nature. Through this objectivation subjectification is made possible. Man goes mediatingly to labour and thereby to work. Hegel left out these two processes, the distinction between thing and object and the step from labour to work. Yet he made possible the basis for these two processes. L. Feuerbach did not grasp the difference between thing and object and thought that the planets, the sun like man objectify the human world; thus, he anthropomorphized the solar system or natural things. (*Das Wesen des Christenthums*, 1841). Through labors' mediation and activity of objectification humanity develops itself. Mammals have also treated natural things instrumentally but such treatment is not a mediating and objective activity. They do not make what they interpose into an object of their work activity. Man learns and teaches how to bring forth this mediating activity, to develop and to vary it further. Finally, he has learned to systematically carry forward everything so that his further development will be unfolded. Mediation and their development transform natural things into objects of labour. (See L. Krader, *A Treatise of Social Labor*, Assen 1979, pp. 187–200). Through labour we objectify the world (See K. Marx, *Grundrisse der Kritik der politischen Ökonomie*, Berlin 1953, pp. 354–374). Labour, mediation and objectification are three aspects of the same process of development of humanity. But Hegel errs when he believes, that the tool is to be more highly regarded than natural objects. To be sure, the invention of tools belongs to the mind, but mind is a part of the labour process which is as physical as it is mental. The mind is thus a part of a greater. Since invention constitutes a part of technic Hegel's theory of invention is correct to this point; but to consider mind higher than natural things is an

anthropocentrism. Mind is a natural object and subject. Man does not stand in the centre of the world as the earthly-divine. As we see, Hegel proceeds from technics to the theory of labour. We begin conversely with the process of reproduction, and thereby with labour, and only then do we take up technics and technology.

53. K. Marx, *Das Kapital*, Vol. I op. cit., chapter 5.
54. In his last, posthumously published book, *Noetics: The Science of Thinking and Knowing*, 2010, Krader outlined a new science of nature in which he distinguished three natural orders according to different configurations of space-time in which they are constituted: the material, the quantum and the human orders of nature. In the first two of the aforementioned series there is no teleology but causality in the first, probability in the second. In the third, the human order of nature, there is teleology—human purpose and design. Marx explicitly rejected teleology in nature in his paean to Darwin's *Origin of Species*, implied it in a subtle way in his comparison of the human architect and the bee in *Capital* and then fudged it again in his appreciation of Milton's poetry in the first volume of his *Theories of Surplus Value*. For Krader, only in the human order is time abstracted from space and space from time. Nature is a manifold of three orders: material, quantum and human. Teleology thus exists in nature but only in the human order thereof. See also the relevant material in: C. Levitt and S. Sander (eds.), *Beyond the Juxtaposition of Nature and Culture. Lawrence Krader, Interdisciplinarity, and the Concept of the Human Being*. New York 2018, pp. 219–279.
55. The great theoreticians of the 18th century, like Bernard Mandeville, Joseph Harris and Adam Smith have highlighted the process of the division of labour. But labour must be organized, combined and then apportioned or divided.
56. According to Krader's thinking in *Noetics*, the natural thing continues to be a material thing but in the human field it becomes a human object—trans.
57. F. M. Feldhaus, *Der Weg in die Technik*, Leipzig 1935. Idem. *Die Technik der Antike und des Mittelalters*. Repr. Olms 1971. R. J. Forbes, *Man the Maker*, London 1958. Technics will be treated in this work mainly as a series of inventions and discoveries.
58. Aristotle, *Politik*, 1253 a-b. Idem. *Nikomachische Ethik*, Book V passim. Techne according to Aristotle signifies art, *ars*; further it means the: artifice, artificial, the achievement of the adept, of practice, of self-mastery and thereby the mastery of external nature. There are two kinds of arts through which we master and know the matter: 1. The arts by which we use things; 2. The architechtonic or those who direct the production of materials (Aristotle, *Poetics*, 47a. Idem. *Physics*, 194b).

    C. Darwin, *Der Ursprung der Arten* (*The Origin of Species*), London 1859. K. Marx (in relation to Darwin's theory of evolution): Correspondence with F. Lassalle, 16 January 1861); with F. Engels, 18 June 1862. Cf. L. Krader, *The Ethnological Notebooks of Karl Marx*, Assen 1972 pp. 82–85, 354f and 392f. (Ger.: *Die ethnologischen Excerpthefte von Karl Marx*, Suhrkamp 1976). E. P. Thompson, *The Poverty of Theory*, London 1978, p. 256, 355, 389, 396.The presentation of technics as a projection of the hand and other organs was discussed in the 19th century. See E. Christian Kapp, *Grundrisse einer Philosophie der Technik. Zur Entstehungsgeschichte der Cultur* (Braunschweig 1877), Düsseldorf 1978, Introduction: H.-M. Sass. M. Daumas, *Histoire générale des techniques* ; Volume 1, *Introduction*, Paris 1962. J. Ellul, *La technique ou l'enjeu du siècle*, Paris 1954. Idem. *Le système technicien*, Paris 1977. L. Mumford, *Technics and Civilization*, New York 1934. Idem. *The Culture of Cities*, New York 1970. H. Schelsky, *Der Mensch in der wissenschaftlichen Zivilisation*, Köln-Opladen 1961. J. Habermas, *Technik und Wissenschaft als „Ideologie"*, Frankfurt 1968. Daumas treats technics in part as did Kapp, as a projection of organization. According to Habermas labour comes from technics and not vice-versa. Thus, technics is abstracted from the other parts of the economic process, like distribution, exchange and consumption. Habermas repeated this abstraction. These authors in their critique of civilization or ideology considered technics as something specific, torn loose from the labour process and from economic life, hence as something simple and primitive, like the *materia prima* of the philosophers of antiquity and the Middle Ages. R. Sonnemann, *Geschichte der Technik*, *Preface*, Leipzig 1978. Here the conception of Jane Goodall is treated uncritically—further concerning domestication, see L. Krader, 'Ecology of Central Asian Pastoralism' in: *Southwestern Journal of Anthropology*, Volume 11, 1955, and idem. on the keyword 'Pastoralism,' in: *International Encyclopedia of the Social Sciences*. David Sills (ed.) New York 1968. Further concerning technics and labour see the sources cited above.

PART II

CHAPTER THREE

Labour Processes in Central Europe, 15th–17th Centuries

3.1 The Population and Its Numbers

The population of Central Europe from the 15th to the 17th century was for the most part based in the countryside, and its main occupation was tied up with agriculture. The total population of Central Europe in 1500 amounted to around 12 million, of which the country population was 9 million or about 75% of the whole. The town population counted 3 million or about 25% of the total. The country population includes the peasants, workers on the land as well as the administration, people of the cloth, servants, traders, the military. Customarily one reckoned that those who were not peasants constituted 5 to 10% of the total population of the countryside. The town population included embossers, iron workers, and miners; yet their labour was not plied everywhere in cities or small towns. The numbers offer a rough idea; the division of the totality in the city and in the country is likewise imprecise, for some iron works were then country based.

In 1300, the entire population of Western Europe, as we define it in Table 1, counted 43 million and in 1500 roughly the same number. No increase in population was attributed to this region between 1300 and 1500; the stagnation was explained by the effects of the plague, especially of the Black Death around 1347/52, and by war.[1] In 1600, the total population of Central Europe rose to 15 Million and in parts of Western Europe to 54 Million. The further development of Central Europe from 1600 to 1700 is separated from the development in all of Europe and from Western Europe. In 1700, the population of Central Europe amounted to 15 million, thus remaining stagnant; in parts of Western Europe it amounted to 59 million and in Europe as a whole 115 million in total. The stagnating numbers of people of Central Europe during the 17th century is attributed to the 30 Years' War and its effects.

The urban population of Central Europe rose during the 16th century from 3 to 4 million, thus keeping up with the increase of the total population step by step. The increase of the urban population of Central Europe which continued during the 17th century, occurred through the surplus of births in relation to the deaths among the population and through the influx of the people from the countryside who tried to avoid the desolation of the country during the war. This means that the number of people in the countryside during the 17th century decreased absolutely and relatively, from 12 million around 1600 to 10 million around 1700. It is estimated that the population of Central Europe around 1650 had sunk to 10 million as a consequence of the war. The losses were mainly confined to the second quarter of the 17th century in Central Europe, which was followed by a population increase. Immigrants from foreign countries are included in this. [The population rebounded although the population increase 1650–1700 did not result in a rural population that was as large as it had been at the beginning of the century before the war—trans.].

Population figures are not the cause of an event, they are more likely the characteristics and expressions of the biological, economic, military, political and peaceful processes of humanity. If we consolidate just these facts presented, the following picture arises:

Table 1: The Population of Europe, 1300–1700 (in Millions)*

Year	Europe	Western Europe		Germany %		Countryside %		City %	
		(a)	(b)	(c)	(c)		(d)		(d)
1300		43		12					
1500	87	44	46	12	14	9	75	3	25
1600	107	54	57	16	15	12	75	4	25
1700	115	60	63	15	13	10	67	5	33

(a) British Isles, Germany, France, Italy, Switzerland.
(b) The above plus the Netherlands.
(c) As percentage of the total population of Europe.
(d) As percentage of the total population of Germany.
*K.T.v. Inama-Sternegg, Bevölkerung, in: *Handwörterbuch der Staatswissenschaften*, ed.: Conrad et al. 3rd edition 1909. All figures and percentages are gross estimates and are only offered for general orientation.

H. Bechtel (*Wirtschaftsgeschichte Deutschlands*, Vol. 1, Munich 1952) disputes the assumptions of Gustav Freytag and Inama-Sternegg that the population of the Holy Roman Empire had been diminished by two-thirds through the effects of the Thirty Years' War. Yet, effects of the war were bad enough that there was no need for exaggeration. The whole of Europe had an increase in population of 10% in the course of the 17th century, Germany on the contrary, had none. [Indeed, it was smaller in 1700–trans.] (R. Mols, in: *Europäische Wirtschaftsgeschichte*, Ed.: C. Cipolla, K. Borchhardt, Vol. 2, Stuttgart 1979. H. Kellenbenz, R. Walter, in *Handbuch der europäischen Sozial—und Wirtschaftsgeschichte*, Ed.: H. Fischer et al. 1986).

The following table provides population figures for major European cities in select years from 1300 to 1700:

Table 2: Population of Cities in England, France, Italy, Spain, and the Netherlands, 1300–1700 City Year (Population in Thousands).

City	1300	1400	1500	1550	1600	1650	1700
Amsterdam			15	35	100	135	180
Antwerp					100		70
Bruges	35					34	
Florence	95	55	70	60	80	70	80
London		35	70	80	250	450	600
Milan			100	50	110	95	100
Naples			230	210	250		215
Paris	100			300		500	
Rome			50	45	110	126	135
Seville				100	150	125	
Venice			115	160	150	120	140

Around 1520 Naples was the largest city in Europe, around 1600 it was Paris, around 1700 London.

These data point to the general directions in the history of the urban population. The numbers are rounded and presented only provisionally. They show smaller or larger swings in the population numbers for cities such as Basel, Rostock, Zurich, Danzig, Augsburg and Nuremberg. We have more data at our disposal for these cities than for the others, otherwise the same could be asserted in relation to other cases. At the end of the period—in comparison to the beginning of the increase in population—it is clearly shown in Hamburg, Breslau, Frankfurt am Main, Leipzig, Bern, Vienna. This urban increase in population can be generalized with regard to Central Europe in comparison to the Middle Ages; we take into consideration the whole, not the individual results. The effect of the plague in the 14th century on the cities of Central Europe can be identified. The population data cannot be abstracted from the social and economic events. These are bound up with the economic development of the entire region in the 15th, 16th, and 17th century. By contrast, the effects of the plague, of war and of the rearrangement of single industries or entire branches of industry are to be taken into account. The losses of Augsburg (45,000 in 1600, as opposed to 20,000 in 1650) of Berlin (13,000 in the year 1625, as opposed to 10,000 in 1645) and Frankfurt am Main (25,000 in 1600, 15,000 in 1650) are imputed to the impact of the Thirty Years' War. Around the year 1700 people in Berlin and Frankfurt, as in Hamburg and Breslau, Leipzig among others, were able to recover.

The role of the state and its centralized administration was expanded and intensified. In this way, the increase in the population numbers of London, Paris, Vienna, Berlin are explained, leaving aside the fact that in this period there came great losses through fire, war and plague. The fortunes of war and the rearrangement of industries, trade, textiles had exerted an effect on the population numbers of Antwerp, Augsburg, among others in this period.

The total population of Central Europe from 1300 to 1500 remained fundamentally unchanged. The great losses of the 14th century, mainly through the plague, were counterbalanced by the natural increase of the population and improved living conditions. The fact that the numbers at the beginning and end of the period are the same, grossly speaking, conceals the great swings within the period. The population in the countryside in the 15th and 16th century increased as a percentage in comparison to the total population numbers and to the portion of it in the countryside. Probably 10% is too low, 25% would be too high an assumption in relation to the total for the urban population of Central Europe; the general tendency lies in-between, at around 15%. The same is valid for Italy, France, the Netherlands and England.

There were small and large swings in the urban population numbers of Central Europe from the 14th to the 17th century. Hamburg, Basel, Breslau, Frankfurt am Main, Freiburg/Switzerland, Danzig, Augsburg, Nuremberg all have lost as well as gained. The increase can be imputed to the immigration to the land, the losses, mainly to war and the plague. The following table provides the size of population for select cities in Central Europe from the 14th to 17th century:

Table 3: Population of Some Cities in Central Europe in the 14th–17th Centuries

City	Year and Populations in Thousands					
Augsburg	1450	1475	1540	1570	1600	1650
	20	18	40	50	45	20
Basel	1349	1429	1446	1454		
	14	9	10	7		
Berlin		1625	1645			
		13	10			
Breslau	1348	1403	1700			
	22	12	40			
Cologne	1400	1550				
	30	37				
Danzig	1403	1415	1437	1470	1550	
	22	40	20	18	20	
Eger	1390	1500				
	7	5				
Frankfurt (Main)	1387	1440	1600	1650	1700	
	10	9	25	15	25	
Freiburg (Switzerland)	1390	1500				
	9	6				
Hamburg	1311	1419	1526	1594	1700	
	7	22	12	19	60	
Leipzig	1474	1550	1600	1700		
	4	7	15	22		
Nuremberg	1431	1449	1500	1520	1622	
	22	20	52	47	50	
Rostock	1387	1410	1500			
	11	14	10–13			
Zurich	1357	1410	1467	1500	1600	
	12	11	5	5	7	

Source: See Table 1.

Around 1700, the urban population of the Kurmark Brandenburg accounted for 40% of the population of the total Kurmark; the portion of the population of the countryside in Central Europe accounted for a third of the total. In relation to the Kurmark it is reckoned that Berlin had developed from a small to a large city, which was traced back to changes in the city's position and its functions. Central Europe from the 15th to 17th century had no centres of large industry, rather its cities were points of trade, administration, garrison, workshops and supply. The fabrication of products of industry through workshop labour, the guilds and manufacture were supplemented by auxiliary operations in the countryside of cloth as well as of metal, wood, horn and leather works.[2]

In relation to the movements of population from the country into the city one can distinguish the coerced moments from the forces of attraction. Sir Thomas More wrote in his book *Utopia* in 1525, that while men are eating mutton elsewhere, in England the sheep are eating men. With this well-known sentence, he wanted to say that the fields of agriculture were kept free for sheep pasture, that is free for wool production. The peasants were in this manner driven into the city. Changes in property law as well as in the practices of agriculture were introduced in the interests of the landed gentry. Bands of robbers had an easier time plundering a farm and especially an isolated one than cities. These negative factors had caused immigration to the towns. Positively its attraction can be explained by the increase in urban enterprises, expanding trade and handicraft businesses and by the beginnings of manufacturing. Further, the formation of the nation state system in large parts of Europe amplified the administrative activities of the cities; and as a result, the increasing military power of the rulers of England, France, Prussia, Austria, Russia and Spain is linked during the 16th to 18th century.

The mechanisms of supply for the city, for the royal court, the garrisons and barracks were developed and narrowly bound up with domestic and foreign trade. Yet, the great bulk of the population remained in the countryside. Towards the end of the 16th century, 2/3 of the population of Flanders was in the country, a third was urban. Development of the population of the Kurmark Brandenburg occurs in the 17th century.[3] In these movements of emigration and immigration expansion of free mobility in the law and of illegal immigration is presumed. Freedom of relocation is related to the already mentioned negative and positive factors of mobility. The legal prohibition against moving to the town was in practice either expressly or implicitly rescinded. The oft cited sentence "town air is liberating" [*Stadtluft macht frei*] assumed this possibility of immigrating into the city, to search out a dwelling, to earn money, to establish a family, to raise children, and to lead a bourgeois life. Yet, that sentence corresponds rather to the medieval legal customs and practices than to those of modern times. Pro forma the legal freedom of movement includes within it the incontestable right of relocation into the town. The goal of town freedom was reached only pro forma in the 15th to 17th century. In substance the possibilities of city life in Central Europe as well as in other parts of the continent were limited by economic conditions. There were few jobs, un—and underemployment were widespread, economic development occurred sporadically, quicker or also slowly or even stagnating. The housing problem in the large cities remained severe and devastating for immigrants from the country and from other countries into the 19th and 20th century.

As with the losses due to war, so too did diseases, like the plague, the Saint Valentine's plague, epilepsy, apoplexy, consumption, typhus, cholera, boils (carbunculus, tumour, ulcus, pustula) syphilis, common pestilence, caused a large drop in population numbers. Medicine in the 15th century had asserted the contagious pestilence was linked with a disease of a nervous character, like consumption. Yet the plague was the main illness; according to the medical view, lung infection, the black death, pestilence, bubonic plague, among others went along with it.

The plague was classified as the infectious or decimating plague. Medicine had separated morbus as a disease from the plague and asserted morbus curabilis est, sed diu durat, 'plague' [morbus is curable but from Diu to Durat—a distance of 540 kilometres—there is plague]: Morbus, of the diagnostic practice in medicine from the 13th to the 17th century was a disease that was curable, however, plague was not; as a means against the plague, no herbs grew in the garden: diu durat, plague', that is, the plague was of long duration. Diseases were the corruption of the body, wheezing, coughing fever, which brought phthisis, along with it coughing and gasping fever. Phthisis was designated as wasting, consumption or marasmus. An attempt had been made to investigate morbidities according to their source. Yellow fever was designated as the West Indian plague in opposition to the occidental or bubonic plague (also pestilential bubo). Disease comes to man out of the air; in this way, poisoned air was called malaria (mal=bad, aria=air). In this sense, Martin Luther had explained the prolonged disease as consumption and lamented cold air. Paracelsus imputed consumption to the pharmacen family—"which affects man with sweat" [*"der dem Menschen ihr Schweiß berühret"*]. The origin of this expression is clear: Pharmakon in Greek means two things, remedy or medicine and poison or ruin and a means for bringing calamity. With the war the bubonic plague was identified as a plague of encampment.[4]

The Black Death appeared 1347/52 as something unusual in the history of the late Middle Ages in Europe. It came from Central Asia over the harbour cities of the Black Sea, mainly on the Crimean Peninsula towards Constantinople and the Aegean Sea. Then it was spread over the Near East from the Nile to Anatolia, across the Mediterranean to Libya, Tunesia, Sicily, Sardinia, across the coastal cities of Italy and the Iberian Peninsula, thereafter across France, the British Isles, the neighbouring states of the North and Baltic Seas, finally across Central and Eastern Europe until it reached Northern Russia. It originated in Asia, travelling over the Silk Road through caravans, thereafter across the sea by means of ships in connection with the silk, slave and fur trade. It was spread by parasites on flea infested rats. Milan was able to avoid the plague because it was not immediately linked to trading ships. It was spread through many cycles from 1347/52 into the 18th century and beyond.[5]

In *Eigentliche Beschreibung aller Stände auf Erden* [Actual description of all classes on earth], the so-called *Ständebuch* by Hans Sachs and Jost Amman from Nuremberg, there emerges the picture of commercial life in the 16th century in wood cuts and in poetry. Of the 114 figures 99 portray the trades, the arts, handicrafts and trade, while the rest appear like scenes out of the ship of fools, like the picture of court jesters, fools, gluttons, profligates, of popes, kings and gentlemen [*gentilons*]. Nuremberg was the great city of metal working; of the 99 trades, there were 26 involving metal workers, such as the copper, knife, scythe, can, brass, gold, and ironsmiths, the bell and candlemakers, cymbalists and goldbeaters, armourers and ring makers, thimble makers, needle makers, nail makers and hook and eye makers, polishers, locksmiths and spur makers, wire drawers and coiners among others. Woodworkers were lathe operators, joiners, sifters, cartwrights, and carpenters. Wool and fustian weavers, silk embroiderers, cloth cutters, hat makers, rope makers, carpet makers and tailors, purse makers, belt makers, shoelace makers, leather workers, parchment producers [*Permenter*], saddle makers and shoemakers created cloth, clothes and leather commodities. Occupations dealing with food were those of peasants, producers of oil, producers of grapes, fishers, bakers, brewers, hunters, millers and butchers. Huntsmen were bird catchers on water and land. Salesmen and storekeepers mediated between producer and buyer, when the tradespeople did not conduct their own business with the producers of commodities. The salesmen were interested in the import of commodities *en gros*, not in the sale of home-made products. These were sold by shopkeepers. Aside from book publishers the producers of the *Ständebücher* did not affect the putting out and manufacture in Nuremberg (see reproductions).[6]

Central Europe was almost but not entirely self-sufficient through its domestic agricultural production; the overwhelming majority of the population from the 15th to 17th century was based on the land, namely occupied with working the land. The importation of foreign products, for example, wool, spices, precious metals, stands in opposition to the economic self-sufficiency of the area. The expansion of the market, wage, and money economy and manufacture in this period led to the collapse of the old social and economic system, that had more to do with natural materials, agricultural products and less to do with commodity exchange, money and credit.

3.2 The Condition of the Peasants

Regarding agricultural relations and the condition of the peasants the concept [*Begriff*] of Central Europe in the 14th to the 17th century was inconsistent.

Europe west of the Elbe found itself—in opposition to the peasants east of the Elbe—in a process of general liberation, which was accelerated in the 18th century. To be sure the East Elbian peasants had greater freedom than the peasants west of the Elbe in the Middle Ages, but the situation of those in the east worsened after the middle of the 15th century. The meaning of the word serfdom varied from one country to another, but the situation of the peasant estate at this time in the west was in the matter of its emancipation in general better than that in the east, although Mark Brandenburg (west of the Elbe) was subject to the same unfreedom as the eastern provinces.[7]

The situation of the peasants was unfavourable and grave in the 16th century. The peasant is the only one to complain about his lot in the *Ständebuch* by Hans Sachs and Jost Amman:

> Ich aber bin von Art ein Bauwr /
> Mein Arbeit wirt mir schwer und sauwr /
> Ich muß Ackern / Seen und Eggn /
> Schneyden / Mehen / Heuwen dargegen /
> Holtzen / und einführn Hew und Treyd /
> Gült und Steuwr macht mir viel Hertzleid
> Trinck Wasser und iß grobes Brot /
> Wie denn der Herr Adam gebot.

> However, in kind I am a peasant/
> My labor becomes hard and sour for me/
> I must work the field, sow and reap/
> Cut, moe and hew against it/
> Chop wood/ and bring in hay and grain/
> Money and taxes give me much heartache
> Drink water and eat coarse bread/
> As then Adam was commanded by God.[8]

His worries did not derive then only from the difficult field work, but rather also from the money economy and the payment of taxes.[9] He was not burdened with corvée but rather with money debt. The prices for the products of urban production are too great for the likes of him, even when he produces wheat, fruit, wine, vegetables, meat and leather for himself. These verses were published 43 years after the great peasant uprising of 1525. The margin squeeze between the products in the country and city were the same in the 16th century as we know in the 20th century. Prices of the country products fell, those of the city rose, and that worsened the situation of the peasants. Slicher von Bath believes, the situation in the east Elbian part of Central Europe would have appeared to be worse than in western Germany, but better than in Poland and Russia in the early epoch of modern bourgeois society.[10]

Peasants in the south and southwest of the Central European region were rebellious in 1423, 1431, 1449, 1459, 1475. The *Bundschuh* movement made its appearance on the Upper Rhein and lasted 24 years, until 1517. In 1503, *Der Arme Konrad* was formed and lasted until the uprising of 1512/13, which was set off by the poor harvest result of the same year. In 1524/25, the great peasant uprising and the peasant war took place in Hessen, in the Electoral Palatinate, in Wurttemberg, in Swabia and Brandenburg, in Thuringia, in Tirol, Salzburg, Upper Austria (Steyr), Carinthia (Friesach), Steiermark (Leoben), in Hungary, in the Confederations (Bern, Zurich, Saint Gallen and Appenzell), in Alsace and in Lorraine. The causes were traced back to money and tax burdens, which were to be redeemed by the serfs, and to the poor harvest result. The peasant uprisings nevertheless had other causes, which we recognize.

In 1476, a shepherd, Hans Böhm, in Taubertal, preached that Holy Mary had commanded him to tell the people to kill the pope and the clerics, priests and the rich. Tithes and interest were only alms. All people, princes, masters, citizens, peasants should work for their daily wages and with their own hands earn their keep in a brotherly fashion. All tributes should be abolished, hunting and fishing should be open to all. Declarations of freedom and brotherhood as well as the right to wage labour and to the abolition of serfdom are repeated in the declarations of peasant liberation. Wage labour became a symbol of freedom and equality. All men should labour for their daily wage. The program of the peasants and herdsmen was expressed in this respect in two ways. For one, wage labour was considered the free employment of all men. But this way of thinking presented above all the wish and desire of servile labourers; wage labour signified liberation from forced corvée service. For another the same program expressed the peasant demands for liberation from all forms of exploitation. Pope and clerics, priests and the wealthy should work for their daily wage as well. In 1460, the *Bundschuh* was spread in the Hegau, in Alsace. In 1502, in one of the *Bundschuh*, the serf Joss Fritz demanded the abolition of all interest and tributes. Serfdom should end, water, forest and pasture should become common property.[11] The declarations of the pursuit of justice are not singular appearances, but precursors of the subsequent demands of the peasant war.

Pentacost 1524, the peasants armed themselves in the Black Forest, at Bonndorf in the provincial county Stühlingen in Hegau, for an uprising,[12] led by the Lutheran minister Doctor Balthasar Hubmaier. The peasants had discussed their tribulations under corvée services. In this case they were unfree in the formal sense. The relationship to the Reformation has often been noticed; that Martin

Luther himself published the document *Wider die mörderischen und räuberischen Rotten der Bauern* [Against the murderous and thieving bands of peasants], in which he wrote: "Therefore to that end should be thrown, choked, stabbed, in secret or openly, by whosoever is able, and consider that nothing can be more poisonous, more harmful, more devilish than a rebellious man …" does not refute this assertion.

The peasants had written down their demands programmatically in the form of articles. The articles whose content was differently composed according to local conditions were passed on from some farms. The best known of these peasant programs is perhaps that of the twelve articles of the Baltrigen group, composed and distributed in March 1525. The peasants did not themselves write down their articles; they had invited a furrier apprentice, Sebastian Lotzer, to compose the twelve articles. The student of Zwingli, Christoph Schappeler had written the preface for the articles. Both had previously composed, printed and distributed several leaflets. The relationship of the movement to writing and the art of printing, as well as to the suffering and the increasing social consciousness of the peasants became even more visible through them.

In the first article the peasants demanded the right to elect and scrutinise their own priest. He should preach the Gospel without any man-made additions. Second, the peasants wanted to deliver the exact grain tithes, as instituted in the Old Testament and fulfilled in the New, and no more than these. Third, the peasants held, contrary to the previous custom that the rulers maintained them as their own people, inserted with the justification: "seeing that Christ saved and purchased all with the spilling of his precious blood." They rejected complete freedom—without any authority, for "god did not teach us that." They argued: "Therefore it follows from the Bible that we are and want to be free." Yet they showed the will to be obedient to the authority. The third article leads to the practical conclusion: "We also have no doubt you will gladly release us from serfdom as true and just Christians as rendered by the Gospel, that we are legally in bondage." The fourth and fifth article explain the peasants' right to venison, fowl, fish and groves, which the rulers acquired disproportionately and in an unbrotherly way. The sixth and seventh articles explain the aggravation of services, which are increased daily; the eighth grapples with wages and interest. Interest should be set fairly "so that the peasant does not ply his labour for nought, for daily labour of any kind is worthy of his wage." In the ninth article the peasants insist that "we" be treated "according to the old written punishment", "and not by favour." In the tenth article complaints are recorded "that some have acquired meadows, of the same field, which however belong to a community." One ought to "compare oneself in a goodly and brotherly fashion according to the shape of the matter." "We shall take the same again into our common hands." The eleventh article deals with the right of widows and orphans to what belongs to them.

In the peasants' war 1524/26 about 100,000 people lost their lives. In one campaign over 5,000 peasants were killed and left for dead, others were taken prisoner. In Brandenburg, a further 80 peasants were beheaded, 69 peasants had their eyes plucked out and their fingers broken.[13]

Peasants were variously oppressed by corvée service and money tribute. The manorial system was not everywhere the same but operated and led according to different terms of the dominant, communal and private law. The regulation of peasant rights in the direction of the private and money economy led to a liberation of the peasants in the formal sense; that means, peasants in the domains and manors were formally-juristically unfree, compulsory services were in the same sense performances by the unfree. In the northeastern parts of Germany during the waning years of the Middle Ages and in the first centuries of the modern era the conditions of peasant unfreedom were continued, while they were abolished early in the south and the west. In part, the peasants won these rights through their own rebellious activities. In general, the principle was ascertained from the 15th and 16th century, that formally-juristically unfree labour stands opposed to the capitalist conditions of economy. In the twelve articles the peasants again took a strong position against serfdom. Their prime example for the labour of the future is wage labour. The herdsman, Hans Böhm, and the composers of the twelve articles, return to this point *expressis verbis* in the eighth article. The alternative to serfdom and compulsory services is wages by the day and piece. This appears in the capitalist era not for the first time in human history, but it now corresponds to the aspirations of the peasants. Objectively serfdom and the performance of compulsory service are replaced by relations of the market and exchange, wage labour and money economy. In place of labour tribute or products in natura, the peasants demanded freedom and finally reached their goal. Freedom is multiple in the formal sense of freedom to leave one's domicile, place of residence or location of work, to move freely. To this is to be added the legal and political freedom, freedom of thought, of belief and of the press.

Capitalist exploitation is the effect of this program. The peasants constituted the vast majority of the population in the transition period, and thus they had formed the quantitative condition for the transition; they sacrificed their lives to achieve their principles. The fate of the peasants is the negative principle for the revolution of feudal society. The positive principles are the active role of the economic system of the market, of money, of wage labour, of the capitalist entrepreneurs and the social system of the parties, of the education system, of writing, of law and of the ethos tied up with it.

The program of the rebellious peasants in the 16th century insisted on the continuation of the old common laws. Wage labour was considered a step forward at the time of the peasant movement of liberation, even when day and piece wages as the conditions of labour in the mines, in the working of materials of the putting-out system and in manufacture were inhuman and frightful. Contemporary movements of wage labourers in Frankfurt am Main, in Nuremberg, in Augsburg, in Joachimstal and elsewhere—the movements and uprisings of apprentices and miners' guilds had taken up only superficial contact with the uprising of the peasants. The relations of wage labour are nonetheless progressive in comparison to the conditions of serfdom and the rebellious peasants were aware of it (see the third article). Progress was and is defined and in part determined through the actualization of the formal-legal system of freedom.

The termination of relations to the past was only partly accomplished during the 15th to the 17th century. Elements of a patriarchal agricultural system were continued into the 19th century in Electoral Saxony, Thuringia, Brandenburg and Hanover. Various forms of landed property were conditioned by the transition to modern bourgeois society.[14] The landed property of the domain and of the manor were widespread east of the Elbe; the domains of the Junkers were in many cases leased so that in northeastern Germany it amounted to a mixture of peasant farms and manorial estates, which continued into the 19th century. Duties to the lord in the form of feudal services, domestic and forced services were maintained into the era of high capitalism.[15]

Peasants in east and western Germany had developed by means of various activities of colonization and rebellion, various property rights and forms of leasing. The peasants east of the Elbe who were settled on deserted farms by landlords [*Gutsherren*] before and during the Thirty Years' War, had no property rights in them in the ordinary sense, for they could not sell or mortgage the property. The peasant could only dispose of the harvest. The right to inherit the property came to them after the fact. These peasants were called *Lassiten* [or those who could bequest possession but not ownership to their heirs—trans.]. In the east there was non-inheritable land possession [*Landbesitz*] also small farmers [*Büdner*], cottagers [*Häusler*], cotters [*Kossäten*] (Cf. *Kote*, *Kotsass*).[16] The lord of the manor stood under compulsion for care, the subjects under compulsion to work. The title bearer of the manor had made the peasants into hereditary subjects, which not all of them were previously. The liberation movements of the 16th century had little impact on the countries east of the Elbe. Hans Böhm, Joss Fritz, Hans Sachs and the Twelve Articles pointed to the fact that the money economy emancipates, that wage labour emancipates. The former is in the country as well as in the town, the latter is mainly to be found in the town. Town air emancipates in both cases, country air emancipates in the first case. The expansion of daily wage labour in the country follows in the late periods. The cottager had his house in the village, but he had no land.[17] Overseer of the villa rustica [Villicus, curagundarius], steward and land custodian of all kinds did not disappear all at once, but rather gradually. Fronhof [Villication or manorial estate] was dissolved in the Steiermark in the 12th century and replaced by late villication [*Rentengrundherrschaft*, whereby labour services were replaced by money payments—trans.]. The path to a money economy was thus prepared and reinforced.[18] In the 15th to the 17th century the rights of peasant landownership became consolidated and there was a generalization of tax burdens. Tax freedom of the privileged estates was reduced. The money economy had led to formal equality in society, for the circulation of money, money tax and money rent was tied up with it.

The struggle over forest, meadow, and water rights is bound up with the division of the commons [*Gemeinheiten*]. But they are not the same thing in this struggle; moreover, the lifting of the commons and the setting aside of the conflict of diverse interests do not necessarily belong together. The peasants in the 15th and 16th century had demanded the right to hunt game, catch fish, gather wood and the right of return viz. to the maintenance of the customs of the common especially in relation to the forests, meadows and water. Here the community kept the meaning of the country community, the town had another history and meaning. The former was derived from the epoch prior to written history, the latter appears in later history and becomes approved and recognized by the state. The abolition of *Flurzwang* [forced regulation within the three-field economy] and of servitude, of land consolidation or of the degradation of the community was related to the villages and farms in the 16th and 17th century. The communal rights to the land were degraded in connection with the liberation of the peasants and the individualization of the rights of property in the land.[19]

The capitalist entrepreneur is fundamentally the representative of private interests and of the private sphere in social life. In the era of modern bourgeois society, he stands in opposition to the public interest and the state. Adam Smith and G.W.F. Hegel have confirmed these oppositions of the 18th and 19th century. The process is also to be found in the 15th to 17th century as well in the conflict between the capitalist and the feudal lord. The latter was simultaneously master of the public and private power; he was neither statesman nor private man alone, but rather both without difference together. In the post-feudal era, the capitalist appears on the side of the private interests, and he puts himself on the side of the state in the course of his altercation with the feudal lords. Conversely, after the capitalist has become master in his own house, he puts himself on the side of state power, manifested implicitly in the 15th to the 17th century, explicitly in the 19th.

The struggle between the two ruling classes in this period was already decided in substance even if not in the formal sense.

The money economy mediated the transition from the natural economy to the new economic and social situation. The money economy already determined the struggle between the money masters and landed authorities, between the new capitalists and the old aristocrats in the 15th to the 17th century.

The peasants in the wars of liberation brought to expression the problem of the struggle over benefits [*Rentenkampf*] when they declared themselves opposed to interest, taxes, land tax in money or in kind [*Gült*], compulsory labour [*Frondienste*] and compulsory collective services [*Scharwerk*]. Further, the problem of the struggle over benefits appears in the dispute between the old masters of the land, that is the aristocrats and clerics, on the one side, and the capitalists, the new men, on the other, and this is reflected in the 19th century in the novels of Balzac and Chekov. But the problem is not put to rest, for there is a further historical dynamic at play.

The passing of medieval and the beginning of capitalist relations concerning the process of production in the countryside could be linked with the struggle over ground rent. However, rent is a form in which the surplus product of the land objectively appears. The peasants produced a surplus, and many of them fought very hard against ground rent in word, in deed, and in life. Hence, ground rent is an important matter, and its alienation from the immediate producers is important as well. The integration of the peasants into the money economy, that is into domestic and foreign trade, into the market for agricultural products, further peasant wages in the form of money, the development of prices and the total income of agriculture constitute factors, which are equally dynamic and important in relation to the theoretical conception of periodization in history. All mysticism aside, the peasants grasped concretely, that this was about the division of plots of land, about the rights to the use of the soil, wages and salaries.

Wilhelm Abel investigated the relation between the social conditions in the countryside and the prices for agricultural products.[20] If prices rose, conditions on the land improved. World depression led to the deterioration of life. These conclusions signify two things: first, the increase and decrease in prices imply the presence of a price and money economy, of market relations, of world trade and traffic; second, the early-modern peasants of Central Europe in the waning years of the Middle Ages to a certain extent, but then, primarily in the first centuries of modern bourgeois society, in the 15th century and thereafter, participated immediately in these relations. If one were to say that the relations of the natural economy were continued, then this assertion would only have a formal significance. In substance, the peasants had participated in the world market already in the 15th to the 17th century and they had already contributed in an essential way to money revenue at first west of the Elbe, thereafter in the territory east of the Elbe as well. In this context one can speak of world money and world trade. Further, Abel researched movements in agriculture, that is depression and the rise of prices concerning production relations, following the expansion and contraction of settlements, the partial and regional desolation of meadows. The decline of the settlements and of production led to a decline in the income of the peasants and landlords. The margin price worked to the disadvantage of the peasants. The income of the lords was not uniformly recouped or handed over. In 1600, Cloister Eberbach on the Rhine had leased some assets against a third of the harvest. The tenants were also obligated to corvée. The cloister had many assets which they owned in a wide circle from Koblenz to Limburg and Frankfurt am Main. The cloister steered a portion of rent, corvée services, money and products in the form of taxes and appraisals of the authorities further to the landlords and bishops. The latter devoured the surpluses of their own peasants and tenants, since the cloister was forced to lend money to the authorities and to tolerate "unadorned blackmail". This led to the "gradual decline of the Abbey Eberbach."[21]

The agricultural economy in Central Europe 1511–1625 had among others the products:

Cultivation of grain: wheat*, rye*, barley*, oats*, millet

Cultivation of vegetables: beans*, peas, carrots, parsnips, corn salad, radishes, small radishes, turnips, fodder turnips, rapeseed, cabbage, onions, peas (large, early), vetches [vicia], lentils, alfalfa

Spun yarn: Flax*, other varieties of flax, hemp, linen*

Viniculture: Grapes, raisins*, wine*

Colored plants: Woad, madder, safflower, dyers saffron, saffron, vinegar

Oil production: Rapeseed, roots, poppy seed, flax and hemp seed

Bees: honey, wax

Cattle: cheese*, butter*, meat*, leather*

Pigs: meat*, leather

Sheep: meat, wool*

Horses*

Fowl: Geese*, chickens*, swans, peacocks

Fish:* Herring, salmon, pike, carp, sturgeon

Wood* and charcoal*

Salt production: Salt*

Beer: small beer*, export beer*, malt*, hops*

*The main commodities in the exact sense. They were reckoned into the development of price and wages 1511–1625. The other products were not *eo ipso* excluded from these accounts.

That the agricultural products were transformed into commodities through market, exchange, price and wage relations, offers no proof that the feudal was replaced by the capitalistic economy. There is also talk of corvée emancipation payment [*Frongeld*] as there was of corvée emancipation services which were transformed into money at the beginning of modern times, that is in the 15th and 16th century.[22] Only when the total relations in the process of production, distribution, and consumption are investigated, can the degree of transformation from the feudal system into the modern bourgeois society be assessed. There is thus not one lone marker that will express or determine the transition. To be sure, some researchers have chosen such activities as double-entry bookkeeping or savings as the spiritual exposition of inner-worldly asceticism, as the express symbol of this transition. The entrepreneurs played an important role, the rebellious peasants and the organization of labourers in sea trade, in mining, and in the print industry are important as well.[23]

The figure of the exploiter was not constructed through simple economic relationships, but rather through several internal levels opposed to one another, secular and clerical. In this case it was the lowly in the abbey itself, the lofty in the land authorities and in the bishopric. The figure of exploitation is complicated by the fact that in part it consists of corvée service and forced collective labour [*Scharwerk*], in part of money tribute, in whatever form it may appear. The agricultural product was sold on the world market. In Lower Saxony aristocratic families arose, which took part in such enterprises and were referred to as aristocratic capitalists.[24] At this time capital did not flow from the countryside to the town, but rather conversely, from the trades and towns to the country, which remains *noble*.[25] In the period of high capitalism, on the contrary, capital was pulled out of the country into the city enterprises. The population increase in Central Europe during the 16th century resulted from the expansion and intensification of land cultivation of all kinds, of trade, of cattle raising, of fishing and of salt production. The same facilitation of the conditions of the agricultural economy also occurred in the Netherlands. The organization of labour in production in the countryside was improved on the coasts of the Baltic and North seas by the specialization of dairy products. The fattening of cattle led to the development of trade with Flanders and Holland, which bore within itself the further development of the money economy. The price revolution of the 16th century was related to the upswing of agricultural production, founded on the increase in the price of grain. This was almost everywhere the case in Central Europe in the 16th century and was linked to the boom in agriculture. Foreign and domestic trade were bound tightly to one another: the upswing was disrupted by the peasant wars, yet the disruption was temporary. The growth of the conditions of agricultural production, of the population numbers and of the transition to modern bourgeois society continued to advance.[26]

On the basis of past customary practices and rights of use the peasants kept their cattle on the common meadows and gathered wood in the common forest. The disparate condition was variously administered, in some cases by a regulation of the stock of cattle on the common meadows; each and every peasant had a recognized right to have his cattle graze there. These rights were reduced in the course of the 15th and 16th century and some traditional customs were lost in this connection. The peasants during the peasant wars complained that their right to fish in the community waters was denied and the right to hunt was taken away because the lords disproportionately acquired the venison, game, fish, wood and meadows of the same farmland, which, however, belonged to the community. The peasants repeatedly returned to the complaints that the lords have behaved in a non-fraternal way. The peasants' idea of fraternity consists in the belief that the ancient rights of commonality of meadows, forest, fish and bird catching as well as hunting in the forest and the rights of using the wood ought to continue without disruption. Thus, in the peasants' conception there was an internal connection between commonality and fraternity.[27]

In the ensuing centuries, the abolition of the commons and the setting aside of the complex conditions were not considered as a singular question. By legislation and quiet forgetting, the separation or division of the commons was carried through in Prussia, elsewhere in the integration, realignment of boundaries, consolidation, or interlinking of the dissolution or expansion of the community. In the bishopric of Kempten in Allgäu land consolidation parcelling [*Vereinödung*] was recorded in the middle of the 16th century.[28]

In opposition to the picture portrayed by Janssen and Pareto of bourgeois life in the 14th to the 16th century, Abel wrote about devastations—devastations of places and of fields—in the late Middle Ages. There followed a period of peasant prosperity, for example, in Schleswig-Holstein and in Fehmarn, as well as in the south and southwest of Germany from the end of the 15th until the beginning of the 17th century.[29] Günter Franz assessed the following epoch of the Thirty Years'

War in relation to the losses of war differently for the city and the populations in the countryside: for the latter 40%, for the former 33% damages. In relation to the total losses he put together the following picture: More than 40% losses: Trier, the Palatinate, Wurttemberg, Mecklenburg, Pomerania, Brandenburg, Thuringia. 40 to 50% losses: in Alsace, Swabia, Franken, Bavaria, Bohemia, Brandenburg, Magdeburg, Hessen, Breisgau, as well as Saxony and Lower Saxony. 30 to 40%: in South Bavaria, North Swabia, parts of Magdeburg, West Hessen. 20 to 30%: in North Trier, Paderborn, Berg, Cologne, Julich, Lusatia, Silesia and parts of Breisgau and Wurttemberg. 10 to 20%: Munster, Bohemia (in part), Moravia, and parts of Lower Saxony and Saxony. 1 to 10%: the vicinity of Hanover and Bremen. Other parts of Central Europe, like Switzerland, Austria (Tirol), Holstein, Aachen and surrounding area, Emden and surrounding area and Burgundy were less impacted by this war.

Franz writes as follows: "In Mark Brandenburg and Mecklenburg, Thuringia and Hessen, Wurttemberg of the Upper Rhein Plane and of the Palatinate there were wide stretches which lay devoid of people after the war."[30] The greatest ravages of war originated in the second half of the period of the war. Thereafter, the situation of the peasants improved, which can be deduced from the general economic growth and the corresponding increase in population numbers. The absolutist state in the late 17th and in the 18th century had assured internal civil peace; civil rights as well as peasant rights had been extended. A further stage in the history of modern bourgeois society corresponded to these formal improvements. The notorious absolutism of the state in the 18th century was welcomed in comparison to the previous chaos.

In the 15th and 16th century the already previously begun dissolution of the single farm and villication [a villa worked under supervision of a manager] systems and the loosening up of living conditions continued. The rights of peasant assets and the right to inherit them had increased. Production on the land had been further extended and the forests were forced back. The extensive cultivation on estates was conducted in connection with the cultivation of land in the east. The cultivation in the three-or-more field system—commonly the summering, the wintering and the fallow—were extended through the intensification of market gardening. The specialized culture of plant species which originated in the New World, for example, potatoes, corn, sunflowers, tobacco and tomatoes were first introduced or enlarged only in ensuing centuries. The development of fruit and wine production, the rationalization of grain production as well as technical improvements[31] of fertilizer led to an intensification of agricultural production in the 15th to the 17th century.

Agrarian production in Central Europe had not only covered personal requirements but also produced a surplus during the period from the 15th to the 17th century. The expansion of arable farmland at the cost of virgin forest in Central Europe, the inclusion of the countries of the east in the transportation system of the agrarian economy, the rationalization in commerce and transport and the intensification in agriculture had led to the amplification of foreign trade as a consequence. Grain, wine, beer, cattle, leather, cheese, butter, meat and the secondary products of the agrarian economy, cloth, linen, oil were exported. The towns had lived from it, domestic and foreign trade had contributed further to the profit of agrarian products. The conjuncture and the turnover in seaport cities like Hamburg, Lubeck, Danzig and in river port cities like Cologne, were increased to the advantage of traders. Conversely merchants introduced spices, silk, velvet among other commodities. Overall, Central Europe was an area of export in relation to agrarian products; imported products were those of cotton, spices, precious metals and some luxury commodities (silk) from the region of the Mediterranean, from Mexico and Asia. Additional colonial commodities like cocoa, coffee, tea, further, precious tropical trees and shrubs and rubber, came to Central Europe only in the following period.

When one speaks of an economic miracle in the period of early capitalism, it thus had its basis in the agrarian economy. Even under the condition of the increase in the city population central European agrarian production could satisfy the increasing demand for the most part. Peasants had nevertheless continued in their rebellious orientation and in their activities in the southern and western parts of Central Europe. During the 16th, 17th, and 18th century, the peasants in Austria, Hungary, Bavaria, in Switzerland, in the Black Forest, in Hesse, on the Rhein and in Bohemia were rebellious. The exceptions were the east German peasants. That there was no uprising among them, Otto Hintze traced back to the effect of Lutheranism. Günter Franz emphasized other causes for the passive orientation of the east Elbian peasants: the lack of city life or of economic progress. "Nevertheless, the resistance against the excess of seigniorial pressure was stronger than one had previously assumed."[32]

The marginal squeeze between peasant and town products to the advantage of the latter was not the only opposition between town and countryside. The town had its villages which lay in its vicinity which it took into protection and defense. The city of Frankfurt am Main had maintained security in the villages of Bonames, Bornheim, Oberrad, Sulzbach, Soden among others. The expressions, *einem Herren hünen* [to be a giant to a man], to belong to him, to be a serf, are in this connection synonymous. The villages were duty-bound to supply tribute in kind to the town, but not to provide compulsory labour. In the area around Frankfurt only the products of bodies of water and meadows were rendered to the Kaiser or rather to the lords-paramount of Hesse. Tributes for the City of Frankfurt consisted in the form of chicken parts taken from servile labour in payment of interest and the best cattle chosen by the lord on the death of the tenant [*Leibhuhn, Besthaupt*]. K. Bücher writes: "When Bechtram von Vilbel made the thoroughfares unsafe, Frankfurt residents of Dortelweil came to his defense."[33] They were right to reject the protection of the city, and this was then assumed by a powerful man. A certain freedom of the village corresponds to the law in the 15th century. Namely, the village had the right to choose between two masters; single persons enjoyed such a right as well. But there ought to be but one dominion. Conversely, many villages had still sought the security of town walls. The inhabitants of these localities had been subsumed under the authority of Frankfurt, such that the town council and its subjects were accountable to it. The village of Dortelweil was not the only case, for several villages in those uncertain times oscillated between two authorities. The obligations of the lord in relation to his subjects were given summary expression in that the lord is responsible to, promises, defends as well as secures and shields his subjects. At that time Frankfurt protected 103 localities and gave them civil law. Mainz had 40 localities; Ulm, Bingen, Worms and Speyer had comparable relations to their surrounding villages.

Dortelweil in the vicinity of Frankfurt can be recognized by the names of its village history; there was a hamlet in the past. Hamlet refers back to the old-High German *wîlâri*, Middle High German *wîler*, which is derived from the Latin *villa*.[34] In the late Middle Ages a distinction was made between hamlet and village, but thereafter both words were loosely taken up in relation to the small towns and localities in the countryside.[35] In 1498 the peasants of Oberrad decided, as they were burdened with a heavy monetary fine by the Frankfurt town council on account of insubordination: "… any serf should seek his master in opposition to the council …"[36] [*… jeglicher seinen leibangehörigen Herrn dem Rat* ***zuwidder*** *zu suchen …*]. Thus, Bechtram von Vilbel was able to enrich himself in two ways, first as a highwayman and second as an exploiter of the Dortelweiler peasants.

The peasant villages of this period, although to a certain degree self-sustaining, were nevertheless still dependent on the industry of the towns. The by-laws of Saxony of 1482 had determined: "No one in a village who is not by some peculiar fashion freed should employ a tradesman." Smithies and weavers of linen, who laboured for the requirements of the village and only in the areas distant from the town, were exempted from this prohibition.[37] Village weavers received needles, yarn, thimbles, and spinning wheels from the town workshops.

The prohibitive declarations [*Prohibitiverklärungen*] by the Nurembergers assured the metal trades their share of the market. Production for the market—within the precinct—had been monopolized by the spectacle makers, wire drawers, trumpet makers, gold, and silversmiths, brass lathe workers and cymbalists. Distributors and precincts were already introduced by the end of the 13th century in Nuremberg. An order in council proclaimed: "No citizen, whether smithy or not, shall transfer a smith to his work within seven miles in all directions, with the exception of hammer smiths." Whosoever transgresses the prohibition, should pay one of every fourth heller.[38] Precincts were variously conceived. On the one hand, there was the concept of the precinct taken together with the protected area of the town. Within the precinct, securing of the civil peace was considered the task of the town of Mainz. It belonged to their administrative and judicial circuit. On the other hand, the precinct was taken together with the opposition between town and countryside—to the advantage of the town, as we have seen. The precinct of Landshut amounted to duum millarium, that of Brandenburg to trium millarium. In 1516 the precinct of Altenburg accounted for 2700 rods, and thus the extent of the city limits came to 630 square kilometres. Within the precinct of Basel in the 14th century seven villages were found.[39]

3.3 Labour Processes in the City: General Considerations Concerning Harmony and Struggle

The Central European town from the 15th to the 17th century looked nothing like its contemporary counterpart. It was small in comparison to today's city; it was also small in comparison to the large cities of classical antiquity and of the Renaissance in the region of the Mediterranean. In 1520, the population of Naples was around 230,000; in 1550, the population of Cologne amounted to around 37,000. Cologne gradually attracted to it the surrounding boroughs, communities, peasant communities, and villages. As already stated, from 1300 to 1500 the population of Central Europe remained basically unchanged or perhaps even declined during the period of the Black Death.

The town at that time had no natural growth, since there was no special excess in births in relation to the death rate. Rather, the town population increased as a consequence of the physical expansion of the city limits; immigration into the towns also had a certain significance in this connection. One can visualize this first factor through city borough designations like "old town" and "new town". Thus, Göttingen in 1319 had a new town, Thorn, an old town and a new town, Dortmund a new city and so on. Braunschweig at the same time was "a federal town of five municipal areas." Historically, Hamburg arose out of the combination of two towns and the same is asserted of Halle on the Saale and of Salzwedel.[40]

Documents trace the founding of Berlin in the 13th century back to three localities, Spandau (1232), Berlin (1244) and Cologne [Cölln] (1237). The localization of cities is customarily linked with their functions as a cultural centre, as trade, transportation and communication, administration, mining settlement or as a Roman colony.

In the 12th book of his work *De Re Metallica* Georg Agricola dealt with the extraction of salt. Salts are not only indispensable for the life and health of people and of domestic animals, but for the industries of leather and metal processing, chemistry and so on, as well. Salt at that time was created and distributed as a state monopoly in connection with the salt tax. Thus, it appears as a means for the wealth of the state and the centralization of power in the hands of the authorities. The role of salt in social, economic and political life is recognized in the names of localities such as Salzbrunn, Salzdorf, Salzkammergut, Salzmine, Salzburg, Salzwedel.

The towns in Central Europe in the 15th to the 17th century were renowned for their handicraft products, such as, for example, Nuremberg for its metal processing. If one speaks of the harmony of city life, the literature in relation to this is ambiguous. Social relations were idealized and described as harmonious; the only disagreement were the hostilities among the master singers in the competition between the guild and future musicians of Nuremberg. Engels and Zimmermann, Kriegk and Schoenlank opposed these ideal-harmonious ideas.[41]

G.L. Kriegk was of the view that as the peasants rose up in the whole of southern and central Germany, the burghers of the towns in those areas were also rising up. Both classes were driven by one and the same spirit, as both had one and the same goal in sight. The peasant revolt was a revolutionary war of the entire underclass of the people in the town and countryside against the privileged secular and clerical estates, "thus a revolution in the full sense of the term." Kriegk writes further of the uprising of the town from 1355 and uprisings of the handicraft guilds against the patricians at Nuremberg and Ulm.[42] Bruno Schoenlank wrote of constant class struggles in Nuremberg over the entire course of the 16th century.[43] The details in both works are treated carefully and reliably. The class struggle in Central Europe in the Middle Ages and in modern times is well described therein. However, in one sense the authors have decidedly exaggerated the significance of the movements. There were at that time contacts to a certain point between the rebellious peasants and the manual labourers in the towns which should be neither under—nor overestimated. Kriegk asserts that a revolution spreads across the town as across the peasantry, but this perhaps goes too far. Engels' position in this question is well-known. Fundamentally, the peasants and the manual labourers did not mutually support one another; neither did the one struggle on the side of the other. The movement was not driven in common—it was not a revolution—the peasants' program did not mention the condition in the towns, and only in specific cases such as in Rothenburg ob der Tauber, Nuremberg or Bamberg, did the manual labourers in the town take up the cause of the peasants or join in the common struggle against the rulers. On the other hand, the historians did not go far enough. They took no notice of the uprisings of the miners' guilds in Joachimsthal, Freiberg, Annaberg and elsewhere during the 15th and 16th century.[44]

In 1525 declarations of sympathy of the paupers of Nuremberg appeared on the side of the rebellious peasants; this was in one sense a fraternization of town folk [*Bürger*] and peasants. Schoenlank described the relation of the two in the following way: Among the fraternal organizations of the apprentices in Nuremberg the radical elements of the Reformation with their primitive utopianism and their radical critique of prevailing conditions found numerous supporters. Book publishing apprentices in Nuremberg secretly and in the absence of their masters published a polemical pamphlet of [Thomas] Münzer. Karlstadt pamphlets too were printed in Nuremberg and eagerly read. Monks who fled the monasteries united themselves with the apprentices. The outbreak of the Peasant Wars pulled in the poor people of Nuremberg as well in sympathy with those who rose up in May of 1524.

Not only the proletariat but the petit bourgeois also sympathized with the peasants. An innkeeper from the suburb of Wöhrd and a cloth maker apprentice [*Tuchmacherknappe*] were beheaded on account of their public declaration that town folk and peasants must stand together to rid themselves of the oppressive excess tax on drink and grain. When a baker's servant made an illegal speech with a peasant and was put into a pit, the baker stood up on his behalf and the council set him free. This clever tactic saved the council; the reform of market money, of the excise tax, expenditure tax and of quit-rent [*Erbzins*] averted the threatening catastrophe.[45]

The interests of the journeymen and the peasants were in general the same. Both were poor. But that which the urban fraternities concretely demanded, had little in common with the program of the rebellious peasants. The dissolution of quit-rent, the reform of market money and of the excise tax on drink and grain were not listed in the peasant program. Schoenlank cited a list of single cases. The apprentice bakers demanded the release of their brother, not fraternity with the peasants. These causes are to all appearances not to be considered as a revolutionary mass movement. Those who judged the struggles of the 16th century in the 19th and 20th century have not freed those events from the historical categories such as reform, revolution, social change of the later period, but rather projected into the past later historical conceptions anachronistically. We will avoid such anachronism as much as possible.

One can speak of a certain utopianism of Thomas Münzer, as Schoenlank opines; he mentioned the ideas and sentiments of the peasants, and of the town fraternities. A member of Müntzer's party, Heinrich Pfeiffer, had resided for a time in Nuremberg, but without exerting a deep impact on the urban working class. The views of Zimmermann, Kriegk, Schoenlank and others are perceptive, but in this regard not balanced. The following were apparently overlooked: In 1525, 70,000 to 100,00 peasants fell in this conflict. Yet no such war took place in the towns.

3.4 The Guild System, the Putting-Out System and Manufacture

The guild system dominated the labour and exchange process in the towns of Germany, such as in Cologne, Hamburg, Augsburg, Frankfurt, Danzig and Nuremberg. Since the producing unit was the workshop or the home, this concerns a small organism for the production of commodities, as we have already seen, as much as with a low and limited number of workers in the production process. The structuration and division of labour remained at a lower level in comparison to manufacture in the factories of later periods. To make this more concrete, we will consider a factory in England in the 15th/16th century. The history of the entrepreneur John Winchcombe, also known as Jack of Newbury, who died in 1519, is well-known from a poem written in the year 1597. The poem is in part a pure invention, composed in poor verse (doggerel), and is in part a romanticized view of the batch processing [*Stapelbetrieb*] of the wealthy man. The King of England, either Henry VII or VIII, was supposed to have exclaimed: "This Jack of Newbury is richer than I." According to this poem, 200 weavers and an equal number of apprentices worked together in a great room; this is not a small workshop but rather a true factory. This is shown not only by the number of weavers and apprentices, but also by their being brought together in one room, and by the relatively detailed and complicated structuration of labour in the process of production for the time: furthermore, 100 women worked with the wool scrapers, 200 girls on the distaff and the spinning wheel, 150 children were employed as sorters of wool and in addition, there were 50 cloth cutters, 20 cloth walkers and 40 dyers.[46] To these are to be added the conveyer and transportation labourers. The numbers appeared to be rounded up and hugely exaggerated. But even if they were halved, or even three quarters of them were removed, the business remains extraordinarily large in comparison with others of the same time, and in this lies the truth of the poetic recounting. Industrialization, manufacture in the factory and the extensive organization and division of labour in the creation of cloth disappeared temporarily after it. The causes of this fate were often investigated: The estates, the town council, the guild system and even the high authorities resisted it. The capitalists in the weaving industry were too weak to follow through with this new manufacturing practice in the 15th, 16th, and 17th century. The labourers on the contrary were engaged in opposition to it. Preparations for the great enterprises as in the 19th and 20th century were too early. Hence, the development of the process of production of great industry was not carried through with necessity or with internal logic.

The organization of labour and of the economy in the towns of Central Europe from the 14th to the 17th century was fundamentally regulated and controlled by the guilds. The guild is an inclusive and exclusive entity, dominated from without and from above; it is a hierarchical organization of labour, which reflects the graduated levels [*Stufenhaftigkeit*] of social life, by which it is determined.

The organization of the workshop was not only small in terms of the size of the undertaking, so that only a limited number of labourers—masters, journeymen and apprentices—would be set together, but furthermore they were separated in space as well. In the production of books there were three or four labourers at the press, two or three at the binder, both separated from one another. Rationalization of the process of production in the guild system was different from the system of manufacture and of the factory.

The ancillary trades of domestic labour in the putting-out system were regulated according to the pattern of the guild organization. A structuring of labour, the preparation of the apprentices in the process of production and the qualification of masters and journeymen conformed to the guilds. The oldest guilds were established in the 12th century. The trades of Central Europe, such as the shoemakers from Wurzburg and Magdeburg or the blanket weavers from Cologne, received, on the one hand, imperial privileges, and on the other hand, town rights; the same was also true for Augsburg, Ulm, Strasbourg, Mainz and Frankfurt am Main. Bound up with this was not only public permission to produce shoes, bed accessories or garments, but also personal freedom of the city, the securing of material life as well as the possibility of owning housing and property and participation in civic-police politics. The maintenance of guild privileges thus depended on the foundation of bourgeois existence and the classification of belonging together with the bourgeois estate.

The *guild* [Zunft] is a corporate body whose provenance is bound up with the verb *ziemen*, *to behoove, to befit*, in the original meaning *to merge, to coalesce*. Similar corporate bodies with comparable economic and social function are found in Chinese, Indian, Islamic and Japanese traditions. The guild in the Germanic tradition is traced back to concrete economic practices in building houses; it is bound up with the conceptual field of *Bauholz*, English *timber*, German *Zimmer*. It is abstract and can be traced back to the conceptual fields of dexterity, expediency and further to regulation, association. The guilds [*Gilde*], which in the late Middle Ages and in modern times, hence in the 14th, 15th, 16th, 17th and 18th century, played *grosso modo* the same economic and social role as did the guild in Central Europe, can also be traced back to a different etymological conceptual field. It is historically bound up with the words, money, *to count* [*gelten*], *to repay* [*Vergeltung*], further with paying taxes, sacrifice. Brotherhood and miner [*Knappe*] in the further Indo-Germanic realm indicate the more abstract conceptual field of guild [*Zunft*] in the sense of rule, association [*Verein*] (see above). Office [*Amt*], professional association [*Innung*], union [*Einung*] give expression to the coming together in the associations and the corresponding structuration of labour in the production and in the sale of commodities in the early history of the market economy.

The Central European tradition of the Guild [*Zunft*] and of the guild system [*Gildewesen*] is traced back to the encounter of various traditions. The capitularies from the time of Charlemagne, hence around 779, speak of ghildonia, confratria (fraternity), confederation (*Eidgenossenschaft*), and of the prohibition of these practices. Yet, the early ghildonia and brotherhood were strengthened in the economy and in law. In the late Middle Ages, the guilds supported and secured the peace of membership and the guild system the peace of the city (compare Anglo-Saxon Frith, i.e. peace guild [*Friedensgilde*]).

The guild [*Zunft*] as a corporate body is traced back to the early Germanic cooperative [*Genossenschaft*], Genootschap, and so on, on the one hand, and on the other to the Roman coporation and the collegium. The German Hansa was in its origin a merchants' guild [*Kaufmannsgilde*] (kopgilde).

The concept of the guild is linked with crafts, concretely with the construction of houses, the concept of the *guild* [*Gilde*] with merchants. Both were hierarchized in the early history of economic and legal practices in the creation and process of trade and commerce. The step ladder of apprentices, of journeymen and of the guild masters appear to be almost the same in several professions and in several towns. The functions of the monopoly in production and sale in a specific field of commodities or of a service, such as that of the master singers, are shown as well in the Italian word *moestranza*, which has the same sense as the German *Gilde*. Also, the word *Zunft* or guild is the same as the Italian *moestranza* or *corporazione*. The structuring and division of labour, training and the welfare of the members as well as of their families, widows and orphans in the same organizations derive from antiquity and the Middle Ages. The progressive accomplishments and functions of the guild and *Gilde* systems are related to the quality of the products, such as their stand in opposition to the falsification of bread, to the forging of coins and so on, not to the quantity of products and the increase in profit.

The contradiction between the professional and creative practices of the guilds and the spirit of the capitalists, which is related to profit, led to the decline of the guild system. The guilds reacted negatively to the new modes of labour and commerce. In addition, they were manipulated as an instrument of the state and authorities in the class struggle. Their functions were in part superseded and overtaken by the new trade unions, in part through the new capitalist forms of organization in the period of the industrial revolution and of high capitalism. The important contributions of the guild system in the development of the structuration of labour in the late Middle Ages disappeared so that diverse figures such as Martin Luther, Hans Sachs, Goethe and Richard Wagner despised the guilds and cursed the guild spirit.[47]

In their history the guilds did not develop in a unitary fashion. Some guilds disappeared, the guild organizations of entire branches of the economy were lost. The towns on the other hand kept others, down to the epoch of high capitalism. The guilds maintained some control over jurisdiction, administration of justice and self-administration. This situation in law can also be exaggerated, for in the last instance the guilds were subjected to the jurisdiction of the town council and dependent on the authorities. The guilds and their membership were subjects in the period of absolutism to royal sovereignty, as Schiller poetically and consciously expressed it in *Wallenstein*.

The integration of the membership in the guild system—according to the ranking of apprentices, journeymen and masters—was related to their dexterity and assurance in the process of labour. The products of the guilds, like Nuremberg's metal goods, were known for their high quality within and without the Central European region. Yet, a contradiction in the further development of these relations of labour developed. The forward moving structuring of labour in the new processes of production and in the new associations of handicraftsmen in the second half of our period, (in the 17th and 18th century) connected with it, abutted the limit of the internal organization of the old guilds and associations.[48]

The guilds in the late Middle Ages and in the early-modern period were closely linked with the public regulation and organization of the skilled crafts and their associations. Guild [*Zunft*], office [*Amt*], Gilde and trade guild [*Innung*] have a common significance and role according to local usage of language and traditions. For example, in the Hansa cities the designation *office* [*Amt*] was used in place of *guild* [*Zunft*] with the meaning of an assembly of independent handicraft masters of a particular profession in a town and each according to recognized trades, yet elsewhere in northern Germany the designation *Gilde* was usual. The appearance of similar associations in Italy, France, Spain, England, in the Netherlands and in the Scandinavian countries under the same conditions and roughly at the same time is well-known. The fortunes of the guilds are varying. They were repressed earlier in the Netherlands and in England than in Germany through the rise of manufacture and factories. Kulischer speaks of the transition to trades' freedom in this context.[49] The concept of freedom is in this case related to formal freedom. Freedom in one epoch is different than that in another. Hence, the guild system in the late Middle Ages was bound up with the freedom of the town, yet later it impinged upon the freedom of the trades, of the process of production and of civil (bourgeois) life.

The guild labourers, in the period from the 15th to 17th century, basically tradesmen in the workplaces of the town, were paid a money wage, but not seldom with natural products as well. Bestowments such as lodging, beer, etc. were points of dispute for artisans in negotiations and altercations between apprentices, guild masters and council.[50] Apprentices as a social estate had the right to move freely. If the council had tried to take this freedom from them, the tradesmen would have fought against it. The freedom was mainly related to the change of place of residence, of the town and of the workplace, hence it was a physical, formal freedom. Master or council had the formal right to fire apprentices, which corresponded to a complementary formal freedom. Since the town labourers usually worked for another person—for a superior, a wealthy man—they were unfree in substance. They could not earn their daily bread except by working under these conditions. The freedom of the miners on the other hand reached further in a formal sense, as we shall see.

While peasants in the south and west of Germany fought for the freedom from corvée and forced collective labour, the town labourers as well as the miners and church attendants were to a certain extent free from them in the 15th and 16th century. The movements of journeymen in the towns (see above section 3.4) have some characteristics in common with the peasant movements, however, they certainly did not go as far as these. It concerns the formal freedom and equality of contract in the towns and the further formal freedoms of the miners. The working class in the towns had already won that which the peasants demanded. The social struggle which found expression in the peasant war and in their program, was about the freedom and equality of the peasant estate in society. The struggle of the labourers in the town as well as that of the capitalist enterprises was related to the formal juridical freedom of both sides and the corresponding equality without the explicit program. If someone could prove that he had signed a contract as an unfree person, as a servant under duress or threat, this was and is invalid in civil law; that which is now explicitly the case, was implicitly present in the early-modern epochs. This legal condition was set forth at the beginning of the capitalist era in negotiations concerning wages and the conditions of labour. Associations of journeymen negotiated with the council. In Frankfurt am Main the production of cloth was organized along guild lines in 1440, namely there were at this time 16 guilds in the textile trades whose members were recognized as independent earners:

Table 4: Number of Textile Guilds and Their Independent Members around the Year 1440

Guild	Independent Earners
Blanket borers	22
Cloth walkers	3
Dyers (2 guilds)	7
Fustian weavers	38
Linen weavers	21
Preparers of cloth (3 guilds)	7
Rope makers	5
Wool weavers (6 guilds)	141

Aside from the actual wool weavers there were the cloth washers [*Zauwer*], *Spansetzer*, wool cleaners or preparers of raw wool [*Wollenschläger*], one who weighs wool [*Wollenwieger*], wool combers. Together there were 6 guilds of wool weavers.

Preparers of cloth, cloth finishers and planers together made up the 3 guilds of preparers of cloth. Beside the dyers there were assistant dyers [*Kumpknechte* or *Kesselknechte*]; 2 guilds. Altogether there were 16 cloth processing guilds. Of those, 115 wool weavers were self-employed; 5 had one son each in the trade, 2 each had a servant weaver. The remaining wool weaving enterprises had neither sons nor menials. Of 3 sons, one worked with cloth finishers, one with preparers and one son with planers; there were no menials. The dyers had 6 members of the guild, of them one dyer's son, 4 menials, in addition to 2 assistant dyers [*Kumpknechte, Kumpenknechte*], who together were active in the same dying house of the weavers' guild. The *Zauwer* were also called tanners [*Kompgenger, Kumpengänger*]. There were 22 blanket borers [*Deckelecher*], one of them with a son, in the entire guild together 4 menials. The number of fustian weavers amounted to 38, 2 menials were added to them. The rope makers had neither sons nor menials in the enterprise.[51] The weaver workshops were small, the number of members in each single business was limited, and the production of commodities was similarly limited. The guild organization inhibited the development of the structuration and division of labour. The maintenance of the traditional organization of labour and its traditions stood in the foreground of their efforts. The "son" was not always or not necessarily the son of the family. We shall return to this question.

In the first centuries of the modern era weavers in Germany, England, France, the Netherlands and other countries in Europe maintained their customs, modes of labour and implements, with which they created cloth and rope. Their primary instrument of labour was the spinning wheel, and their traditional mode of labour was supported by the council and the authorities. Newer methods employed in the fabrication of commodities were considered harmful and were suppressed by officials and the guild system. The history of the introduction of new modes of labour in the cloth producing industry is instructive in this context. It has to do with the elimination of the old qualified labourers, their replacement by inexperienced youths, and the rationalization of the process of production, the sinking of wages through child labour and by the introduction of new tools such as ribbon looms, cord mills [*Schnurmühle*], and mill chairs [*Mühlenstuhl*].

The ribbon loom was introduced into Central Europe in the late 16th century. At that time, it had four to six webs, 16 to 18 gears, and it could be powered by a water wheel. The council at Iserlohn was concerned that this invention could turn a large number of labourers into beggars, and consequently their use in the production of cloth was prohibited. Possessors of the new tools of labour kept them secret in the majority of locations in Europe. In the 18th century the public mention of this instrument was avoided. It doesn't appear in the *Encyclopédie* of Diderot and d'Alembert. This silence, however, is no proof that the French did not know of it; it only shows that knowledge of it was not published, spread and generalized. The Italian cleric D. Secondo Lancelotti from Perugia told the following story in 1636: A certain Anton Moller was supposed to have seen an artificial machine in the year 1579, which could complete at one time the work of four, six or more weavers. But since many poor men who were dependent on weaving would die of hunger through the introduction of such machines, the council prohibited its use and had the inventor suffocated (*affogore*, suffocated or drowned). Everything is third hand; no other source confirms this report. Anton Moller is unknown. Perhaps this story about that invention itself is only invented. Yet we can attest that towards the end of the 16th century in several cities of Europe there were these ribbon looms and other mechanical spinning wheels, and that the weaver guilds, the council and the town officials offered resistance to their introduction. In the sixties and seventies of the 17th century the ribbon loom was banned by the council in Nuremberg, Frankfurt am Main and Cologne. In 1681 it was banned in the entire empire. In 1719 some merchants complained to the *Hofrat*, yet the prohibition was renewed in Kursachsen in 1720. In 1728 the ribbon loom was acquired by the king. The receipt reads that since conditions had changed and in other provinces of the empire the prohibition had lapsed, so it was decided to confer upon the loop makers the freedom to publicly make use of the ribbon looms and cord mills [*Band*—and *Schnurmühle*].[52]

The history of the weavers' guild is linked with the transition to the industrialization of cloth production, the expansion of domestic and world markets, the increasing influx of merchants and with the rising exploitation of labourers. The struggle over the maintenance of the stratum of qualified labour and the employment of unschooled children had changed the conditions and led to the employment of new machines. One can hardly speak of an industrial revolution here, but some steps in this direction were undertaken. Beckmann is an eyewitness, someone who introduced the events. His critical treatment of this history has been lost to memory. Later researchers have only repeated the history of the actual or fictional Anton Moller. However, the truth of the literature consists in the fact that the weavers, the council and authorities had set themselves in opposition to the employment of ribbon looms in the textile industry.[53] By 1728 this new merchant class had much greater influence than previously. In this way they could relieve the guild masters and organizations of their role. In the late Middle Ages and in the first centuries of the modern era the maintenance of commercial stability was the top priority of the guild system in Central Europe. Its policing contribution to the internal peace of the city was duly recognized. There was an expectation that the medieval drinking/political societies would extinguish any conflagration. Each member of the guild was required to serve in the military, and this requirement the members of the guilds shared with the other burgesses. Their contribution to the maintenance of civil order by means of their policing function was fulfilled in general through the professional obligations of service. The guild system formed a corporate body like the village or town communities. In fact, this concerns a structuration of corporations, which had determined the internal and external life of the town. The exclusions, like the prohibitory system, the abolition of free competition or the limitation of it by the guilds, were criticized by several authors in the 19th and 20th century. The journeymen were repressed and exploited, the guild system as a whole was subjected to the town authorities, so that the assault into the sphere of freedom of the individual by the authorities came about.

There are two moments involved in this critique, one negative and another positive. The limitation of freedom, the regimentation of free competition and of free trade and the incursions into the freedom of the individual are to be judged negatively in the guild system and in civil (bourgeois) life from the standpoint of later epochs. There are objective proofs for the repression and exploitation of the fraternities and the association of apprentices. Yet the repression is relative, since the unfree peasants were desirous of the formal freedoms in the towns. The objective moment of the guild and apprentice organization served as a symbol and was taken over and given expression by other estates. The main theoreticians and ideologues of capitalism in the 18th and 19th century strove after free trade and free competition. The freedom of the working class in the capitalist system was positively valued and subjectively, ideologically, formally and objectively expressed. The formal freedom for the peasants, workers and tradesmen is linked to the improved conditions of labour and to rising profits. In the same way there was a connection between the freedom of the labourers and that of the capitalist entrepreneur. The freedom and equality of both sides in the negotiations and contracts over wages and the conditions of labour are dependent on one another. Under these conditions it concerns the expansion of formal freedom and equality in civil (bourgeois) society. The interest of the constitution of the guild was not related to the increase of revenue or of profit. In this sense it was not established capitalistically. The main emphasis of this guild constitution lay on the employment of the members of the guild, on the safeguarding of the estate and of the town, on the maintenance of the family enterprise and of the social welfare and the care of widows and orphans upon the death of the master, that is of the head of the family. The state dominated and regulated the journeymen organizations through the guild system. Guild, council and state oversaw the quality of the respective products and the fulfilment of agreements.

The number of guilds is not the main issue here. They can increase or decrease as a result of coincidence or external events of the estates-based life in the town. In fact, the number of independent trades in Frankfurt am Main decreased from 1554 in the year 1387 to 1207 in the year 1440. The guild organization of the town was able to continue, nevertheless. The same process of rise or fall in the numbers can also be tracked in the 16th and 17th century in Frankfurt, Cologne, Augsburg, Vienna and in smaller towns like Heidelberg.[54]

The Church took up these practices and efforts in the Middle Ages in the abstract idea of the just price. The just price did not exist, but rather expressed the wish for stable maintenance of prices, that is the wish for security in economic life. The guilds established and represented a constitution, which was concerned with the same security. The organizations of apprentices in part gave expression to the class struggle, in part they exerted themselves for the same goals as that of the Church and the guilds; guilds and journeymen organizations were regulated by the Church, the councils and the state. The constitution of the guild was criticized. Guild operations had little to do with rising profit, as little as with the rationalization of the labour process, which developed in the period of high capitalism. To be sure, these capitalist tendencies were also present already in the time of Fugger and Agricola, yet the guild system fought against them. The Romantic School in the 19th century expressed their disdain of the guild system in poetry through their inner connection to high capitalist ideology. Alongside of this, poetry praised just as much the old creations of handiwork and despised the mass products of the capitalist factories.

The regulation of the guild system by the council points to its historical development. In the 15th and 16th century the council enacted the guild system in Central Europe. The membership, the leadership of the guild, the length of labour time, wages, the recognition and withdrawal of the same from the guilds and associations, the number of enterprises and the number of apprentices and journeymen in an enterprise, the extension of the precincts, the prohibitory system, the quality and even the quantity of the products of the guilds were so regulated. In the second half of the 17th century—in connection with the rise of the absolutist state—the authorities repeatedly took over the regulation of the guilds. The King of Saxony was *eo ipso* a member of the guild system. In Braunschweig the head of state enacted the constitution of the offices and of the guilds [*Gilden*]. In Brandenburg, the Grand Elector Friedrich Wilhelm had initially decided to cancel the guild system, and after that, to maintain it, yet with a changed constitution. Morning assemblies and the jurisdiction of the guilds and associations were limited, the economic customs and misuses, like price fixing, falsification of material and not carrying out of orders, were dominated by royal decree, punished or threatened with fines.[55] Whether the new regimen of the guild in fact changed something concretely is an open question. However, the new enactments of the guilds reveal a strengthening of state power and the immediate regulation of economic life through the instances mentioned above. The new governance of the guild reveals a centralization of state power in the second half of the 17th and over the course of the 18th century, which was bound up with the formation of the national state in Germany and in Central Europe.

The guilds [*Zünfte*] and *Gilden*, the associations of journeymen and the communal organizations, were, as we have seen, corporate bodies. They survived the admission, the participation and the withdrawal of individual members of the corporation. The guild was responsible for the behaviour of the individual guild member and for the membership as a whole: hence in Braunschweig, for example, for the relationship to the council and to the state. The guild had an internal governance which was administered through the general regulation of the council. The guild system was a richly structured organism of handcraftsmanship, and it had maintained the customs of the old communes. Some of them, such as the goldsmiths of Frankfurt am Main, referred to themselves as a brotherhood or fraternity (fraternitas, confratria). This guild constitution continued in a weakened form into the 19th century, and the weakening in comparison to the high point in the development of the guild which had been attained in the 14th/15th century, is related to the number of guilds, the number of members and the juridical compulsion of the guild, which dominated the labour process in the 15th century.[56] The further development of capitalism through the expanded liberation of wage labour, of commerce, of the market and of manufacture, was directed against the guild system of the past. The dispute over free trade with the state system belongs to this past as well.

Through the councils, patricians and the wealthy families controlled town life in Central Europe in the period from the 15th to the 17th century; the Grand Electors dominated the empire, the towns and the guilds through the Reichstag. The Catholic Church which had a powerful hand in this period prior to the Reformation, was weakened by Lutheranism and Calvinism. When the secular dynasties had lost and squandered their money through war, the early capitalist families were ruined. The following period is that of mercantilism-cameralism.[57] The men of state had discovered how the merchants could serve state politics; it was not the main intention of the state to increase private capital. The capitalists were powerful enough in the 19th century, to take the state into their service; in the previous period they were not.

The generation of commodities in the 15th and 16th century was mainly carried out in small enterprises. The producing units in the town were above all the workshops for metal processing as well as for the production of cloth, leather goods, foodstuffs, means of construction and of transportation. Domestic labour was plied in a smaller unit of production than that of the workshop. The number of trades, apprentices and masters, who worked together in the workshop, was delimited by the limited accumulation of capital, by traditional practices and through the legislation of the council and of the guilds. As we have seen, the council had determined the magnitude of the enterprise—that is, how many labourers may work in the single enterprise—according to each trade in the town. Their determinations, through the edicts and decisions, had an effect not only on the quantitative size and productive extent of the enterprise, but also on the accumulation of capital, the use of the means of production and on the structuration and division of labour in the process of production and distribution.

Professions in the guild system were passed from father to son. In the year 1387 114 trades were counted in Frankfurt am Main with a total of 350 trade plying masters, 47 sons of masters and 9 servants. The son could be the biological son, or a person recognized as a fictive son by the guild and council. In the year 1440 the number of independent gainfully employed Frankfurt masters reached 1,498, that of the masters' sons 77 and that of the servants 38. In spite of striving for social stability, the number of professions did not remain unchanged. There were in Frankfurt in 1384 148 types of occupations, in the year 1440 the number increased to 191. The numbers are valid for the following branches of the trades: metal processing, heating and lighting fuel, textile and leather trades, wood and horn processing trades, trades involved in preparing foodstuffs, trades of clothing, cleaning and construction.[58] The number of masters' sons and servants rose in the 15th century, and so the guild system was strengthened.

In 1588 in Heidelberg there were 139 men, 27 servants, 130 women and 28 maids in primary production (vintners, fishers, millers, construction workers, gardeners); in the trades (metalwork, textile trades, leather and hemp trades, wood processing, food processing, clothing and construction trades) there were 450 men, 334 servants, 412 women and 172 maids.[59] The workshops were exceedingly small, as small as were the towns at that time in comparison to the cities in the epoch of high capitalism. In comparison to the workshops and ergasteries in Athens and classical Rome as well, in which 30 or 100 or even 500 slaves worked together, the town enterprises in Central Europe were small; the number of those employed in foundations and cloisters in the period from the 15th to the 17th century was varied. This not only had to do with the number working together in the enterprises but, above all with the structure of labour, with the qualification of the labourers, their technical prowess, their wages, the total capital, the workshop including their heating and lighting, the creation and outfitting of the enterprise as well as the instruments of labour and other means of production of the same. In comparison to the workshops and ergasteries of antiquity, the workshops of the early-modern period could produce more with a smaller workforce. The productivity and the structuration of labour rose, the rationalization in the labour process, technology, planning, the market economy and capital did as well. These indications of progress are especially noticeable in mining; Agricola, Biringuccio among others, as we shall see, made telling observations in relation to it.

Schoenlank described the opposition between the poorer and wealthier handicraft masters of Nuremberg in the 16th century. The poor masters sought work in the home to earn their daily bread, but that was prohibited by the council. The ring makers of Nuremberg, a branch of brass smithing, who finished brass rings for curtains, horse bridles, and the like, were prohibited by the council, from working for another Nuremberg master. Lodging with another master was also forbidden. Impoverished masters were forbidden with a penalty of five pounds of new hellers, to work in place of a journeyman. The declassé masters were no small obstacle in the way of industrialization of the town and for the development of the movement of journeymen. On the other hand, the Nuremberg merchants advanced the development of house industries, and the rich masters fought against the small ones. The council tried to prevent the masters of means from employing the poorer masters in cottage industries. In this way, the council could itself determine and limit productivity in the process of production. Hence, on March 4, 1542, the council ordered that among the smiths producing augurs, gimlets, piercers or borers, no master shall give any kind of employment of completing or carrying out labour to another of his fellow masters under penalty of two pounds new heller.[60]

There was no separation of creation and sale of the product envisaged in the guild system. Those who produced sold their product as a commodity in their stores. This can be graphically seen in the different town guilds in the *Ständebuch* from Hans Sachs and Jost Ammon; the handcraftsman working in his workshop, which also served as his commodity store, together with his wife or his journeymen and apprentices (see the drawings from the *Ständebuch*).[61]

The bitter struggle of the guild in England, the Netherlands, France and Germany against the introduction of new tools and methods of labour continued over the course of the 16th and 17th century. As mentioned, the inventor of the stocking frame had to flee England. Similar stories are known from the Netherlands and France. The struggle for the guilds was temporarily successful and as a consequence led to the prohibition on the employment of newer tools and the organization of labour bound up with it.[62] The guild system engaged in sharp opposition to the rationalization and the increase of productivity in the labour process (see above).

The miners' association [*Knappschaft*] was in its origins an independent association of labourers, who had much in common with the other guilds. In the 15th and 16th century the miners' guilds, the metallurgists (*Hüttenwerker*) and smelters (*Schmelzer*) were organized into fraternities, distinct from one another. In Saxony the territorial prince was integrated pro forma into the professional association; the mining administration kept the miners' association under its control.[63]

The workshops in Nuremberg around 1300 tried to keep the economy within specific limits by means of the law. It was thus so ordered in that period: "No master, or no workshop shall transfer to smiths other than his own workshop with the three servants and the *Bolzenreicher* [Person who hands over bolts to the carpenter. Found only in Sombart *Der Geist des Kapitalismus*]. No one shall lend or give money for it; neither shall one take money for it from townsfolk or from strangers. Whosoever violates these rules must pay a fine of one of four hellers [*den vierten Heller*]."[64]

The guild organization in its provenance appeared in history as the result of the structuration of working life, of the separation of town and countryside, as well as the spheres of production strictly separated and closed off from one another. This result was formed by the pressure of the guild, with the limitations of production, with the exclusion of free competition, with self-administration, exclusive jurisdiction, and the freedom of the trades.[65]

The laws of the guild organization were identified with the actual practice of the same, which in a later era appears to be inexact and exaggerated. Some masters and journeymen belonged to several organizations. The organization of enterprises differed from one town to another. The guild organizations of the enterprises were not the same in all cases. In Frankfurt am Main some enterprises ceased to exist between the 14th and 15th century; the creation of necessary commodities for daily use was replaced by other enterprises: pan smith [*Pfannenschmied*] which appears on the list of trades from 1387, is not represented in the list from 1440. In 1552 the number of masters in Frankfurt amounted to 777, the number without guilds were 228,[66] 77.3% guild masters, and 22.7% without guilds.

Through the domestic transformations of the labour process in Central Europe the guild organization was changed. In part they could adapt to the new systems of production and enterprise, in part not. To the new processes of the 17th century and thereafter the old modes of labour had to yield. W. Stieda emphasized the general and internal conditions. Manufacture and the organization of the factory to a large extent replaced the workshop and practices of cottage labour. Free movement expanded among broad strata of agricultural labour. Schoenlank added an external factor:[67] The Thirty Years' War destroyed the power position of Nuremberg; general economic decline led to the fall of handicrafts. Nuremberg did not stand alone in Central Europe.

The view that the Middle Ages was a period of civil peace and the class struggles began in the modern era, is frequently propagated. These conceptions were already expressed by Janssen and Pareto. O. Johannsen shares this opinion when he auspiciously writes: "the old patriarchal relation among masters and their people disappeared in the first epochs of the modern period. The first signs of the class struggles made their existence known."[68] B. Schoenlank and G. Schanz voiced something similar regarding medieval manual labour: "So long as the relation of servitude and authority in which the labourers found themselves was only a time limited transition and point of access to independence of the masters, the condition of the patriarchal character remained in effect."[69] Endres pointed to another, perhaps unknown fact at that time. Class struggles showed themselves already in the Middle Ages: an uprising of Nuremberg craftsmen took place in 1348/49 and again in 1355 as has already been discussed. Since then the craftsmen were strictly subordinated to the patrician council.[70] We don't limit ourselves to these single cases. We mentioned above the dispute between O. Brunner on the one hand, Reininghaus and Elkar on the other, concerning the meaning of the concept "the entire house." The class struggle does not begin with modernity; it was spread over the class relations of the Middle Ages as well as of modern civil (bourgeois) society. This is not about isolated facts, also not about a matter of style. Recent research shows itself to be more sensitive in relation to the fate of the poor, of the suppressed and exploited and in relation to their class interests, expressions and struggles. We have already noted a comparative treatment of the history of the peasant wars by G. Franz.

The private sphere in the social life of Central Europe in the period of transition to modernity has shown itself as active and stronger in practice in comparison to the Middle Ages; this is related both to the parts as well as to the whole. The peasants and labourers in the countryside, the town proletariat and the capitalist entrepreneurs express their opposing interests; the dispute between the private estates on the one hand and the public sphere of the state together with the nobility and the Church on the other was sharpened in France;[71] in Germany, however, this was not or not so much the case .... An accord between the middle class and the autocracy was introduced in England, the Netherlands and Germany in the 17th and 18th century; the agreement was not signed, yet the two classes could live together.

The relations of production and the system of distribution, exchange and circulation of money took devious paths and have—according to later opinions—even taken false steps. Detours were the guild system, the organization of the Hansa, the so-called *Fuggerei* and the system of putting out, whose old forms were revolutionized during the 17th century. The research of von Kriegk, Schoenlank, Stieda and Kulischer, Endres and Reininghaus have shown that the guild master and the council inhibited the organizations of journeymen in the 15th and 16th century. As a result, the latter lost their initiative. Manufacture and the mechanization of the factory system transformed the world of high capitalism. In general terms, wage labour, credit, commodity and market processes advanced from the late Middle Ages into the beginning of modernity. Thus, we observe discontinuities in the process of elaboration and continuities which continue forward through the interruptions.

Kulischer in his influential work put together the system of putting out with cottage industry, the class of small masters and home labour and all forms tied to the guild system.[72] The putting-out system came to Central Europe from the region of the Mediterranean and from Northwestern Europe in the late Middle Ages. It was really not a unified system. The enterpriser of the putting out workshop [*Verleger*] was a trader or merchant, who advanced money to the craftsman. The advance was in some cases an occasional matter, in others it occurred on a regular basis. The merchants were sometimes united with the craftsmen in the same guild, but under other circumstances they were not. The putting-out system was important for the production of fustian and the creation of linen in Central Europe. No new forms of the system of commercial enterprise were established, but new marketing negotiations were carried out, whereby the old enterprises founded on handwork remained unchanged.[73] The renewal initiative arose on the side of the entrepreneurs, who sought profit, and not on the side of the craftsmen.

The putting-out system was expanded after the development of the printing industry with regard to the production of books, brochures, proclamations, leaflets, advertisements, calendars and toys. The enterpriser in this putting-out system had advanced the printer a sum of money in this case. The Frankfurt printer Georg Raben printed the work *Die eigentliche Beschreibung aller Stände* 1568 for the publisher Sigmund Feyerabend. The collaboration of the poet Hans Sachs and of the best-selling illustrator Jost Amman was arranged by the enterpriser. The same publisher had also in the year 1568 published in conjunction with the printer G. Corvin the edition of the work in the Latin language with the title: Πανοπλια omnium illiberalium mechanicarum aut sedenterarium atrium genera (Overview of all illiberal, mechanical or settled arts).

The Πανοπλια contains roughly the same images by Jost Amman as the *Ständebuch*. The text was composed by Hartmann Schapper. In 1574 the same Frankfurt publisher had a new edition of the book printed by a third printer under the title: *De Omnibus Illiberalibus sive Mechanicis Artibus* with the same text and the same wood cuts.[74] Feyerabend's publishing activity is related to contracts with three printers, two authors and the one artist. The publisher also wrote a preface in which he celebrated the printing enterprise of Hans Kuttenbergers (Johann Gutenberg) from Mainz.

The typesetters conducted a workshop separated from that of book printing. In the *Ständebuch* he worked alone, "poured the writing at the printers / made from bismuth, tin and lead." Thus, he could work by contract for several book printers. The book printer organized the letters; two journeymen in one workshop set them together and made words from them; the master worked with the press, his servant jerked the cudgel, and in this way printed a sheet of paper. "Thereby some of the arts came to the light of day. The art of book printing was first plied at Mainz. The bookbinder binds all kinds of books in parchment or boards. He mounts it with a good enclosure and buckles and stamps it for decoration. Some are embossed with gold letters for he makes much money with it."[75] (See images)

The publisher had expended the money for the book and received a profit from the enterprise. Feyerabend had taken over the developed Gothic type from the Augsburger, Johann Schönsperger, and from the Nurembergers, Johann Neudörffer and Hieronymous Andreae. He had begun as a type founder and a book adorner in Augsburg and in Mainz, then travelled to Venice, returned to Frankfurt and founded his publishing house in 1560. He had established ties not only with Jost Amman, but also with V. Solis among others, who prepared the wood blocks and book images for his books. Their role in the spreading of the arts and of the sciences was known to the book industrialist.[76]

Calendars, books, toys, indulgences in the realm of the Church and printing in the commercial world were the creations of book publishing. Each copy in the same edition is like all the others. The reliability of the copies was assured in this case, which was important for contracts. Both sides could be assured, that the spelling and misspelling are the same and that the mistakes of copiers could normally be eliminated.

The virtues of the high capitalist process of production are already present in the early book enterprises. Control over the quality of the identical published copies, of the time saving through the speed of dissemination of copies and the mechanization of the industrial process are the early achievements of the book and print publishers. The dissemination therewith of writing, the development of the public system of education and the modernization of the process of information are bound up with the print shops and with the system of book publishing.

The putting-out system was not plied in a uniform but rather in a differentiated fashion, according to the branch of industry. The ways and means of how the process of labour was structured, constituted the great contradiction between the putting-out system in the print shop and in the production of needles. In the latter there were several products created as commodities and sold by independent craftsmen, in the former, only one commodity was sold by the putting out enterpriser, who controlled the entire distribution process.

The poet sold his poetry, the form cutter his wood cuts, the printer his books, to the publisher. Poems, wood cuts and books are commodities, which are not distributed in the process of production, but rather are bought and sold. The book is supplied in the publishing house and is demanded by the buyers. The printer has purchased the paper, the ink, the letters and the book bindings as commodities from their producers. The type founder purchased metal, bismuth, tin and lead for the letter foundry from the smelter; he has refined the metal in his furnace and ordered the letters. Inside the book printer's workshop, the ink, paper and letters are not sold but distributed; they are not commodities in the process of distribution but rather parts of the process of production.

The iron wire is sold to the merchant-entrepreneur issuer of needles; in this case the wire is a commodity. However, the issuer distributes the sharpened filament; the domestic labourer receives it from the issuer not as a commodity, but rather as means of production in the process of refinement. The pledge of the sharpened filament is a transitional form in trade. The domestic worker is dependent on the issuer and cannot move freely; he receives the material for finishing, and it is pledged against a sum of money. The issuer is the only one who plies this trade with the iron wire as an advance against the pledge. The craftsmen have only one trader to whom the product is sold or supplied and one single supplier of iron wire. The iron wire in the production of needles is not a commodity under these conditions; only the final products are commodities.

The historical relation between the workshop labour and domestic labour was explained by G. Schanz using the example of the Swabian needle industry.[77] The expansion of sales led to the domestic industry. For now the pin and sewing needles could no longer be sold at the same location by the artisans. It had to occur to the issuers to whom the needle workers transferred the commodity and who assumed the enterprise of needle-making at his risk. The issuer was the one who completed the needle-making. The half-completed needles were supplied to him and the last processes of hardening, of activation and release, of polishing, of sorting and packing of the needles fell to him. The masters in the end were reduced to purely domestic labour. They received from the issuer the sharpened wire for refinement.[78] In one variant of the same system the issuer offered the artisan for his use money, material or both as security against the pledge. The craftsmen maintained the tools in the production process as their property; the merchants had offered money in advance of the products and in all cases only they sold the products.

The putting-out system is based on the trade, commodity, market and money relations of the late Middle Ages. The possibilities for its expansion were partially actualized. The guild system, on the contrary, with its lower level of productive forces in the period of high capitalism and monopoly set itself in opposition to the development of these productive forces.

The guild system in the Middle Ages became a system of structuration of labour in the creation of cloth in the towns, in the processing of metal, glass, leather and wood as well as in trade with their products. In the first centuries of the modern period the guild organization of the town enterprises were continued and increased. This increase and the specialization in the labour process of the guild and guild organizations which arose along with it reinforced the demarcation between the different guilds, prevented their working together, led to the elimination of outsiders in the same branch of enterprise and supported monopolistic and privileged tendencies in production and in trade.[79]

The issuers in Straßburg introduced the so-called truck system. That was the practice of the issuer to recompense their workers for a portion of their past labour through the promise of new work.[80] This practice signified a possibility for increased profit for the merchants; for the workers it meant lower wages. The putting-out system, which could avoid this conduct, was continued in the printing industry.

The guild and putting-out system had developed comparative customs and practices. They did not form a unified system, yet they were shaped by practices of resistance to the expansion of the capitalist system. They tried to regulate profit, the accumulation of capital, the structuring of labour, the magnitude of enterprise and technical innovations and whenever possible, to contain them, at first with success; but in the end their world disappeared. The guilds and putting-out workshops [*Verlage*] in the 15th and 16th century reacted defensively to the achievements of the modern period in the organization, structuration and division of labour and in the training of the labourer, to the introduction of new technology and in the accumulation of capital. The activities of the guild and the putting-out system were often condemned from the standpoint of the period of high capitalism and convenient quotes from the contemporary sources were sought out in order to awaken among today's readers the impression of the narrow-mindedness of the past guilds and merchant entrepreneurs in the putting-out system [*Verleger*].

Some guilds in Central Europe continued into the 19th century. In the 17th century the authorities were undecided whether they should repress the guild system or tolerate its continuing existence. In Brandenburg, Braunschweig and in other parts of Germany the officials discovered, that they could control the workers' movement to a certain extent through the guild organizations which on their part kept the journeymen, masters and apprentices under control.

The medieval guilds [*Gilden*] had various tasks: the structuration and division of the social labour of production and distribution of commodities; the enforcement and maintenance of the monopoly of exchange and market processes; the securing of civil peace; and the undertaking of the welfare of its membership. These tasks are bound up with a determinate social condition of the past. Thus, the guild system was negatively assessed with the rationale that it prevented progress in the process of production. Other social organs assumed the securing of the peace of the towns and so on. The social practice in the period of high capitalism can also be negatively judged. The ideologues and representatives of this period were little concerned with the welfare and social assistance of the poor; their main interest was the increase in productivity and profit, in the rationalization in manufacturing commodities and the increase in turnover. The views of the old guilds [*Gilden*] and of the council can be positively judged: they saw that the new practices of labour, machines and capital accumulation, would lead to unemployment, child labour and the immiseration of the population. On the contrary, the bad practice of the monopoly of trade, which was developed in the old guild system, continued in contemporary trade practices. The condemnation of the guild system, which was practiced in the 19th century, appears to be a one-sided type of treatment of its historical process. Currently there is an effort to assess the tasks of the guilds in a more balanced fashion.

3.5 Merchants, Trade and Calculating Skills [Rechenkunst]

3.5.1 Arithmetic, Calculating Skills

The merchant class in modern times had a close relationship to the exact calculation of money, to the measure of commodities, such as ore or cloth, to that of time, of space, and of human skilfulness and animal capability, taking cognizance of them and developing them further.

In order to solve the problems of the economy and merchant class, a few advances in arithmetic were made in the period from the 15th to the 17th century. These advances were founded on contacts of the Europeans in the region of the Mediterranean, on contacts with the Near East, especially in Italy, and beyond that to India. At the same time the arithmeticians and geometers opened the entrance to the classical books of Euclid and in part to those of Archimedes. The merchants of this period could do two things: to reckon with the abacus on lines with pennies as well as with the system of numeration and multiplication tables. It came to a contest between the two arts of reckoning, which the system of numeration won early in Central Europe. In other countries, such as in Russia, China and Japan, it was reckoned with the reckoning table or the abacus into the 20th century. In 1522 Adam Ries published a book with the title *Rechnung auff der linien und federn in zol, mass und gewicht* [Reckoning on lines and springs in inches, mass and weight]. The corrected edition of the book with the title: *Rechenbuch auff Linien und Ziphern in allerley Handthierung Geschäften und Kauffmannschafft* [Arithmetic book on lines and numbers in various handling businesses [*Handthierung*] and merchandizing] appeared in 1574. A woodcut of an unknown master with the drawing of the arts of arithmetic and of measuring and determining the content of barrels was copied on the title page. Two men are sitting at a table, the one reckoning with numbers and a feather pen, the other on lines with reckoning pennies; a third stands in front of the table and is thinking, perhaps as a referee judging the outcome. On the right in the same illustration are two men occupied with the examination or inspection of barrels to determine their measurements [*Visierung*] (see illustration).[81]

Achievements in the art of reckoning with numbers which originated in Italy were notable. Instruction in the use of numbers in the *Rechenbuch* point to the fact that the number zero reached Central Europe from India through the Arabs and Persians;[82] arithmetic and the significance of numbers and the decimal system were introduced into northern Europe.[83]

The method of Ciriacus Schreittmann is scientific, objective, systematic and palpable. It is not only related to the introduction of the decimal system. Adam

Ries stood in the middle of a development which was useful to the merchant class, and in the title of his book the application of arithmetic in business practices is prefigured. The many objectives of the work composed by Erhart Helm were the calculation of profit, of weight, of the rate of exchange, of the shipping of crucibles of coin templates, of loan-sharking, of engravings, and of the examination and inspection [*Visierung*] of barrels; it appears as an appendix to Adam Ries' book.

In 1470 the Indo-Arabian numerals appeared in Augsburg. Prior to that Roman numerals were written down, but not used for arithmetic. Hence, reckoning tables and reckoning pennies were employed. In 1202 Leonardo Pisano had propagated the number system in his book *Liber abaci,* in which the significance of numbers and zero as a cipher was expressed. Johann Widmann published the book *Rechnung auff allen Kauffmanschafft* [Arithmetic for all Mercantile Communities], in which the plus and minus signs were represented. The intended readership for his book is indicated in the book's title.

Trade between Venice, Genoa, Pisa and the Near East from Syria to Algeria was developed into a regular phenomenon. This had to do with the exchange of wood, wool, and cloth against silk, spices, jewels. Bookkeeping expanded over Lucca, Siena, Pisa, Florence, Genoa and Venice. In the same cultural-historical context the work of the counting board appeared, written by Leonardo, son of a family from Pisa in the year 1202.[84] Only later were calculations made with numbers and multipliers. With both systems the rate of exchange and of commodity trade with money prices or various coin values could be calculated quickly such as with Florentine, Venetian, Pisan, Frankfurt, Nuremberg, Augsburg or Hanseatic coins, and further with lot, heller, pennies, gulden, schillings, ducats, florins, pieces, blots, kreuzers and albus. In this way the difference, the remainder or percentage could be calculated. The transfer of commodity purchase and sale, the recording of exchange on account, commodity exchange or take was calculable. Quantitative losses in traffic or transport with regard to exchange, that is, fares and impurities of commodities [*tara* and *fusti*] could be ascertained and time as well, turnover or *Sald* und *Tumin* could be calculated. And the calculation of rent and leases, negotiations with various participants in business or corporation, wage and salary calculation and likewise in calculations in chemistry, in mining and in assaying, as well as in the calculation of allocation and alloying could be executed. The creation of feather pens and ink (also derived from calamari, octopus), paper, papers for business and books, things of contemporary office supplies, had undergone a brisk internal development. The Nuremberg calculating table was necessary for the abacus [*Rechenbrett*, *Rechentafel*].

In the 15th century the Italian mathematician and merchant Leonardo of Pisa (Pisano, aka Fibonacci) brought out a simplified system of signs and calculation that was spread widely across Europe. The links between the merchant class and mathematical science were close-knit and deep, in accordance with the traffic between Central Europe and the Mediterranean. At first the direction of development of the two fields of trade went from south to the north. Regiomontan studied Greek mathematical science with Cardinal Bessarian in Rome and he published his Greek texts in Nuremberg from 1474. Pacioli defined exchange as follows: Exchange is nothing other than replacing [*stechen*] (commutare) one commodity with another with the idea of improving one's condition.

Michael Stifel (Stiefel), Apian (Bennewitz or Bienewitz), Christoph Rudolff, Heinrich Schriber (Grammateus), Adam Ries and Wolfgang Schwieker published books concering merchant matters and the art of arithmetic/calculation [*Rechenkunstbücher*]. Grammateus composed the work *Buchhalter durch Zornalkaps und Schuldtbuch auff alle Kaufmannschafft, ayn new kunstlich buech welches gar gewiss und behend lernet (…) notürfftig Rechnung auff Kaufmanschafft …*, Nuremberg, (s.d.), Vorrede Wien 1578. Wolfgang Schweicker composed *Zwifach Buchhalter sampt seine Giornal desselben Beschlus auch Rechnung zuthun* 1549.[85]

Out of economic and scientific intercourse double-entry bookkeeping arose and was made available. Those like Werner Sombart who have designated double-entry bookkeeping as the foundation of the capitalist era, had a narrow viewpoint, overlooking in general the extensive intercourse and the system of merchant practices (arithmetic, measurement of barrels, exchange of commodities) with geometry and mathematics. Central Europe had developed a connection with Italy, as the Store House or Establishment of the Germans (Fondaco dei Tedeschi) in Venice shows. The Italians had their link to the merchant practices and the artists and scientists of the Near East. The Arabs on their part, had intercourse with the Persians and Indians. There was no hard and fast line of distinction drawn between merchant affairs, arithmetic and mathematics. Arithmetic was in this sense not run in a guild-like fashion. Teachers, scribes, mathematicians and merchants had retrieved their common endeavour from antiquity as well as from the contemporary Mediterranean region in the 15th and 16th century, further from Asia, hence ex oriente lux. Jakob Köbel, the town scribe of Oppenheym, had composed *Das new Rechenpüchlein wie mann uff den Linien und Spacien mit Rechenpfenningen Kaufmannschafft und tegliche Handelungen leichtlich rechen lernen mag* 1518 (corrected for the third time and printed in Oppenheym). The same scribe published in 1535 a *Geometrie, von künstlichem Messen und Absehen allerhand Höhe, Fleche, Ebene, Weite und Breyte, als Thürn, Kirchen, Baw, Baum, Velder, und Äcker (…) mit künstlich Jacob Stab*[86]*, philosophischen Spiegel, Schatten und Messruten.*

The lines, spaces and reckoning pennies point to the preparations and practices with the abacus. Köbel at this juncture had not yet introduced the numeral system.

In later proceedings he brought out a book of arithmetic with lines and numbers in 1544, in which he gave instruction in the measurement of barrels [*Visierung*], the weight of coinage, the measure in ells of all mercantile commodities. It is thus to be inferred that the new art of arithmetic with numerals was extended. Adam Ries, as we have already seen, broadened the calculation with numbers of Indo-Arabian provenance in 1522. In his book he had taught lines (abacus) and numerals, or the art of numeration. In 1526 Christoph Rudolff published his *Kunstliche Rechnung mit der Ziffer und mit den Zahlpfennigen* in Vienna.[87] Books of arithmetic were prepared for girls as well as for boys.

More influential were the works on the *coss* or unknown variables by Christoph Rudolff, Michael Stifel and Adam Ries. The word *coss* is of Italian provenance (*coso*) and was in this sense applied to algebra. It was especially related to calculation with unknowns. Cosa, *thing*, as a concept comes from the Arabic sai, *thing*. Adam Ries published a book, *Die Coss* in 1524. In 1494 Luca Pacioli had written about the *cosa* or unknown in his *Summa de Arithmetica.*; today it is designated with an "x". Calculation with the abacus harkens back to the Italian masters of the abacus, of which the most talented was Leonardo of Pisa. Calculations in general with the abacus as with the (Indo-Arabian) numerals, were called by some people Venetian arithmetic; "die brauchen die Kaufleut zu mal gern" [the merchants need this only too gladly], as it reads in a written document from Munich in 1480. The mediators of arithmetic from antiquity and from Asia were the Arabs and Jews in the 12th, 13th, and 14th century.[88]

A number of words in the German world of the German merchant class and the commercial practices of the early-modern period are traced back to the Italian language. *Agio, Bilanz, Brutto, Debit(o), Diskant, Giro, Kasse, kassieren, Kassierer, Konto, Kredit, Lombard, Manko, Netto, Numero, Obligo, Posten, Rabatt, Renditen, Rest, Risiko, Saldo, Sporko, Strazze, Syndikat* are borrowings of this sort. Conversely, words such as *Banco* (=bank) are borrowed from German vocabulary by the Italian and return to the German from there. That *Risiko* and *Syndikat* furthermore are traced back to the Greek is also known. Words such as *Depositär, Kommanditär, Indossament, Protest, Rimesse, Traitta, skontieren, Komturei, Faktor, Faktorei*, have their connection to Italian commercial usage and vocabulary. The florin survives in the coin symbol FL, fl., mediately from Florence.[89]

Words like *Kosten, Pfennig, Preis* and *Sold*, which originate immediately from the Latin or from vulgar Latin of the Middle Ages have another history. The etymology of *Risiko* is contested. The word is borrowed from the Greek, but it is related to modern Greek and has the meaning here of foot of a mountain or cliff. This is a source of danger for the mariner, but this connection is a supposition.

Risk can also be traced back to *rhizo* in classical Greek, the root of an herb. Rebate supposedly stands in a metathetic relation to baratto, cheap, well-priced. Two etymologies are suggested for penny [*Pfennig*]. The one leads back to the Latin *pannus*, piece, cloth, rag, with the justification that cloth served as units of money in antiquity. The other leads back to Latin *pandus*, weight, that which is weighed, gold coinage. Collateral [*Pfand*] and pound are linked to both etymologies. Reckoning pennies appear to be more closely linked with weight than with cloth. Further derivations of these roots in today's linguistic usage are post, position, pendulum and suspend.

"Reckoning board" is the translation of the Italian *abaco*, *abacus* in Latin, which is traced back to *abaq*, Hebrew אבק: dust, אבקה powder. The board was originally covered with powder upon which the numbers were drawn.[90] Archimedes composed a book *Psammites* (Sand Calculator). His famous portrait shows the mathematician in front of his reckoning board.

The accomplishments of Fibonacci, Pacioli, Meister Dardi of Pisa, Cardano, G. Peurbach and Regiomontan made possible the transition to the algebra of L. Euler, C.F. Gauss and E. Galois. Together these people of the early-modern period built the foundation for the merchant class, commodity exchange or *Stich* in the domestic market and in world trade of the capitalist era. Adam Ries, Chr. Rudolff, M. Stifel, Apianus, Stevin, Widmann and Köbel contributed to this foundation in Central Europe.

Risk in business, in merchandising and in the enterprise was assumed; one expected it and it was calculated. Risk was connected with the investment of money and capital. One advanced and risked capital for possible profit, or went bankrupt, bust, for the greater the risk, the greater the profit or loss. In opposition to this thought and the hope and anxiety associated with it, stood the practice and theory of the medieval *iustum pretium*, of the just price[91], along with which the risk of trade and the exchange of commodities was supposed to be lessened or overcome. The lessening or overcoming of the risk *im Stich* [precarious] was considered in relation to the just price from the standpoint of the Church. Whether commerce was carried on that way in fact remains an open question, which is left to the medievalists. Risk was at that time considerable in another relation. The cooperatives [*Genossenschaften*] in the Middle Ages and in the modern era were partly composed of traders. They were in fact adventurers, who had risked their goods on long trips. They had conducted distant trade with locally produced commodities, like amber, metals, leather, herring or cloth with the East, the region of the Mediterranean and Scandinavia, England and Russia.

The worldview of merchants and traders was shaped through their Italian relationships not only by word, but also through practices like bookkeeping. Matthäus

Schwarz represented the Fugger interests in Venice in the early 16th century. Thus, he mastered bookkeeping and regarding balance wrote: "The debt book is compared to a scale, that the Italians call bilanza." The balance [in bookkeeping] according to his practice looks like the mechanical instrument [to measure weight]. We shall return to the mechanization of worldview in the early-modern era.[92] The Pagament or copper-bearing silver did not come from Italy, only the word for it did; a word that also signifies coinage silver, since this material contains copper among other elements.[93] It is to be assumed that *kaputt* refers back to *caput*, the front part of a ship, and has a word history which is mediately tied up with risk, cliff or the foot of a mountain. (see above).[94]

3.5.2 Merchants and Trade

We have considered the relationship between the new arithmetic and the merchant world. In several studies by Ehrenberg, Strieder, von Below, Brentano, Max Weber, Sombart and also in the overview of the theories by Schumpeter, the main emphasis of the historical dynamic in the transitional process from the feudal to the modern bourgeois period was put upon the practices of the class of entrepreneurs, of mercantile capitalism and of the merchant class. Marx, on the other hand, emphasized the role of the physical movement of peasants in this transitional process. The movement of peasants from the countryside into the town and later back again to the countryside, the liberation movement of the peasants, the associations of journeymen and the miners' associations point to their historical dynamic in the transformation of feudal society and in the formation of the new. We have pointed to the contribution of the liberation movement of the peasants to the transformation of the old society in outline and directed attention to the struggles and uprisings of the associations of journeymen. The two movements each deserve a special study for themselves in understanding the upheaval of the feudal and the construction of the capitalist society. The period of transition from the 15th to the 17th century only appeared as such considered from the standpoint of the later, especially of contemporary society. People of the early-modern era like Fugger, Dürer or Luther had not considered themselves as premature or transitional people. They were not a road, a way or a means, and they did not understand themselves as such.

The new society had formed an economic and social system. From the standpoint of later epochs, it would seem that the earlier bears in itself some characteristic features of the feudal and some of the following capitalist period.

Some characteristic features like the guild system in the legal sense, corvée and forced collective labour ceased to exist. Some types of enterprise like the Hansa and the Patrician or family council in the town disappeared or were transformed. The main problem of this section of our study is the role of the entrepreneurs; we consider them as an aspect of the then contemporary society and economic system and assess their role in the transition to modern bourgeois society.

The business venture appears in the Middle Ages in connection with pilgrimage, in modern times with the investment of capital; in the 17th century the enterprise of the *Pegnitzschäferei* [literally of Pegnitz sheep tending – a reference to a group in Nuremberg organized to monitor German language usage–trans.] was mentioned.[95]

Tied to the business enterprise were: the economic processes of the circulation of money, of wage labour in the factory, the commodity as an outcome of commercial trips and of production by wage labour in the factory, and further, the exchange of commodities in the market, the advance of money to meet the demands of enterprise, wages and land rent, and of credit and debts. Risk, profit and the price of commodities stood in the foreground of the business venture, as we can learn from the words of Martin Luther, Adam Ries and William Shakespeare. The calculation of profit is linked with that of loss or the annulment of both. The arts of writing and arithmetic are so employed that they led to reportage. Writers and calculators are essential components of business enterprises, whether in the person or in the function of the entrepreneur or the enterprise. The new system of education, the art of writing and book printing are the results of these processes in modern times. We have seen that the calculation of credit and debts interconnects with the art of arithmetic and with the rise of bookkeeping out of it.

Perhaps equally important, if not more so, is the concept of the company [*Gesellschaft*] and connected with it that of the associate or partner, shareholder, member of a partnership. These are legal persons in an enterprise who are participants in the ventures. They are possessors of money who risk their credit in an enterprise mediated by contract. The juridical persons of both kinds, the individuals and the corporations, constitute the list of associates.

If we broaden the field of activity across the political and philosophical sciences, we come in this way to the social contract.

In the years 1512 to 1514 the Roman patrician Mario Salamonio composed his theory of the state, *civitas*, and of society, in which he had considered the state as a kind of *societas*; in this sense *societas* is a partnership or company of patricians. The assembly of the partners lies in the basis of a contract, *pactio, pactum*. A society is founded either explicitly or implicitly on the contract.[96] The idea of the social contract can be traced back to the Middle Ages and antiquity. Salamonio and other representatives of this view in modern times linked it with the theory of the contract of business enterprise and venture. The contract in commerce, in limited partnership and other social contracts lay implicitly or explicitly in the foreground of political, juridical and philosophical thought.

Several thinkers in the 16th and 17th century traced their conception of law and the state back to the social contract.

Bourgeois society was conceived by Salamonio, by the opponents of absolute monarchy, like some Calvinists and Huguenots on the continent, as well as by Thomas Hobbes and John Locke, later by J.J. Rousseau and Immanuel Kant, as the result of a contract. Some of these jurists and philosophers distinguished two kinds of contracts in this regard: a contract between persons, who establish a society or wish to do so, and a rule or contract of state. The former is a contract among persons of the same level, that is among equals or persons of the same station. The latter is a contract between unequals; on the one side the subjects, on the other the authority, for it will determine the relation between subordinate and superior.[97]

Society was conceived as the rendering of the Latin *societas* by Salamonio and in part by Luther. The former wrote about the *civilis quaedem societas*, that is bourgeois society, as a kind of state, *civitas*: civil society is founded on contract and without it is inconceivable. Luther spoke about the society *monopolia*, that is the trading and producing society, which monopolizes the market for its commodity. Other societies without contract were not considered. In the 17th century Thomas Hobbes had presented a human condition, in which the people lived without contract. In this condition life is nasty, brutish and short. It is the condition of continuous war of all against all, *bellum omnium contra omnes*. The basic idea that we voluntarily come together as equals is ascertained as the foundation of society in commerce and in civil life. The difference between the two ideas that we voluntarily join and depart in the commercial society, while the membership in the enterprise negotiate as equals, and in civil (bourgeois) society enter as subordinates, stimulated a wide-ranging dispute. That means that at one time we were free and relinquished our freedom. We have lost the right to exit the state like we step out of a coach.[98]

The notion of the *societas*, which derives from Roman law, was erected on that of contract. Contract in Roman private law was conceived of differently than in modern civil law. In antiquity contract was taken up as a binding agreement between parties, but in opposition to contemporary practice only a closed circle of debt contracts was recognized in Roman law.[99]

Pactum (*Pactio*) and *contractus* in Roman law are translated as *Vertrag*, as contract. The slave was not capable of contract. The notions, too, of contractual freedom and stipulated liabilities were prominent in antiquity and modern times. The concept of a *societas* in both cases was founded on a preceding contract. Both ideas of the juridical and of the political-social contract were mentioned only later. The legal contract is the only one recognized today as valid, and it is inextricably bound up with the ideas of liberty and equality. Equality and liberty in the formal sense were related to the entire civil society in modern times—in fact only in the 19th and 20th centuries.

The legal contract appears as one of the most important means of securing and expanding formal freedoms and equalities, which characterize bourgeois society. The system of civil rights of liberty and equality has enjoyed an enthusiastic reception in modern times. Those who have advanced this system became enthusiastic and have extended the legal contract in fantasy to the social contract and the state contract. The legal contract has an objective foundation and function in bourgeois society, its content is actual, although formal. The social contract is the result of a mythopoetic invention, and it has neither a social, political, juridical, nor historical foundation or role. It only appears because people have looked at the legal contract with enthusiasm. Normal citizens are free pro forma, even though norms are variously conceived. There is a system of norms and variabilities within the system of civil society.[100] The contradiction between free trade and the obligation of companies on the one hand and the incremental unfreedom of civil society on the other, led to a series of uprisings and revolutions in England, North America, France, Germany, the Netherlands and elsewhere from the 16th to the 19th century in order to broaden the formal freedoms among the people and to generalize them. A second contradiction lies in the derivation of the concept society [*Gesellschaft*] and journeyman [*Geselle*]. *Societas*, *Sozietäre*, joint-stock owners [*Gesellschafter*] are linked to the idea of equality, while the journeyman was conceived as an original member of an entourage of the house, of the prince and others.[101] The associations of journeymen in the 15th to the 17th century were subordinate to the council in the German towns. The history of the word craft, trade, guild [*Gewerk*], trade union [*Gewerkschaften*] is the opposite. While society [*Gesellschaft*] is generalized, the trade union today is related only to the working part of the whole.[102]

Society or *societas* was related to the juridical relations of civil society. Civil society is a formal idea, identified by some with the state, by others with the system of law. Until the 19th century—and in the justification of the contemporary social sciences—it is targeted as a formal institution and consciously expressed and systematically presented and conceived. It has to do with the celebrated systems of bourgeois society in the entire period from the 15th to the 19th century, of natural law, of the social contract and of the theories of human rights and tyrannicide bound up with them (cf. Molina, Suarez, Victoria; further Salamonio concerning the Huguenot *Monarchomachia*, like Hobbes, Spinoza, Locke, Rousseau and Kant among others have emphasized).

The joint-stock company is conceived of as the model for society as a whole. The former ought to be constituted through the contributions of associates and the like. According to this account it's on target and rational, that is rationally constructed. *Ragione* in Italian in the 14th and 15th century was related to the accounts of business affairs (*lista dei conti*) (*affari*) and to their interests.[103] Normally, the joint-stock company has the purpose of increasing money for the owner of the stock. It is a rational enterprise or can be rationally run, even if the commodities produced are employed irrationally. Human society is neither now (nor in its origin) rational. A future reason in society is not hereby excluded. Human society is the result over thousands of years of traditional relations and actions. The joint-stock company is newly invented and established daily. The notion of a joint-stock company is very old.

The joint-stock company was and is a corporate body; *societas* is in this sense ambiguous. In Roman law state and community [*Gemeinde*] like municipium and colonia, corporations and at the same time associations, collegium, *sodalitas,* sodality in private law.[104] Associations and companies, *societates*, are distinguished by their construction. The means of creating an association is its organization, the subsuming of the members constitutionally under the authority of the association, so that the totality, the corporation becomes free or capable of action and dealing with assets. The means of establishing a society on the other hand are obligation, credit and contract.

In this way the opposition between the legal, transactional and the association capable of action, of the corporation and of pure societies is given. The *societas* of Roman private law is the expression of a contract between legal persons. The partnership [*Sozietät*] is not capable of action or of dealing with assets. The parties in the contract are legally capable. They are bound through mutual obligations to determinate performances in a given period of time in order to reach a common goal. The *societas* is not a legal subject, only the associates are legal subjects. The professional association is likewise not a legal subject, only the associates, *socii*, which have founded a *societas* are such.[105] In one sense society in the social contract is identical to the *societas*, the contract is in this case a contract like others as well. In a further sense the social contract is *toto coelo* different from the other contracts. It is a mythical contract.

The joint-stock company in modern times is a corporate body, a corporation or an association, which, independent of the individual members or stockholders, is legally capable. It is not only the result of a contract, and it is not identical with the contract. It is capable of action and of dealing with assets. The transition from the Roman concept of *societas* to that of the modern bourgeois concept of society depends upon the changed legal condition of the society, its relationship to the process of economy and state as an invention of modernity. Medieval activities in this connection are excluded.

The state, *civitas, res publica*, in Roman antiquity was treated as a corporate body, and this method of treatment, was taken up in the Middle Ages as well as in modern times from different angles and by various representatives. In the ancient as well as in the new systems of law, persons who stand in a formal relation to the state are also considered legally capable of acting. The joint-stock company based on a formal contract, assumes this relationship as a legal person and appears in this relationship as a corporate body in relation to the state.[106]

The question is often posed whether the joint-stock company is an invention of the 16th or 17th century. In Germany, in any case, the word "*Aktien*" [stock] appears in the middle of the 16th century in the sense of instruments payable to bearers.

Such securities were also mentioned in Genoa in the 15th and 16th century. The difference between the practices of the 15th and those of the 17th century appears to be bound up with the speculation in securities in the later period. Everyone is in agreement that the San Giorgio bank in Genoa was a joint-stock company since 1409. The bank came out of a merger of groups of state creditors and was transformed into a stock-owned bank through dividends. The main enterprises which could be called organizations in capitalist form in Central Europe during the 15th and 16th century, are the Welser, Imhof, Tucher, Paumgartner or Fugger in Upper Germany. By the way, the joint-stock companies appear in Styrian and Upper Austrian iron ore trade in the 15th century.[107] The Hansa appears as a transitional form.

The commercial societies and companies in the Middle Ages have a connection to the joint-stock companies of modernity, but they are to be distinguished from them.[108]

The German Hansa founded a league or union, which was active in the common interest. The union was not a state, that is not a federal republic, but it possessed some characteristics of authority. The union membership negotiated independently with the states on the North and Baltic Seas like England, the Scandinavian countries, and so on. Yet the Hansa towns did not form a state like Venice. The city states of Italy entered into the intermediate stages in the history of state authority just like the Hansa towns. They do not lie on the same plane, but rather point to the limits of state power in the hands of the papacy and of the Holy Roman Empire in the 14th to the 17th century. In the late 17th and 18th century absolutism of state power was in the hands of the Grand Elector Friedrich Wilhelm, later taken over by Frederick the Great, Maria Theresa and Joseph II in Central Europe; in Spain, France and England this occurred earlier, and only later in the Italian Risorgimento of the 19th century.

The German Hansa, the guild system, the putting-out system and the family enterprises of the Upper German commercial firms achieved a large turnover and a great level of commercial activity in the first centuries of the modern era; however, they limited their activity or even disappeared altogether in the 17th and 18th century. The causes of their blossoming and their decline are varied. Their development appears as a contingent one. Their history is that of the forms in the capitalist organization of the earlier epochs in modern times, as Jakob Strieder has shown.

The joint-stock company like other companies of this kind are forms of economic enterprises in the capitalist era. Yet there is a further connection between these forms of organization of the modern era and the ideas in Roman antiquity concerning the nature of the corporation in general. On these grounds we have linked the statements of Sohm, Mitteis and Kaser in the development of law. The theory of society in which we live as people, has a formal, external relationship to this earlier idea of society. The reason why the social sciences have chosen the concept of society can be explained historically. The followers of Saint-Simon, the utopian socialists as well as Auguste Comte, John Stuart Mill and Herbert Spencer played a special role in relation to it.

The Hanseatic society was a formal cooperative [*Genossenschaft*], which had been formed by patricians, guild members, guilds [*Gilden*] and offices. It arose in the late Middle Ages, that is roughly in the 12th century, and continued to develop until the 15th to 17th century. It pointed to the strength of domestic and foreign trade of that epoch, of the importation and export of commodities, to the monopolies and the extent of their enterprises. Their linkages over the coastal towns of Lübeck, Hamburg, Bremen, Danzig, Konigsberg, Riga and across the inland towns of Cologne, Dortmund, Lunenburg and Goslar as well as the expansion of their trade to London, Deventer, Visby, Dorpat and Novograd concretely confirm the extent of their reach. The turnover of their trade was correspondingly great for the conditions of the Middle Ages as for that of the early-modern period. They imported and exported cloth, fish, salt, butter, hides and fur, grain, wax, wood, beer, copper, iron, oil, flax, Rhine wine, Westphalian linen and silver. Their trade was plied in all directions over the Baltic and North Seas with great energy. Technically the Hansa society played a part in the transformation of sea travel; they integrated the types of ships from the cog to the hulk and further to the caravel, in part developed and in part appropriated them. The hulk, which had a single mast, remained the most important ship of Hansa trade to the 17th century. The caravel possessed up to three masts and could carry a load of more than 300 tons.[109]

If we compare the load of the Hansa ships with ship loads in the region of the Mediterranean, the following picture emerges:[110]

Table 5: Ship Cargo (on Average), Hansa and Venice, 1300–1700

	Year	Tonnage
Hansa	1300	75 (cog)
	1400	150 (hulk)
	1470	300 (caravel)
Venice	1450	200
	1500	400
	1650	600 to 700

Thus, the ship's cargo was extended step by step in Venice and in the Hansa towns. The economic driver in this development came from the region of the Mediterranean.

The historical development of the cog ship and of the hulk ship was closely connected to the elaboration of trade on the Baltic and North Sea and with the technique in shipbuilding there. The larger caravel arose in the region of the Mediterranean and had a peculiar kind of construction. It was also used for military purposes, but to be sure without great effect.

Many explanations of the decline of the Hansa have been advanced. In part they trace the disappearance of the Hansa in the 17th century back to the external conditions of the Thirty Years' War and the decrease of production, of consumption and demand under these conditions, of the extension to the wars of the English, Spanish, Dutch and Scandinavians; in part internal conditions were made responsible. In their internal organization the Hansa was a system of town cooperatives [*Genossenschaften*], offices and guilds [*Gilden*], determined by the guild system and dominated by the patrician system in the Hansa cities. The difficulties of the guild and patrician systems brought about the decline of the Hansa in the 17th century, as we have seen from our standpoint.

There are further contradictions to be observed in the commercial-technical realm. The Hansa was a cooperative [*Genossenschaft*] in the medieval sense. The inner structure of this cooperative was a loose one, and it is not comparable to the modern bourgeois corporation organization which is strongly internally segmented. The guild system of the early-modern period could not take over the manufacturing process in relation to the structuration and division of labour. In the sense of technical production, the guild system had in many cases offered resistance especially in relation to the introduction of new processes of labour, for example, in the creation of cloth. That led to a further contradiction, since the Hansa art of shipbuilding was progressive, and it mastered the new kinds of construction first of the hulk and then later of the caravels. The cloth and metal processing guilds had continued their traditional production processes in the first centuries of the modern era. On the one hand, the traditional processes of labour had diminished the turnover of commodities because they could not compete with the production of commodities in England and in the Netherlands. On the other hand, an internal rationalization of the labour process did not occur in Central Europe, since some branches of production were operated according to an ancient, others, on the contrary, according to a new kind and mode. The Hansa in Central Europe had not appropriated the formal and external regulation of entrepreneurship and not adapted to the new forms of organization of the capitalist system.

The commercial constitution of the Hansa merchants had not led to the concentration and accumulation but rather to the fragmentation of capital. They plied their single businesses and did not expand them. They appeared as a rule to have founded neither family firms nor the broader capitalist companies. They invested their goods and sought profit in sea trade, but in single enterprises independently of one another.[111]

Hence it led to a further contradiction between the training of skill in the arts of shipbuilding and seafaring and the lack of perfection of technique in Hanseatic entrepreneurship. It formed no corporate bodies. We will consider some examples of these enterprises.

The English East India Company founded in the 17th century was an early example of companies that traded in capital shares, and thus were a model for the further development of the joint-stock company. The company was led 'democratically', the leadership lay in the hands of the totality of participants, who on an annual basis confirmed the directors in their offices by the decision of the majority and raising of hands. All commodities brought with from India were sold at public auction. Each participant had the right to inspect the company books. When the ships returned, the participants assembled, and the East Indian letters were publicly read out.

In every way the English East Indian Company was the opposite of the Dutch East Indian Company, which was not led democratically but rather oligarchically, bound by the spirit of speculation and enlarged by a great collection of capital. Their foundation was the collection of seafarers and merchants from Amsterdam and London who had invested their capital in shipping companies and foreign travel.[112] The concept of democracy is relative since only the well-off owners of stock had the right to vote in the English company—the poor in England and the people of the East Indies absolutely none. The English company was a corporate body in the modern sense.

The Jihlava commercial cloth company was an organization of capital, which can be considered an early joint-stock company. Jihlava in the Middle Ages had a significant cloth-making guild. Yet in the 16th century the sale of products declined, and the guild sought to support the economically needy masters by means of the then often practiced limitation on the number of journeymen and of the number of pieces that single weavers were allowed to produce.

The sinking rate of sales and the lack of working capital, wool, alum, dyes and so on were connected to the failure of the putting-out system, which was driven by advances provided by the cloth merchants. Thus, the Jihlava weavers decided to establish their own company and were supposed to take over the domestic putting-out enterprise, the production of cloth and the sale of the products. The statute or plan of the company was confirmed by imperial officials in 1592. It was built on the model of the Styrian iron trade company in the 15th and 16th century. Membership in the company consisted of citizens of all estates and classes of the city of Jihlava in possession of capital. This had to do with a publicly registered corporation that is registered and recognized. Whether shares were involved is unknown. The town folk had carried their basic capital [*Legegelder*] together, the poorer groups in two's, three's and so on, the rich singularly. Whether individuals and groups were legal persons and part owners of securities or stock is a possibility which we leave open. In any event the cloth company was a legal person and counted as a corporate body. The total capital of the company was insufficient for business needs, and thus it borrowed significant sums, namely several thousand guilders from merchants in Styr, Prague and other cities; the Jihlava cloth company, exactly like the Styrian iron trade company, had thereupon issued bonds at a fixed rate of interest. The company was required to assume responsibility for the bonds; the shareholders were responsible only insofar as they were members of the company. Explicit confirmation of the liability of the shareholders or groups of shareholders was not ascertained and the limitation of liability, possibly related to the value of the capital investment of each shareholder, is likewise not established. The members of the company were the ones who produced the cloth.

The company as a corporate body was also a putting-out enterprise [*Verleger*]. It had sold the wool that it bought in Bohemia and Moravia to the poorer Jhilavan cloth and hat makers, in part as advanced payment, and made off with the finished commodities. These were sold in the fairs and markets in Austria, Hungary and in the Siebengebirge. The other cloth merchants in Jihlava continued their economic activities, and therefore this is not about a company monopoly. Not only citizens of Jihlava, but rather all who had substantial capital, could participate in the founding of a Jihlavan cloth company.[113]

A social system consists of parts, factors and conditions which reciprocally effect and oppose one another. Let us consider the previously mentioned case of Jack of Newbury. England, at the end of the 15th and beginning of the 16th century, had a cloth factory and system of manufacture that was quite highly developed, not only in relation to the conditions of that period, but also in relation to those of a later era. The class of entrepreneurs of this sort made great strides in concentrating the production of woolen cloth in their hands. However, their external role and political influence were weak. The royal government had considered them as a danger to the traditional organization of the guilds [*Gilden*] and to the majority of small craftsmen. It was forbidden in England to bring together in one workshop a weaver and a cloth fuller [*Walkergewerbe*]; employing more than two apprentices in cottage industry outside the town was prohibited as well.[114] The guild pressure on parliament was greater than that of the rich factory owners, which was later reversed. Yet all were part of one and the same social system.

If we turn to Upper German trade in the period from the 15th to the 17th century, we discover from a number of historical points of view similar, from other points of view on the contrary, different conditions. Monopolies, cartels and the beginnings of the concentration of capital are present in the activities of the rich families in south Germany. The patricians of the monopolies of South German trade in Augsburg, Nuremberg, Ravensburg and Ulm during the 15th and 16th century had established companies, dominated the city council, and had taken financial power into their hands. Their firms were predominantly family companies. The marriage ties among the families had concentrated finance and politics in their hands.

The Ravensburg company appears to have been the largest family company according to the number of its members continuing over several generations. The period of their activity is related primarily to the 15th and 16th century. The Bimmel family had a firm in Augsburg which continued through the enterprises of the father, the sons and of the families Haug, Langenauer, Link, and others married into it. They became a financial power across wide parts of Europe.

Especially in the course of the 15th and 16th century family firms developed in southern Germany. Blood relatives and relatives through marriage, brothers and brothers-in-law continued the original small family businesses founded by the father of origin and developed them into lasting and self-expanding enterprises.[115] Their activity was not limited to trade and financial enterprises.

The Fugger family was active in trade, in weaving, in the metal industry and in high finance in Augsburg during the 15th, 16th, and 17th century. It had a leading role in almost all areas of business in Upper Germany and beyond in further parts of Europe, from Flanders and the Netherlands in the north, to Italy and Spain in the south. The Fugger family was founded by a member of the weavers' guild in Augsburg. Over several generations in the 15th and 16th century it expanded its economic activity and its influence. Jakob Fugger (1459–1525), the wealthy man, was a member of a line of trade, production and finance enterprises at that time. The family firm organized, among other involvements, activities as competitors of the Ulmer and the Barchent weaving works in the area of Weissenhorn.[116] It was active in mining in Tirol and Hungary especially in the copper and silver mines and also in the Oberpfalz and in Bohemia. It conducted the business of credit in Spain, France, Flanders, the Netherlands as well as in Germany. Against a loan from Jakob Fugger of 121,600 florins in the year 1496, Kaiser Wilhelm had mortgaged the revenue of the Tirol mines. At this time trade with copper and silver was the main preoccupation of the Fuggers. This trade was closely bound up with credit transactions. The war against the Swiss Confederation three years later increased the Kaiser's need for money, which did not improve in the ensuing decades of the 16th century. The Fuggers conducted similar business with the Spanish. The assets of Fugger's trade per year contributed around 3 million gulden, of which 270,000 florins or 9% was accounted for by mining and mining components among which was 60,000 from Tirol and 210,000 from Hungary. The commodities of the house amounted to 380,000 florins, 12% consisting mostly of copper. The accounts receivable amounted to 1.65 million florins or 55%. The Spanish accounts receivable came to 507,000 florins and the liabilities of the same to 340,000 florins. The liabilities of the firm totalled 870,000 florins. Anton Fugger, the nephew of the wealthy Jakob Fugger, asserted in 1554: "The appetite for war should reasonably wither away easily for these great men." Like his uncle he wanted to make "profit as long as he is able."

Nevertheless, these merchants and bankers did not understand that their fate was bound up with that of the dynasties. Since the losses of the Hapsburgs, Spanish, French among others were so high, the Fuggers also suffered as a result. The total losses of the Fuggers up to the middle of the 17th century amounted to 8 million guldens. Up to half of the claims and liabilities against the Spanish crown were lost. Their claims and liabilities against the French court and the Dutch treasurer remained largely unpaid. The fortune which the Fugger had won over the course of 200 years, disappeared. Anton Fugger was forced to admit in his will, "… on account of protracted processes of war the sending of goods could only be done with difficulty, so that we could not bring our trading goods to a conclusion and to carry our debts …". What remained in the end of this were some landed properties which were desolated and greatly burdened by the results of continual warfare.[117] [Thus, by the middle of the 17th century—at the end of the Thirty Years' War, the fabulous Fugger fortune had largely disappeared—trans.].

The other great houses of Upper Germany did not fare essentially any better. In fact, the commercial, shipping and credit enterprises in the 16th and 17th century made unsafe transactions. The Nuremberg merchant, Hans Paumgartner, was involved with mining in the Tirol in the 15th century, that is as a member of a known copper syndicate. His son Hans Paumgartner the younger married into the Fugger family and became known as the banker of the house of Hapsburg, first as Emperor Maximillian's money lender and afterwards to King Ferdinand. Together with the Fuggers and Haug, in 1544 the Paumgartners had loaned to Ferdinand silver in the value of 100,000 florins. The Paumgartner sons had suffered a heavy fate; David lost his fortune and ended on the gallows; Johann Georg who sat in debtors' prison for five years, from 1565–1570, had to relinquish all his fortune and was forced to flee to foreign lands.

The Welsers belonged to the oldest houses in Augsburg. In the 15th and 16th century they were just as involved with the Habsburg money business as the Fuggers and Paumgartners. They were active in Portugal, Antwerp, Italy and beyond that in East Indian trade and had a branch of the house together with Imhof in Nuremberg. The Welsers in Nuremberg had mostly engaged in commodity trade and money transactions like the Fuggers, Imhof, Paumgartner among others. They had their factories in Genoa, Venice, Aquila and Milan, in Vienna, in Antwerp and Lyon. They participated in the rich silver pits in Schlackenwald, had lent a great deal of money to Duke Schlick together with Hans Nutzel and could expand their enterprise. The well-known silver ore mines of Joachimstal were found in the Schlackenwald. The Welsers were often mentioned at this time in relation to money transactions together with Fugger and Imhof. In Antwerp, Spain and Lyon these families allowed themselves to be enticed into speculative money matters. The Welsers were mixed up in the financial crisis of 1537–1562. In 1580 their large land holdings in Antwerp had to be sold. Matthäus Welser became the Imperial tax collector [*Reichspfennigmeister*]; he remained a creditor of the Kaiser with great sums of money. On the day after his death in 1614 his brother was declared incapable of payment, and the Welser catastrophe followed suit.

The Höchstetters in the 16th century rose very high by means of speculation with Tirol silver and copper businesses among other things; however, they got into money difficulties and debt and were not able to avoid the collapse of their businesses. A similar story is told about the Manlich family, which became wealthy in the course of the 16th century and went bankrupt in 1574. Similarly, the Neidharts had been able to conduct large commercial transactions until 1570 and went under in the following years; their total wealth consisted almost entirely of income from foreign ventures. Florence, Pisa, Venice and Genoa which earlier played a great role in world trade, had lost their commercial significance in the 16th century. The focus of trade was shifted to the north but by the 17th century the centre moved to the hands of the English and Dutch.

The importation of colonial commodities, intercourse with India, America and Africa and the wars in Europe in connection with the devastation of the cities and of agriculture changed the trade map. Nuremberg which was so important for the metal processing industry, Augsburg for money and credit transactions, relinquished their leading positions. The Hansa cities were also changed. The confluence of the Weser and other rivers temporarily fell into foreign hands.[118]

The formation of banks, of other credit institutions and of joint-stock companies are forms of processes of capitalist organization. Speculation with money and commodities, wars and loans for purposes of war are external events in the life of the people. Yet the warlike activities, the conquests and devastations are not external events of imperial and royal enterprises. The money and trade princes functioned as mediators in the 15th, 16th, and 17th century.

The forms of economic and social processes are bound up with the substantial processes of the same. However, this linkage is a mediate one, since both, legal and administrative forms as well as the social and economic substance, traverse an apparently separate history. The history of the juridical, property and political forms of administration is for a time—a time which stretches over centuries—other than that of the process of labour in production, distribution and in the exchange of the products of social labour. There is no automatic or mechanical connection between the two.

Human life without the formal side is unthinkable and impossible. There must be a form for the labour process, however the forms do not always correspond to our expectations; they are not apposite or customized forms. In the transition to the period of high capitalism we have seen that several forms were assumed; some continued others abolished. The previous era of feudalism did not immediately disappear. The domination of the aristocratic estate continued into the period of high capitalism. The juridical forms in agriculture had changed after a protracted struggle.

Sombart praised the adventurers of the early capitalist era. The pirates, the warriors, condottieri, sea robbers and conquerors formed the romantic streak in the early capitalist spirit.[119]

Romanticism has its early history. It begins in the Middle Ages with the song of the minstrels, *trovatori* and troubadours. Only this romanticism is a streak in the spirit of those people who stayed at home. The question is whether the pirates and condottieri were romantic spirits or whether they had been dominated by a romantic streak. Most of them were murderers, robbers and rapists. The interactions of the forms of speculation among the merchants and bankers as well as among the authorities, the princes and the emperor in the period of early capitalism is palpable. Both sides, the private sea robbers as well as the public power, were seekers of adventure at the cost of the common folk, that is, of the peasants and the town proletariat. Adventurers made people into slaves, exploited and killed them.

The merchants, patricians and the middle class served as mediators between the process of labour and the state regime. This is in relation to production and trade in the towns. The landowners, the Church, the bishoprics did not behave any differently than did the authorities; they did not serve as mediators in this process.

Notes

1. R. Mols, in: C. M. Cipolla (ed.), *Wirtschaftsgeschichte Europas*, Vol. 2, Stuttgart 1979. K. Helleiner, in: *Cambridge Economic History of Europe*, 5.4., Cambridge 1967.
2. The figures and percentages are generally trustworthy, if they have a connection with other figures and percentages, so that they appear meaningful. We shall not ascertain anything specific and definitive, only propose a picture.
3. A. de Maddalena, in *Europäische Wirtschaftsgeschichte*, Vol. 2, C. M. Cipolla, K. Borchardt (Eds.), 1979. Concerning the Electorate of the Mark Brandenburg, Cf. Inama-Sternegg, *Bevölkerung*, loc. cit.
4. K. F. Helleiner, *Cambridge Economic History*, Vol. 4, 1967. F. Braudel, *Civilisation, matérielle ...* (see above) 1979.
5. Health science established the provenance of the Black Death from Central Asia and its path across the Black Sea. The aetiology of the Black Death should be researched further, since geographical knowledge is sufficient. The aetiology of the bubonic plague is known. The occidental rat flea xenopsylla cheopsis is one of the most important carriers of this plague. The flea has a parasitic relationship to several rodents such as rats (rattus norvegicus). One of the rodents, the marmot, whose fur was sought after in medieval Europe, came over the Silk Road, over the lower course of the Volga, the Black Sea and the Mediterranean to the Near East and Europe. The plague was known in Astrakhan and Alexandria, 1346 and 1347, 1348 in Toulouse, Bordeaux, England and Ireland, 1349 in Norway, 1350 in Denmark and Germany, 1351 in Poland and 1352 in Russia. In 1497 Hieronymus Brunschwygk published his *Liber de arte destillandi de simplicibus* (The book of the correct way to distill singular things). In 1500 his *Chirurgie, Dis ist das Buch der Cirurgia, Das ist Hantwirkung der Wuntarzny* was published. From his hand came likewise in 1500 the book *Liber pestilentialis de venenis epidimie* (The Book of the poison the plague). He was active in Straßburg and his books appeared in that same place. Aureolus Bombastus Paracelsus of Hohenheim composed several books about chemistry, surgery and medicine for wounds as well as about general medicine. He disputed the view of medicine of the Galen school. In his stormy life he moved several times. Most of his writings appeared posthumously. Brunschwygk and Paracelsus employed chemicals against human diseases and thereby achieved contributions to iatrochemistry.
6. Hans Sachs and Jost Amman. *Eigentliche Beschreibung aller Stände auf Erden*. Publication by Sigmund Feyerabend. Frankfurt am Main 1568. The publishers commissioned the so-called *Ständebuch* and wrote a preface. Hans Sachs described: "the estates, arts, handicrafts and trade/

and composed in German rhymes/very useful and humorous to read/ and also replete with artistic figures by Jost Amman."

7. W. Abel, G. Franz, *Geschichte des deutschen Bauernstandes*, 2nd. Edition, Stuttgart 1976. F. Lütge, *Deutsche Sozial—und Wirtschaftsgeschichte*, 3rd edition 1966. G. Knapp, *Landarbeiter in Freiheit und Knechtschaft*, Leipzig 1909. Theodor von der Goltz, *Geschichte der deutschen Landwirtschaft* (1902), Stuttgart 1963. B. H. Slicher v. Bath, idem.
8. In the Latin edition of the *Ständebuch* Hartmann Schopper, [πανοπλια. Frankfurt am Main 1568] treated the peasants, rusticus, in the same manner: »Pauper et obscuras inglorious incolo sylvas, atque gravern vitam raroquinetus ago. Insidias avibus moliri, figere damas, Claudere nunc rivos, et dare rursus acquis. Sunt vigilanda mihi, Laber improbus instat ubique Sen ver, aut aetas, aut fera venit hyems. »
9. The peasants in the 16th century complained about forced collective labour [*Scharwerk*] and corvée: "I must do compulsory collective labour all day long so that I may not work my field. I have a young master, really a nasty one, for whom I must perform compulsory collective labor [*Scharwerk*] and compulsory labor [*Fron*]." Jacob Ayrer from Nuremberg, 1544–1605.
10. B. H. Slicher von Bath, in *Cambridge Economic History of Europe*, Vol. 5.m Cambridge 1977.
11. G. Franz, *Geschichte des deutschen Bauernstandes*, 2nd Edition, Stuttgart 1976. Idem. (ed.) *Quellen zur Geschichte des Bauernkrieges*, Munich 1963.
12. Lütge (*Deutsche Sozial—und Wirtschaftsgeschichte*, p. 220ff.) is of the view that one cannot speak of an impoverishment of the peasants of Southwest Germany at the time of the last great uprising. The economic causes were not the primary ones. They were, however, religious and political. That which was apparent was also overlooked here: The twelve articles speak about the abolition of serfdom, of interest and taxes, about the maintenance of community practices, and about the care of widows and orphans. These articles express the economic program of the great peasant uprising. On the title page of the article letter issued by the rebellious peasants is the picture of an armed band of peasants. The title of this letter reads: „Operation/ Article and instruction/ thus having been undertaken by all bands and clusters of peasants/thus were duty-bound together: M:D:XXV:" It had to do with an issuance concerning the crowd from Baltring for the further instruction of other peasant bands and groups. On the title page of the twelve articles it was written further: The fundamental and legal main article of all the peasantry and hangers-on of spiritual and secular authority, of which they feel themselves aggrieved. This refers to all peasants and not only those who have united themselves into troop units, an army or groups. Further to this: M. Kobuch and E. Müller (eds.), *Der deutsche Bauernkrieg*, Weimar 1975. From the state archives in Dresden and Weimar.
13. Th. v.d. Goltz, *Geschichte der deutschen Landwirtschaft*, Vol. 1, Part 2, §2. Günther Franz, *Der deutsche Bauernkrieg*, 10th edition, Darmstadt 1975. Idem. *Zur Geschichte des Bauernkrieges*, 1963. H. Kellenbenz und R. Walter, in: *Handbuch der Europäischen Wirtschafts—und Sozialgeschichte*, W. Fischer (ed.). 1986.
14. J. J. Rousseau had written: "The first who called out, this property belongs to me, and found another who was so foolish as to find it convincing, was the founder of bourgeois society." Many have taken up this idea differently, like property is theft and so on. G. W. F. Hegel (*Rechtsphilosophie*, 1821) distinguished between possession and property. Possession is the foundation of inequality (loc. cit, §49). Taking possession (§54) is in part the immediate corporal seizure, in part the formation, working the land, the culture of plants, the taming, feeding and raising of animals, in part it is the designation (§§55–58). One can alienate property. Possession becomes transformed into property through external recognition of it and thereafter it can be

sold. The Hegelian system of freedom, of possession, of taking possession and of property aligned itself with the program of liberation of the peasants. Hegel asserted: "… nature is not free and thus it is neither right nor unjust" (§49). Freedom is the fundamental condition of justice; the rebellious peasants already said it; they concretely grasped that there is a connection between freedom and justice, in the succession of concrete freedom, namely the abolition of collective compulsory service and serfdom, towards justice. Hegel expressed it abstractly. Freedom in the program of the peasants as well as in the Hegelian system is formal-legal freedom, that appears at first concretely and thereafter abstractly. On the one hand, it is formally bound with property, on the other hand, with justice. That which is taken as possession, is transformed through recognition into property. The assumption of recognition is the presence of the bourgeois legal system. (This is a circular argument, to follow Hegel; not so among the peasants). Marx declared his agreement with the Hegelian system of possession and property. The practical foundation of both theoretical systems is traced back to the sayings of the peasant movement. Hegel's conception of universal freedom is based on the investigations which he begins in the German Middle Ages.

15. Georg Simmel (*Philosphie des Geldes*, Munich 1930) had written: "The slave holder, like the landowner had the personal interest, to maintain his slaves or his peasants who were duty-bound to perform services, in good and performance-ready condition." "The liberation of the peasants must so to speak be paid with a liberation of the employers, that is, with the cessation of the care which those who were unfree enjoyed." (p. 317f.) That is correct in part, but also in part a romanticization of the unfree conditions of labour, and it was said only after the liberation of the slaves and peasants. During the epoch of the struggles for liberation the productivity of the unfree and free labourers were compared, to the benefit of the latter. (Adam Smith, *Wealth of Nations*, 1776):

    1. The welfare from the side of the lord is a patriarchal idea of life relations on the domain or slave plantation.
    2. When little is produced, when that is, productivity is low, welfare thus has little significance.
    3. The rebellious peasants concerned themselves not only with the freedom of wage labour, but also with the return of the old communal rights, which was important for their own welfare.
    4. No one asked about the intentions of the slaves and serfs. Their opinions didn't count. That is the reification through the unfree conditions of labour, not its objectification. Simmel looks at the labourers as pure objects, that is not as humans, only as things.

16. J. Kulischer, *Allgemeine Wirtschaftsgeschichte*, Vol. II, 1928, 2nd edition, Munich 1958.
17. G. F. Knapp, *Die Landarbeiter in Freiheit und Knechtschaft*, 1909. F. Lütge, *Geschichte der deutschen Agrarverfassung*, 2nd edition, Stuttgart 1976.
18. F. Lütge, *Geschichte der Agrarverfassung*, loc. cit. p. 83. Otto Johannsen (see above) describes the transport and supporting labour [*Förderarbeit*] of the peasants for the mines in the Harz.
19. Grossmann, *Handwörterbuch der Staatswissenschaften*. J. Conrad et al. (eds.), 3rd edition 1911 (keyword *Gemeinheitsteilung*). Idem. W. Lexis, (keyword *Abbau*).
20. W. Abel, *Geschichte der deutschen Landwirtschaft*, 3rd edition, Stuttgart 1978. Idem. *Agrarkrisen und Agrarkonjunktur in Mitteleuropa vom 13. bis zum 19. Jahrhundert* (1935), 3rd edition, Hamburg 1978. Cf. B. H. Slicher von Bath, in: *Cambridge Economic History of Europe*, Cambridge 1977, Chapter 8, in which the significance of Abel's contribution is assessed.
21. W. Abel, *Geschichte der deutschen Landwirtschaft*, loc. cit., p. 201.
22. W. Abel, ibidem. F. Lütge, ibidem.
23. We have already alluded to the connection of these moments and will refer to them further.

24. W. Abel. Loc. cit., p. 203. The history of the cloister Eberbach is related to the period of boom of agricultural economy, 1551–1600, in Europe; for example, the export of rye from Danzig grew more than 100,000 tons annually around the year 1600. The cultivated wheat on the island of Fehmarn in Lübeck Bay became so renowned, "that people in France, Spain and Italy paid dearly for it." W. Abel, *Agrarkrisen und Agrarkonjuntur*, op. cit., p. 113.
25. Karl Marx had a differentiated view in relation to the land in Europe and in India. The Russian sociologist, M. M. Kovalevsky had argued that feudalism in India had been present prior to the period of colonization. Marx found this risible and wrote in this connection: "Because 'benefices,' 'farming out of offices' [but this is not at all *feudal*, as Rome attests] and commendation are founded in India, Kovalevsky here finds *feudalism* in the Western European sense. Kovalevsky forgets, among other things, serfdom, which is not in India, and which is an essential moment. [In regard to the individual role of defence, however (cf. Palgrave), not only of the unfree, but also of the free peasants by the feudal lords (who play a role as wardens), this plays a limited role in India, except for the wakuf]. [Of the poetry of the soil which the Romanic-Germanic feudalism had as its own (see Maurer) as little is found in India as in Rome. The soil is nowhere noble in India, so that it might not be alienable to commoners!]." Marx contributed here negatively to the question of periodization, insofar as he excluded India from the feudal period. The farming out of offices was practised in ancient Rome, in India, as well as in medieval Europe and thus had nothing in particular to do with feudalism. As the *differentia specifica* of Romanic-Germanic feudalism one finds the poetry of the soil and the nobility of the land. Marx positively contributed to the question of periodization, insofar as he considered serfdom as an essential moment in European feudalism. Thus the moments of serfdom and of feudalism were particular characteristics of the history of Europe. Lawrence Krader, *Asiatic Mode of Production*, Assen 1979, p. 202, 383. Karl Marx, *Formen vorkapitalistischer Produktion*, H.P. Harstick (ed.), Campus 1977.
26. W. Abel, *Agrarkrisen und Agrarkonjunktur*, 3rd edition, Hamburg 1978.
27. See above the sermons of the shepherd Hans Böhm, further the Zwölf Artikel of 1525. §§ 5, 6, 10.
28. J. Hasemann, *Gemeinde*, in: Ersch und Gruber, *Encyklopädie*, 1853. W. Lexis, *Abbau* in *Handwörterbuch der Staatswissenschaften*. J. Conrad et al. (eds.) 3rd edition, 1910. F. Grossmann, *Gemeinheitsteilung*, ibid. Th. von der Goltz, *Geschichte der deutschen Landwirtschaft*, vol. 1. 1963, p. 406ff. The separations, and so on were introduced by the legislation of the 18th and 19th century.
29. Abel, *Agrarkrise und Agrarkonjunktur*, ibidem. F. Lütge, *Geschichte der deutschen Agrarverfassung*, ibid. Janssen and Pareto, see above.
30. G. Franz, *Der Dreißigjährige Krieg und das deutsche Volk*, 3rd edition, 1961, p. 177f.
31. Potato cultivation was ushered in in the 18th century and spread at the end of the century by starvation of the years 1771/72. W. Abel, in: *Handbuch der deutschen Wirtschafts—und Sozialgeschichte*, Vol. 1, 1971, chapters 13, 20.
32. Günter Franz, *Geschichte des deutschen Bauernstandes*, § 13. Otto Hinze, *Kalvinismus und Staatsräson in Brandenburg, Gesammelte Abhandlungen 3*. 1943. In this overview, Emden and surroundings, Schleswig among others, were left out. Emden was at that time a centre of Calvinism, yet the peasants of this region at this time were not rebellious. Perhaps the peasant-religious pastors also here, as in the East, were in the service of the lords (Franz, loc. cit., p. 195). An important factor was the effect of eastern colonization on the lives of the peasants.
33. K. Bücher, *Die Bevölkerung von Frankfurt Main im XIV. und XV. Jahrhundert*, Tübingen 1886, p. 484.

34. This concerns the history of the word, not to that of the village. Towns had their hamlets. Johan Kepler was born in Weil der Stadt (Württemberg) 1571.
35. Grimm, *Wörterbuch*.
36. Bücher, loc. cit., p. 481.
37. Sprandel, in: H. Aubin, W. Zorn (Eds.), *Handbuch der deutschen Wirtschafts-und Sozialgeschichte,* Stuttgart 1971, p. 339.
38. Schoenlank, *Soziale Kämpfe*, loc. cit., p. 178.
39. K. T. v. Inama-Sternegg, *Deutsche Wirtschaftsgeschichte*, Leipzig Vol. 3, part I, pp. 28–34. Duum millarium amounted to 2, trium millarium to 3 miles. 2,700 rods = 14, 175 kms. A circumference with a radius of 89 kms. and an area of 31.24 square kilometers.
40. K. Hegel, *Städte und Gilden der germanischen Völker im Mittelalter,* Vol. 2, Leipzig 1891. Naples: see C. M. Cipolla, *Before the Industrial Revolution*, op. cit.
41. F. Engels, *Der deutsche Bauernkrieg* (1850), 3rd, edition. W. Zimmermann, *Allgemeine Geschichte des großen Bauernkrieges,* 1841–1843. The passionate presentation of the peasant wars by Engels was based on the work of Zimmermann. In the 19th century the view of the peasant war was closely connected with the ideological struggles and the insurrection of 1848.
42. B. Schoenlank, *Soziale Kämpfe vor dreihundert Jahren*, 2nd edition, Leipzig 1907.
43. G. L. Kriegk, *Frankfurter Bürgerzwiste im Mittelalter*, Frankfurt am Main 1862, p. 371 and passim. Kriegk was the city archivist of Frankfurt am Main.
44. We return to the movements of the miners' guilds. Rudolf Endres 'Einwohnerzahl und Bevölkerungsstruktur Nürnbergs im 15–16. Jahrhundert.' *Mitteilungen des Vereins für Geschichte der Stadt Nürnberg,* Vol. 57, 1970 emphasized the socio-economic tensions and protested against the exaggerated views. The idealizations of harmony and of discord come not only from the left but also from the right, in both the 19th and in the 20th century.
45. Schoenlank, loc. cit. p. 25f. Endres (loc. cit., p. 268) had already taken this up. He considered the call for the lifting of the excise tax, the oppressive tax on drink and grain, as the call to "social change". Schoenlank conceived of this as a purpose of the reform program. A fraternalization of peasants and town folk occurred in Rothenburg ob der Tauber, as well as in other towns; however these remained isolated cases.
46. Thomas Deloney, *The Story of John Winchcombe, Commonly Called Jack of Newbury,* 1597. There are no fewer than ten structures of labour put together and executed in one large room. The poem appeared 78 years after Winchcombes' death. In part it has to do with oral tradition. The moral of this story is also known. Aside from the donation of money for the establishment of a church, there was almost nothing further to report about Winchcombe, about the year of his birth or his career. He disappears from the history of capitalism. In the course of the 16th century we read about the fate of English entrepreneurship. In the 16th century a prohibition was levied against cutting or dyeing of cloth outside of the city of Norwich, and similarly the prohibition against the processing of woolen blankets outside of the town of York. Paul Mantoux, *La révolution industrielle*, (1905), Paris 1973. Monteux referred to the undertaking by Winchcombe in part as a workshop, in part as a factory. If the data are true, it appears as a factory with respect to the size, structure of labour and its concentration in one room. The prohibitive system of Nuremberg in the 16th century is comparable to the English.
47. On the history of the words *Gilde* and *Zunft*: Grimm: *Deutsches Wörterbuch*. IV/I, 4, 1949 and XVI, Leipzig 1954 (Hgs.. Wunderlich and G. Rosenhagen). F. Kluge, W. Mityka, *Etymologisches Wörterbuch der deutschen Sprache*, 20th edition, Berlin 1967. J. Pokorny, *Indogermanisches etymologisches Wörterbuch*, Francke 1959. We're citing the examples primarily from the Germanic

languages, German, English, Dutch. The legal history of the guild system: O. Gierke, *Das deutsche Genossenschaftsrecht*, 4 volumes (repr.) Graz 1954. The economic history of the guild system are treated in the works of W. Stieda, J. Kulischer, G. v. Below, F. Keutgen, G. Mickwitz and passim in this work.

48. W. Stieda, *Zur Entstehung des deutschen Zunftwesens.* Jena 1877. *Das Zunftwesen. Handwörternuch der Staatswissenschaften,* Conrad et al. (eds.), 3rd edition, 1911. The guilds are distinguished by their provenance and through their role or function. Guilds, professional associations, gilds corresponded to the system of cooperatives (*Genossenschaftswesen*) (O. Gierke, *Das deutsche Genossenschaftsrecht,* Vol. 1, 1868, §§ 32–38). Kin lineages were unified in gilds. To this are to be added the commercial guilds (§ 37) and the cooperatives (*Genossenschaften*) or guilds of handicraftsmen (§ 38). The guild was a free association, like that of the town, a communal entity writ small. Guilds were political, military and professional bodies, religious organizations and ethics police as well as social, spiritual brotherhoods. J. P. Davis [*Corporations* (1905), New York 1961] wrote about the guilds as peace association and further about the social-religious gilds, the church guilds, occupational gilds, as well as the commercial and handcraftsmen guilds. The history of the guilds in Central Europe is diverse. On the one hand, Bruno Schoenlank (*Soziale Kämpfe vor dreihundert Jahren,* 2nd edition, Leipzig 1907) repeatedly asserts: "In Old Nuremberg there were never any guilds." On the other hand, Inama-Sternegg, G. Schönberg, K. Hegel, W. Stieg, K. Bücher, R. Endres enumerated the guilds in Cologne, Frankfurt am Main, Nuremberg, in the Hansa cities and elsewhere. Guilds were introduced in the later history of Nuremberg.
49. J. Kulischer, *Allgemeine Wirtschaftsgeschichte des Mittelalters und der Neuzeit,* Vol. II, 1958, Chapter 28. Wilhelm Stieda, *Zunftwesen,* ibid.
50. B. Schoenlank, *Soziale Kämpfe.* The apprentices negotiated and struggled with the Nuremberg council over the gifts.
51. K. Bücher, *Die Bevölkerung von Frankfurt am Main im 14. und 15. Jahrhundert,* Tübingen 1886.
52. The bitter struggle of the guilds in England, the Netherlands, France and Germany against the introduction of new tools and methods of labour continued and went beyond the 16th and 17th century. The inventor of the stocking maker loom had to flee England. We know similar stories from the Netherlands and France. The struggle was temporarily successful for the guilds, and had as a consequence the prohibition of employment of the new tools and the organization of labour associated with it. The guild system strongly set itself in opposition to the rationalization and the increase in the productivity in the labour process (see above).
53. In 1676 there were supposedly riots in England and in Cologne on account of the introduction the new ribbon looms. Josef Kulischer (*Allgemeine Wirtschaftsgeschichte*, II, p. 111) sees Anton Moller as the inventor of the ribbon loom. Then he was supposedly drowned by the council in Danzig. It is improbable that this concerns the history of Anton Moller, as related by Lancelotti, even if he discovered this machine all on his own, which is equally highly improbable. We eschew the further investigation of this question. Nevertheless, we take from this story the fact that the weaver guild and the council in Danzig around 1579 or 1586 set themselves against the new machines. Other guilds and towns behaved in a similar fashion. To content oneself in acting in the way portrayed here, was sensible from their standpoint, but not however from the standpoint of industrial progress.
54. K. T. Inama-Sternegg, B. Schoenlank, G. L. Kriegk, G. Franz, R. Elkar, W. Reininghaus, R. Sprandel, H. Kellenbenz ibid., R. Endres see below.
55. W. Stieda, ‚Zunftwesen', *Handwörterbuch* (see above).

56. W. Stieda (see above), *Jahrbücher für Nationalökonomie und Statistik,* Vol. 8, 1867. G. Schönberg, *Zur wirtschaftlichen Bedeutung des deutschen Zunftwesens im Mittelalter.* G. L. Kriegk, *Bürgerzwiste.*
57. The name *mercantilist* is only appropriate, says John Hicks, if we consider the history from the standpoint of the state and its rulers. They become *mercantilists* when they imagine that the merchants could serve as an instrument for mainly not mercantile purposes. John Hicks, *A Theory of Economic History,* Oxford 1973, p. 162. All of this is the music of the future for the Central European state in the 16th century.
58. K. Bücher, *Die Bevölkerung von Frankfurt am Main in 14. und 15. Jahrhundert,* Tübingen 1886, pp. 118, 121, 215f., 238.
59. F. Eulenberg, 'Berufs–und Gewerbestatistik Heidelbergs im 16. Jahrhundert,' *Zeitschrift für die Geschichte des Oberrheins,* N.F., Vol. II, 1896. Here, a comparison with Frankfurt am Main, p. 111, Table 9 is undertaken.
60. B. Schoenlank, *Soziale Kämpfe,* loc. cit., p. 46f. and 161. J. Kulischer, *Allgemeine Wirschaftsgeschichte,* loc. cit., vol. II, p. 118.
61. H. Sachs, Jost Ammon, *Eigentliche Beschreibung aller Stände.*
62. Kulischer, loc. cit., chapter 8 and 12.
63. Leuthold, 'Knappschaft.' Ersch and Gruber, *Encyclopedie,* Leipzig 1885. The miner's association "is the entire society of miners and those who have anything to do with mining" or the totality of those involved with working the pits who as shareholders in a pit constitute a social union with the name guild under the direction of their master. Already in the Middle Ages the cottagers, the winch servants, smelters and mining masters gathered into one association. Through this association the territorial authorities had control over the miner's association. Such regimentation arose not just in modern times, but earlier as well. This opinion is contested by H. Wilsdorf (*Bergwerke und Hüttenanlagen,* Berlin 1971).
64. B. Schoenlank, *Soziale Kämpfe,* 2nd edition, Leipzig 1907, p. 48.
65. G. Schönberg, *Jahrbücher für Nationalökonomie und Statistik,* Vol. 8, 1867, p. 7. He points to the opposition between the old freedom of the trades and the new freedom of trade and competition.
66. K. Bücher, *Bevölkerung von Frankfurt,* loc. cit., p. 735. *The Pan Smiths,* p. 118ff., 215ff.
67. B. Schoenlank, loc. cit., p. 145.
68. O. Johannsen, *Geschichte des Eisens,* 3rd edition, Düsseldorf 1953, p. 245.
69. B. Schoenlank, G. Schanz, *Gesellenverbände. Handwörterbuch der Staatswissenschaften,* 3rd edition, 1909. W. Sombart represented a closely related view.
70. R. Endres, 'Einwohnerzahl und Bevölkerungsstruktur Nürnbergs,' *Mitteilungen des Vereins für Geschichte der Stadt Nürnbergs,* Vol. 57, 1970, p. 269.
71. Voltaire set himself against the Church in France; at the same time, he was befriended by the King of Prussia.
72. J. Kulischer, *Allgemeine Wirtschaftsgeschichte,* loc. cit., Vol. 11, chapter 8, 9.
73. F. Furger, *Zum Verlagssystem als Organisationsform des Frühkapitalismus im Textilgewerbe,* Stuttgart 1927. R. Sprandel, in: H. Aubin, W. Zorn (eds.), *Handbuch der deutschen Wirtschafts – und Sozialgeschichte,* Stuttgart 1971, chapter 14.
74. Some wood cuts were taken out of later editions and replaced by others.
75. H. Sachs, *Eigentliche Beschreibung aller Stände,* 1568.
76. A. Ruppel, *Johann Gutenberg,* 2nd edition, Berlin 1947. A. Kaps, *Deutsche Schriftkunst,* Dresden 1955. K. Dietrichs, *Die Buchdruckpresse,* Mainz 1930. S. H. Steinberg, *500 Years of Printing,* 3rd edition, Pelikan 1974. M. Clapham, in: C. Singer et al. (eds.), *A History of Technology.* Vol. III, Oxford 1958. The staff of a print shop around 1450–1460 amounted to 15–25 men, 2 or 3 print

founders, 3 to 6 typesetters, 6–12 printers and their boys and so on. In the *Ständebuch* by Jost Amman and Hans Sachs there is an image of the setter's room with one setter and his boys. The book binder and type founder each worked in his own workshop. The investment of capital for such enterprises was, in the notion of commerce at that time, large, as the process between Gutenberg and Fust indicates. Gutenberg borrowed 800 Gulden twice for his enterprise from Fust, a substantial sum. Rudolf Blum, *Der Proceß Fust gegen Gutenberg*. Wiesbaden 1954.

77. G. Schanz, *Kolonisation und Industrie in Franken,* 1880. Josef Kulischer, *Allgemeine Wirtschaftgeschichte*, loc. cit., p. 115.
78. See the contributions by R. Sprandel, H. Kellenbenz and W. Zorn, in: H. Aubin, W. Zorn, *Handbuch der deutschen Wirtschafts- und Sozialgeshichte,* Stuttgart 1971.
79. H. Haussherr, *Wirtschaftsgeschichte der Neuzeit vom Ende des 14. bis zur Höhe des 19. Jahrhunderts,* 4th edition, Cologne 1970. Haussherr calls the guild system vile. It was that in later epochs. Richard Wagner in the 19th century, thus the period of high capitalism, condemned the guild music of the master singer of Nuremberg as pedantic, spiritless, laughable and despicable. However, one has to take issue with this condemnation. Nuremberg had no guilds in earlier times, but rather only in the 15th and 16th century, when the metal creations of the town were valued and sought after in all of Europe. Italian ambassadors reported on this Nuremberg industry; the blurb read: the Nuremberg *Tand* goes through every land—*Tand* can be understood as a commodity. *Tand* is also a toy. The master singer and the master metal workers came out of the same guild system, that evinced the same advantages and disadvantages. Hans Kellerbenz, *Nürenberger Handel um 1540. Mitteilungen des Vereins für Geschichte der Stadt Nürenberg*, Vol. 50, 1960. K. Menninger, *Zahlwort und Ziffer,* 3rd edition, Göttingen 1979.
80. R. Endres, *Einwohnerzahl ... Nürenbergs* (see above).
81. Die Geschichte dieser Rechenweisen bei Karl Menninger, [The history of these modes of reckoning according to Karl Menninger], *Zahlwort und Ziffer,* 3rd edition, Göttingen 1979.
82. Albrecht Dürer, in the *Unterweisung der Messung,* wrote about the system of space, not about numbers: The point is beginning and end of all corporeal things; it occupies no space, it is indivisible and thus exists in two modes, in corporeal space and in spirit [mind]. One can paint a point with the tip of a feather, which is a corporeal point and has, no matter how small it might be, thickness, length and breadth. The point in the mind has no dimensions, hence exists without thickness, length or breadth. 0 as a number, zero, exists in the system of numbers and is also portrayed. C. F. Gauss distinguished between the space of corporeal things and their movements from the mental realm. He also said that the system of numbers exists not doubly as with space but rather as a simple. This thought is new. Archimedes has shown in this regard that the point is without length, breadth and thickness. Dürer grasped this thought and he added to it that there are two points, a corporeal and a mental. Gauss drew the conclusion: space is twofold. The point can also be treated dimensionally so that the number of dimensions can be reduced to zero and the extension in each dimension can be reduced to zero as well. In this treatment zero is a number and also a geometrical figure indicated by a point.
83. The extension of the decimal system in Europe is traced back to the region of the Mediterranean in the 15th and 16th century: Pellos 1492, Adam Ries 1522, Christoph Rudolff 1530, Ciriacus Schreittmann 1578 and Simon Stevin with his book *De Thiende* (*Das Zehnte*, 1595 in the Netherlands) spread the decimal system and double-entry bookkeeping. The decimal system originates in Asia and was used earlier by the Indians, Persians and Arabs. Johannes Tropfke, *Geschichte der Elementarmathematik*, 4th edition, K. Vogel et al. (eds.), Berlin 1980. C. S. Smith, 'A Sixteenth Century Decimal System of Weights,' *Isis*, Vol. 46, 1955. In his *Probierbüchlein*

Schreittmann had written about weights (Part 2, Chapter 3, p. 17 verso ff.): "*Von den Namen dieser Gewichtlin.* [About the names of these weightlings]. The weightlings are called elementlings, or atoms, *Stüplin* or minutlings." Each name is bound to a property of weight, which is to be observed: "They are called elementlings because all other weights are created and composed of them as other earthly things have their origin and life from the divine elements. Atoms or *Stüplin* on account of the fact that they are indeed light and are like the dust that the son reveals [aufzeucht] in its shine. Minutling on account of the fact that they are in fact small and are to be reckoned to the smallest part among all weights." The present system of the chemical elements out of which the material world is composed is implied in this passage, but not however elaborated. The elements consist of atoms. The weights, after their properties of regulation, of composition, of smallness and of lightness have been observed, were integrated according to the decimal system. When ten of these elements are put together: "I stamp them with a pointling, after 20 a second one, after 30: I stamp them with a third pointling. The third is three times as heavy as the first." "To understand what each of their weights signify. If you want to know what each of the twenty-two weights signify you should take note that the weights are put on the cipher numbers or other common measure on the lines." Thus, the problem of the choice between the reckoning with Indian numbers or on the lines with reckoning pennies remains undecided in 1580. Ciriacus Schreittmann, *Probierbüchlin. Frembde und subtile Kunst, vormals im Truck nie gesehen, von Woge und Gewicht/ auch von aller handt Proben/ auff Ertz, Golt, Silber und andere Metall etc. Nützlich und gut allen denen so mit subtilen Künsten der Bergwerck umgehen. Frankfurt am Mayn bei Christian Egenolffs seligen Erben,* in Verlegung Doct. Adami Lancieri, Doct. Johannis Cnipii Anronici Secundi und Pauli Steinmeyers 1578.

84. Leonardo da Pisa, *Liber abaci,* 1202. The close relationship between the development of the merchant class and that of arithmetic can be shown in the example of the activities of Leonardo da Pisa and Pacioli in Italy and of Widman, Köbel, Stifel, Rudolff, Adam Ries, Apian, Grammateus among others in Germany.
Fibonaci determined the rules of the purchase of goods: a single man cannot buy or take. In his book he wrote, only two can buy or sell. In his arithmetic with the unknown (*cosa*, thing) he made a contribution to the development of numbers theory. In the reckoning of debts one could reckon with negative numbers, thus: 17–8=9. He did not use this sign, but he mastered the theory of it. Down to the 18th century some philosophers had not believed in the existence of the negative numbers. Fibonacci had recognized a debit as the solution of an equation and in this way had taken up the reality or actuality of the negative numbers. Debts existed in actuality. Pacioli popularized but did not invent bookkeeping and double-entry book entry. In 1494 Pacioli included a chapter in his book *Summa de arithmetica*, which contains "il metodo veneziano":, that is the Venetian method of double-entry bookkeeping is contained. In Venice, double-entry bookkeeping was already in use.
85. The book by Grammateus is entitled: *Buchhaltung durch Zornal (Kaufmannsbuch) Kaps (Warenbuch) und Schuldbuch,* 1549. J. Tropfke, *Geschichte der Elementarmathematik*, 4th edition, Vol. I, K. Vogel et al. (eds.), Berlin 1980. Further to be researched would be the role of Naples, Sicily, Calabria and Barcelona in trade with the Near East.
86. Mariners used Jacob's staff at sea, to measure the height of the sun and of the stars.
87. Adam Ries, 1492–1559, was a master of arithmetic in Erfurt, *Rezeßschreiber* (*Bergschreiber*). *Gegenschreiber*, *Zehnter*, and Court Arithmeticus of the Elector of Saxony. He directed a famous school of arithmetic. He died in Annaberg, the important centre of mining. Jacob Köbel was a mathematician and astronomer and contributed to the development of the astrolabe. His career

of studies [*sein Studiengang*] was linked to Copernicus. His *Rechenbüchlein uf den Linien mit Rechenpfennigen* and *Ein neu geordnet Visierbuch* appeared in 1515, his book *Mit Kreiden oder Schreibfedern durch die Zifferzahl zu rechnen* appeared in 1520.

88. J. Tropfke, *Geschichte der Elementarmathematik*, 4th edition, Vol. I, K. Vogel (ed.), 1980. B. L. von der Waerden, *A History of Algebra*, Berlin 1985. Grimm, *Deutsches Wörterbuch*, K. Menninger (see above). M. Stifel (Stiefel) wrote: *Die Coss Christoph Rudolffs mit schönen Exempeln gebessert*, Königsberg 1553/54.
89. F. Kluge, W. Mitzka, *Etymologisches Wörterbuch der deutschen Sprache*, 20th edition, Berlin 1967. A. Schirmer, *Wörterbuch der deutschen kaufmännischen Sprache*, Stuttgart 1911; M. Wis, *Ricerchi sopra gli italianismi nella lengua tedesca*, Helsinki 1955.
90. F. Kluge, W. Mitzka, *Etymologisches Wörterbuch der deutschen Sprache*, 20th edition, Berlin 1967. C. Battisti, G. Alessio, *Dizionario etimologica italiano*, Florence 1951.
91. R. Kaulla, *Die geschichtliche Entwicklung der modernen Werttheorien* (1906), Vaduz 1977, 2nd part. Id., *Die Lehre vom gerechten Preis. Zeitschrift für die gesamte Staatswissenschaft*, 1904. E. Schreiber, *Die volkswirtschaftlichen Anschauungen der Scholastik*, Jena 1913. S. Haguenauer, *Das justum pretium bei Thomas Aquinas*, Stuttgart 1931. J. W. Baldwin, 'The Medieval Theories of the Just Price.' *Transactions of the American Philosophical Society*, N.F., Vol. 49, Part 4., 1959.
92. M. Schwarz, *Copia und Abschrift ab und von Matheus Schwarzen eigne Handschrift, was das Buchalten sei. Die Musterbuchhandlung mit Beispielen dem Fugger-Geschäft in Venedig entnommen*, 1516–1550. Cf. Alfred Weitnauer, *Venezianischer Handel der Fugger, nach Musterbuchhandlung des Matthaeus Schwarz*, Munich 1931.
93. P. R. Beierlein (ed.), L. Ercker, *Beschreibung: Allerfürnemsten Mineralischen Erzt/ unnd Berckwercksarten* ... (1580), Berlin 1960.
94. Kluge, Mitzka, id. Caput also has the meaning of beakhead, beakhead figure, ship's nose.
95. Die Pegnitzschäfer , or the *Order of Flowers on the Pegnitz* , a society founded in 1644 by the Lord von *Harsdörfer* zu Nürnberg (which is known to be located on the Pegnitz) to improve the German language and to purge it of foreign words and additions. The members called themselves Pegnitz shepherds. See *Brockhaus Conversations-Lexicon* 1809. Also Grimm, vol. 24, p. 1704 and Meyers *Konversations-Lexikon*, vol. 15, p. 538, 1909.–trans.
96. Salamonio was a jurist, philosopher and politician and *Capitano del Popolo* in Florence in 1498. He came forward as an opponent of the papacy as the worldly rule in Rome. His book *De Principatu* appeared in 1544, cf. Mario D'Addio, *L'Idea del contratto sociale dai sofisti alla riforma e il 'De Principatu' di Mario Salamonio, 1954.*
97. The theory of the social contract belongs to the early period of our epoch and did not survive it. Yet, this theory is bound to the concept of natural law. See Otto Gierke, *Das deutsche Genossenschaftsrecht*, Vols. 3 and 4, 1954. In Vol. 4, the theory of the state and corporation down to the middle of the 17th century is the subject, that of natural law to the beginning of the 19th century. The main point of our consideration is the relationship between society and limited partner and the problem bound to it in the early period.
98. M. Luther, see above. T. Hobbes. *Leviathan*. 1651. Salamonio, see above.
99. M. Kaser, *Das römische Privatrecht*, 2nd. edition, Munich 1971. The extent of debt contracts reaches across many further areas of activity in the present than in antiquity.
100. We have discussed this system; see L. Krader, *Dialectic of Civil Society*, Assen 1976.
101. In the medieval *Schwabenspiegel* the princes too were counted in the retinue of the emperor.
102. The shareholder of a pit [*Gewerke*] was a participant in a mining enterprise. From the 15th to the 16th century some had worked, and above that profited from the labour as shareholders. Trade

union was only related to the working class in the 20th century, and in fact only to a portion of it. Excepted were the non-organized workers.

103. Battisti, Alessio, loc. cit. These meanings of the word are also attested earlier. It is not about the meaning of the word in Italian, but rather about the conceptual field of European commerce in the capitalist period.
104. Kaser, *Das römische Privatrecht*, loc. cit., p. 302ff. The partnership [*societas*] is not mentioned. Only the [late] *societas publicanorum*, the "society" [*Gesellschaft*] of the tax and customs lessees [*Steuer-und Zollpächter*] [p. 308]. Whether the state, the *Municipium*, and the *Colonia* are corporations in the same sense than private law associations [*privatrechtliche Vereine*] is a problem that we won't be dealing with.
105. R. Sohm, L. Mitteis, L. Wenger, *Institutionen. Geschichte und System des römischen Privatrechts*, Munich 1930, p. 207f., 435. The *universitas* (p. 199) counts as well as a corporation or association. Kaser (loc. cit., p. 304) says, the *universitas* is sometimes conceived of as a corporation, sometimes not.
106. O. Gierke, *Die Genossenschaftstheorie und die deutsche Rechtsprechung* (1887), Graz 1963. The joint-stock company is recognized here as a legal person and treated as a legally capable corporate body.
107. Strieder, *Geschichte kapitalistischer Organisationsformen*, loc. cit., p. 110ff, 125f.
108. Strieder, idem. G. Schmoller, *Jahrbuch für Gesetzgebung, Verwaltung und Volkswirtschaft im Deutschen Reich*, Vols. 14–17, 1890–1893. R. Ehrenberg, *Das Zeitalter der Fugger*, 2 volumes, Jena 1896. Philippe Dollinger, *Die Hanse*, 3rd edition, Stuttgart 1981. H. Kellenbenz, W. Zorn, R. Sprandel, in: Aubin, Zorn, *Handbuch der deutschen Wirtschaft- und Sozialgeschichte*, op. cit., 1971.
109. Dollinger, *Die Hanse*, loc. cit.
110. C. M. Cipolla, *Before the Industrial Revolution. European Society and Economy 1000–1700*, London 1976.
111. Strieder, *Organisationsformen*, loc. cit. Dollinger (*Die Hanse*, 1981) cited single cases of the formation of consortiums; loc. cit., Second Part. The consortiums appear not to have lasted long.
112. R. Ehrenberg, *Das Zeitalter der Fugger*, vol. I, Jena 1896.
113. J. Strieder, *Organisationsformen*, loc. cit., p. 142ff. Strieder had shown that this was about a corporation of Jihlavan cloth makers, which was established by means of capital investment. It is an early form of the capitalist company or society; it is probable that a company established in the 18th century was an authentic joint-stock company. The iron trade company was the active moment, to which the cloth companies reacted, driven by necessity to relinquish their previous guild-like treatment.
114. P. Mantoux, *La révolution industrielle*, Paris 1973. In Frankfurt am Main the system of prohibition was continued into the middle of the 19th century. On account of the locksmiths the iron traders were not permitted to sell any chains for roping, trees, spans, springs and ships, further for wheel-headed nails, shackles, window frames and tap wrenches; for the benefit of knifesmiths and swordsmiths they were not allowed to sell swords, sabers, rapiers, and blades; for the benefit of the gunsmiths no guns; for the girdle makers no spurs, riding sticks, stirrups and currycombs. J. Kulischer, *Allgemeine Wirtschaftsgeschichte*, 1958, vol. II, p. 139. Other prohibitions in Schoenlank, von der Goltz, Kellenbenz (see above).
115. Strieder, *Organisationsformen*, loc. cit., 3rd book, chapter I.
116. H. Kellenbenz, in: Aubin, Zorn, *Handbuch …*, chapter 18.
117. R. Ehrenberg, *Das Zeitalter der Fugger*, Vol. I, Jena 1896.

118. Ehrenberg, loc. cit. J. Strieder, *Organisationsformen.* loc. cit., 3rd book, 2nd chapter. J. Kulischer, *Allgemeine Wirtschaftsgeschichte,* Vol. 2, chapter 16. H. Kellenbenz, in: Aubin, Zorn, ibid., chapter 18.
119. W. Sombart, *Das Wirtschaftleben im Zeitalter des Frühkapitalismus. Der moderne Kapitalismus,* Vol. 2, 1. Half volume, Berlin 1969, chapter 4.

PART III

CHAPTER FOUR

Machines, Mechanics, Time and Geometry

The machine is a tool, but not all tools are machines. The bodily organs of humans and animals are tools, or they can serve as tools in the process of labour, but they are not machines. Thus, the answer concerning the nature of machines can be answered in the negative: in the past, people tried to consider organs and bodies as machines; yet this way and means of looking at machines essentially fell into disuse. Machines and machinery are those tools which do not consist of muscles and bones of living beings. A machine is set into motion through muscle power as well as through other natural forces, wind, water, gravity, steam and heat, electricity, electromagnetism, organic and inorganic forces, atomic energy and so on. The machine is principally defined as a tool whose components can be distinguished from the driving forces which move it. The lever, the wedge and the inclined plane, the crane and the various mills, like the peddle, water, and windmill; the wheel in its various kinds, like the water, peddle and spinning wheel, then the wagon, the hammer, the knife, the nail, the pulley, the gate, the scale, the chain, the rope, the bellows and the smelter are called machines. If the component parts of the tool in general do not or cannot be distinguished from its driving force [*Triebkraft*] and moving force [*Bewegungskraft*], and further, if both forces are also indistinguishable from one another, thus it is not at all or only with difficulty recognized as a machine. In the 17th century a mechanical worldview prevailed.[1] We direct attention to the fact that mechanics and the mechanical were differently conceptualized in the 17th century than in the 20th. That the differences which are rooted here were insufficiently perceived explains in part the conceptual difficulties of the mechanistic worldview of the 17th century. The theory of the tool as a projection of the organ also has great difficulties but it has the one advantage in that it differentiates the projections of the organs from the driving force. The hand as an organ is different from the hammer, which counts as a projection of the fist, and does not serve as the hammer itself. The theory of technics as the projection of human organs—as, for example, the hand or a part of it, like the fingernails, was discussed by Ernst Kapp. His conception is one of the basic components of the modern theory of technics. We concern ourselves primarily with the tasks and ideas in the matter of technics in the 15th and 16th century.

The component parts of the machine are simple, like the wedge, which counts as *machina simplex*, or it is assembled out of many parts and is called *machina composita*. The complicated machines arise out of the simpler ones. Machines are also to be distinguished in another sense, namely, those which are not physically separated from the driving or moving force and those which are outfitted with an independent driving force or force of movement. The machine which is set into motion can be distinguished from the stationary machine. The movable machine has the means to eliminate the friction of the entire tool, to minimize or to overcome it: to wit by means of the wheel, the pulley, gravity and of electromagnetic or chemical means. Oil, fat, and lubricant were introduced to reduce or master the effect of friction. Theoretical mastery of the principles of statics in mechanics was in the past the basis of implementation, for the creation, for activating or actuating the machines; now, however, the principles of dynamics like thermodynamics, electrodynamics, aerodynamics, quantum dynamics and so on are applied.

Stationary machines are distinguished from portable ones. The stationary machine has a driving force, which sets it in motion, like the hand does the pulley, and heat, the oven. These machines are driven, but not moved. A cart which is set into motion is a machine. The complicated machines of the stationary sort are called abstract machinery, industry and even large-scale industry like in chemical factories. The mechanism is two-fold: the abstract principle and the concrete tool. The abstract instrument of labour is not a machine, yet it can well express the principle of the same.

The driving force is conceptualized as a motor, which sets in motion the machine in the mine, the ship and the wheel. Human and animal muscles, wind and water were the major driving forces of transport in the 15th and 16th century. Heat, chemical forces in general and gravity were now employed for the activation of stationary machines, for the furnaces in glass manufacturing, in the smelters, in the salt works or in the assaying arts. Wheels and the moving force for such furnaces are likewise parts of the stationary machine.

These principal observations are not only valid for the entirety of machines and the treatment of machines in the 20th century, but also for those in earlier epochs—of the 15th and 16th century—albeit there abstracted from the dynamic, that is, thermodynamic, aerodynamic, electrodynamic and other principles. Aerodynamics was in the earlier epochs implicit in the weather machine and in the bellows, thermodynamics in the bloomery furnace [*Blähofen* (*Blau*—or *Blasofen*)], and the force of gravity was empirically applied in the art of hay drying. The sailboat, the mechanical clock, the water wheel and the weather machine also possess the principles of dynamics—in part empirically through experience, in part abstractly conceived and practically treated. Through the practical application of mechanical and chemical principles in the process of labour, the transition from the earlier epochs of modernity was formed primarily into that of the industrial revolution and high capitalism.

Artistry is also of two kinds: it is either a kind of machine, like the rag and chain pump in mining, or the way and means of how a machine is set to operate or to be put in motion, and how it is applied in the process of labour. Technics is artistry in a second sense. A mechanism can be distinguished from the machine in that this is a tool from which the God descends deus ex machina in classical tragedy. The machine in modern times is increasingly less set into operation by human and animal muscle power, and increasingly more through the application of mechanical and chemical laws.

The mechanism in opposition to the machine can be considered as that object—including the tool and the instrument of labour—which is put into service or set in motion through the application of mechanical laws. The driving force or moving force can be mastered by men—they can introduce them and turn them off as well. The concept of mechanical laws and of their effectiveness is changed in the course of history. The laws of mechanics laid out in the 15th and 16th century, are different than those in the 20th century. Nevertheless, we shall understand the concept of mechanism as the object which is put into service or set in motion through the application of mechanical laws. The concept of mechanism is thus related to the object as to the process of operation and of movement. In the past the laws of celestial mechanics were conceived as absolute and their scope as eternal.[2] Man as microcosm possesses the force of motion of muscles, nerves and bones; the universe as macrocosm possesses the force of motion of gravity. These forces are the natural characteristics of the material word. Albrecht Dürer distinguished geometry from mechanics. Isaac Newton made the same distinction 150 years later.

Mechanics was in this sense practical and illiberal. Now, however, it is conceived of as practical and theoretical, liberal and illiberal. In the 17th century the universe was considered as a machine, as the *theatrum machinarum* or as the showplace of machinery and of the mechanics of the heavens. Their laws were geometrical, necessary, introduced in accord with strict evidence. The physicists and mathematicians showed that the mechanism of the universe, of the heavenly bodies and of space, ran continuously and without limit. By this means they solved the problem of the *perpetuum mobile*, in theory and in practice. The movement of the heavens continued ad infinitum. Herewith the concepts *perpetuitas* and continuity are related to the world machine.

In 1525 Albrecht Dürer in his *Unterweisung der Messung* [Instructions in Measurement] presented this artistry for the workman, the painter, the goldsmith, the sculptor, the stone mason, the carpenter, The art lover, the highly intelligent and the youth. In this book, Dürer asserted: "The highly astute Euclid had put together the foundation of geometry. Whoever understands it well, has no need whatsoever for the following described matter." He presented the distinction between geometry and mechanics in the following way: to demonstratively grasp artistry means to grasp it exactly. In this sense he wrote: "As soon as I want to deconstruct a hendecagon in the circle, I take a quarter of the circle's diameter and obtain eight equal parts of it itself, and move with this length around the circle; if it happens coincidentally then it is found *mechanice* but not *demonstrative*. Further, if I should make with agility a 13-sided figure thus I tear out of a centre a circular line. Afterwards, I tear out a half diameter.a.b. and cut it with a point.d. from one another in the middle and use the lengths.e.d. thirteen times around the circle. It is however also *mechanice* and not *demonstrative*."[3]

We have already seen that Hartmann Schopper in his edition of the *Ständebuch* of 1574 *De Omnibus Illiberalibus sive Mechanicus Artibus*, that is, had written "about all illiberal or mechanical arts." Geometry belongs to the liberal, mechanics to the illiberal arts. The mechanical arts were also called *sedentaria*.[4] Dürer treated both arts, the liberal and illiberal, and he mastered the difference between geometry and mechanics and the concept of geometric proof. He wrote: "Three kinds of things can be measured. First, a length that has neither width nor thickness, then a length that has width and thickness. These both begin and end with a point. But a point is a thing that has neither size, length, width nor thickness, which can be made or which we can conceive in our senses." "And thus, a point occupies no space, for it is indivisible. And from mind or thought it may be placed at any end or location." "Now when this point from its first beginning is extended, it is thus called a line."[5] After Dürer had defined the point and the line geometrically and differentiated them from their pictorial treatment, he presented the straight line and circle line, the wavy line and helical line, the solid or cube and the ball or sphere. In this way he distinguished the idea of the object in the mind from the corporeal manipulation of it. The former way of treatment is geometrical, the latter mechanical. Mechanical means nimble, agile, fleet as well as without spirit, thought or feeling. Point, line, magnitude, length, width, thickness are not corporeal things which can be produced by hand. The point is a thing, that one can conjure in the mind. It is indivisible and occupies no space. The relationship between indivisibility and inextensibility of the point appeared in the geometrical thinking of G. W. Leibniz 150 years, and in the mathematical system of H. Grassmann, 320 years after Dürer. C. F. Gauss had introduced the difference between the two kinds of research of space at the beginning of the 19th century. Space in external nature is to be conceived differently than space in the mind. 300 years earlier, Dürer had so presented the concept of space that the point, which was demonstratively conjured, is presented differently than the point which is mechanically treated. A system derived from this was published by G. T. Fechner as well in the 19th century. Dürer expressed himself further in this regard: "For I may with my mind throw a point high into the air or let it fall into the depths, however I cannot reach it with my body." To treat the point geometrically or pictorially or mechanically, these are two tasks that are different from one another. Now Dürer traced back and grounded the mechanical labour of the workman on the geometric idea. That which the cabinet maker, carpenter or architect makes is already outlined in the mind; yet in the mind one can sketch the outline exactly, with the hand only approximately. Dürer said, the master has mastered the rules of the art, and with his tool creates the table, the house or the picture in practice. Marx said, the architect, no matter how poor he may be, has the house in his head and then builds it with his hands. Dürer means the right workman has learned and mastered the art of measurement and then mechanically works it out. These thoughts agree with one another.

Dürer studied in Italy and took over the laws of perspective from Filippo Brunelleschi. Dürer's theory is different from that of the Italian masters. Leone Battista Alberti identified the laws of perspective and pictured them in conjunction with his *demontrationes*.[6] Yet, as Panofsky says, these *demonstrationes* were in no way models of geometric processes, but rather actual pictures.[7] Dürer presented practical manual labour *mechanice*, and the theoretical labour *demonstrative*. The line is invisible and is understood in the mind [*Gemüt*] through the straight cleft. "For by such a means the inner understanding must be shown in the external work." The purpose of Dürer's work is not mathematical education in theory, but rather the practical instruction in measurement, so that what appears before one's eyes would be better understood in order to improve craftsmanship.

Dürer's theory of mechanics appears in the following century in Newton: "The ancients held *Mechanics* (according to *Pappus*'s statements), to be very important for the study of nature, and the moderns, after abandoning substantial forms and hidden characteristics, have begun to trace the appearances of nature back to mathematical laws. It appeared appropriate in the given work, *Mathematics*, to carry it to the point that it relates to *Physics*. The ancients presented mechanics in a two-fold way, as *rational*, which moves forward with exactitude by means of evidence, and as something *practical*. To the latter belong all manual skills from which the name mechanics is derived. Since, however, artists are not used to working exactly, *mechanics* and *geometry* can be distinguished to the degree that everything exact counts as geometry, everything less exact to mechanics. The errors committed should not however be ascribed to the art, but rather to the artists. Whosoever works in a less exact manner, is an imperfect mechanic; on the contrary, whoever can work in the most exact way would be the most accomplished of all mechanics."[8] The development of this line of thought reaches out from Dürer over Kepler, to Galilei and Newton. We have already pointed to Dürer's relationship to the Italians and to Euclid.

The perfect mechanic created the universe according to this idea. In the 17th century, this creator was called God or nature. Celestial mechanics was presented as complete, adequate, exact and accurate. Errors and mistakes arose from the thoughts of men, of the physicists and mathematicians like Galileo Galilei, Descartes and Newton, whose method did not suffice and was not strong enough, to present the effect of God or of nature. Our geometry and mechanics, the science of space and of the movement of natural bodies are not the same things. The preparation for this idea is already present in Dürer, Gauss and Newton.

Ernst Mach defined mechanics in the following way: The investigation of motion and of the balance of masses leads to the name mechanics. According to Herbert Goldstein the object of classical mechanics is the investigation of the motion of material bodies. With regard to Dürer's and Newton's concept of mechanics, we have already spoken. Kant traced the mechanical philosophy back to the simple elements or physical atoms. He wrote in this connection: "The way of explanation of the specific diversity of materials through the quality and composition of their smallest parts, as machines, is the mechanical philosophy." Machines are the simple tools of external self-moving forces.[9]

Dürer conceived mechanics practically, geometry theoretically, as the basis for the practical activity of man. Leonardo da Vinci compared the arts of poetry and painting in his diaries. It was said that painting is a mechanical art in a double sense: first, because the painter works with his hands, in order to bring out the creations of his mind and second, because the artistic creations are sold for money. The works of a painter on copper will take longer to produce than poetry. Leonardo honoured mechanics as the paradise of the mathematical sciences, as he said, because through it the harvest of mathematics is achieved. He did not consider the world as a machine, but rather as a living being. Mechanical force has an active not a corporeal life. We cannot see this force, and it is not accessible to the other senses.[10]

Galileo Galilei had said that numerals are the language of nature. Descartes wrote nature is not a Goddess, but rather nothing other than matter. Spinoza expressed himself: *Deus sive natura*, God or nature; he did not exactly write: *aut Deus aut natura*—either God or nature. While Galilei wanted to comprehend nature through numbers, Descartes and Leibniz had attempted to explain the world as a machine.

Mechanics and mechanism in the workshop were already developed in antiquity. The laws of statics in mechanics were worked out by Archimedes and in modern times by S. Stevin in Holland. Mathematics and mechanics are not the same and were conceived in the 17th century as the same neither in extent nor in method. In the 20th century some researchers conceived rational mechanics as an aspect of mathematics. In the 17th century this assertion was given prominence as a problem. Galilei had shown that the laws of celestial mechanics—those of statics and dynamics—were the same as the earthly laws. Newton ascertained that the laws of gravity were the same in both areas. The motion of the heavenly bodies could be calculated if it were assumed that geometry for this region is complete, the circles perfect, the lines absolutely straight, and so on. In the empirical-terrestrial sphere everything is inexact. Not only our thoughts, but rather in addition the instruments and mathematical calculations of the genial thinkers are weak. Thinkers from Dürer to Gauss had determined that the point in mind and the point circumscribed with the feather are not the same objects. Mechanics is thus not simple, but rather multiple and complicated. Newton drew the conclusion, and Dürer problematized the concept of mechanics.

Some thinkers were convinced that the world is a machine; the human body is according to the same conception a world machine writ small, hence a microcosm.[11] Technics and science are aspects of the labour process. The relation between parts and whole is seldom an object of research. Our task is not to examine this relation in general, but rather in a determinate area and in one period as a contribution to the problem of periodization.

In the 17th century progress was made in the practical analysis of the vacuum. Otto von Guericke had developed a vacuum pump. J. B. van Helmont had researched water, steam and gas; he had analysed the concept of gas as chaos and derived the word gas from chaos. Weight exerted pressure on the body and air pressure can be measured. Van Helmont had brought out a corpuscular theory of air. According to his conception, air had small pores, like skin, and these pores supposedly contain foreign particles as well, like a gas, which in turn is conceived of in terms of corpuscles. Between the corpuscles and the particles air is supposedly empty. These corpuscles are also referred to as atoms.[12] Evangelisto Torricelli, Galileo Galilei, van Helmont and Blaise Pascal contributed to the theory of the vacuum and of air in connection with the development of aerostatics and aerodynamics. The instruments for the examination of the vacuum were suction tubes, gas bottles and glass tubes filled with mercury. The chemical property of mercury—it is a metal and at the temperature of the human body is not hard and solid like the other metals, iron, copper and so on, but rather liquid—was fundamental for their experiments. The vacuum was in theory presented in relation to the concept of the ether. In the 16th and 17th century, the suction power of the tube and capillarity, then the action of sprinklers and pumps and that of the fluids, like that of water, were observed and explained through nature's abhorrence of a void, called *horror vacui*. This *horror vacui* can be comprehended emotionally or as a personification of nature. Galileo Galilei interpreted it neither as an emotion nor as a personification of nature, but rather considered it as the *resistenza del vacuo*, as the force of resistance like the other natural forces, gravity and so on. He thought the resistance of the vacuum is a measurable force, and he sought to accomplish these kinds of measurements with a sealed column of water with a boot pump. The attempts were unsuccessful because the theoretical conceptions like the *altezza limitatissima*, the limiting height or the highest limiting value of the water which determined the upper limit of value for the resistance, were faulty. His instruments were not suitable for the practice. Torricelli had the notion of the resistance of the vacuum, but did not assume that of the *altezza limitatissima*, and instead of raising the water above 18 Italian Ells, he carried out experiments with mercury in a glass tube about a meter in length. In this way he came upon the theory and practice of measuring air pressure, which is fundamental for the assembly of the modern barometer. Blaise Pascal later wrote about the weight of air and further—through mountain experiments among others—developed the barometer as well as its theory.

Subsequently Otto von Guericke conducted experiments in the field of aerostatics. In antiquity, the air together with earth, water, and fire were understood as one of the four elements of nature. In the 16th and 17th century as well this conception of nature was propagated by Agricola, for example. Guericke did not consider air as an element but rather as the scent of bodies. Air is thus not a primitive or original in nature, that which constitutes a characteristic of the element, but rather that which is derived from corporeal being. Air has the characteristic of compressibility and in general of the change in volume through heating, which is ascertained by means of a rise in temperature and through the reduction of heat. He created the vacuum by pumping out a water-filled vessel. He conducted further experiments in relation to the air vacuum by enclosing a small water-filled wooden barrel in a larger one; he pumped out the water from the smaller into the larger and observed that here, too, the water flowed back into the smaller one. He took a large hollow copper ball and further a glass ball into his experiment for he could observe that the wooden barrel was leaky. On this basis he showed that air had a pressure which could be measured. The pressure is not constant but rather variable; it varies according to the warmth or coldness of the air. Air has weight which changes according to temperature and pressure. These experiments by Galileo Galilei, Evangelista Torricelli, Blaise Pascal and Otto von Guericke were expressed and summarized quantitatively in Robert Boyle's law and later by Mariotte. Further, Guericke tore apart a ball consisting of two composite halves first pumped empty with a great bang by the force of 16 horses.[13]

Mechanism can be understood concretely or abstractly. Concretely mechanism appears as an *automaton materiale*, as something material, physical, palpable.[14] In abstracto, mechanism is to be understood as the effect of the laws of mechanics. These laws are not formulated today in the same sense as in the past, and in the future, they will probably change once again. To interpret the world as a machine or as a mechanism is a consequence of reverie. This way of thinking was taken up enthusiastically by means of the victory of machines developed in the early capitalist period and of their principles, and thus one tried to explain everything mechanically at that time.

4.1 Mechanical Clocks and the Consciousness of Time

4.1.1 Mechanical Clocks

Mechanics, the machine and mechanism have their connections to the theory of geometry, to the philosophy of nature, to the mechanization of the worldview, to the development of physical theory and to the practice in the workshop. The development of the mechanical clock in the late Middle Ages and in early modernity is bound up with the theory and practice of mechanics and with the transformation of the concept of time, of the measurement of time and of the consciousness of time. It was already common in antiquity to divide the day into twenty-four hours.[15] Some machines like the sundial, sand clock and water clock were already invented for the measurement of time. The calendar or reckoning in years, months, days and parts thereof is documented among almost all peoples. The concept of a particular length of time, large or small, and the division of the same into smaller or larger parts has a written history in the Near and Far East, in Central America, in Europe and in South Asia.

Mechanization of the measurement of time in Europe during the late Middle Ages was introduced by many guilds and by artisan activities. In the *Divina Commedia* Dante mentioned the chiming clock. It is probable that a mechanical clock was conceived abstractly and outlined in the 12th/13th century. Mechanical clocks in the 14th and 15th century were both large and small; the large ones were tower, cathedral and wall clocks. The small ones were pocket watches which could be carried with one. Both kinds of clocks point to the wealth of the towns or of the persons who could acquire them for themselves. They immediately became an object of social status. Towns in Europe were proud of their clock towers; individuals were proud of their watches. In the 15th century this was made palpable in the name *Nuremberg's egg* or little egg [*Eierlein*], perhaps mistakenly through the mix-up with the word *Ührlein* [little clock]. Mechanism, town ornaments or body adornment, and the growing consciousness of time were bound up with one another. We won't pursue the competition concerning the invention of the mechanical clock or of the little egg of Nuremberg, which became a matter of honour. As well, there was speculation and conflict concerning the function of the early mechanical clocks, whether the hour was numbered or struck in the cloister or Church or in the town, whether in the service of labour, of the observatory, of prayer and so on.

As soon as the mechanical clock was developed, many European towns adopted them. The clock towers and cathedral clocks were assembled in the cities and cloisters in England across Europe to the Adriatic coast. Wealthy citizens and rich churches paid handsomely for them.

The mechanical problem of the measurement of time, namely the maintenance, storage and regulated release [*Freisetzung* (detent)] of mechanical force, was solved early. The storage and release of force was concentrated and regulated in the mechanical clock. These arts, so it was thought, were all practiced by guilds of metal workers. Metal workers in the 14th century constructed wheel clocks which resulted in the production of highly artistic clocks. Their gear trains were similar to the open winches. In the 16th century mechanical clocks were miniaturized by the metal guilds and transformed into pocket and dress watches.[16]

Christian Huygens invented a pendulum clock and the escape wheel for the clock in the 17th century. It was ascertained in the Netherlands that the clockwork escape mechanism had a connection to the construction of the late medieval crossbow. The cathedral and castle clocks in Salisbury and Dover in England were not manufactured by makers of the crossbow; however, in Cologne, Aachen, Arnheim, Wesel, Bruges, Deventer, Gand, Leiden, Nijmegen, Rotterdam and Zutphen, the arbalest makers were brought in to fabricate, regulate and repair mechanical clocks. They built the clocks at Ragusa and Lille. It can be observed that the bolt nut of the arbalest and the clockwork escape mechanism are similar to one another if not exactly identical. The *semicirculus* or the half-circle shaped escape mechanism of the clock and the bolt nut of the arbalest are homologous creations. Leonardo da Vinci and Richard von Wallingford sketched the cross-shaped escape mechanism of the clock according to the template of the homologous part of the arbalest. The opposite direction of the process of thought is not excluded. In both cases there is a close connection between the artistry of arbalest making and that of the clock.[17] The mechanical clock in Milan was built with a weight pull, hence with a different principle than that of the arbalest. Up until now over 50 great mechanical clocks were found in Europe dating from the 14th and 15th century.[18] The most well-known public clocks of the 14th and 15th century are shown in Table 6.

Table 6: Mechanical Clocks in Europe in the 14th and 15th Centuries

Country	14th Century	15th Century
Bohemia	Olmütz Prague	
Denmark		Roskilde
England	Dover Castle St. Albans Glastonbury Salisbury Norwich	
France	Chartres Lille Perpignon Cluny Lyon Rouen Dijon Paris	Bourges
Germany (or in the German-speaking World)	Aachen Nuremberg Breslau Stralsund Cologne Strassburg Frankfurt am Main Wesel Munich	Danzig Magdeburg Hildesheim Villingen Jena Worms Lübeck
Italy	Bologna Milan Ferrara Padua Genoa Parma	Venice
Netherlands	Arnheim Ghent Rotterdam Brugge Leiden Zutphen Deventer Nijmegen	
Sicily (or Dalmatia)		Ragusa
Sweden	Lund	
Switzerland	Basel	Lucerne

It is probable that further investigation will discover still more clocks of this sort. For time measurement sundials are more exact than mechanical clocks, but they count only the sunny hours. Classical and the most recent research on the reciprocal interaction between the workshop and the science of chronometry have referred to this topic. The gear wheel was applied in the development and construction of the clock, of the water mill in mining as well as in the processing of grain.[19]

The small clock or egg of Nuremberg originated in Nuremberg, from which the pocket watch was developed. It exhibits the same characteristics as that of the tower clock, namely, the mastering of the useful labour process required for the manufacture of the clocks, for the origin of the consciousness of time, for the wealth that is required for the creation, origination or purchase of the clock and its repair, and interest in the civic or personal aesthetic, that is, the clock tower or the egg as ornamentation. In this sense, Hamburg, like other cities in Europe as well, had commissioned an instrument for civic ornamentation in the 15th century, which exhibits the same principles of the Church and City Hall clocks.

The day was divided into hours, the hours into minutes, the minutes into small fractions. The measurement of time in the 15th century was accomplished approximately as it was in the 19th and 20th century. The gear wheels of wood were created for the great clock of Nuremberg in the 15th century. The principle of exact time measurement was instituted in a practical way by the spatial shift of the gear wheels. The counting of the submultiples of minutes was reckoned by the number of expired "teeth" of the clockwork. The relation between space and time as well as the reciprocal action of the measurement of space and time was already conceived in the 15th century. The precision of this measurement of seconds was traced back to the principle of the clock; that is, the clock is the optical-spatial translation of the movement of time, of experience, of the counting up and of the consciousness of the passage of time, as well as of the motions of the celestial bodies and of life. They were not only counted up in hours, minutes and seconds by the clock but were also visible and made audible by the bells. The arts of time, space and arithmetic are bound up with the metal, wood, glass and other industries and arts. This assumes the idea that time was valued in general and, further, that a particular value was placed on the exact reckoning of the units and the extent of the course of time. The time of the living being, and the time of inorganic bodies, is the same. The mechanization of the worldview, the measurement of the weight of commodities of grain, oil, metal, wood, meat, leather, salt, wine and beer, geometry, the arts of arithmetic and stereometry in the practice of merchants and likewise in pharmaceuticals and astronomy and finally chronometry were elaborated together.

The principle of mechanization is not one and the same in the course of history. Archimedes principle was changed in the course of development in modern times by Leonardo, Stevin, Newton, Gauss and Einstein. Statics was based on four principles from Archimedes down to the epoch of Stevin and Galileo: the principle of the gear, of the inclined plane, of the composition (parallelogram) of forces and that of the virtual displacements in the actions of machines. Only in the 16th and 17th century were the two last-named principles of statics given expression by Stevin and Galileo. Galileo and Newton had founded and developed the other department of mechanics, dynamics, in a classical form during the 17th century. Celestial dynamics or the laws of motion of heavenly bodies served as the model for the laws of all bodily movements. Space and time were taken up in an absolute sense by Newton and Leibniz; that means, space and time were treated separately, and both were considered in the absolute sense as not further analysable, both considered *non plus ultra*. In Newtonian and Leibnizian mechanics space is a kind of extension.

Descartes took a further step and asserted that the nature of matter and the body was the same; both consisted of a substance which is extended in length, thickness and breadth; nature is matter and matter is extension. Time, according to Newton and Leibniz, had extension. The relation of the extension of space and time was investigated by A. Einstein in the 20th century. The space of Newton and Leibniz was considered absolute in another sense; it had the three coordinates of our optical experience. Dürer had already written about this, as we have seen. Leibniz, in opposition to Newton, had grasped space relationally. Only in the 20th century were the three coordinates of optical experience, thus length, breadth and thickness, which were seen as generally valid for the universe in general, called into question by Einstein's theory of relativity. Space and time in this theory were taken up together as spacetime; this is relative as there are no preferred coordinates. All three dimensions of space—length, breadth and height—stand in right angles to one another, and thus enjoy a constant or preferred coordination. The space of our sense experience, in particular our optical perception, is an objective datum of the material world and its corporeal movements, in which three and only three dimensions of space are found. This notion of space is constant and presupposes the concept of mechanics in the 16th as in the 20th century. The concept of space in quantum mechanics is related to other notions of dimension. We showcase here only the constants in the principles of research of nature between the 16th and 20th century, however we are otherwise more concerned with variables than constants. Nature is no atom, rather it is divisible; it is a composition of particles according to corpuscular theory. Newton was of the opinion that light as well is composed of particles and their movement. C. Huygens represented the view that light was wavelike and not of the particle kind. In the 20th century both conceptions are valid; it is wavelike and corpuscular.

Usually two opposed principles are featured in the creation of mechanical clocks in the 14th and 15th century. It is assumed that the mechanical clock with the weight pull came into existence in the late 13th century and in the middle of the 15th century with the main spring—each with a corresponding practice of winding up. The clockmaker Paulus Almanus, Paul the German, left a handwritten document, in which 30 mechanical clocks in Rome in 1475 were described.[20] These mechanisms were also used in the art of war. Relations between the art of war and the art of pyrotechnics, of metallurgy, of the art of clock-making and of mining have been emphasized multiple times and are well-known.

The mechanical clock, the accurate measurement of time and the application of these products in manufacture, mining, in the art of seafaring and astronomical observation were developed at the same time. The great successes in the workshop are recognized as objective events and have a rational basis.

In this case a rational worldview led to its changing into irrationalism. The reflection of the rational macrocosm as the great clock and God as the great clockmaker is a mystical conception of the universe; the conclusion, that the clockmaker in the workshop is a little God, is a micro deity, is derived from it. Mechanics in general and celestial mechanics in particular are treated here metaphysically, not scientifically.[21] Time is also measured in a purely practical fashion. In the 16th century the counting of the months of the year began with January. Years and leap years were calculated (Adam Ries). 1556 and 1560 were counted as leap years, each with 366 days; the normal year was reckoned at 365 days. 52 weeks and 1 day are a normal year, 52 weeks and 2 days a leap year. 7 days are a week. One day and a night amount to 24 hours. A normal year has 8760 hours and a leap year 8784 hours. 4 years have 35,064 hours. An hour has 60 minutes, a minute has 60 seconds, a second has 60 tierces. Julius Ceasar initially created the calendar with the assistance of the famous mathematician, Sosigenes.[22] This calendar was introduced by Caesar in the year 45 before the turn of the calendar. Sosigenes was an Egyptian Greek, an astronomer and mathematician in Caesar's service. Most recent research has not refuted Ries' conception. Sosigenes accused the Greek mathematician Eudoxos that his theories did not salvage the phenomena of the celestial bodies (*sozein ta phainomena*).[23]

The development of the mechanical clock, advances in the art of metal working, in chemistry, in the work of mining, in assaying, in geography and astronomy, in physiology and in mathematics had a deeply reciprocal effect on one another. Mechanics was either envisioned concretely as a mechanical clock or abstractly, that is, as lawful [*gesetzmäßig*]. The concrete idea points only to the extent of human imagination, to poetry and fantasy. The most abstract of all notions is an interesting mixture of metaphysics and empirical physics. The mechanical worldview proceeds from the notion that the universe, the solar system and life are explained by the investigation of mechanical laws. It is not possible to refute a metaphysical conception through empirical research in cosmology or biology, in geology or in anthropology. Hence, we have nothing to say in this context about the metaphysics of Descartes or Leibniz.

The science of mechanics is researched and conceptualized differently today than in the past. In the 17th century mathematics was not separated from empirical mechanics. Today they are treated separately. It is also likely that mechanics will change further in the future (see above). Since the laws of mechanics change, the mechanization of the worldview and the mechanistic worldview itself will change.[24]

In different parts of Europe during the 15th, 16th, and 17th century mechanics in the labour process was advanced, and tools were continuously made more complicated. The mechanical clock in comparison to the sundial is only one example among others in this connection. We have already spoken a little about mechanization in the art of weaving and we will later examine more closely mechanisms in mining. Machines were more reliably constructed in the 15th, 16th, and 17th century, better controlled and regulated in waterpower, in meteorology, in haulage and in transportation. The risk in the investment of capital was taken up as well as the risk of death for the labourers. The development of the art of seafaring had made voyages across the ocean possible and led to the exploitation of ore deeper underground. The number and complexity of tools in the process of labour were increased.[25] The easing of corporal labour was seldom mentioned, because it did not happen. Agricultural labour, as Hans Sachs mentioned, remained hard and bitter for the peasant. Schoenlank and Kriegk repeatedly pointed out that it was no different with labour in the town.

In the 19th and 20th century systematic attempts to limit physical effort in the factory were undertaken, and it was concluded on this basis that the alleviation of these efforts and the easing of physical labour were bound up with the increasing quality and quantity of products and the productivity of labour.

4.1.2 The Measurement and Consciousness of Time

With the dissemination of the mechanical clock in the towns, a change in the consciousness of time came about. Peasants followed the seasons with regard to harrowing, sowing and harvesting. All human beings have a daily and yearly rhythm of life, of labour, of consumption of the fruits of their labour in common. Through the mechanization of clocks people in the centre, west and south of Europe came to have a changed concept of time. Labour time was reckoned in hours; the measurement of time was taken up by all estates and classes; wages in the town were linked to labour time, and this had to do with the transformation of the consciousness of time. Time flows, yet it is imprisoned in hours and minutes. It is ascertained in ceremonial-clerical seasons of the year, weddings and by peasant labours, yet in the town it was conceived of differently. The changed interaction with the measurement of time is expressed in poetry:

Dasz es erst sey die zehent Stundt

sprich doch es habe lang zwölffe geschlagen.

(Kaspar Scheidt. Grobjanus 1551)

That it is only the 10th hour

Yet say that the 12th hour has chimed.

The daily wage had explicitly fixed the day and the hour as reckoning unit for the recompense of labour. Human life and labour time were divided into days of labour and thereafter no longer reckoned according to the season. Martin Luther went further in the matter of the reckoning of wages and salaries and believed that there was an abstract, no longer concretized unit of value, namely the common or foundational labour time, whose compensation ought to serve as the reckoning unit for the valuation of the achievement of commercial labour. The merchant who wants to reckon his fair profit, should make a rough estimate of the time and magnitude of his labour and seek that which a common day labourer earns in a day. "Thereupon reckon how many days you strove to procure and earn your commodity and how great the labor and danger you faced in so doing. For great labor and a lot of invested time should also earn a greater reward." Labour time, so Luther thought, is valuable in and for itself. The monopolies have set themselves against the word of God, and the great commercial companies equally so, because they earned in a short period that which cost an honourable man much labour time. He said further: "How can it happen in the eyes of God and the law, that a man can become so wealthy in such a short time, that he might want to buy out King and Emperor."[26] His chief example of commercial usury was related to the practices of the Fugger company, for it was in the position to buy out the princes in Rome and Vienna.[27] It was often said that Luther's economic views were derived from the Middle Ages. We show here that Luther's opinion, his conceptions and practical examples are related to modern times.

These assertions in the 16th century point to a change in the treatment of time, of labour practices and of time consciousness. We do not speak of an increase in the consciousness of time, because the peasants were just as much influenced by the passage of time, but rather of a qualitative change in form in relation to the reckoning of labour time and with the consciousness of time bound up with it. The changes are not traced back to the invention or production of clock towers or cathedral clocks, of the egg of Nuremberg, and so on. The development and diffusion of clocks as well as the changes in the consciousness and reckoning of fractions of minutes in astronomy are various expressions of the changes in society and the processes of labour.

Agricultural labour and the rhythm in agricultural production would no longer be the determining factor of time consciousness; they are replaced by the labour processes in the towns. And even if the peasants remained the overwhelming majority of the population in the 15th, 16th and 17th century, labour in the town became the driving force in the process of change in the treatment of time and of coming to grips with time. These changes were related to the countryside. The peasants wanted everyone to be paid a daily wage.

The increasing accuracy in the measurement of time is bound up with the increasing accuracy in the measurement of the process of labour, of space, of weight, of the mechanical processes and of the geometry of volume. Accuracy and reliability increase in social information activities. The printing press provides for the exact, reliable and secure repetition of the wording of a law, a document, an act, a decree, an instruction, a book, a contract, and so on. The same processes and kinds of treatment in the factory—through the mass assembly of products of the same type, of the same quality and of the same performance ability and defectiveness—are the characteristic features of the modern economy.

The working day and wage were reckoned differently according to the season. In Nuremberg the measure of the day consisted of 12 hours of the same length from midnight to noon and no less than the many hours from noon to midnight, which was counted by the clock. Alongside of this there was another, called the great clock, according to which the daily hours used to be counted according to the character of the changing length of the day from sunrise to sunset, so that together they amounted to 24 hours. In high summer 16 daylight and 8 hours of night were reckoned. In the deepest winter it was vice-versa. The effective working day in construction in Nuremberg in the 16th century amounted on average to 10 or 11 hours; 7 in the winter, at most 12 in the summer. In an order in council at the time, which fixed the wage and labour time of the roofer, construction workers, plasterer [*Klaiber*], stone mason, white washer and carpenters, it read: "And namely they should throughout the entire year go to work every day early when the clock strikes [*wann es den Garaus schlägt*] they should end their labour. So, that the day is 8 and 9 hours long, they should break for refreshment [*sollen sie zur Suppen abgehen*] when the great clock chimes three and return again to work at four and at night when the clock strikes one cease working. When the day is 11 hours long, they should also go to dinner [*zur Suppen abgehen*] when the clock strikes four and at 5 return once again to their labour and at night, around one, cease their labours. When the day is 12 hours in length, they should go and return twice to their labour, namely the first time early to dinner when the clock strikes three and return at four. The other time they should leave off their labour at vespers when the clock strikes seven, be at work again at eight, and cease their labour at one at night." The working day was similarly regulated when the day was 13 and 14, 15 and 16 hours long. In this way the rhythm of labour and civic life were determined by the striking chimes of the clock.

Labour time in the 14th, 15th, 16th and 17th century in the towns of Central Europe was long. Many trades still carried out their work by candlelight as well. For the helmet, hood and weapon smiths as well as the pewterers in Nuremberg, 14, 15, 16 hours of labour daily was something common. In comparison to these conditions of labour the hours of labour of construction workers appear to be an elite matter. Apprentices demanded throughout not a shortening of the working day, but rather a shortening of the work week through the guarantee of a free workday to wit that of the *good* or *blue* [*hungover*] *Monday*. The struggle was carried on in connection with a piece of folk hygiene, with the access to the bathes on Monday, which was lifted during the Thirty Years' War. In the 15th and at the beginning of the 16th century the good Monday was generally recognized but thereafter revoked. The struggle was over a half day holiday, at times weekly, at other times every second week.

Time in social life and in social labour was observed, divided and measured with increasing exactitude. The measurement of time was related to daily wages and to the price reckoning of the products. If the prices of provisions fell, so too would wages. The time of the labour process and of the wage was counted in increasingly smaller units of measure. Our point of departure is not the measurement of time, but rather we begin with reciprocal effects of daily wage labour, of the money economy, of money prices, of the trade of commodities and chronometry bound up with them.

People and time under these conditions were treated mechanically, labour time was counted mechanically. The effects of these conditions do not lessen over time, they are only controlled more exactly and more sharply.

The struggle for free time was not only about the good or blue Monday. The Reformation had regulated the holidays and the need for official holidays was more lively contested as a result. At the end of the 16th century the local journeymen [senior journeymen, male head servants *Örtengesellen*] and the common society of the Nuremberg fustian weavers-handicraft [*gemeine Gesellschaft des Nürnberger Barchentweber-Handwerks*] complained: "We have had as compensation for our efforts and labour 7 fixed days, the way other workshops still have it, but for us here 5 were cancelled and only 2 remain, Carnival and St. Martin's Day." [„Wir haben auch hiervon uns einer Ersetzlichkeit unserer Mühe und Arbeit sieben Tage fest gehabt, das auswendig auf anderen Werkstätten noch ist, aber allhier seien uns deren fünf abgebrochen und halt uns nur zwei, als die Fasnacht und Lichtgans (Michels-oder Martinsgans)]."[28]

In the period from the 13th to the 17th century the duration of labour and daily wages were not fixed immediately by the contracts among entrepreneurs, company managers and labourers, but rather through the decrees of the town councils. These regulations extend over the late Middle Ages and the first centuries of the modern era. For apprentices and child servants, life was joyless, the chance of better relations was small, the effort for daily bread great, the exploitation of menials painful and embittering.[29] They were forced to deal with the council and to assert their views and rights through the increasing number of worker uprisings. The explicit or implicit labour contracts were related to the negotiations between the organizations of apprentices and the council.

4.2 Wage Labour and the Politics of Wages in the Early Capitalist Period

We have considered the meaning of wage labour from the side of the rebellious peasants in the 15th and 16th century, of the contracts in civil law, of the guild system, of the entrepreneurs and of the journeymen's organizations. It is foundational for the conception of the capitalist period in European history. The daily wage, wage labour and the money form in recompense did not appear for the first time in history. They were introduced sporadically in antiquity in the various parts of the Near East, in Asia and in the region of the Mediterranean. In distinction to the earlier practices, wage labour is widely and increasingly more systematically elaborated in the capitalist period. This social labour is free in the formal sense, voluntarily recompensed and not coerced. Concerning the wage, it is either negotiated in an immediate process of negotiation, or in comparison with other payments of labour. We shall consider more closely some examples of wage labour in the early capitalist period.

In modern bourgeois society wage labour is the predominant form of labour. In opposition to slavery and serfdom it is pro forma free labour and expresses the immediate, reciprocal relation between the labourers and owners, the master or capitalist in the enterprise. The formal unity and the unmediated reciprocity of the relation between the wage labourers and the capitalist entrepreneurs are set out as the equality between the two sides in the juridical sense. Freedom and equality in relation to the two sides appear in the historical form of an explicit or implicit contract, in which recompense, in whatever form, is determined by the duration of labour and its conditions. Recompense has the different forms of wage or piece wages, money or natural wages, among others. The determinations of the working day according to the season, summer and winter, as well as of the working week and the holidays were brought into labour contracts through negotiations. The representatives of the labourers were the fraternities of journeymen or the journeymen federations, the miners' association [*Knappschaft*] and more of the kind in the late Middle Ages and in modern times. The proxies of the company owners, masters and entrepreneurs were for the most part the council. The wage labourers entered into contract negotiations through their representatives on the basis of equality. In this way the immediate relations of the labourers and the entrepreneurs transformed into mediate ones. The council had also tried to represent the labourers, the journeymen and apprentices as well as the masters; its orientation in this matter corresponded however only to the side of the patricians and the wealthy.

Freedom and equality of the negotiating partners in the wage labour contract were recognized early. Revocation of the reciprocal relations were ushered in by strikes, unrest and uprisings on the side of the journeymen and apprentices and by the lockouts and cessation of wages on the side of the council and entrepreneurs. The organizations of the journeymen were transformed under some conditions into organizations of masters and journeymen; thus, there were no trade unions in the epoch of early capitalism in the sense of their existence in high capitalism. The masters were in part entrepreneurs and in part an elite of labourers in the early epoch. The shareholders were then copartners, stock owners or associates in the mining companies.

Wage labour continued to develop at the expense of serfdom and of forced labour in the 15th and 16th century. Originally this recompense was a mixture of money as an annual wage, wage in kind and assorted emoluments, such as that, for example, taken from the data of Inama-Sterneggs, which concern the Austrian foundation [*Stift*].[30] In the decade of the 60s of the 15th century the money wage was the predominant form of recompense of the foundation. The transition to the money economy was already initiated.

Comments to Table 7: In the hammer mill as well, labour was in part recompensed by payment in kind. Payment in kind lost its significance in later times.

Money and payment in kind in any case constitute the opposition to corvée and compulsory collective labour as they were practiced in the Middle Ages. Payments in kind are mainly the products of the labour process, such as grain, hay or meat for the peasants, iron for the hammer craftsmen.

The transition to the wage and money economy in the countryside in the 15th century is shown from the details of a manor in Saxony. We observe how the money economy has penetrated the life of the laiety and of the clerics.

Table 7: Annual Expenditures of Knight Hans von Honsperg in Clöden (Saxony) in 1474. Wilhelm Abel, *Geschichte der deutschen Landwirtschaft*, 3rd edition, Stuttgart 1978, p. 141

Expenditure	Schok (New Pennies)	Percentage (Rounded Off)
Cattle	12.0	7.5
Clothing	44.0	28.0
Food	27.0	17.0
Inventory	13.0	8.0
Wages	62.5	39.5
Total	**158.5**	**100.0**

Wages fell into two categories, one for the craftsmen (smiths, coopers, potters among others) and one for the labourers, who belonged to the activities of the household and economy of the manor (servant, maid, dairy woman, steward, maintenance sergeant [*Schirrmeister*], cook, waiter, herder, custodian, scribe). In the second category 21 people were engaged. The total wages contributed just under 40% of the total of the manor. The 62.5 *Schock*[31] of new pennies were converted into 5.920 tons of rye, and the money value of the entire operation for one year, which came to 158.5 *Schock* of new pennies, was translated into 15,010 tons of rye. The expenditures for iron, a fish net, rope, skeins, a cart and fencing were reckoned together in the inventory. Expenditures for cattle were related to the oxen, calves, chickens and geese but the keeping of sheep was excluded from it and reckoned to the expenditures for food. 27 *Schock* of new pennies were expended on food, of which 10 *Schock* were for hops, wood for brewing and spices, 9 for fish, 3 for figs, raisins, almonds and rice, 5 for honey, salt and so on. The money value of clothing is reckoned only for the members of the knight's family, which amounted to 70% of the money value of the wages or 44 *Schock* of new pennies.

In 1538 Sebastian Franck wrote: "Now let the peasants in the meanwhile immediately give a farm and estate for a thousand guilders, which could hardly be sold for half the price and give a cart of hay for 4 or 5 guilders, a cow for 10 guilders, and equally a horn also for 1 guilder, the tail for 2, the skin for 3 guilders, so that

that none of the parties can complain about it. Thus the butcher must give a pound of meat for 7 or 8 pennies, the tanner a skin for 4 to 5 guilders, the shoemaker a pair of shoes for half a guilder; the stove setter, tailor, smith may not like it when they comport themselves in this way and give a penny chamber pot for 1 kreuzer, the smith the horseshoe for 3 kreuzers, the wainwright the wheel three times the expense he incurred. Thus, it is exactly as before, that it was inexpensive; but that all things are more expensive and the kreuzer plays the role of the penny."[32]

In Nuremberg we have the following data for the daily wage for construction workers (in pennies):

Table 8: Wages (in Pennies) for Unskilled Labourers, Journeymen and Masters, in Construction in Nuremberg by Selected Years

Year	Unskilled Labourers	Journeymen	Masters
1490	18	20	24
1559	24	28	32
1597	36	58	77

In 1559, the winter wage from October to January rose by 20 pennies for the journeymen masons, and the summer wage from April to September by 36 pennies. In the winter, work was 8 hours a day and in summer, 12 to 13 hours. Nothing was said about the situation in February and March.

In 1543, excavators earned a daily wage of 24 pennies, which meant almost 19 pennies over the course of a year.

The day was strictly related to the duration of the working day and with its recompense. At the end of the 16th century the wages in Nuremberg for construction work amounted to the following:[33]

Table 9: Summer and Winter Wages in Construction in Nuremberg by Classification at the End of the 16th Century

Classification	Summer Wage	Winter Wage
Masters	84	71
Journeymen	60	55
Paddle mixers	46	42
Common labourers	42	38

The council decreed an edict regarding the daily wage, when the prices for provisions were low, "and therefore saw this as a reason to set the previously daily wage rather lower, than to raise it or bid it up." In 1597 a pound of meat cost 10 pennies, 1 Simra (=16 Nuremberg *Metzen*) of corn 4 ½ florins.

Labour time in the construction sector in Frankfurt am Main in the 15th century was reckoned in two ways, from Saint Gallen's Day (the 16th of October) to the Day of Our Lady (*Becliben*, the 25th of March) called the shortest period, and on the contrary, from the Day of Our Lady to Saint Gallen's Day which was called the longest period. The wage (without food for the roofer [*Steindecker*] and the construction worker who produces and puts clay on the inner walls of a house [*Kleuber*] in the longest period amounted to 5:4 in relation to the wage of the same guilds in the construction sector during the shortest period. For the thatched roofer [*Schaubdecker*] the wage amounted to 4:3 in the same seasons. The guild of the *Opperknechte* (the unskilled workers) [*Handlanger*] in other parts of Germany) belonged to the skilled construction workers. The daily wage of the unskilled workers [*Opperknechte*] was the lowest, which the Frankfurt council had recognized, and can thus serve as an example for the common wage, which Martin Luther (see above) had imagined.[34]

Tables 8 and 9 above point to the fact that the wage and money economy in Central Europe were related to the agrarian sector already in the 15th century. We won't generalize this observation, because large parts of the agricultural economy, especially east of the Elbe, was still primarily feudal—thus driven by corvée obligation and falling therefore outside of the circulation of money. The spread of wage labour was implemented as a rule in the town, but sporadically in the country as well.

The general data and statistics in Central Europe during the 15th, 16th and 17th century have been thoroughly researched and yet there is no systematic summarization because the details are fragmentary. Hence, only a few examples of daily wages are mentioned in that period. The shoemaker journeyman in Nuremberg in the 17th century earned 8 kreuzers daily on average, the junior apprentice in the same sector earned 4 kreuzers daily. For the carpenters the weekly wage was set at 4 to a maximum of 8 Batzen. However, the difference between the domestic and foreign journeymen was known. The latter received 6 Batzen as a wage, and thus lay in the midrange of the weekly wage for a journeyman carpenter.[35]

At this time commodity prices in Central Europe strongly increased, wages less so. Hence Abel reckoned the following developments of prices and wages in Hamburg from 1511 to 1625: wages of masons increased by 265%, carpenters' wages rose by 209%, weavers' wages rose by 225%, women's wages rose 138%. The price of rye in the same period increased by 376%. The prices of beans were linked to the prices of grain. Everywhere in Germany from 1500 to 1600 wages rose by 150%, prices of the products of the various sectors on the contrary by 200% and the prices of grain by 300%, that is greatly higher than the increase in wages. It was no different in England, France, Austria and Poland.[36]

Until the Reformation the workers had in addition to Sundays 48 holidays annually; after the Reformation workers had just 18 holidays. Real wages for the unskilled labourers, like the unskilled labourers in construction, sank in the 16th century. They earned the equivalent wage for a working day in 1500 of 4 pounds of meat, in 1600 of 2 to 2 ½ pounds of meat, in 1500 for 25 to 30 working days of 1 *Sümmer* [bushel] of grain, in 1600 for 80 working days 1 *Sümmer* of grain. During the 16th century wages for the unskilled labourers rose by 200%, for the journeymen just shy of 300%. For real wages there was no improvement. In the same period, meat prices rose 300–400%, the price of beer 300%, the price of wine 500–600% and the price of grain 400%.[37]

In 1563 manual labourers in Styria [*Steiermark*] wrested authority from the merchant entrepreneurs of the domestic iron industry [*Eisenverleger*]. An iron trade company was established, in which each townsman who could acquire a capital investment could be a member. Every wainwright received an advance from his buyer who was his hammer master [*Hammerherr*], and he in turn was given an advance by his Styrian dealers. It was the master wainwright above all who had the advantage from the expansion of oven capacity and from the transition to the heavier standard. In the hammer enterprise the journeymen fared increasingly poorly and the women who worked there fared even worse. Sinter washers received for the tenth washed iron [*Wascheisen*] 20 pennies each. This was mostly the labour of women. The medieval-patriarchal relation between the master wainwright and their people disappeared. The common Sunday meals ceased as did the *Fasching* hospitality and the housing cost in domestic chores as well. In the movement of the journeymen, the class struggle was made noticeable, not for the first time, however. The history of the class struggle of the journeymen organizations in the Middle Ages is known.[38]

In 1583 the ironworks in the town of Styr went over into the hands of the workers from the merchant-entrepreneur putting-out distributer [*Verleger*] in lieu of payment in money. Traders, hammer master [*Hammerherr*] and shareholders came together in a putting-out enterprise [*Verlag*]. The dealers gave the hammer masters [*Hammerherrn*] an advance, and the master wainwright received an advance from the *Hammerherrn* according to the schedule, to set his workshop into motion, to appropriate tools and raw materials and to pay the workers. The original wage of accord or piece wage increasingly receded in favour of the weekly wage. The dealers who were the merchant entrepreneurs [*Verleger*] of means in the putting-out system, acquired the iron ore without difficulty and turned it over; the poorer ones found little or no market for their portion. The enterprise was built by the participation of the shareholders. Each shareholder was supposed to have a *Verleger* in principle who would advance him money, or should himself be a *Verleger*, who could take out his portion from the yield of ore. The town council of Styr should have allowed the passage of the requirements in the iron hammer works and in mining in the region. There arose in the area of Saxony during the 16th century the tin plate trade, the pewters in Amberg. However, the difference between native and foreign slowly disappeared. More shareholders were miners, at the same time small capitalists and hewers.

The feudal hewers took over partial sections in the putting-out system in mining. They worked at their own risk, their income in the best case was set above the level of the wage workers. Little by little the wage labourers moved forward in place of the shareholders. As a consequence, there came about the differentiation of the shareholders into two classes, those working and those not working in mining. On the shareholders' part an agreement was made on behalf of everyone in the feudal system [*Die Lehenschaft*] and in opposition to autonomous mining and against a quota of the part devoted to supporting the mining claim. The shareholders kept the better part of the mining for themselves, the remainder they conferred on others, which is to be concluded from the mining regulation of Meissen of 1328, from the mining regulation of Tirol of 1408 and of the mining regulation at Breisgau from 1517.[39]

The founding of the iron trade company in Styr can be compared with the founding of the General Iron Trade company in Löben and the Cloth Trade Company in Iglau. Some poor weavers were forced to accept putting-out. Over time the private people as a matter of the course of business had no longer accepted putting-out. Thereupon the founding of the company occurred.[40]

In the region of the Mediterranean the population increased, purchasing power in the domestic market was elevated, the system of credit and finance expanded. This had to do with greater income for the entire macro economy and with new foreign markets, this in connection with the increasing productivity through new entrepreneurial activity, through lower prices, more rational processes of production, entrepreneurs producing in advance, through a stronger measure of taking risk into account, new customers and investments and through increased competition among the entrepreneurs. The economy as well as productivity was strengthened by technic.[41] The poor remained poor, the rich established their wealth in the period of capitalism not on the exploitation of corvée, but rather on the exploitation of wage labour and of capital.

4.3 Labour and Society, Public and Private Interests

The labour relations of the capitalist system are everywhere socially organized. In the collective, communal or in the communistic society social labour is correspondingly organized [i.e. as collective, communal or communistic labour]. The emphasis of wage labour relations is closely linked to the interest of the group. The town council, the guilds, (*Zünfte, Gilden*) unions (*Innungen*), offices (*Ämter*), associations (*Verbände*), fraternities (*Bruderschaften*), associations express group relations in the 15th century.[42] The individual appears not as founder, but rather as participant in these activities, relationships, spheres of interest and conflicts.

What is present implicitly or hidden in the period of early bourgeois society, appears clearly in later epochs. The keen thinkers and observers first saw that there were two opposite spheres of interest in modern bourgeois society—the public and the private. Adam Smith and Hegel directed general attention to the duels between these two spheres.[43] The conflicts did not come to the fore so starkly three hundred years earlier, but they were already present. The town council in Augsburg, as in Mainz, Frankfurt am Main, Nuremberg and elsewhere represented the interests of their members, that is the wealthy, the patricians, the old bourgeois families; the imperial cities represented the interest of the Empire and of the territorial princes. The council guaranteed civil peace through the system of guards, gatekeepers, custodians, soldiers, highway officials, judges, of the wall and road structures. It was inclined or forced to introduce compromises with the journeymen organizations in order not to jeopardize civil peace. It was forbidden to the masters to conduct negotiations with the journeymen. The council was supposed to determine the wages and working conditions for the entire city according to each branch of business operation and the qualification of labour. Public power in the form of the council had not recognized the independent interests of the private sphere, of the entrepreneurs.

Through wage relations, labour time became a commodity, which had a determinate price in the labour market. The labour market is like all others, with a seller of a commodity, of labour time and labour capacity, and a buyer of the same. The market was widespread in the capitalist system, especially in the private sphere.

The uprisings, the wars, the unrest and the uncertainties of civil life at the beginning of this system transformed society, the system of towns and countryside, of the economy, of politics and of religion in Central Europe. The capitalist system and modern bourgeois society continued to develop in the waning years of the 17th century under new conditions. Civil peace was transformed and established on the basis of the new national and territorial state as well as on its new absolutism. The economic relations of free trade in conflict with mercantilism and cameralism had replaced the preceding system of guild, council and patriciate. The later system is a further development of the earlier one. Capitalist practices of wage labour, of money, commodity, credit and market system were continued under later and more conducive conditions.

We judge the process of development objectively as advantageous for the people of Europe. Quantitatively the creation of riches and of commodity exchange from 1450 to 1700 and later were further multiplied. We judge objectively and qualitatively the process of development as advantageous for humanity, for civil rights and civil peace were deepened, multiplied and expanded in the late 17th century. The freedom and equality of the lower strata and of the outsiders of society were secured and supported. With that said this development had already begun in the 15th and 16th century. The two spheres, the public and the private, did not come into conflict in the earlier periods. Only in the 18th century did this come about; before that time the dispute of labourers with entrepreneurs in the labour process had been mediated by the council. Only later did it come to an immediate conflict between the working class and the class of capitalist entrepreneurs.

The council in the period from the 15th to the 17th century had decided how much could be earned, what the length of the working day should be, and how large the enterprise could become. The early-modern town council decreed and regulated how many workers would be allowed to be hired in an enterprise in a given branch. The town council also decided which enterprises should be conducted inside town and which should be located within and without the town wall. Moreover, the council had determined the quality of life through the control and punishment for the counterfeiting of bread, coins and so on. The public interest was not identical with the private interest but the difference in this case did not so stridently come to the fore as it did in the 18th and 19th century. The public power of the state and of the council was greater than the private power of the entrepreneurial class in the 15th and 16th century in Central Europe. The absolute state assumed the power of the council in the 17th and 18th century. The private sphere and the private interest of the capitalist class became strong enough to dominate the power of the Central European aristocracy and of the state only in the 19th century.

The great political event of modern times in Europe was the surfacing of nation states: first England, France and the Netherlands, then the national states in central, southern, northern and eastern Europe. When Hegel said, Germany was no longer a state, he meant it was not a nation state: Germany was a collection, a *mixtum compositum*, a mélange of a wide variety of small states. Through the development of the capitalist system the current composition of nation states formed in their development and their defeats. Feudal power was dispersed, the power of the states in the capitalist period became concentrated. In Central Europe in the modern era the power of the dynasties and of the Catholic Church was constricted, limited and weakened, over the course of time. In the epoch of early capitalism in this part of the world, political power was strengthened by dynastic absolutism whose period of efflorescence was the second half of the 17th and 18th century until roughly the French Revolution. The influence of the state upon the economy was centralized in the form of high cameralism. (Autocrats in Berlin, Vienna, Dresden and elsewhere, gathered around them economists that were commonly referred to as cameralists.) These economists established no unitary school of economic science; in fact, they were mainly servants of the princely and imperial courts in the period of developing capitalism. The Thirty Years' War, the peasant revolts, the wars of the Reformation and Counter-Reformation from the late 15th century to the middle of the 17th century, had brought the people to the point where they welcomed the absolute rule of the autocrats in the 18th century. On their part, the princes secured civil peace within the empire, and extended religious tolerance and civil rights. Lessing, Goethe and Schiller gave expression to the tone of the period. That which the king had proposed was good, but not enough. The poets wanted still more freedom, more equality.

The cameralists were no free spirits as were the poets. They were statesmen who influenced the further development of the political economy. They were primarily advisers in the service of their masters. Increasing economic activity did not lead immediately to the expansion of bourgeois political influence. In practice the princely court considered and used the bourgeois merchants as a possible extension of state power. The bourgeoisie as a social class had not yet elaborated its social consciousness as a class. They were, rather, more the subjects of state politics. Both sides, the cameralists and the merchants, determined the role of citizens in service to the state.[44]

The cameralists fundamentally demonstrated their service to the public power and their interests. They investigated and pondered, how state power and their wealth were to be increased. Another name for their activity is police science [*Polizeiwissenschaft*]; crudely stated the German cameralist corresponded to the Spanish *politico*. The major interest of this group was the furtherance of the growing industry and agriculture, at the same time preferring production in the domestic market, not that of foreign trade. Insofar as they represented a theoretical conception, this stood in connection with a systematic expansion of advancements of this kind right up to autarky or the self-preservation of the state. Their second major interest was the administration of the economy in the service of the state. Industrial or agricultural development should serve as the source for the increase in state income. Diomede Carafa, Jean Bodin, and Giovanni Botero endorsed this line of thinking. We shall not pursue it and not criticize it, but rather counterpose such views to the private interest. The German-speaking cameralists, like Melchior von Osse, Georg Olbrecht, Veit Ludwig von Seckendorf in the 16th and 17th century, Johann Heinrich Gottlob von Justi and Joseph von Sonnenfels in the 18th century, were no advocates or representatives of the private interest as was their contemporary, Adam Smith.[45] The direction of the national economy by the state and mediately through the advisers of the state with the view to increase state income and the state budget, does not lie in the immediate sense in the interest of the private man as a capitalist. The great cause for him, understood by Adam Smith, is his profit, which is not identical with state income. It was already clear in the 18th century, that the increase of state income did not lie in the interest of the private capitalist as a social class. The intervention of the men of state in private affairs was unsuccessful for this reason. The statesmen were ineffective and understood nothing of private commerce or the merchant class.

Hegel included the opposition between the two spheres, of the private and the public, in his dialectical understanding of bourgeois society. The original dispute between the spheres in the earlier period of modernity was more implicit than explicit. Osse, Olbrecht and von Seckendorff had represented the state and its interest. The opposing interest of the bourgeois class did not achieve prominent expression, because this class at the time was weak. The working class was weak as well, for the public hand of the town council had repressed the journeymen. The journeymens' organizations were suppressed by the communal politics of the council. The state and council as organs of the public power were mighty. The private sphere of the capitalists, of the entrepreneurs, of the traders, of the associations of miners, of the organizations of the journeymen and of the fraternities was entirely in opposition to the organs of the public power.

The struggle over the wages of the journeymen and miners [*Knappen*] as well as the wage politics of the council are to be understood in this connection. Class relations in the town during the 15th, 16th and 17th century were qualitatively the same as in the following centuries. In this respect Hegel's conception of history provided an important contribution for the understanding of the earlier epochs of modernity. The guild masters and the journeymen were regulated as private persons by the council. The representatives of the state in Brandenburg, Kurhessen, Braunschweig and Saxony in the second half of the 17th century had decided to keep the guilds and to administer them directly. The town council in the later epochs was a remnant of the imperial town system of the past and had become irrelevant. The guild system as an expression of the private sphere in central European society was dominated by the electoral instances in reference to the relation of masters, journeymen and apprentices to one another and to the customers. The public hand had been thereby strengthened, and it had made reference to this strength. The private sphere of the bourgeois class in the period of high capitalism followed, then abolished the guild system and changed its attitude in relation to the state.[46]

In this early-modern period, the state was strengthened at the cost of the Church and of the town council in Central Europe. All are representatives of the public hand. Lastly, the state made the public hand into its monopoly everywhere in the world.

With regard to the quality of life of the miners [*Knappen*] and the journeymen in the period of early capitalism in Central Europe, F. M. Feldhaus made the following remark: "The information which we can take from the files of the Fuggers (who were not only the bankers of the emperor and popes, but also the owners of the monopoly of wholesale world trade in copper) is thought provoking concerning the condition of the workers and provokes us to reflect. Day and night shifts were encouraged. Wages were low; distress and poverty very high. Women and children also worked in the ironworks; there were many accidents caused by machines, but there was no workers' welfare; at best there were alms. Debts of fired workers or dead miners [*Knappen*] were collected by pawning things necessary to life, and the remainder went through the business ledgers for many years. Two widows of miners [*Knappen*] who died in the Spanish mines of the Fuggers were only supported after a lengthy back and forth, but everything was subtracted again 'from the earnings of their sons.'"[47]

The poor in Esslingen and Württemberg (Heilbronn) as well as in Mühlhausen (Thuringia) were manual labourers and those without possessions who made up more than 50% of the population of these towns; the middle class constituted a third, and the rest were wealthy. In Constance 61% of the population were poor and possessed together 2% of the wealth of the town; the wealthy constituted 2% of the town, and 40% of the town wealth belonged to them; the middle class amounted to 37% of the population with 58% of the wealth. The assets in these towns refer to the end of the 16th century. In 1378 24% of the population in Rostock was poor. In 1550 the wealthy amounted to 0.5% of the population of Rostock, the poor (around the year 1520) 63%, the manual labourers and small merchants 20% and the upper middle class 15%.

From the payments of taxes in Augsburg in the 16th century we have the following picture of wealth: in 1558 0.9% wealthy, 4.8% belonged to the middle class; in 1576 there were just as many wealthy, while 5.8% counted as middle class. In Nuremberg in 1500 6–8% of the population belonged to the wealthier upper stratum, the poor or the lower stratum amounted to a third of the population; 450

burgesses were able to live with a good income. In 1568 416 townspeople had more than 5,000 florins, of which 250 had more than 10,000.

The continuing structuration of labour in the municipal industries and the immigration of unskilled labourers led to increasing poverty. The excess population in the 16th century had increased. In 1449 10% of the population, in 1662 12% of the population were homeless in Nuremberg. 300 poor brass smiths [*Rotschmiede*], thimble makers and eyelet and hook makers [*Heftleinsmacher*] in the year 1522 could not nourish their families and asked for support.[48]

The patricians pitted the journeymen against the masters, in order to keep the manual labourers down.[49] By itself, economic development, which had aimed to unify the masters in the organized manual trades, caused the consolidation of the servants at the opposite pole. The movement of journeymen on an extended level begins in the 14th century.[50] The connection of the mechanization of the process of labour with the movement of liberation of the peasants and the rise of capitalist entrepreneurs in Central Europe during this period has already been emphasized in this work.

Notes

1. See E. J. Dijksterhuis, *Die Mechanisierung des Weltbildes*, Berlin 1956, Chapter III; he shows this worldview by means of the example of the activities of William Gilbert, Descartes, Pierre Gassendi, Robert Boyle and Otto von Guericke.
2. E. Mach, *Die Mechanik*, 9th edition (1933), Darmstadt 1976. E. J. Dijkserhuis, *Die Mechanisierung des Weltbildes*, Berlin 1983. H. Goldstein, *Klassische Mechanik*, 8th edition, Frankfurt am Main 1985.
3. H. Schopper, πανοπλια *mechanicarum aut sedentariarum*, Frankfurt am Main 1568. Idem., *De Omnibus illiberalibus sive mechanics artibus*, Frankfurt am Main 1574.
4. A. Dürer, *Unterweisung der Messung mit dem Zirkel und Richtscheit in Linien, Ebenen und ganzen Korporen*, Nürnberg 1525.
5. A. Dürer, *Unterweisung der Messung*.
6. Leone Battista Alberti's book *De Re Aedificatoria* (*Concerning Architecture*) was competed in 1450 and posthumously published in 1485. Georg Agricola's *De Re Metallica* (*Concerning Mining and Metallurgy*) was posthumously published in 1556. The volumes have not only the Latin language but also the form of the title and their posthumous appearance in common. Both were moved by humanistic principles, both have ascertained scientific laws, and both have taken up art and the practice of working men.
7. Erwin Panofsky, *Albrecht Dürer*, 4th edition, Princeton 1955 (Ger. Munich 1977). Panofsky showed that Dürer depicted the geometry of the manual labourers and of the workshop for the mathematicians. Cardano, Tartaglia, Benedetti, Kepler, Galilei and Cataldi had perceived the mathematical and artistic ideas of Dürer. Dürer presented the infinite as a thing that is present in the mind—not in front of one's eyes. It is a point no matter how small it may be. The point that we see or draw with a feather, we are able to reach physically, the infinitely small on the other

contrary, not. The infinitely large is similarly to be conceived. Dürer mastered the difference between the infinite and finite body.

8. Sir Isaac Newton, *Mathematische Prinzipien der Naturlehre* (1686). J. P. Wolters (ed.), Berlin 1872.
9. E. Mach, *Die Mechanik* (1883), Darmstadt 1976. Herbert Goldstein, *Klassische Mechanik*, 8th edition, Frankfurt am Main 1985. Immanuel Kant, *Metaphysische Anfangsgründe der Naturwissenschaft*, 1786.
10. The mechanical investigations of Leonardo reveal that he was one of the most exceptional physicists of his day. Several historians of mechanics and of technics, like H. Grothus, F. Schuster, O. Werner, E. Solmi, F. M. Feldhaus, P. Duhem, A. Maier and I. B. Hart, have highly praised Leonardo's knowledge in these areas. He investigated mechanics through experiments, yet he was not a systematic thinker in this field. After the invasion and victory of the French in Milan he was forced to leave the city. Afterwards he studied mechanics together with the mathematician Pacioli (see above).
11. See the following section. There is no all-encompassing history of mechanical philosophy. Medicine and physics were mechanically conceived by many thinkers in the 16th and 17th century. Santorio, professor of medicine at Padua published his book *De medicina statica* in 1614. He investigated mechanics, in particular statics in physiology. In this little book the notions of Galileo Galilei were related to medicine, and there the modern investigation of metabolism was founded. In England William Harvey researched the circulation of blood. He observed that the heart moved 540 pounds, 245 kilograms of blood, hence three times the weight of the human body per hour. The ideas of Harvey were likewise traced back to the mechanics of Galilei. Charles Singer, *A Short History of Scientific Ideas*, Oxford 1982. Singer treated the development of medicine from magic to science in: *From Magic to Science*, New York, 1958. E. J. Dijksterhuis (*Die Mechanisierung des Weltbildes*, Berlin 1983) touched but little on the history of medicine, even though it stood in a close relationship to the mechanical view of the world, as Singer has shown. On the other hand, Dijksterhuis has pointed to technics as a source of science; he gave emphasis to the interaction of the two in this context and critically, and really negatively, condemning the statements of F. Borkenau and A. von Martin. Dijksterhuis examined the problem of mechanization on the basis of research in mathematics, mechanics, astronomy and chemistry. A. Maier, *Die Mechanisierung des Weltbildes*, Leipzig 1983. In this work the emphasis is on philosophy. M. Boas, 'The Establishment of the Mechanical Philosophy,' *Osiris*, Vol. 10, 1952. M. B. Hesse, *Forces and Fields: Über die Korpuskular Theorie*, Greenwood 1970. K. Lasswitz, see above. P. Rossi, *I Filosofi e le Macchine*, Milan 1962. As the full title of his book reveals, E. Mach (1883; 1976) presented *Die Mechanik in ihrer Entwicklung historisch-kritisch dargestellt.* Not only celestial mechanics is treated here but also aeromechanics, that is, physics in the immediate terrestrial surroundings. Some of the problems of the workshop are also highlighted, but not systematically, only here and there. The disadvantages of this work are the gaps. Van Helmont and the early development of gas theory are missing; chemistry is only treated in relation to physics. Concerning his positivistic worldview we shall speak of elsewhere, but not here. Our task is not to investigate this relation in general but rather on a particular area and in a period as a contribution to the problem of periodization.
12. J. R. Partington, J. B. van Helmont, *Annals of Science*, Vol. 1. 1938. Comparative thoughts were expressed by Ciriacus Shreittmann.
13. E. Mach, *Die Mechanik*. E. J. Dijksterhuis, *Die Mechanisierung des Weltbildes*. M. Boas, *The Establishment of the Mechanical Philosophy* (see above).

14. I. Kant said that Leibniz wanted to explain the world mechanically; the Leibnizian explanation assumed the *automaton spiritual,* because it was driven by ideas; Leibniz intellectualized appearances. Kant, *Kritik der reinen Vernunft,* 1st edition, 1781; Anmerkung zur Amphibolie der Reflexionsbegriffe.

The conception of the Leibnizian mechanical philosophy led Kant to the conclusion, that mechanism was an *automaton.* The automatic effect of mechanism is twofold: *materiale,* corporeal, and *spirituale,* mental [spiritual, geistig].

After Regiomontan and Michael Stifel, Christoph Rudolff from Silesia developed the decimal system further in his work concerning *die Coss.* His books on arithmetic appeared in Augsburg in 1530 and later. Xylander (Wilhelm Holzmann), introduced *die Coss* or algebra among the Germans in the translation of works from Diaphantos from the Greek (Heidelberg 1575). Schreitmann and Stevin later applied the decimal system, the former to the art of assaying, the latter to astronomy, coinage, visor arts or stereometry, as well as to all merchants.

C. Rudolff, *Kunstliche Rechnung mit der Ziffer und mit den Zahlpfenningen,* Vienna 1526. M. Stifel, *Deutsche Arithmetica inhaltend die Hausrechnung, die deutsche Coss.* Nürnberg 1545. Idem. *Die Coss Christoph Rudolffs mit schönen Exempeln gebessert,* Königsberg 1553.

Pappus of Alexandria around 300 after the turn of the calendar brought out the following system of the mechanical arts. There are in it threefold practical arts necessary for life:

1. The art of *magganarioi.* The ancient mechanics called them this, those who made the tools, which simplified manual labour. They have great weight against nature; their tools set the weight in motion by means of a small or weak force.
2. The art of machines for warfare. Those who built these machines were called mechanics as well. With catapults they could throw objects of stone, iron and other materials across a great distance. There mechanics were called *organopoioi.*
3. The machines for waterworks. Those who made these machines were called *mechanopoioi.* Through their art they could lift water from a great depth. The ancients also called magicians (illusionists) *mechanics* or *thaumasiourgoi.* Many of them, like Hero in his *Pneumatika,* used the arts of weather or wind. Filippo Pigafetta, 1581, repeated the thought of Pappus, that by means of mechanics large weights can be set in motion with small or weaker force. *Magganon* means the machine of war to hurl stones and arrows, lat. *ballista. Magganarios* according to the ancient Greeks, meant: swindler, magician, illusionist as well.

Automaton and *automatic* have a different meaning in the 20th century than in classical antiquity or in the 18th century. *Automaton* can be understood as that which is self driven, as voluntary or as that which is coincidental. The thing lacking will is an automaton, and the voluntary recedes in this case. The automaton has no self-determination. Automatic is that which happens without a loss of time. The effect of mechanical motion under this condition can be reckoned without the quantum of time and in independence of external moments. A machine is automatically driven without self-determination according to the notion in the 15th and 16th century. The mechanical clock was so conceived in this period. The *engienen* (machines) were understood as automatons, not as self-motors or self-actors. The mechanical view of nature had been changed from the 17th to the 18th century. Since our laws of mechanics are other than the laws of the 17th century, there is a different mechanical understanding in the 20th century than in the 17th.

15. This is based on the duodecimal system of numbers which was widespread in the world far beyond Eurasia. The Chinese divided the day into 12 units, which for the Europeans each unit would be two hours. There was a struggle between the two systems. The conceptions of Fibonacci,

Pacioli, Schreittmann, Stevin among others were refuted by the French philosopher of nature Buffon, who argued on behalf of the duodecimal system in the 18th century. Duodecimal societies were established in vain. The philosopher Leibniz supported the founding of arithmetic on the binary system. The decimal system in Europe was victorious over the duodecimal system in the measurement of temperature and space; the Celsius system of the measurement of temperature, further meters and kilometers, were widely employed. Even in weights the decimal system dominated. In the measurement of time the system of the twelves remained the victor in the counting of hours and months. However, this victory of the duodecimal system in the measurement of time is contradictory, for the chronological order of the year, decades and centuries is related to the decimal system. In everyday life the decimal system is dominant for counting, coinage, the reckoning of weight and distance, but not in the measurement of time. Ten thousand has another history of meaning. The Chinese have the word *wan*, Japanese *ban*, ten thousand; the Greeks have *myriad*, which can mean long, many, eternal. רבבה *Rawawah* in Hebrew means ten thousand, a large amount, an indeterminate large number. *Groshundert* is the compound of elements of the decimal and of the duodecimal system. Karl Menninger, *Zahlwort und Ziffer*, 3rd edition, Göttingen 1979. Georges Ifrah, *Universalgeschichte der Zahlen*, 2nd edition, Frankfurt am Main 1978. Tobias Dantzig, *Number*, 4th edition, New York 1954. Bernhard Karlgren, *Analytic Dictionary of Chinese and Sino-Japanese*, Paris 1923. Ludwig Koehler, Walter Baumgartner, *Lexikon in Veteris Testamenti*, Leiden 1958.

16. O. Johannsen. *Geschichte des Eisens*. 3rd edition, Düsseldorf 1953. It is possible that metal workers in the 13th century also built mechanical clocks.
17. A. Lautink-Ferguson, *Nature*, Vol. 330, 1987.
18. Among these clocks from the 14th century 5 were in England, 6 in Italy, 9 in the German-speaking areas, 8 in the Netherlands, 8 in France and one or two in other countries. Further, in the 15th century 15 or 20 mechanical clocks were installed, among them a weighted clock [*Waguhr*] with a pull weight and a gear wheel clock.
19. The method of discovery is varied. Sometimes the clock is present, even though in a changed condition, sometimes on the contrary, one reads in the archives, that a certain clock is exhibited with *engienen*. F. M. Feldhaus, *Die Technik*, Potsdam 1931. Idem. *Die Maschine*, Basel 1954. C. M. Cipolla, *Clocks and Culture*, New York 1978. D. Landes, *Revolution in Time*, Harvard 1983. H. A. Lloyd, *Mechanical Timekeepers*, C. Singer et al. (eds.), *A History of Technology*, Vol. 3, Oxford 1957. K. Maurice, *Die deutsche Räderuhr*, Munich 1976. L. Reti, *The Unknown Leonardo*, New York 1946. Lautink-Ferguson (see above).
20. K. Maurice, *Die deutsche Räderuhr*, ibid., vol. 1. H. Tait, *Clocks and Watches*, British Museum 1983.
21. J. J. Baumann, *Die Lehren von Raum, Zeit und Mathematik*, Vol. 1 (1868), Frankfurt am Main 1981. K. Lasswitz, *Geschichte der Atomistik vom Mittelalter bis Newton*, (1890), Hildesheim 1984. E. T. Dijksterhuis, *Die Mechanisierung des Weltbildes*, Berlin 1983. P. Duhem, *L évolution de la mécanique*, Paris 1905. E. Mach, *Die Mechanik*, (1883), Darmstadt 1976. F. M. Feldhaus (see above), S. Sambursky, *Physical Thought*, New York 1975. G. T. Fechner, *Über die physikalische und philosophische Atomlehre*, 2nd edition, Leipzig 1864. E. Cassirer (*Individuum und Kosmos in der Philosophie der Renaissance*, Leipzig and Berlin 1927) treats the problem macrocosm/microcosm in the 15th and 16th century as a network of analogies of the metaphysical kind.
22. Adam Ries, *Rechenbuch auf Linien und Ziffern,* Frankfurt am Main 1574. The division of seconds into tierces was theoretical, the hours in 4 years are counted one after the other. "Terz" [tierce] as a fraction of a second in not listed in Grimm's dictionary. In 1474 Cardinal Nikolaus von Cuso criticized the deplorable condition [*Übelstand*] of the Julian Calendar. Reform of the calendar

was introduced in the 16th century by Pope Gregory VII. The ideas of Nicholas von Cuso, of Pope Gregory VII, as well as by Dürer, Luther and Adam Ries, point to a deep consciousness of time in the 15th and 16th century—in practice as in theory.

23. Adam Ries wrote about the number of days and months of a year: "To know that a year is reckoned as 365 and ¼ days is to complete the breach. Thus, one waited for a long time, until 4 years had run out, before giving the fourth year an additional day for 4/4. The next year prior to Christ's birth was a leap year and received 366 days. This is the reason why the number of years is divided in 4 (to recognize a leap year) and without remainder, is a leap year, that 1556 as well as 1560 are leap years, then divided in 4. Leaving no remainder, the years have such an order. Initially established by Julius Caesar with the help of the famous mathematician Sosigenes, it has now defended itself more than 1600 years. Yet the years are in fact a little too long. There is nothing more to be said about this here." The months are in length and in succession the same in the 15th and 16th century as they are today. Adam Ries, *Rechenbuch auf Linien und Ziffern*, corrected edition, Frankfurt am Main 1574. Whether the years 1600 and 2000 are leap years or not was an open question. For us the year 2000 is not a leap year.
24. E. T. Dijksterhuis (see above) suggested the distinction between mechanical and mechanistic. Mechanization is related to the view of the world according to his conception. Mechanics as we have already seen, is related to the analysis and composition of the laws of mechanics under given conditions. Mechanics is the conception of the sciences according to a mechanical model, whether it be of the science of celestial bodies, of life, of psychology or another field of the consequence of mechanical laws. The unlimited application of mechanical laws to life, to psychology, to human society and history in the same sense as they are applied to the movement of celestial bodies is a fantasy. The program of the mechanical philosophy of the 17th century is inadequate for the explanation and theory of the world, of nature and of the human being.
25. F. M. Feldhaus, *Die Maschine* (see above), idem., *Die Technik* (see above). A. P. Usher, 'Machines and Mechanism,' in C. Singer et al., *A History of Technology*, Vol. 3, Oxford 1957. R. A. Salaman and F. Braudel listed the tools in the practice of manual labourers. They underestimated the number of them in Jost Ammans images in his *Eigentliche Beschreibung aller Stände auf Erden*, the so-called *Ständebuch*. They only listed the number of tools in the workshop of the carpenter, but other tools which were not illustrated in the woodcut, the carpenter had in common with the lathe workers and joiners. Such tools which did not appear in the carpenter's workshop, ought to be added. Yet the conclusion by Salaman and Braudel is correct: there were increasingly more tools and instruments of labour introduced into the labour process in the 15th, 16th, 17th, and 18th century. (R. A. Salaman, in: Singer et al., *A History of Technology*, vol. 3. F. Braudel, see above).
26. M. Luther, *Von Kaufhandlung und Wucher*, 1534. He also mentioned danger or risk as a factor in the reckoning of time and value.
27. W. Roscher, *Geschichte der National-Oekonomik in Deutschland*, Munich 1874.
28. In relation to the *The Protestant Ethic and the Spirit of Capitalism* the following is to be noted: Those who treat this ethic or spirit, have focused on the entrepreneurs. The working class is supposed to have been moved by another spirit. On the one hand, the discussions of Max Weber, Ernst Troeltsch and Werner Sombart have taken the ethic of the capitalist class into account, on the other hand, we have taken up the investigations taken up by Schoenlank and Schanz who emphasized the standpoint of the labourer. The labourers were concerned with pay, free time, working conditions, like fresh air, light and warmth, in opposition to the entrepreneurs concerns regarding profit, risk and asceticism.

29. B. Schoenlank, G. Schanz, 'Gesellenverbände (Deutschland).' *Handwörterbuch der Staatswissenschaften,* 3rd edition, J. Conrad et al. (eds.), Jena 1909—Bruno Schoenlank, *Soziale Kämpfe* (see above).
30. Further all those in service obtain bread, wine and cheese (payment in kind) according to rank. K. T. v. Inama-Sternegg, *Deutsche Wirtschaftgeschichte,* Vol. 3, 1. 1899, p. 425. Of the attendants distributed among 28 kinds of workshops, nine sorts of workshops were counted as having the additional money value of clothing as part of their recompense. Six received in addition tips, ten an additional recompense in payment in kind, brats and intestines for the prelate's cook, wages in crops and hay for the *Stadler* and major domo. All of the 33 to 35 attendants were fundamentally recompensed with money. The bakers' underlings' portion of bread was replaced with money. The attendants of the foundation were subsumed under the prelate in the hierarchy of the church. The foundation produced no commodities, neither was it self-sufficient, but rather dependent on alms, to which the sundry emoluments of the master cook and of the 1st kitchen attendants refer. Reapers and thrashers worked for daily wages, insofar as they did not serve in forced collective labour. The transition to the money economy and wage labour developed but not however completely. The arborist, the publican, the smith, the sacristan, the assistant organ player, the mariner and *Sagmeister* were only recompensed with payments in kind. The master carpenter as well as the book binder received a daily wage, and additionally clothing for each with a money value of 6 shillings. The wages amounted to 737 shillings per annum. Inama-Sternegg provides the sum of 753 shillings. The difference is 16 shillings. If we halve the difference between the herewith provided reckoning of the annual wage and that of Inama-Sternegg and divide it equally, the annual wage of the master carpenter and of the book binder amounts to 8 shillings (re-calculated). The value of clothing amounts to 66 shillings 20 pfennigs. If we figure that 1 shilling (Austrian, also Swabian) has 30 pfennigs, then the sums of Inama-Sternegg agree with ours. The difference of money wages of 16 shillings are distributed to the daily wages of the master carpenters and of the book binders. Otherwise the question involving the sums of Inama-Sternegg is inexplicable. The halving of the difference is only a conjecture, in order to simplify the solution to our problem not however the problem of economic life. For the computation of the Austrian shilling and pfennigs, see Adam Ries, *Rechenbuch auf Linien und Ziffern,* Frankfurt am Main 1574, p. 108 verso and 109.
31. Schock was a unit of measure of 60 pieces of something. See Grimm, pp. 1430–1434. Schock was a currency notion in Saxony, Bohemia and Silesia. See Friedrich Albrecht Riemann: *Vollständiges Handbuch der Münzen, Maße und Gewichte aller Länder der Erde.* Quedlinburg und Leipzig 1830, S. 304 f., 24, 115. Other translators render it as „shock Groschen."
32. S. Franck, *Deutsche Chronik,* 1538. Abel, ibid.
33. B. Schoenlank, *Soziale Kämpfe vor dreihundert Jahren, Altnürnbergische Studien,* 2nd edition, Leipzig 1907. R. Endres, *Zur Einwohnerzahl und Bevölkerungsstruktur Nürnbergs im 15./16. Jahrhundert. Mitteilungen des Vereins für Geschichte der Stadt Nürnberg,* Vol. 57. 1970.
34. K. Bücher, *Die Bevölkerung von Frankfurt am Main in XIV. und XV. Jahrhundert,* Tübingen 1886.
35. B. Schoenlank, *Soziale Kämpfe ...,* ibid. Since the system of coinage was uneven, we make the following comments. In Nuremberg, Franconia, Thuringen and Meissen were 30 pennies = 1 lb. The gulden had 252 pennies. 1 gulden in Nuremberg and Franconia had 816 pennies. 1 groshen = 12 pennies, 1 gulden = 21 groshen, 1 gulden had 15 Batzen, 60 kreuzers are a gulden. 14 Batzen 4 kreuzers are a gulden. In Frankfurt am Main and in Swabia the value of coins were different. In Frankfurt 1 Nuremberg kreuzer was 4 1/5 pennies. The parts of the shilling in

Swabia and Austria are equal to the parts of the pound in Nuremberg. Adam Ries. *Rechenbuch.* Frankfurt 1574. Beer was no longer given in Nuremberg. In 1658 for a pound of pork 4 ½ to 5 kreuzers were paid, for a pound of beef or veal 4 ½ kreuzers and in the year 1597 4 ½ florins for 16 Metzen grain.

36. W. Abel. *Agrarpreise und Agrarkonjunktur*, 3rd edition, Hamburg 1978.
37. R. Endres, *Zur Einwohnerzahl … Nürenbergs,* 1970 (see above). Add to this tips and allowance for dangers (for the roofers). Vespers' money amounted to 4 pennies, cash money 2–4 pennies, that was banned by the council in 1597.
38. O. Johannsen, *Geschichte des Eisens*, 3rd edition, Dusseldorf 1953. B. Schoenlank, G. Schanz, R. Endres, R. S. Elkar and Winfried Reininghaus committed themselves to oppose the sentimental treatment of medieval labour relations.
39. J. Kulischer, *Allgemeine Wirtschaftsgeschichte*, Vol. 1, Munich 1958.
40. J. Strieder, *Studien zur Geschichte kapitalistischer Organisationsformen*, 2nd edition, Munich 1925 (see above).
41. H. Kellenbenz, *Technik und Wirtschaft*, K. Borchardt (ed.), *Europäische Wirtschaftsgeschichte 16–17. Jahrhundert*, Stuttgart 1979.
42. For further information regarding these forms of organization please see Chapter I above.
43. Adam Smith, *Wealth of Nations* (1776). G. W. F. Hegel (see below).
44. In this sense, the notion of John Hicks, who was mentioned above, is understandable. The mercantilists had considered the merchants as a tool in service to the state. The cameralists were the mercantilists of Central Europe. Joseph Schumpeter, *Geschichte der ökonomischen Analyse* (see above).
45. Schumpeter (loco citato, Part II, chapter 3), The principles of taxation of Diomede Carafa were continued by Adam Smith. In *The Wealth of Nations* the state as a harvester of taxes was not more than a night watchman. For the cameralists, theory and practice is an endorsement of the public interest, the teaching of Adam Smith that of the private. The scholars of a previous generation, like G. Schmoller and J. Kulischer, put the emphasis of mercantilism on the creation of privileged industrial enterprises of the town companies. Mercantilism was "one of an expanded economic politics on a larger territory." This viewpoint is part of a larger problem, that relates to the role of the state in the political economy.
46. G. W. F. Hegel in his *Enzyklopädie der Philosophischen Wissenschaften*, 1830. Part 3, § 544, treated the counter-position of the private person, of the corresponding interests and of the state in a historical-concrete fashion. "The estate authorities include all those who belong to civil society in general and to this extent are private persons,and who take part in the exercise of governmental power especially in regard to legislation, namely to the *universality* of interests, which does not relate to the appearance and action of the state as an individual (like in war and peace) and therefore does not belong exclusively to the nature of the Elector's power."

"For as *private persons* the members of the assembly of the estates are to be taken first, they are to serve as individuals for themselves or as representatives of the many or of the people." The privileged corporations serve as examples of the private interest of bourgeois society in the feudal condition. Here we relate the formation of the private interests, in opposition to the public, to the class oppositions. We have observed the two oppositions in their continuing development in modern times. The guild system was unambiguous in its origin, and it was treated lastly as an association of private persons by the instances of the state. In the middle of its historical course it served as an instrument of public administration.

47. F. M. Feldhaus, *Die Maschine im Leben der Völker*, Basel 1954. This is not only about the Fugger concern, but rather also about capitalist enterprises in all countries at that time.
48. The numbers of poor, of the middle class and of the wealthy from different parts of Germany in the 16th century in: R. Endres, *Zur Einwohnerzahl … Nürnbergs*, 1970.
49. The patricians of the German towns, Augsburg, Nuremberg, Mainz, among others were subordinate to the noble estate in the empire. The towns were free imperial cities, the patricians were masters in them, and they dominated the council. The German patriciate was distinguished from the ancient Roman and from the medieval patriciate in Venice, Genoa and other Italian cities mainly through the fact that these were the upper stratum. The Roman patrician was an aristocrat (nobilis), the Venetian a member of the first estate. The German patrician in the 15th and 16th century was not a gentleman (Gentilon) who, as Hans Sachs says, could be elected Duke, so that governance was still open to him (Hans Sachs, *Eigentliche Beschreibung aller Stände*).
50. Schoenlank and Schanz, *Handwörterbuch* (see above).

CHAPTER FIVE

Mining and Metallurgy

The primary sources for the knowledge of mining and metallurgy, of the art of assaying and of the art of glass making in Central Europe in the 15th, 16th, and 17th century are the writings of Agricola, Ercker and Kunckel. The work of Biringuccio in this context is indispensable. To these the writings of Rühlein von Calw, C. Schreittmann, Z. Lochner and C. C. Schindler, Modestin Fachs, Becher and Glauber are to be added as well. The illustrations and drawings of the best-known artists, which accompany the writings of Agricola, and the drawings of unknown artists, reproduced in the writings of Ercker and Kunckel, are an important addition to this knowledge. Dürer is the guide of the art to the wood cut and copper point. Jost Amman played a meaningful role as his successor in the art of the woodcut in relation to the guilds and estates. For the knowledge of mining and metallurgy are likewise to be added in wider circles the writings on arithmetic and medicine of Euclid and Galen, Apianus, Regiomontan, Köbel, Ries and Stifel, von Fibonacci and Pacioli, then the writings on perspective and measurement by Alberti, Leonardo da Vinci and Dürer and the writings of Luther, Calvin, Machiavelli, Botero and Bodin.

The changes of consciousness and their expression over the course of the 15th and 16th century can be followed by means of these sources. The artistic, technical, religious and scientific processes in the writings and images did not cause the social and economic events, but rather gave them expression, profile, understanding and made them visible and through their internalization transformed them.

We can retrace the origin or historical development of books on mining and metallurgy and the art of assaying. An early work, if not the earliest in this area, was Ulrich Rühlein von Calws (Kalbus) *Ein Nützlich Bergbüchlein* [*A Useful Mining Pamphlet*] without year or location, probably written around 1500. The author was professor of medicine in Leipzig. In the *Bergbüchlein* the young Knappius is instructed by the experienced miner Daniel on the system of mining. Further editions appeared in the 16th century in Worms, Nuremberg, Erfurt, Frankfurt am Main and Augsburg. A later edition was completed with attention to the art of assaying.

Georg Agricola (Bauer) was born in 1494 in Glochau (Saxony), attended the University in Leipzig and subsequently was active as a schoolteacher in Zwickau. He returned to Leipzig and studied medicine, the classical languages and other sciences there. In 1524 he emigrated to Italy in order to continue his medical studies. He was engaged for two years in the Manutius-Publishing House in Venice as a scholarly collaborator on the edition of Galen's works. Agricola also attended the universities of Bologna and Padua. In 1527 he returned to Germany and received a position in Joachimsthal as a town physician and pharmacist, which had been created shortly before (1516). He broadened his knowledge of languages, particularly of Greek and Latin, above all in the field of mining, in addition to continuing his medical practice, and in 1530 he published a small work in Latin, *Bermannus sive de re metallica* (On the Essence of Metals).[1] His great work, *De Re Metallica*, was written in 1550 and published in 1556 in Basel. He moved to Chemnitz 1530/1533 and remained there until his death in 1555. He published further books in the scientific field: *De natura fossilium*, 1546, *De mensuris et ponderibus*, 1533, *De ortu et causis subterraneum*, 1546, *De peste*, 1554, among others, which were all instructive in relation to medicine, mining and minerology. In 1540 the work *De la pirotechnia* by Vannoccio Biringuccio appeared in Venice, and in 1574 the *Beschreibung: Allerfürnemsten Mineralischen Erzt—unnd Berckwercksarten* by Lazarus Ercker appeared in Prague. The main works of Agricola, Biringuccio and Ercker complement one another, but the most extensive of all is *De Re Metallica* by Agricola. To this can be added the work of Johannes Kunckel on the manufacture of glass.

De Re Metallica by Agricola is subdivided into 12 books:[2]

1. On the vocation of the miner and metallurgist
2. The search for the ore vein
3. Concerning veins, chasms and strata of rock
4. The measurement of campsites. The offices of mining personnel
5. The opening of camp sites. The art of one who draws boundary lines [*Markscheide*]

6. The tools, implements and machines in mining
7. Assaying ore
8. Preparing ore
9. Smelting ore
10. The separation of pure metal
11. The separation of silver from copper. From iron.
12. Concerning salt, soda, alum, vitriol, sulphur, bitumen. Concerning glass. (see images)

The work contains woodcuts by Basilius Weffringer from Joachimsthal and by two illustrators from Basel, Hans Rudolf Manuel Deutsch and Zacharias Specklin. The art of assaying is treated in the seventh book by Agricola, in greater detail in Lazarus Erckers' *Beschreibung: Allerfürnemsten Mineralischen Erz/ und Berckwercksarten.* The art of glassmaking is briefly treated by Agricola in his twelfth book, adequately in Johannes Kunckel's *Ars Vitraria*. All three volumes are masterpieces.

The works of Agricola and Kunckel in particular point to the close relationships between Italy and Germany in economics, in the labour process, in technics and science. These relationships are to be noted in the example of Dürer in the fine arts, Regiomontan in mathematics, Copernicus in astronomy and Jakob Fugger in the world of merchants. The relationship of German to Italian arithmetic was mentioned above. The lines of connection led not only from Italy to Germany. Book publishing began in Mainz, Frankfurt am Main and Strasbourg and thereafter was propagated in northern Italy and in the Netherlands. Vannoccio Biringuccio took over and treated more fully some matters from Rülein von Calws *Bergbüchlein*, other matters from Agricola's early work *Bermannus*, whereas, conversely Agricola treated some things better than all the others in *De Re Metallica*. Rülein von Calws and Agricola had both studied medicine and earned their keep as physicians.

Vannoccio Biringuccio, born 1480 in Sienna, was active in Rome, Naples, Sicily, Florence and elsewhere as an architect and foreman, and died in Rome in 1539. Shortly following his death his work *De la Pirotechnica* (the ten books on the art of fire), appeared in Venice, which was organized as follows:[3]

1. The metals (gold, silver, copper, lead, tin, iron and steel, brass)
2. The semi-minerals [*Halbmineralien*] (mercury, sulphur, gravel, vitriol, alum, arsenic, orpiment, yellow arsenic, salt, cink spar or Smithsonite [*Galmei*], saphera, pyrolucite, magnetite, ocher, glazed stone, quartz, glass)
3. Assaying and preparation for smelting
4. The separation of gold from silver
5. Metal alloys

6. Concerning the art of molten pouring
7. The process of smelting of metals
8. Small foundries
9. The technic of working with fire
10. Artificial fuels and the production of fireworks in war and ceremonial occasions (see images)

Lazarus Ercker, born in Annaberg in 1528, died in Prague in 1594. He was named asseyor of precious metals and later mint master at Goslar. Subsequently he was a cross-check assayer in Kuttenberg and bookkeeper in the chancellery in Prague; then he became the chief mining master in the Kingdom of Bohemia and mint master in Prague. He published a small *Probierbuch* 1556, a small *Münzbuch* 1563, and in 1574 his *Beschreibung: Allerfürnemsten Mineralischen Erzt/ unnd Berckwercksarten.* The work is known as *Das Große Probierbuch.*[4]

The works of Agricola, Biringuccio and Ercker complement one another in such a way that, taken together, they render a complete picture of the systems of mining, metallurgy, assaying and smelting in the 16th century. The works of Agricola and Biringuccio overlap. The main difference between the two lies in the fact that in the first 6 books by Agricola, the vocations, the labour processes, technics and administration of the mines are treated exhaustively and systematically, while they are only presented briefly and in passing in Biringuccio. The tenth book by Biringuccio promises the treatment of pyrotechnics, a theme which does not appear in Agricola. In addition, iron and steel and in particular the refinement of raw steel is represented more completely by Biringuccio than by Agricola. However, these are briefly dealt with by both of them. Only later was the industrial significance of steel recognized. When those in the know and the experts talk about coal, what was mainly meant was charcoal; bituminous coal had limited significance under existing conditions at that time.

The main topic of Ercker's central work is the art of assaying, which was not presented so comprehensively either by Argicola or by Biringuccio. More extensively than the other metals the works of Agricola and Biringuccio treat the precious metals, and in this they expand on one another. The description of the reverberatory furnace for the smelting of ore is found in Biringuccio's work, not in that of Agricola.

Biringuccio believes that gold originates from sulphur transformed by the effect of heaven, time or nature. Otherwise Biringuccio takes a position against the transformability of metals and thus against alchemy. The opinions of Agricola and L. Ercker in relation to the transformability of the metals are also negative. More comprehensive in comparison to Biringuccio is the occupation with extractive metallurgy from gravel in the 7th and 8th book by Agricola, from the digging out of the ore, and the roasting and washing of the ore. The lighting for the workers underground was mentioned by Agricola and described especially in the images of his book.

Biringuccio took a stand against usury, against securities, that is, against bank certificates and the financial side of the mining industry. Agricola had much to say in the first six books of his work *De Re Metallica* about the organization of mining, the structuring of labour pertaining to mining, the technics of measurement of pits and the art of surveying mines, about the tools, instruments, arts and machines in mining. No work from the 16th century or later—down to the 18th century—contains so many details regarding this field as the main work by Agricola. With regard to the participation of the shareholders of the pit he had the following to say in book 4: "Earlier the owners or the shareholders [*Gewerkschaft*] possessed those ores that the hewers, standing on the floor of the tunnels, with shovels, whose grip was usually maintained for a long time, were able to move." In Agricola's time, on the contrary, a determinate height and width was awarded to the inheritor of the tunnel [*Erbstöllner*], who was responsible for water removal from the tunnels of the mines, so that the owner of the mine did not have to endure losses, if the shovel handle should be longer than normal. The effect of new tools was taken in stride in the labour of mining. Every pit rich in ore which had water removed from a tunnel and which was supplied with air in the mine, thus to each of the owners of the tunnels [*Stöllner*] the ninth of the ore taken from the floor of the tunnel was given; what was taken from under the floor of the tunnel belonged to the owner of the next deeper tunnel. The master miner is responsible for demarcating the tunnels from the mining pits. The shareholders mark with boundary stones in the presence of jurors the contiguous mine fields. The participation of citizens of the town as witnesses in modern times replaced this custom in distinguishing the fields bounding one another. Further, says Agricola, the shareholders, the owners of the tunnels or of the mine field pay attention to the dispositions of the mine master and of the mining rules.

Table 10: Number of Mine Shares by Category of Holders in Joachimsthal

Category	Mine Share Certificate Amounts
Shareholders	122
Landlord	4
Town	1
Church	1
Poorest of the Poor	1
Total	**129**

The shareholders receive the profit or suffer the losses from the enterprise. In order to drive the work of mining, the shareholders distribute mine share certificates. In the silver pits of Schneeberg the mining share certificates amounted to 128, in Joachimsthal to 129 (see Table 10).

Only the shareholders paid a *Zubuße* [payment in times of need by the owners of a mine to support mining operations—translator, Langenscheidt German-English Dictionary]; the lord of the manor did not pay but rather made available a large amount of wood from his forests in the construction of the pits, for the machines, buildings, smelters, for the furnaces and charcoal. Agricola adds: his countrymen called a pit colliery *Zeche* [after a local communal drink], and the money that the shareholders paid, was called a *Zubuße*. The iron pits remained undivided or had two to four partners, seldom more.

The investment of capital and the profit accruing to it appear to have been significantly higher in the precious metal pits than in the iron pits in the 16th century. The difference in the possibilities of profit in the period of high capitalism is worthy of note. Wood, as Agricola says, is a necessary matter for mining. If the forest is lacking, then the pit is built in the vicinity of a river in order to float the logs down to it. The locations containing many minerals normally do not have field crops, for the trees are also damaged.

The miners are either shareholders themselves or wage labourers. What they require for their living needs has to be imported. A longer or more problematic route increases the costs in mining that negatively affect not only the pit workers but the load carriers and the drivers as well. Agricola remarks that their pay and the increase in costs in this connection is less a burden for the workers than it is for the partners. If the wage labourers are unhappy with their wage on account of the increasing costs and demand higher wages from the owners of the pits, this action can have unfavourable economic consequences for the shareholders. The wage labourers have the right to remove themselves from the pits; the partners or joint owners [*Teilhaber*] cannot stop them (Agricola, *De Re Metallica*, 5th book).

The art of the glassmaker, as has already been stated, is treated, but not exhaustively by Agricola and Biringuccio. It is mentioned by Ercker. In 1612 *L'arte vetraria distinta in Libri sette* appeared in Florence. In 1662 it was translated into English by Christopher Merrett and supplemented. Johann Kunckel translated it again and augmented it further: *Ars vitraria experimentalis* or *Vollkommene Glasmacherkunst / Lehrende … Commentario über die … sieben Bücher P. Anthonii Neri, von Florenz—und den darüber getanen Anmerkungen Christopheri Merretti, M.D … Das reinste Crystall-Glas … Maler-Farben, die Salze dazu, drei Bücher …, 200 Experimente von Glasmalen, Vergülden und Brennen, die Öfen dazu,* Amsterdam and Danzig 1679.

The work by Agricola contains 292 woodcuts, that by Biringuccio, 57, that by Ercker, 41, and 24 copper points are found in Kunckel's work; all are artistic, beautiful and valuable from the scientific standpoint. We are particularly interested in the work by Agricola, because he exhaustively describes the offices, professions and the tasks of manual labourers as well as those of administrators in mining. But Biringuccio too provides some clear indications concerning those activities in the first half of the 16th century in Central Europe.

At the beginning of the 16th century Biringuccio had visited the Archdukedom of Austria and saw a large valley between Innsbruck and Hall, which was surrounded by many mountains which he described in the following way: "A well-watered river flowed through the valley. In almost every mountain surrounding it ore was obtained, to wit mostly copper or lead, that almost always contained silver. A number of people from the area had already begun to build; they had determined the locations to be worked through the indicators which came to light. They had begun at the foot of the mountain, since beginning at the lower elevation is more advantageous for the draining of water, for driving in and out, for the transport of the miners, to lighten their hauling, and for facilitating the ore and wall rock or country rock or waste rock [*taube Steine*]; this way and means of mining also avoids or minimizes the danger of collapse and increases the comfort and security of the process. Moreover, it is less costly. If one begins to build at the foot of the mountain, every 50 ells takes one a half an ell higher with the tunnel.[5] They drove a tunnel almost two miles long before they came to the ore. Water constituted the greatest difficulty as a rule, also the greatest danger for the miners, because there, where much ore was found, there was also a lot of water present. Yet the water did not present the greatest problem for these people, but rather the rock. When the miners had arrived with the tunnel in line with their indicators, they came up against a hard limestone stratum. With much labour they succeeded in punching through the more than 1 and ½ rods thick stone and only then encountered a rich vein of copper. Between two walls of limestone they bored out a massive cavity, where more than 200 miners were at work. They worked day and night in shifts, without daylight, only by the light of their lamps. Out of the mouth of the tunnel a large amount of in part select—in part crude—ore was removed. The ore was copper ore that contained so much silver that it was called silver ore. To their profit they still had the copper which was mixed with the silver. This mining was administered by the mine owners, who were responsible for the large number of unskilled laborers who were necessary for the maintenance of the water, for the construction of wheels, pumps, pipes and linkages as well as other water maintenance devices. Through the middle of the pit there ran a trench which collected water, which ran off from various cracks. With the runoff and intake, one was soaked."[6] Thus far we can follow the description by Biringuccio. We return to the remarks by Agricola in this regard.

5.1 Mining Freedom

In the Middle Ages as well as in the early period of the modern era miners were free. In the states of Central Europe this freedom meant free mobility, tax preferences, freedom from military duties and self-jurisdiction. In the early Middle Ages compulsory collective mining labour was performed for the lords of the manor, but in the late Middle Ages (12th century) mining was propelled by the shareholders through their capital investment and by the wage labourers. The freedom of mining was in this regard linked with the freedom of capital investments, with the declaration of freedom of the locations of resources of certain minerals and fossils like ore and bitumen, and with the establishment of free organizations of shareholders or communal associations (*Genossenschaften*) of free shareholders. In the communities of Upper Germany every resident [*Bürger*] had the right, with the discovery of a deposit of ore, to demand the surveying by the authorities of the specified land for mining. The custom of the principles of mining law [*Bergregal*] spread across the Steiermark, Upper Palatinate, the Harz Mountains and beyond. The *Bergregal* arose from the declared constitution of mining freedom in the 12th century; this contained the proper privilege of the residents of the borough who exploited the ore and fossils. An open statement regarding the extraction of salt was excluded from it. The feudal lords offered resistance to the freedom of mining and received some counter privileges in return.[7]

In the 15th century and later the system of mine share certificates [*Kuxsystem*] was dominant, in which the elements or shares of a given mine were distributed in theory among 128 participants. These shares were simultaneously linked with additional payments [*Zubußen*] of the participants. Each share owner was thus required to lay out a sum of money for the enterprise, for the operation and administration of the mine. We can speak of 129, 130, 132, 134 owners of mine certificates. One who inherits a certificate [*Erbkux*] which belongs to the property owner of the mine, was freed from the cost of enterprise or of the additional payments. Free certificates [*Freikuxe*] were also those of the Church and hospitals. One share was issued to the state, one to the poor. The landowner did not pay additionally for his portion, but rather supplied the mine owners the required amount of wood from his forests, as we have seen, without compensation, for the expansion of the pits, for the machines, for the structures and the smelting furnaces.[8]

The miners or pitmen [*Knappen*] were paid a daily or piece wage. The miners' association was the entire company of mine workers. The shareholders were partners in the mine and in part also miners. The totality of all those participating in the pits constituted the communal association [*Genossenschaft*] of shareholders. The owners and partners were separated from the pit workers, the shareholders worked for themselves, and the miners [*Knappen*] were designated as those who worked for others in the mining industry.

The communal associations [*Genossenschaften*] of the mining trade of both kinds—of the shareholders and the miners or pitmen [*Knappen*], according to Gierke—belonged to the bourgeois class [*Bürgerstand*]. In the Middle Ages they shared some characteristics with the core communal associations [*Markgenossenschaften*], for example, their specific location, others with the town guilds. In the mining community in the Harz region, whose main settlement was located in Goslar, the association of miners and metallurgy workers (miners and foresters, *montani* and *silvani*) constituted a civil corporation. They stood between the merchants and the guilds (minters, shop keepers and manual labourers), participated in the town regiment, sent deputies to the signing of statutes and were asked by the town council for their agreement with every change in the law. The forestry works in the Harz forest constituted ipso facto a *Markgemeinde*, which in addition to mining and the smelting of metal also utilized timber. For the mining and smelting of the Harz region, the totality of all miners and foresters formed an independent, autonomous communal association [*Genossenschaft*] subject to the jurisdiction originally of an imperial governor, later to that of the town council of Goslar. The shareholders themselves maintained the administration under the mining judge or mining master; their general assembly met at Goslar under the influence of the council, according to the rules of mining, the peace of the mines and mining rights. In the court of the master miners they dispensed justice as aldermen in matters of taxation law, in serious cases of criminal law, on appeals before the mining court, and they appointed most of the mining officials, like bailiffs [*Fronbote*], court marshals [*Fronknecht*], court scribes [*Schreiber*], sworn jurors of the court [*Feuerhüter*] and so on.

In the large communal association [*Genossenschaft*] of all those involved in the enterprise of mining [*Gewerke*] the owners of the smelters and the owners of the mine were separated from one another. The masters constituted a particular brotherhood and confronted the dependent labourers, hence the unskilled workers [*Knechte*] and the miners [*Knappen*]. In the craft guilds property and labour were not yet divided, for the mine owners [*Bergherren*], feudatories [*Lehenträger*], and renting-owners [*Mietsinhaber*] as a rule still built their pits as masters themselves with their master workers and miners and pitmen [*Knappen*]. The miners in Goslar and elsewhere were autonomous and privileged communities [*Gemeinheiten*] with a communal associative [*genossenschaftlicher*] constitution. Only later, with the development of mining, its rules and mining regulation, did the territorial princes take the leadership of the mining system into their own hands.

The communal association of mining [*Berggenossenschaft*] was put together by the membership of the shareholders. The guild-like corporation of mine workers, according to which the proportional share of the total wealth of the mine led to the sole foundation of membership, appeared only from the 15th century. A common mining property, to be sure, already existed in the 14th century, when the pits were in fact shared among the single cultivators according to fields or shares; thus the construction of a pit was customarily done at communal expense according to specific quotas of the totality of owners who possess it.

As was the case with the guilds, the association of communal members [*Genossen*] was at first founded on the relationships of the miner as an individual person, whether he was a master, foreman or servant. The history of the mining right of Rammelsberg in the edition of Gottfried Wilhelm Leibniz points to this origin of the constitution of the association. The individual character of the enterprise was later changed and adopted the system of a community [*Gemeinschaft*]. From a community of wealth there grew a communal association [*Genossenschaft*], and the communal association [*Genossenschaft*] in turn trailed off again to a community of wealth. Out of this origin the special purpose organization [*Zweckverein*] and the joint-stock company arose.[9] Gierke poses the question on the basis of material collected by Leibniz about the nature of the mining man, whether he was a master, a foreman or a simple miner [*Knappe*]. We will not investigate further the personal side of this question, since it has nothing to do with the period in question. The main point of the formulation of the problem is the nature of the communal association [*Genossenschaft*] as the transitional form to the joint-stock company in the 14th and 15th century.

The miner, whether master, foreman or simple miner [*Knappe*], was excused from military, war and defence service, as a freely mobile individual; in addition, he was freed in that period from taxation under certain circumstances. His freedom was not absolute and not universal; taken in a strict sense there can be no talk of servitude of the miners [*Bergknappen*]. Doubtless some of them were servants, but servitude signified an unfree condition, which did not correspond to the situation of the wage peasants [*Lohnbauer*] in the 15th and 16th century. Gierke contributed something inexact in this connection. The association of people involved in mining in Goslar consisted of masters, foremen and miners [*Knappen*], who were not servants but were formally free. The unskilled labourer in mining was not a serf, but rather a wage labourer, paid in part a wage per piece work, in part through weekly wages, in part in money form, in part in produce. The mining guild [*Gilde*] was a *Genossenschaft* with a common interest, a closed membership, a specific leadership and a permanent constitution. One can ask the question whether the people involved in the mining industry established a guild [*Gilde*] or a *Genossenschaft* in this sense in the 15th and 16th century. The interests of the foremen, of the hewer and of other unskilled labourers were the same in relation to the maintenance of the freedoms of mining; in relation to wages and conditions of labour, on the contrary, they were not. Earlier we spoke of the romanticizing and idealizing of the conditions of labour in the late Middle Ages. In one sense the people involved in mining were organized like a guild [*gildemäßig*], as Gierke says, in another sense they were not. The structuring and division of labour in mining was set up differently than in the guild system [*Zunftwesen*]. In the period from the 14th to 16th century and even the 17th century the organization, structuring and division of labour in Central European mining was relatively highly developed. Many labourers—200 at a time, as Biringuccio says—came together in one shift in a tunnel, to dig out ore. These data are not a poetic tale like those about Jack of Newbury's factory. The structuration of labour in the English and German textile industry was strictly controlled and supervised by the guilds [*Zünfte*], the merchants and the authorities in the 16th century. By contrast the fate of mining was different. Not weaving but rather mining and metallurgy had shown themselves to be a model for the further development of industry in Europe during the late 17th and over the course of the 18th century.

Freedom was related to the miner's right to an unhindered and tax-exempt change of position from one enterprise to another and from one location or spot to another; this freedom was in force for the various labours of those associated with mining. They also received salt and flour without additional charge while others were required to pay tax on them. Although the miners were exempted from military service, they had, for example, participated during the siege of fortresses in undermining the siege, receiving a wage in recompense.

The historical processes and periodization can be considered from several standpoints. The movement of peasant liberation, the social struggles of the labourers in the town enterprises, and the labour of mining and system of smelting lie at the centre of our treatment of these matters. The printing industry, seafaring, fine arts and science can also be seen as the determining processes and characteristics of the new epoch in the history of Central Europe. Mining in the Holy Roman Empire took its large upswing in the 15th century. The form of undertaking of the capitalist enterprise was already formed and had been developed into the predominant form of economics in this field. The transformation of the medieval organization of guilds to the modern bourgeois and capitalist form was established in mining and smelting earlier than in the other branches of Central European production. The printing industry in the middle of the 15th century was worked by private persons. The arsenals in Central Europe were not enlarged by capital investment of this sort. They were administered as public enterprises by the state from the 15th to the 18th century. Both are closely linked with mining and smelting. That which was asserted about the arsenal and war industry, was also said about coinage. The mining and smelting industry showed the same accompanying phenomena and the same social difficulties as those which the working youth [*Kläuberbuben*] had separated and cleaned the rubble from the *Zagel* [a stage of iron refinement in the smelting process—trans.] or the impure ore in the period of high capitalism. If they were strong enough, they entered into the service as *Truhenläufer* [men pushing mining carts in the tunnels—trans.] and *Huntezieher* [men who pull mining carts in the tunnels—trans.]. In the smelter system, many youths began as charcoal burners [*Kohlenbrenner*] and wood cutters [*Holzknechte*]. The career trajectory was hard in the blast house or smelting works. It was no different in the knife industry which was linked to the smelting works. 150 journeymen worked for 300 master knife makers in Styr as did ten times as many maids.

A miner's strike in Schneeberg in the year 1496 was beaten down and suppressed by threats or otherwise by strikebreakers. Additional strikes of miners are known in Joachimsthal and Mansfeld. Already at the beginning of the 16th century the entrepreneurs established so-called anti-strike associations. If the miners protested it was not only a matter of wages and subsistence goods, like grain, fat or cloth, which the labourers received, but also about labour time. The entrepreneurs or managers of the mines had tried to decrease the wages for labour time by not attributing to the hewers the time it took them to enter into the deep tunnels. For the attribution of the time to enter the tunnels had been the normal practice in the pits (see Agricola in the following section). Furthermore, it came to a question of Sunday rest. Ludwig the Wealthy had permitted work to continue in the salt mines of Reichenhall (Upper Bavaria) on Sunday. A treaty with the Archduke of Saxony in the year 1520 was supposed to prevent the emigration of miners from one mining precinct to another, and to this extent it influenced mining freedom. An agitator, who instigated "among the miners, indignation, revolt and agitation", that is, a call to strike, should be deported and banned from finding work in another mine of the opposing party.[10] His name was registered in a book. Not only the accumulation of capital, the mechanization of the enterprise and the rationalization of the labour process, but also the black book, the strikebreaking activities of the entrepreneurs and, on the other side, strikes and unemployment were characteristics of mining and metallurgy in the 15th and 16th century. Labour relations and conditions of the 19th and 20th century, were not only present in a seminal state or *in nuce*, but rather in full bloom in the earlier periods.

The beginnings of the capitalist epoch present no simple problem. The latest researches assume that capitalism begins in the 16th century or even later and that the Middle Ages continued into the end of the 15th century. This way of thinking should be relativized, for the posing of the problem should vary according to the industry which has been chosen for consideration. If one begins with the miners' guilds [*Gilden*] and guild associations [*Zunftverbände*] of other branches of production, the medieval conditions in Central Europe thus continue, and it is no different in the areas of non-industrialized trades in home construction. We concern ourselves with the mining of metal because in our work we don't pose the problem of the continuation of the medieval process but rather give emphasis to the beginnings of the capitalist system. A second question in this context asks whether the appearance of capitalistic processes in mining and metallurgy in the 15th and 16th century is systematic or sporadic. Strieder pointed out the gritty and filthy as well as the progressive side of the process. Relations between the two sides are taken into account in the 15th and in the 20th century. Mining does not stand alone there in the earlier period, but rather has a close connection to coinage, to the metal works in the town, to credit institutes and the banks, to the circulation of money, to printing, to transport, to the war industry and foreign trade. Mining is, in this sense, a systematic and not a sporadic appearance in the 15th an 16th century.

It was to be sure in the interest of the authorities to advance progress in the circulation of money and to operate mining capitalistically. However, the princes, the clerics, as well as the secular members of the ruling class and the representatives of the authorities had demanded precious and non-ferrous metals for their enterprises. Gold, silver and copper were found, dug out and refined. The entrepreneurs, shareholders and merchants, the mine workers, hewers, smelters, smiths, drivers, assayers and coiners created and distributed ore, metals, and finally money for wages and profits. This process began in the Middle Ages sporadically and interruptedly, then in the capitalist period it was developed quickly, permanently, uninterruptedly and systematically. Another scene comes to the fore if town and house construction or weaving are taken into account; in comparison to these, however, shipbuilding, seafaring and shipping companies appear rather closer to that of mining in relation to the increase in productivity and profit in the epoch of the early-modern period.

5.2 Structuring of Labour in Mining During the 14th and 15th Centuries

The structuration of labour in mining is treated by Agricola, *De Re Metallica*, Book 4, in three main sections about manual labourers, pit foremen and district administration. First, he names as the main kinds of manual labourers in mining those designated in Table 11 (see page 306 and images).

Table 11: German and Latin Names of Manual Labourers in Mining

German	Latin	English
Berganschläger	Ingestores	Shovellers
Berghauer	Fossores	Miners or Diggers
Erzpocher	Discretores	Bucker
Häspler (Haspler)	Vecrtarii	Lever Worker (Windlass Men)
Schmelzer	Excotores	Smelter
Seifner (Wäscher)	Loteres	Washers, Buddlers, Sifters, etc.

Other manual labourers mentioned are: mountain climber [*der Bergläufer*], trench cleaner [*der Grabensäuberer*], helpers [*der Handpreu* (*Heimpreu*)], trolley pushers and pullers [*der Karrenläufer* (*Huntestößer*)][11], carters [*der Fuhrknecht* (*Fuhrmann*, *Karrenführer*)] the brineman or salt maker [*der Salzsieder*], the smith [*der Schmied*], the shaft sinker [*der Sinker*], the lumberjack [*der Holzhauer*], the bottom sweeper [*der Dregger* (*Drecker*)], the carrier or porter [*der Lastträger*], transporters, delivery men [*die Förderleute*], the carpenter, (*der Zimmermann*); the pit boys [*die Bergbuben* (*Grubenjungen*, *Treckejungen*)], youth responsible for heating [*der Wärmbub*], the water carrier [*der Wasserknecht* (*Wasserheber*)], youth workers in a Göppelhaus [*der Geipel* (*Göppelbube)* a *Göppel* is a machine powered by muscle, wind, water and other means, often by horses; *Göppelbube* is the youth who drives the machine, and the *Göppelhaus* is the building in which the machine is housed], bargain man [*der Lehn—und Gedingehauer*], the carter or wagoner [*der Wagenknecht*], the pipe fitter [*der Rohrschmied*], the hammer smith [*der Hammerschmied*] (he also had a hammer journeyman and a *Handpreu* or helper), the salt expert [*der Salzkünstler*], the gold washer [*der Goldwäscher*], the glazier, [*der Glaser*], the tin smith, pewterer [*der Zinngießer*]. There were many kinds of smiths. The hewers were variously divided according to wage and labour conditions. The pieceworker [*Gedinghauer*] did stonework for a piecework wage according to time and by the *Lachter* (app. 1.8 meters of measure). A rate was concluded with the pit master in the presence of a jury. Manual labourers were paid a weekly or daily money wage as well as by piece rate (see above). Wages were paid out in cash according to the rules of mining and the hammer mill. Salt miners [*Salinenarbeiter*] and hammer mill workers on the contrary were paid in salt or iron as well. In addition, this applied as well to *Bergmannsbauer*, small peasants, who were mainly miners. Apprentices in mining were not paid—rather, on the contrary—they had to pay the master for their training. Other craftsmen and manual labourers had different designations and tasks in the various mines of Central Europe. The smelter appeared to have been a highly rated miner.

The second division was constituted by the administration of the pits, tunnels and strata (see Table 12, p. 209).

Table 12: German and Latin Names of Administrators in Mining

German	Latin
Steiger (mine supervisor)	Praefectus fodinae (Pit) Praefectus cuniculi (Tunnel)
Shift Master	Praeses fodinae Praeses cuniculi

Other designations of these offices are: *Hutmann* [supervising position], watchmen, supervisors. For the mining machines there were also the stamp mill (ore crusher) [*Pochensteiger*], the mining sink-hole supervisor [*Pingensteiger*], (*Bingensteiger*), the *Kunststeiger* and their assistants, further: *Kunstmeister, Kunstknechte, Kunstschmied, Kunstjung.*[12]

The masters are: the wood master, the master builder, the master smith in a hammer mill [*Hammermeister*], also the master in the weather and in the *Göpel*—[see above] and *Wasserkunst.*

The third division of the offices in the system of mining in Agricola's time was the representatives of the authorities as well as of the district administration. They are as follows in Table 13.

The offices of the chief mayor, of the *Berghauptmann* [head supervisor of the mine] and of the *Oberhauptmann* [a supervising head] were named by Agricola as well. The smelting works had the following administration: the director of smelting, [*Hüttenkampfer*], the smelting master [*Hüttenmeister*], the smelting labourers [*Hüttenschaffer*] and the recording secretary of the smelter [*Hüttenschreiber*].

From these data we can obtain an informal and general impression as to how labour in mining was structured and divided during the 15th and 16th century.

Table 13: German and Latin Names of District Administrators in Mining

German	Latin	English
Austeiler	Distributor	Cashier
Bergamtmann	Praefectus Metallorum	Mining Prefect
Bergmeister	Magister Metallicorum (or Metallorum)	Mining Master
Bergmeisterschreiber	Scriba Magister Metallicorum	Mining Master's Clerk
Bergschreiber	Scriba fodinarum	Mining Clerk
Gegenschreiber	Scriba partium (*Kuxe, Teile*)	Share Clerk (Counter-Clerk)
Gemeiner Siegler	Publicus Signator	Notary
Geschworene (Jurors)	Jurati	Jurors
Zehnter (Zehender)	Decumanus	Title Gatherer

We shall later take up the details of concrete enterprises in the metal branch in Agricola's time. Agricola was able to ascertain in *De Re Metallica*, Book 1, that silver and gold extraction was already being practised in the middle of the 8th century, as the oldest privileges of the inhabitants of these towns reveal to us. The oldest documents from Goslar give hints of the lead works in the 10th century and the documents from Freiberg of the silver works in the 12th century. In a way similar to Lucretius in *De Rerum Natura*, Agricola presents in detail his overview here of the utility of the metals for people. From this we can derive the importance of the same for life in his time. At the top of his list Agricola refers to the profit for the mining people, who devote so much effort in digging up the earth. The labour was not only hard and dismal, but also dangerous to health and life, for the mining hewers quickly died from the toxic pit fumes which they inhaled, soon faded away emaciated by inhaling dust which caused their lungs to fester and, soon enough, from accidents, crushed by mountain cave-ins, and in passage through the mine, from falling down the shafts and thereby breaking legs, arms and necks. One ought to add the danger from water, which Agricola and Biringuccio mention. Agricola treats the danger to health *ex professo*, because he himself was a physician in Joachimsthal.

Agricola (*De Re Metallica*, Book 6) describes in greater detail the accident cases and diseases of mining folk as well as the means used to protect them from them. Water, which in some shafts rose in large amounts and was extremely cold, could damage the lower legs, especially the muscles. The mining people were thus to wear high boots, which might protect their legs from the coldness of the water.

The dry pits brought even greater affliction, for the dust, which the pit labour raised up, reached into the lungs and caused breathing difficulties, asthma, lung festering and vertigo in the body. In Altenberg in the district of Meissen there was black smelter smoke which caused [*ausgenagte*] wounds and ulcers gnawed out down to the bone. A kind of cadmium ate up hands and feet. Poor weather also caused breathing difficulties in the shaft. To combat this, weather machines were engaged. Some pits produced their own vapours and expelled instead of exhales poisoned air. In addition, through the setting of fires in the entrances a thin vapour was blown out. When the vapours increased, the workers who travelled out of the shafts into the shoots of their passages, fell down on account of the effect of swollen hands and feet. Now and then workers fell out of the carriers and broke arms, legs and necks, or they drowned in the slime. The liability was that of the foreman whose negligence was responsible for the lack of reliability of the ride. Moreover, the pits caved in. Rammelsberg near Goslar collapsed, and as a result 400 men lost their lives. In Altenberg in 1546 a part of the mine collapsed and crushed 6 workers. The collapse dragged a house with mother and child into the depths. In order to avoid this, the mining people had to frequently erect or extend arches. Apart from the shafts running out of ore, Agricola adduces 5 reasons why the shafts were no longer worked: 1. The strong flow of water. When lifting out the water cost more than the process of earnings acquired, then the shafts would be given up. 2. Bad weather. When this could not be improved by artifice or expenditure, operations in the shaft or in the entire tunnel were shortened. 3. The appearance of vapours. When it was impossible to eliminate or thin them out, the shaft was put out of operation. 4. The awful and pernicious mining ghost. Each miner fled from it, when it could not be exorcised. 5. The unsafe mine construction from cave-ins. Subsequently the mine collapse would habitually follow. Warlike unrest provides a further reason for giving up mining in an area. Water not only brings difficulties for profitability but also for the health and life of the mining people.

Agricola then shows the utility of the metals in the creation of consumer goods in daily life, in the cultivation of fields, in cattle raising, in the blunderbuss or bombards in war, which can knock down a fortress. He also referred to their utility for usurers, merchants and finally for the mining people themselves.

Agricola was in his character, illuminated in his writings and by the remarks of those who knew him as well, a well-intentioned and generous man. He had a scientific training and wanted to have nothing to do with magic or superstition. In this way he spoke out against the use of divining rods in the choice of prospective locations. He was sceptical in relation to magical wands and incantations, and the application of forked branches from the common hazel he compared to the sale of bad shares. The true mining man, who is a pious and serious man, does not employ the magic wand. Agricola himself wants the mining man to become knowledgeable and understanding of the nature of things and that he only observes the natural attributes of entrances to the pits. He was just as sceptical concerning astrology. He went further in his opposition to the alchemists. Out of courtesy he held his tongue in his relationships to the magicians, but the alchemists, even though he had recognized their achievements for chemistry or metallurgy in earlier times, he could only curse. He returned time and again to the disingenuity of the alchemists. One alchemist is worse than the next; they are swindlers, they are hated in the highest degree; they are punished by death. Lazarus Ercker's opinion in this matter was no different.[13]

The metals with which Agricola, Biringuccio, Ercker and other authors were concerned in the area of mining and the art of assaying in the 16th century, are mainly: lead, gold, copper, silver and tin, that is the non-ferrous and the precious metals. The other metals and minerals which were treated are iron, pyrites, mercury, saltpeter, sulphur, bismuth, alum, and antimony. In the ore-laden mountains of Saxony, the famous discovery was made in the middle of the 15th century, perhaps the most important of them all in 1445 on the Altenberg, 1460 at Schneeberg and at Annaberg in 1470. Silver ore as well as copper, lead, tin, zinc, bismuth and cobalt ore were discovered there.[14]

Thanks to the factors of profit and of the costs of production it was worthwhile to excavate deep into the ground for precious and non-ferrous metals when they were mixed in with them. In 1480 pits the size of 100 *Lachtern* were constructed on Schneeberg in Saxony; in 1482 after the principal tunnel to remove water was dug, an additional depth of 100 *Lachtern* was achieved. Customarily the pits were operated with six to eight men, a large pit at Marienberg on the other hand was operated by 58 men; 2 pits were worked with 14 and 3 with 12 men. In 1515 in Tirol in the mining district around Schwaz and Kitzbühel 10,000 mine workers worked in 274 pits, averaging 37 workers per pit.[15] A large enterprise of mining for precious metals only rarely had reached a work force of 200 men.[16]

Through the reports of Agricola and Biringuccio we have a concrete idea of Central European, in particular, of Austrian and Bohemian, Middle and Upper German mining in the 16th century and of the refinement of precious as well as non-ferrous metals there. The technique of mining was developed in the Middle Ages and the foundational sciences of geography, metallurgy and chemistry were further developed, sometimes, to be sure, in a form which was not entirely free of superstition. However, in the 15th century the entrepreneurs and the technicians had newly organized the necessary activities for these sciences. The qualified labourers, the entrepreneurs, the technics and the sciences were articulated, and they made possible developments of mining in the Harz region, in the Upper

Palatinate, in Mansfeld, in Tirol and in Hungary. The waterworks, the separation of metals and *das Saigern* (the art by which with the help of lead, silver could be extracted from copper ore which contained silver—see page 198+ Vol. 16 Grimm), had been expanded in the second half of the 15th century, offering technical progress in mining of great significance. The rag and chain pump and chain of dippers, which could lift leather sacks with an iron cable 35 or 90 *Lachter* (or almost 200 meters), were introduced at this time.

The separation of copper from the ore [*Das Kupfersaigern*] gained currency in the 60s and 70s of the 15th century. Capitalists in Nuremberg, Augsburg and Leipzig founded liquifying smelters [*Saigerhütten*] and liquifying trade companies [*Saigerhandelsgesellschaften*] with a great capital outlay. The company Schwarza and Mansfeld established in the year 1472 had an original capital of 6,000 Florins.

The operation of a *Saiger* smelter [*Saigerhütte*], which produced 7,000 zentners (=385 US tons app—trans.) of copper, consisted of 8 smelting furnaces, 10 *Saiger* furnaces, 3 gas stoves and 2 *Dörröven* [a specially designed oven in which the fuel materials (wood, peat) are heated, dried and kilned to a high degree. archive.org › stream full text of "Idioticon der österreichischen Berg und Hütten …"—trans.].[17] It united the qualified labourers, the operational articulation of their labours, the technics of the production of copper, the required entrepreneurs and their capital to do it, the supply and demand in the copper trade. The training of qualified labourers in mining and metallurgy took place in the enterprise itself.

In the Falkenstein Tiefbau (see below, p. 327) 500–600 water pumpers worked daily; the number was conditional upon season.

In this section we have viewed for the most part the work of the men in mining, however, the sources also reproduce a picture of the labour of women. Women did not work underground. Women did not appear as hewers, nor did they have anything to with the mined iron and the trough, the symbol of mining. Neither were they smelters or smiths. They performed unskilled labour for less remuneration. Agricola depicted somethings about the labour of women in a pictorial way in relation to the theme of the preparation of ore for smelting.[18] The main task of the women was to work at the sorting table [*Klaubentafel*]; several women were kept busy with the sorting of ore. Further, they worked with the sieve made of iron filament weavings and with woven baskets in the placement of the ore. Women were also involved in washing the ore from the washing pits [*Schlämmgraben*] with tarps [*Planen*] and pre-washing gold ore on stoves with traverse strips. Above ground, men and women worked together without inhibitions. The tools of the women were mostly the sieve, the basket and the tarp [*Plane*]. At sorting the ore, they worked by hand and without tools.

The labour in mining was performed in part in the form of wage labour, paid either by the day or by the piece, in part by the shareholders, who themselves had invested their capital in the enterprise. The structuration of labour in 15th and 16th century mining was not fundamentally different from what was the case in the 18th, 19th and 20th century. This was streamlined in opposition to the structuration of labour in the guilds, which means that it was related to the increase in productivity. It showed the readiness of the labourers and the entrepreneurs to introduce new methods of labour and new machinery. It was not a retrospective industry which remained static. The further development of mining leads in the direction of large-scale industry in Central Europe. The shareholders in mining originally had some characteristics in common with the medieval *Genossenschaften*, guilds and mining guilds [*Zünften und Gilden*], and to this extent Gierke was right. But the shareholders in the 15th and 16th century exhibited still further productive characteristics and types of treatment, which were characterized by industrialists in the same class relations, class oppositions and class struggles as in the period of high capitalism. The shareholders are in part owners of share certificates, who later founded capitalist joint-stock companies, in part they are members of the working class, which established the trade unions of today. Gierke's conception offers less of an explanation than that of Strieder, Johannsen and others, who investigated the developments in the area of the entrepreneurs and of class struggle in mining.[19]

5.3 Labour and Processing in Mining

Mining in the Middle Ages was bound up with sovereignty over the mountain, which was expressed through wording concerning territorial sovereignty; the wording was related to that "which lies and stands" "in plano et in monte", which means: related to the sovereignty over soil and ridge. Through such legal and folk formulas, the appropriation and exploitation of mountains, valleys and patches of land were regulated. It was formulaically expressed as follows: "min acker, min matte, holz und velt, getwing und ban und grund und grete, und alles min got."[20] ["My farmland, my meadow, wood and field, mastered and corrupted and ground and level, and all of that belongs to me." This quote in Middle High German may not be rendered accurately in contemporary English. See Grimm, Wörterbuch and Matthias Lexer, Mittelhochdeutsches Lexikon, both are online—trans.] The separation between the ownership of land and of the wood, the ownership of mines and water rights followed into modern times. The *Genossenschaften* and companies, which had managed collieries and mining, made a valid agreement with the authorities regarding the privileges of taking over the ore pits. The wood share [*Holzkux*][21]—or the free share [*Freikux*] was granted to the owner of the forest.

He became a participant in the enterprise, without being burdened with additional penalties. The landlord provided the wood for the pits, not the wood for the smelters; he had no rights in relation to the granting of mining rights themselves. In the Middle Ages the granting of mining rights still rested with the landlords. The territorial princes for the most part then assumed the granting of these rights in the modern period, and these rights in mining were granted to the mining entrepreneurs through the representatives of the territorial authorities. The transition to sovereignty of the modern national state is bound up with the new customs in the granting of mining rights. The new political practices in this area are related to the new granting usages. Family operations which in the Middle Ages had often or customarily constituted the communal form in mining, were driven back and replaced, little by little, by the capitalist forms of organization.

We will now introduce some data and offer some remarks concerning the organization of mining operations and the organization, structuration and division of labour in this area. The 15th and 16th century was a period of greater transformations in the setting up and composition of the operations in the credit and banking system, in trade and the process of production in Central Europe. To the extent that the arrangements of business operations increased in this period, so too did the structuration of labour increase. The structuration of the enterprises was indicated by the size of an operation and in the rise of its sales, in relation to the expansion, extent and its internal organization. Labour had an inner connection with this development, because the structuration of the enterprise and that of the labour process were dependent on one another. Their further development was closely bound up with one another.

The fusion of pits in Upper Germany developed in the 15th century. (The fusions of pits in the Middle Ages were, on the contrary, emergency associations compelled by operational-technical concerns.) Such fusions occurred particularly in the production camps of the ore-laden mountains; they were introduced in the 15th and 16th century in the interest of the shareholders, their profit and on account of the accumulation of capital. In this sense they were expanded in the capitalist mode and unfolded according to capitalist rules. Production was separated from trade; the mining operations were production and not distribution corporations. The shareholders were in part co-workers in the system of mining and at the same time, its owners. The fusion of pits according to the new, not to the medieval kind, is attested in 1462.[22]

The work of mining in Freiberg was accomplished with hammer and pick from the 14th to the 19th century. In the Middle Ages in this mining district the hand winch was the main tunnel driving machine. In the 15th century the horse capstan [*Pferdegöpel*] was introduced and in the following century the reversible water wheel or *Wassergöpel*. A tunnel depth of up to 250 meters could be reached with the horse capstan, with the reversible water wheel one could get to a depth of 550 meters. The great discovery of silver in the Erzgebirge, the founding of the mining towns of Schneeberg, Annaberg, Marienberg, Joachimsthal and the exploitation of the coal field near Rammelsberg occurred in the middle of the 15th century. The pits around Freiberg were taken into operation in the 15th and 16th century. Unrest and strikes by the miners in Freiberg had begun in the middle of the 15th century.[23]

Figures like Fugger, among others, played a double role in the leadership in production and distribution, and, in this way, they formed a model for the further development of the capitalist system and the spirit which belongs to it. The mergers were related to non-ferrous and precious metal mining, not to iron mining; the main interest of the Fugger concern was concentrated in the area of copper and silver. The aggregation, accumulation and concentration of profit and of capital were actualized in the iron industry only in the following epoch. The large capitalists had unified the production and distribution of non-ferrous and precious metals in their hands. Nonetheless, the internal organization of the centres of production were kept separate from the commercial operations, which were also led by the Fuggers, the Welsers, among others. The credit institutes were distanced from both the centres of production and the commercial operations and driven by particular undertakings. In the Middle Ages and in the guilds of modern times the enterprises such as, for example, the weavers' guild, were simultaneously points of production and of commerce; there were some exceptions among them, mentioned above, enterprises which were temporarily repressed in the 16th century.

Table 14: Number and Types of Mining Workers in the 16th Century

Number of Workers	Type of Worker
41	Day labourers: reel pullers mountain climber, pit cleaners, lumberjacks
28	Borers
12	Carpenters in the construction of water wheels and trenches
10	Carpenters concerning wells
3	Smiths
2	Carters
2	Saltmaker, Brineman
2	Mining foreman
1	Watchmen
1	Wood master
1	Master builder
103	**Total workforce**

The founding of large enterprises in the non-ferrous and precious metal mines came early in the modern period through relatively large capital investments as well as the possibilities for turnover and profit. The establishment of large enterprises in the non-ferrous and precious metal mines also occurred in the other metal branches. In 1567 in Auleben (Upper Germany) a large saline concern reached the numbers reported in Table 14 (see above).

This investment was not itself under private management, but rather in the hands of the territorial sovereign. In precious metal mining only rarely was there a complement greater than 200 labourers. The greatest number for the complement in mining was found in the extraction of iron.

Agricola mentioned the main categories of mining people. We are able to add to it something about the wages in an impressionistic way, because a total overview is not available. Table 15 shows that in 1527 in regular service the weekly wage of mining people in Schemnitz and Hoderitzsch amounted to:

Table 15: Weekly Wages (in Pennies) of Mining People in Schemnitz and Hoderitzsch in 1527

Type of Worker	Wage Earned (in Pfg.—pennies)
Smelters	100
Carter	100
Mill workers	100
Smelter workers	100 (extra wage could be 124–150)
Oberreiter (see below)	100
Mine supervisors	90 or 100
Wagoners helper	62
Miner's boys	24, 28, 30, or 32

In the Klingspute 7 hewers were paid a 100 Pfg weekly wage each, 5 with 70 Pfg each in regular service; a trolley pusher received 40 Pfg.[24]

A systematic presentation of the professions, offices and wages are missing, for the data were not provided for all mines [*Zechen*]. The designation of the professions varied from one place to another. The difference between a wage of the hewer, smelter, carter, of the smelter mill worker [*Mühlschaffer*], smelters [*Hüttenschaffer*], as well as of the persons ordered by the Bishop to work in the mines [*Oberreiter*] and of the supervisor *Steiger* or *Hutmann* [supervisors] on the one hand and the remuneration of the mining apprentices on the other, is very great. Experienced mining people earned three or four times as much weekly as the mining apprentices or the trolley pushers. The wages were trebly categorized: the smallest remuneration amounted to 24–40 Pfg, the middle category 62–70 Pfg, the highest level 100 Pfg per week and more.

It is possible that the smelters, carters, *Mühlschaffer*, *Hüttenschaffer* and *Oberreiter*, that is the qualified labourers, received a higher remuneration than the *Steiger*.

We add to these occupations those related to the mining of precious metals. They include: the distiller of silver [*Silberbrenner*] (Purgator argenti), the master coiner (Magister monetarium), the coiner (Monetrarius).[25] Agricola mostly treats the situation of the non-ferrous and precious metal districts.[26]

Agricola had little to say about the deposits of iron or hard coal, which might pique the interest of the 20th century reader. On the other hand, Agricola accurately appreciated the significance of those metals in relation to copper, silver, gold, lead and tin in economic life. He emphasized the smelting of iron in the 9th book of *De Re Metallica*, not however, the labour of mining, because this labour had not played a large role in Joachimsthal in his time. The system of smelting was of central significance for the non-ferrous and precious metal industry. The iron industry found itself in transition from the immediate treatment of the ore in the production of industrial iron and steel, to the mediate treatment of the same in the production process. We have seen that the in-between move in the production of steel constitutes the creation of raw iron; this had been instituted in Agricola's time. The oven in his time was also in a phase of development from the bloomery hearth to the blast furnace, and the bloomery hearth [*Rennen*] was developed for refining. Some of Agricola's remarks in this context are to be explained through the fact that the transition was not completed in the 16th century. The duration of the smelting process with charcoal is different than with hard coal, for the temperatures are different. Thus, Agricola reports, that the bloomery master [*Rennmeister*] first throws the charcoal into the crucible and on top of it sprinkles the ore mixed with lime. Then a layer of coal follows, which is sprinkled with new ore, and in this way the bloomery master repeats the process, until a weakly increasing mound is formed. This gradually melts together after the coals are lit and a powerful fire is fanned by the wind from the bellows. The work of smelting can be finished in eight hours, but on occasion it took ten or twelve hours. The workers, including Agricola himself, guarded the labour process. They knew, that the ore and the wood were of varying quality. Agricola remarked on this that iron ore of specific quality was smelted in one furnace.

Agricola had very precisely observed how labour time in the mines was regulated.[27] The 24 hours of day and night, so he reported, are divided into three shifts; each shift of 7-hour duration. The remaining three hours between the shifts are the in-between hours, when the miners came into the pits or departed from them.

The first shift, called the early shift, begins at 4 o'clock in the morning and lasts until 11 a.m.; the second begins at noon and is called the mid-day shift which ends at 7 p.m.; these two are the day shifts. The third is the night shift; it begins at 8 p.m. and ends at 3 a.m. The night shift is authorized by the officials only when it is necessary. Grounds for such an authorization include the bailing of water from the shafts and the opening up of a passageway. Then the labourers remain the whole night through, working by the light of their pit lamps. In order not to fall asleep they seek to lighten the difficult and long labour through song which sounds refined and pleasant. In some regions the miners were forbidden to ride out two consecutive shifts; elsewhere it was permitted, because it was not possible to live from the wages of only one shift, especially when rising prices pressed heavily on the workers. When the labourers go on a shift and when they depart is signaled by the ringing of a large bell, which Italian commentators called *compana*. When the shift master hears it, he bangs on the woodwork of the shaft and in this way gives the miners the sign to depart.[28]

The description of the shift work in the pits enlightens not only the organization of labour, but the consciousness of time which predominated in the 16th century as well. This stands in close connection with the consciousness of time as it appears in the process of smelting, and in connection with the development and prevalence of the mechanical clock tower, wall clock, cathedral clock and pocket watch, which were mentioned above; Luther had discussed the reckoning of labour time. The clock mechanism was perfected in the 14th and 15th century; its use in measuring time in the labour process was introduced in the 16th century, according to reports. Time in its various treatments formed the inner connection of procedures, and it generates the consciousness of both time and procedure. In mining, this process is related to the work of the hewers, the strikers [*Anschläger*], transport and delivery personnel, heavy weight carriers [*Schlepper*], ore hewer [*Erzpocher*] and smelter, and to that of the shift—and mine master. Finally, Agricola links the labour process to the hiring and firing of the workers and to the wage, for the workers, whether by the week or by the piece, were all wage labourers.

What is more, we have seen that Petrarch, Dürer and other genial men were conscious of their period as a world epoch. They expressed themselves with regard to time in history in relation to antiquity and apprehended the arrangements and practices of antiquity literally from the reports of Plinius, among others. Agricola had ascertained the differences and commonalities between the antique and modern practice of mining. Yet his consciousness of history was different from that of Dürer. The latter had laid out a clear practical and theoretical classification of historical periods in their chronological succession. The main historical division and the formal categories of the historical periods, as we consider them today, have been determined together with our formal historical consciousness fundamentally by Dürer and two or three others of his contemporaries. Dürer subdivided and analytically treated the immediate and the mediate past. Agricola, on the contrary, had grappled with his contemporary processes of labour in mining. He hardly treated the Middle Ages as a piece of the past. Without having described it in so many words, the Middle Ages for Dürer was present as a historical period. The works and days[29] of antiquity were on the contrary presented and treated in part as embellishment, as was the fashion in the period of the Italian *Rinascimento*. In part, however, it was treated fantastically, and in part, practically, and relevant to his time.

Agricola wrote in a practical way about the structuration of the labour process, how the master miner apportioned the labour on weekdays and how the workers in the pits dealt with it. On Monday, Tuesday, Thursday and Friday the master miner rode out to the pits and specified what was to be done or had a look at the boundaries of the mines which were contested. On Wednesday he met together with the jurors and on Saturday with the mining scribe [*Bergschreiber*]. The jurors were *decem viri*, members of a ten-man council, with a good reputation who are aware of and observe the pits, the veins of ore and the wages. These jurors visit all pits in a period of 14 days at least once and are advisers to the master miner. The mining scribe records details regarding the pits, the vein of ore, the condition and the location of the same. The scribe also makes entries regarding the owners. When someone searches for the right to the pit, he inscribes the name, the day and hour of the application. The counter-writer [*Gegenschreiber*] records the names of the shareholders of each pit, further of the sellers and buyers of the shares, and reports on it four times a year. Aside from the owners of the free shares, the shareowners are required to pay the additional amount [*Zubuße*]. If the shareholders don't pay within the month, they are struck from the list of shareholders. The mine administrator pays the wages for the *Steiger* and the labourers from the additional amount and buys the goods necessary for the mining. He buys as cheaply as he can at the time: iron tools, nails, as well as wood, boards, containers, transportation ropes [*Förderseile*] and tallow [*Unschlitt*].[30] The financial officer of the region [*Zehntner*] gives the mine administrator enough money per week to pay the wages for the hewers and to get hold of the necessary objects for the operation of the pits. We have to a large extent reported what Agricola had to say about time in general and about labour time in particular, and through that which was just presented the reader can obtain an impression about the procedures and consciousness of time in the labour process during the 16th century.

For the appraisal of the labour process in mining, the images in *De Re Metallica* are no less significant than the text itself. Agricola appears to have worked closely together with the illustrators. In the 9th book the tin shaft furnace [*Zinnschachtofen*] and the pouring of the tin rolled into bales [*Ballenzinn*] were presented. Four smelter workers are shown one of whom was employed as tin smith or pewterer, the second with an iron hook, the third had a broom with which he stirred a trough, the fourth got the rolled tin into a basket on his head. Two additional men were portrayed of whom one wrote notes in a book, the other, his assistant; ostensibly this scene is current and represents the way Agricola himself worked.[31] This image provides us with an idea of the collaborative work in an enterprise—13 tools are drawn in and labelled with letters. In the same book 46 parts of a bellows are laid out, together with a man who is busy with its assembly. This image describes the tool and its parts, how it is created, and how large it is in relation to the human body. The following drawing renders the frame of the bellows as well as human figures and that of a dog. On the next picture a bellows is portrayed set into operation; an additional human figure is shown. From these images we get the impression of how people worked, to what purpose, and the size of the things with which they worked. In this way one obtained immediate entrance into the world of the miners. Deficiencies in the first edition of Agricola's work were corrected in the second edition. Three images are rich in fantasy: the one portrays the washing of gold by the Argonauts on the mystical Vlies, the second depicts the extraction of soda at the Nile, the third shows the air ventilation [*Wetterversorgung*] by waving a large cloth, this according to Plinius, *Historia Naturalis*. The other 289 images are palpable, objective and precise representations of the processes of labour and technics in the mining and smelting of his time. The main focus of our research concerning Agricola until now has been the technical assessment of his work. We are pointing to the wealth of material concerning labour which the work contains.

We do not begin with technics or technology. The tool and the manner in which it was employed, are the result of previous labour. The tool is a visible, palpable product of an abstract and concrete human process. If emphasis is given to the technical side of the creation process, the result of the process is achieved. The technic is also a means for other processes, but not alone, not in and for itself, only in connection with human activity, labour, exertion and agitation with the human hand and the human head. The tool, abstracted from labour, does nothing, it is only rusted by oxygen or moved by the wind. Labour can do nothing without tools, instruments of labour, means of production and distribution. However, labour has its internal structure and planning. It has the relation to the past and present labours of others. Technique in the employment of the tool is a result of labour in the process of production and learning.

Agricola and Biringuccio recognized the works of antiquity, but that does not mean that they had mastered the historical events as a process. Neither saw a process, but rather only a juxtaposition of two sides—antiquity there, the present here. The ancients, to follow Biringuccio, were invested at the top, where the ore is unearthed, and followed this through the shafts into the depths, wherever it was found. Agricola asserted the same: the ancient miners dug a shaft from the ground level to the bottom of the shaft and thereafter drove a tunnel forward. Neither author evaluated medieval usages; these they left out, and without further ado depicted the practices of the 16th century. Biringuccio says that the miners in his day treated the matter better. For reasons of comfort and security in relation to the entrances and exits to overcome the danger of cave-ins and the difficulty in draining water, and in order to lighten the work of extracting ore and the waste rock [*taube Steine*], miners in modern times positioned themselves at the foot of the mountain, and not as previously, at its summit or behind it. Since Agricola and Biringuccio left the Middle Ages out of their works, later researchers tried to fill this void.[32]

In the 12th, 13th, and 14th century in Trient, in the Harz, in Saxony, Silesia, Bohemia, Moravia, and Hungary mining was in general still relatively superficially operated, and miners pursued strips of the veins of ore less deeply into the shafts. The extraction of the ore from pits of this kind required neither an expanded structuration of labour, nor higher and more progressive technical qualification. In the Black Forest down to the 14th century no compulsory mine labour [*Fronberg*] greater than seven fathoms [*Klafter*] square was in operation. In the 15th and 16th century the structuration of labour in mining had been intensively and extensively developed. The difficulties of water and problems with weather were being mastered. In 1480 the Schneeberg in Saxony was worked to a depth of 100 fathoms [*Klafter*], and in 1482 was worked a further 100 fathoms [*Klafter*] deeper, after the water drainage tunnel was completed (one fathom [*Klafter*] corresponds to the size of a man's body). Some pits even reached a depth of 270 meters. In 1500 the St. George Pit, about which we have already spoken, was about 300 meters deep. The extraction of silver ore from the Schneeberg had already reached a stage of development in the seventies of the 15th century, that appeared to set the standard for the future.[33]

Water was extracted from the pits with the rag and chain pump. The windlass men [*Häspeler*] used an iron chain outfitted with leather bags in their labour. The art of the bellows [*Bulgenkunst*] which constituted a further development here, was a contrivance for lifting out water by employing leather sacks made of large skins as a conveying vessel [*Fördergefäß*]. Through the rag and chain pumps water could be retrieved from depths up to 35 *Lachtern*, through the arts of raising water [*Bulgenkunst*] from up to 90 and even to 100 *Lachtern* (more than 200 meters). In Bohemian tin mining during the period from 1500 to 1550 the shafts were driven to a depth of 200 meters. The rag and chain pump was developed in the late Middle Ages. It was developed further still in the 16th century and outfitted with a chain basket, from which the leather pipes hung down. The iron chain allowed the leather pipes to fall into the pit, in order to lift water from the depths. Two workers were required to empty the leather pipes.[34] The weather machines [*Wettermaschinen*] were operated with equally extensive and large and complicated measures.

In Agricola's time the name machinery was given those installations, like for example, pumps, water wheels, devices related to weather, pyrotechnics, pumping stations, and machines to extract ore and water. Each machine by means of which a load is lifted from a depth, is of such an art, as the machine to drive miners into the shaft or to exit from the shaft is a driving skill. The winch is also an artifice for mines and water is extracted by horses.[35] In Book 6 of *De Re Metallica* the simple and complicated tools, the devices and machines in mining were depicted. In this book Agricola begins with the simple mining iron or pick iron [*Bergeisen*], then the mining pick with a handle, exhibiting the size of the tool and depicts it. The miner's wedge is mostly 3 hands and 2 fingers long and 6 fingers wide; on top it is one hand and 6 fingers wide and extends gradually to form an edge. Simple tools are those which the hewers use in the tunnels to extract the ore and rocks; they are made of iron and outfitted with a wooden handle. They are not called crafts [*Künste*] but rather tools. Complicated tools were the weather machines [*Wettermaschinen*], the mill wheels, the water wheels, the furnaces, the bellows, the windlass or winch-driven hauling engine, the rag and chain and other pumps. In these crafts [*Künste*] and machines metal played a subordinate role; wood for the wheels, the teeth of the applied arts, the pipes, the scaffolding, the drums, the waves, the gears, the levers were fabricated of wood. The chains of the hauling engines, of the taps of the craftsmanship of can making [*Kannenkunst*] or of the bucket conveyers and nails were made of iron. The barrel was wooden, the baskets in mining were made of wood or leather as were the parts of the bellows [*Bläsebelge*]; the containers used in smelting and in assaying were made of ceramic or glass. The simple wedge was not a practical art [*Kunst*], but it was certainly a tool. The wooden water wheel was a practical art [*Kunst*] or a complicated tool. A tool, whose main part was made of iron, was not an artifice [*Kunst*]. The machine in this context was first employed in the 17th century. The stoves and ovens were made of wood, bricks or tiles.[36] Air was delivered to the depths of the mine through bellows, water wheels, pumps and windmills. The bellows and wheels were driven by horse or with human labour power.[37]

The developments of technics in the 15th and 16th century, were related to other areas of mining as well as to smelting, to the printing industry and to the seafaring arts. The calculation of costs and of the profitability of the new arts and mechanisms, exercised diverse effects on developments in mining. The complicated mechanical installations for the water and weather systems of the locations of the ore sites were costly, and only in the cases of adequate profit was it worthwhile introducing such innovations. The silver mines in Tirol (and in a few other camp sites) were sufficiently profitable, to justify the costs of the new technical installation. In 1515 the mining district of Falkenstein in Tirol inaugurated a shaft which finally reached a depth of 240 meters. The power of 600 labourers was necessary to remove the water from the shafts. In 1538, 240 labourers who worked 8 large handpumps in three shifts, were employed in the removal of water. In 1554, a water apparatus was installed which lifted out the water from a depth of 218 meters. Two men worked on it. The qualification of the miners who created the new water installation, and of the labourers working with the water apparatus, who operated the machine, was higher than those who pumped out the water at the beginning of the century. The organization, structuration and division of labour continued apace. The services rendered by more than the 600 unskilled labourers, were replaced by two men. The main point of our investigation concerns the connection between the work force, the labour time and technics. Here we refer to the time necessary for the workers to learn how to master the new crafts [*Künste*], further with the labour time for the construction of new machines and the labour time necessary to operate the water installations, to keep them running, to carry out necessary repairs and to install new parts. Only after the corresponding prerequisites were created, could the 600 men be replaced by two.[38] Yet, they failed to reach the original depth of 240 meters. The excavation of the ore in the deeper shafts and the profit from the metal was relinquished, in order to concentrate on the more intensive exploitation of the higher shafts. The costs were less, the productivity per hour of labour was higher in the later periods than in the earlier ones. The process of production was in this way rationalized and the profitability of the enterprise was heightened.

The increased qualification of the labourer had been developed in close connection with the progressive structuration and division of labour. To this is added the new means of production, like the chain of dippers, the practical arts in relation to weather and the reversible water-driven water wheels for the extraction of ore, and so on. We reckon to this the time for the training of the labourers as well. This necessary social task was already mentioned by Rülein von Calw; Agricola agrees with this.[39] Ore and metal were sold and treated as commodities. In this connection, the costs of the operation, the labour costs, the expenditures for means of production and of possible profit or loss were calculated. Profit was calculated along with the market prices for silver, lead, tin, iron and other metals, as well as the costs of transportation and storage, the payment of taxes, interest and other charges. It can be said that the mining of Upper Germany in the 15th and 16th century was practiced according to the capitalist mode. The enterprises had expanded in this period—they sought after increased turnover and profit—workers were better qualified and received higher wages, technics were developed according to prospects of the possibility of profit. The miners as wage labourers had tried to increase their wages and to improve their working conditions. These social and economic relations between the entrepreneurs and the labourers were in the immediately preceding centuries of the late Middle Ages (in the 15th and 16th century in Tirol, in Upper Germany, in the Harz, and so on) at times sporadically, at times systematically developed and set forth in the following centuries.

Technics were considered as the driving force in this matter, but such a consideration would be only a simplification of the historical process. Technics, the applied arts [*die Künste*] and sciences are in one sense parts of the labour process. Technics and the practical arts are in a second sense parts of the means of labour in general and of the means of production, distribution and means of advancement in particular. Technics as part of the labour process is developed or retarded according to the social and economic relations, prospects, interests and oppositions. In the cloth producing industry some inventions and processes of production were suggested in the 15th and 16th century, but then repressed, prevented or discontinued. The textile branch in the period of early capitalism in Central Europe showed itself as a realm which appeared to be dominated by medieval usages. The guilds [*Zünfte*] in the production of cloth were not oriented to profit in the capitalist sense, but rather to production to cover social wants and to maintain the social position of the guilds. Family life in the given form was to be continued and technical innovations were only then employed when they did not threaten existing social conditions.

The textile industry of Central Europe from the 15th to the 17th century can only be thought of as capitalist in a transitional and preparatory sense. A similar consideration concerns agriculture in this historical epoch. It is not relevant for the printing industry, for mining and smelting, for commerce, for the system of banking and credit and for shipbuilding. For these industries and branch industries were already conducted capitalistically in a systematic sense during the 15th and 16th century. We have observed this process in mining. Others have described it in other branches regarding the residual and exploitative side as well as the positive, progressive and productive side.

Technics can be continued with speed, but only under certain conditions. The question remains namely whether the company, the workers, the entrepreneurs and authorities are prepared to develop, to take on and to employ the technics. In

Central Europe during the early period of modern bourgeois society few showed themselves ready to assume the innovations in the production of cloth.

F. M. Feldhaus, who researched much in the history of technics and who had shown his social conscience in the critique of the famous Fugger alms and donations, treated technics in another sense, which was limited to the practices of the mechanical arts and handicraft. He said: "The miners formed a closed estate, which kept its knowledge secret and only passed it on from mouth to mouth in a way similar to that of the mason's guild [*Bauhütten*]. The first published booklet only appeared in the year 1505. The small images in the several editions of this well-known piece of writing didn't bring out much in terms of technology."[40] 1505 is dated too late. The matter of the keeping secret of knowledge in mining, in smelting and in the art of assaying had been changed in the time between Ulrich Rülein von Calw (1465–1523) to Agricola (1494–1555), Vannoccio Biringuccio (1480–1537), Lazarus Ercker (1530–1594), Ciriacus Schreittmann (n.d.), Georg Engelbert Löhneyss (1552–1622), Modestin Fachs (n.d.), Antonio Neri (1576–1614), Merritt (n.d.) and Kunkel (n.d.).

Technics includes not only the use of hammer and pick, of the handpump of the chain of dippers and of the hauling engine in mining. It is used concretely in education, in trade, by merchants, in bookkeeping, in the credit system, in architecture, in projects and dealings with formulas and with planning in the process of labour. Technics in this sense is practical and theoretical, concrete and abstract.

The material and visible side of technics concentrates attention on the tool that can be handled and seen. The other processes of technics can be easily overlooked. Labour as a concept is left out of this technical conception of history—in part, because till now no comprehensive theoretical mode of consideration has been worked out related to labour; in part, because some aspects of labour are not visible like its structuration and division. Children are able to point to strange and palpable appearances and to observe them. Yet the theorists of the past and present emphasized other matters which apparently are not as evident. The sort of treatment of the historical process is related to the colourful, the conspicuous, palpable human creation as well as to boring theory. Actually, we begin with the great men, with their great discoveries and inventions, thus with politics, war or new formations in religion. Yet in the broader scientific development other processes emerge which determine the activities of men and their undertakings, actions and inventions. Our main question remains: how the process of labour was established, transformed, structured, combined and divided? In this the entrepreneurs and the workers play their roles.

Technics and the transformation of technics constitute a part of the labour process and its transformation. We have earlier steered the reader's attention to the class of entrepreneurs, its commercial habits and its spirit according to the reports by Schumpeter, Sombart and Strieder, Weber and Troeltsch. They discovered the driving force of the transition to capitalism in the activities and in the spirit of the class of entrepreneurs, just as Feldhaus had discovered this driving force in the history of technics. The class of entrepreneurs is a part of society, technics a part of the labour process. Society in its various parts is changed, the labour process stands in reciprocal interaction with social transformations. The class of entrepreneurs and technics are parts of an extensive and deep-reaching process of economic and social transformation, which determined the transition to modernity.

5.4 The Iron Industry in Central Europe in the 15th and 16th Centuries

It is well-known that the hard coal and iron industry forms the foundation of high capitalist production in the 19th and 20th century. In the beginnings of the capitalist age, the production of hard coal was limited, the iron industry, on the other hand, was important. In this relation the role of Central Europe in production and trade was fundamental. The following table shows the production of iron in various parts of Europe in the 16th century:

Table 16: Amounts of Iron in Europe in the 16th Century (in Tons). O. Johannsen for 1500, F. Braudel and J. V. Nef for later estimates. These numbers are rough and only relatively admissible.

Location	Around 1500	Around 1525
Biskaya		15,000
England	5,000	6,000 (1536–1539)
France	10,000	10,000
Germany	18,000	30,000
Lüttich	2,000	8,000 to 9,000 (1569)
Nassau Provinces	3,000	
Other Countries of Europe	10,000	
Other Districts of Germany	5,000	
Ostalpenländer (Steiermark)	10,000	8,000 to 9,000
Sweden	5,000	
Upper Palatinate (Oberpfalz)	10,000	

Iron mining arose early in the Middle Ages in the Black Forest, in Steiermark, in Kärnten, Haardt and in the Odenwald, in the Upper Palatinate and in the Erzgebirge.

Around 1500 Germany stood first in the production of iron in all of Europe and kept this position over the course of the following quarter or third century. The production of iron in the Central European countries increased; it also increased in Germany. The numbers are not available for all of Central Europe, but German iron production in the period from 1500 to 1525 increased from 18,000 to 30,000 tons (167%). In England, the countries of the Alps and in France, the production of iron at this time remained more or less static; in Liège, on the contrary, it quadrupled. Germany together with Styria produced 45% or 50% of the entire quantity of iron in all of Europe. Yet, in the second half of the 16th century, England had taken over the leading position in the production of iron in Europe and maintained it during the subsequent industrial revolution till the 19th century.

Iron, which was produced in the 15th and 16th century, was of different kinds. Crude iron, soft iron [*Deucheleisen* (*Deicheleisen*) see the entry for Deucheleisen (Metallurgie) at https://de.linkfang.org/wiki/Deuchel_%28Metallurgie%29–trans.], cast iron, wrought iron, pig iron, horseshoe, steel iron, sheet iron, iron wire were still called various names according to the raw product, the user or function. The quality of the iron was determined by its provenance, that is by the natural characteristics of the iron ore and the refinement of the metal. Osemund-iron came out of Sweden through the Hansa cities, which had played an important role in the fabrication of wire, thus in the production of nails, staples and needles. The production of wrought iron in various parts of Europe had roughly the same relations and the same distribution as iron production as a whole.

Table 17: Europe: Wrought Iron Production in 1500. Rudolf Sprandel, *Das Eisengewerbe im Mittelalter*, Stuttgart 1968.

Location	Hundredweight	Percentage
England	66,000	11.1
Erzberg (Inner Austria)	100,000	16.8
Erzgebirge	80,000	13.4
France	45,000	7.6
Hüttenberg (Inner Austria)	48,000	8.1
Iberian Peninsula (incl. Biskaya)	31,000	5.2
Italy (Elba, Tuscany, Upper Italy)	35,000	5.9
Loraine, Wallonia, Eifel	16,000	2.7
Rhein—Elbe	35,000	5.9
Switzerland	9,000	1.5
Upper Palatinate	130,000	21.8
Total	595,000	100.0

In 1500 Central Europe had produced more wrought iron than the rest of Europe, as Table 17 shows. The Upper Palatinate, Erzgebirge, Rhein-Elbe region, Erzberg and Hüttenberg together covered 66% of European wrought iron production.

The extraction of iron in the 13th and 14th century in Central Europe was in part operated agriculturally, in part by guilds, in part capitalistically and in part by monks in monasteries. The capitalist features had increased in the 15th century, but the organization of iron production was still carried out by various systems. Previously, the owner of the smelter was the master operator, but in the later period he kept himself away from the operation. In Siegerland the ore and cooperatively managed wood lots belonged to the smelters in the early period, in the 15th century the smelters and hammer mills separated from one another. The development of specialization in the production of iron goods in Upper Germany occurred at the same time and in the same way. In the Middle Ages there had been relatively little specialization in the refinement of metal. The most important iron towns in Upper Germany and Austria were Amberg, Steyr and Wetzlar. In the 15th and the 16th century, metal refinement including the iron industry in Nuremberg, Regensburg and Augsburg strongly increased, especially in connection with the increasing extraction of iron in the Upper Palatinate.[41]

Quantitative processes in the production of iron were closely tied to the qualitative. Specialization in the production of iron commodities belong to the qualitative processes. Styr became a centre for the production of steel, the Upper Palatinate for the production of sheet metal and Osemund in Sweden for the fabrication of iron wire. The historical development can be followed in the iron works of Inner Austria. In the 13th century, iron in the Styrian Erzberg was produced in part in monasteries. In the course of the 13th century the smelting furnaces of the iron works increased two and a half fold, and the products had accordingly increased two and a half fold. In the 14th and 15th century the number of hammer mills was increased independently of the monasteries as did the number of their products. The hammer works were expanded in connection with an increase in the production of iron ore in the 15th century from Erzberg to Waidhofen, Semmering and Murau, thereupon from Kärnten and Krain, Salzburg and Bamberg to the Save. The export of iron commodities was operated together with the increasing import of raw iron and iron ore, for the Styrian ore proved to contain less iron than the ore from the island of Elba. Hapsburg iron production was in this respect becoming more active and had taken up closer relations with the Mediterranean region.

The iron trade, the importing of ore and the exporting of products, had steadily increased in this development. Through it the merchants became wealthier; credit and commercial capital, as well as capital in the process of production could be increased through increasing profit. This period in history was commonly called that of commercial capital. But such a characterization is a simplification of the economic process. The great enterprisers of this epoch were the merchants and bankers, but the hammer mills [*Hämmerwesen*] and metallurgy and smelting (*Hüttenwesen*) and the metal industry in general and the production of iron in particular had strongly increased.

The iron industry was operated in modern times less by monastic monks and more by the laity. Blow moulding plants [*Blaswerke*] were separated from the hammer mills [*Hammerwerke*]. The size of hammers greatly increased. In the 15th and 16th century, Nuremberg had achieved an increasing significance for the production of gold, silver and copper coins and for the production of iron commodities as well. The number of hammers at Pegnitz increased within the town itself and outside; the industrial hinterland expanded to 50 kilometres beyond the city gates. A close tie between the Nuremberg iron enterprises and the rise of sheet metal production in the Upper Palatinate was apparent.

The expansion of the factories did not lead to an increased number of workers, but led, nevertheless, to the broadening and intensification of production, and to the rationalization of the manufacturing process. Rationalization succeeded through the changes in the organization of labour and in technics through the increasing size of the smelting furnaces, the import of new products and the development of the means of labour. The import of iron from Elba constituted an advance in this relationship, and the assumption of the leading role by the laity in the production of iron was a further step of this kind.

The monks were not wage labourers like the lumberjacks, colliers, miners, founders and smiths in the 15th century. The wages for these professions were partly paid in money, in part in kind. From 1387 onwards, the smiths in the Upper Palatinate received permission for a small garden [*Liebung*] for cabbage und beets from the pertinence [*Pertinenz*] of the iron smelters. The permission was granted beside a money wage.[42]

Mining freedom emerged in Braunschweig, Hanover, Brandenburg, Bohemia, Bavaria, Franken, Saxony, Thuringia and Austria. Freedom to prospect freely on foreign soil and to look for iron was generally recognized in Central Europe.[43] In the 15th century, the privilege of prospecting, of cultivating the forest, and of a writ of escort was widespread in Upper Germany. In 1464, a boom occurred in the Upper Palatinate iron industry, which was closed down after the great catastrophe of 1620. This development can be read off the following Table 18:

Table 18: Number of Seasonal Workers in Mining (Average). H. Wilsdorf, *Bergwerke und Hüttenanlagen*, 1971.

Years	Workers
1400–1465	500
1465–1550	1,000
1551–1620	1,500

The numbers of seasonal workers are related to the major mines in the historical development of the Sulzbach district. In the third period, for example, in 1595/96, in a mine of this kind of 11 shaft installations, 6 had 57, and 5 had 41 hours per weekly labour time. In the two years mentioned, the mine had excavated 121,000 tons of ore.

In the 15th and 16th century, the number of operations had increased, while the extent of the enterprises had grown. The circulation of money had proliferated, and the demand and supply of metal products increased with the increasing economic activities in Central Europe. These developments took place in different ways. While in Augsburg and Nuremberg the undertakings lay increasingly in the hands of the large enterprises like Fugger and Thurzo, the hammer mills [*Hämmer*] and smelters in Salzburg and in Siegerland were rather operated cooperatively [*genossenschaftlich*]. Each participant in these cooperatives had excavated his own ore from the earth and dulled it [*verblies es*] with his own coal; each master had a small number of miners, smiths and journeymen in his operation.[44]

As we have seen, the transition away from the organization of labour based on the single manual labourer in the putting-out system—the cottage industry—became ever-increasingly widespread.

In the Schwabach needle industry, the expansion of the turnover of products brought with it the transition to the cottage industry. In the Middle Ages, the craftsman had produced sewing needles and stick pins locally and sold them locally. At the beginning of the modern era, the *Verleger* [domestic entrepreneur] arose, who gave over the iron wire to the labourers and took over the semi-finished iron commodity. He paid the cottage workers for their product and made it ready for the market. The one who finished the product had to deal with the final process of hardening, of filling up and bleeding, of polishing and sorting the needles and thereafter with the sale of the commodity. They themselves were manual labourers and had organized the labour process and assumed the task of finishing the product. It was forbidden for non-manual workers to undertake a putting-out business. In the ensuing development of the system, the masters had become simple cottagers, the *Verleger*, pure entrepreneurs. Those who received the barbed wire refined it further for a wage. In the fabrication of knives in Solingen those who finished the product were transformed into *Verleger*. In the 16th century, different kinds of knives proliferated, and their production became more complicated. Previously, the same manual labourer was simultaneously a smith, *Reider* [one who brings together knives and blades] and finisher [*Fertigmacher*]. Only the sharpening of the knife was done by a wage labourer. In later epochs, the *Verleger*, who himself was a finisher, bought the iron which the knife smith, the hook and eye maker and the ribbon weaver worked on for a wage in his putting-out institute. Credit, wages and the prices of commodities were regulated by the *Verleger* according to market relations; the independent handicraft masters at that time from then on were re-formed into a part of the working class.[45]

The iron wire [*Drahteisen*] was used to finish nails and needles. The nails were of two kinds, black nails and white nails, and the smiths were accordingly called black and white smiths. The white nails were produced from iron mixed with tin. The wire arose from the twisting or spinning of the iron threads, the threads made of the forged metal. The wire was used to produce musical instruments, like the lyre, as well as for nails, needles and ringed armour. The tin-plated rolled wire was marinated with warmed-up acid, commonly vinegar, and shaken around in a jug. The marinated nails were continuously shaken and heated in an iron pot with tallow and tin. Conrad Celtis had described the wire mill during his stay in Nuremberg from 1487 to 1492. Albrecht Dürer had represented it pictorially in 1497. The wire smiths now no longer worked by hand but rather by milling and cutting with the wire mill. In the work of milling and cutting, the iron leaves were prepared, cut and thinned out. The pliers dart forward and move back, taking hold of the raw iron and smoothing it out to a round wire, which is then wound. The wire pullers in Nuremberg and Augsburg process iron from the Upper Palatinate.[46] In Westphalian Sauerland (Süderland) the towns of Iserlohn (Eisenwald) and Lüdenscheid arose; wire pullers settled there. In the 14th and 15th century the employment of waterpower by means of waterwheels and watermills was developed. The pulled iron was put through holes and thereby made into rolled wire. The steep slopes of the region were unsuitable for fields and meadows but were suitable for the production of wire by means of waterpower. The tax for using the waterpower was paid in the form of a levy on wax. Around 1600 the levy on wax brought the authorities 36 pounds of wax annually. Meanwhile, the predominance of a class of capitalist entrepreneurs in the production of wire occurred. Remuneration in kind receded in proportion to money wages, and the wire pullers' workshop developed from cottaging to the Zoggam-pulling room. Further development of iron wire into rolls required greater sums of money, which only capitalist entrepreneurs could acquire and lay out.

The cooperative [*genossenschaftliche*] organization of wire production was transformed into a capitalist one. In the Märkisch wire industry, the *Reidemeister* became entrepreneurs who were simultaneously finishers. *Reider* and ship owners have this same etymology. Johannsen mentions the stately position of the *Reider* in society following the saying: "En Reidemeister singet mit in de Kerke, he hölt sick dotan sine Lüe" (Leute) ["A shipowner sings (with other congregants) in the church, and in this way he gets his people." The English is rendered from the Low German—trans.]. The steel wire served above all in the production of sewing needles and had been developed in Nuremberg in the 14th century, as needles with eyes [*Öhren*] as well. In the 16th century, that is 200 years later, the wire pullers in Aachen made their needles out of steel wire. The most important tool of the wire pullers was the drawing die, which was the creation of the tinsmith. Tin-smithery was developed in the Upper Palatinate; white tin from Nuremberg was sold in the Netherlands for the production of needles and defensive armaments. The armor industry in Augsburg was developed for shields; in Augsburg and Nuremberg the thimble industry was expanded for mass production. A further specialization appeared: blade and knife fabrication were located in Solingen, cannons and artillery pieces were manufactured in Siegerland and Frankfurt am Main.

Peasants in Dalarna (Sweden) had processed Osmund iron, which was prepared from scrap iron, primarily from scrap iron hoofs and hoof nails. This was created for the production of steel in refining, whereby soft iron was an in-between and byproduct of the process. In Siegerland in the 13th to the 15th century steel production arose by the pouring of steel from the fine iron [*Edeleisen*] of Müsener Grundes. The equipment and smelting of ore were first put into operation by means of bloomery hearths and wolf furnaces; in the 15th and 16th century by the blast furnace. Malleable iron at that time was produced directly from ore; then, after the advent of the blast furnace it was a more refined product. Malleable iron was of two kinds, welding iron and welding steel. The power source was the muscle power of animals and humans, as well as water, fire, gravity and the wind. Iron was employed in general for tools, utensils and weapons; Iron was not used for construction material, which were those of wood, earth, bakestones, bricks, stone, loam, clay, straw and leaves.

The late medieval cooperatives [*Genossenschaften*] of the smelters in Siegerland in the area of Salzburg had on average 12 smelters and smiths. The entire crew of a smelter in the 16th century on average amounted to 100 men; the number would later rise to 300. Looking over the entire iron industry in the Upper Palatinate we obtain the following picture in the following table:

Table 19: The Number of Workers, Iron Industry of the Upper Palatinate, 1475

Type of Worker	Number of Workers	Percentage
Carters	3,245	27.5
Excavators	606	5.1
Manual labourers	404	3.4
Mining people	750	6.3
Smelters and hammer smiths	1,159	9.8
Unskilled workers in hammer works	479	4.0
Wood cutters and colliers	5,180	43.8
Total	**11,823**	**100.0**

This iron industry nourished a quarter of the total population of the Upper Palatinate in the 15th century. The peasants left their fields lie fallow in order to travel to the hammer mills [*Hämmer*].[47]

The same picture is valid for the Harz region and Inner Austria. These statistics will refute the conception of the purely sporadic appearance of the capitalist system prior to the 16th century.

A general history of mining in the 15th and 16th century will include the non-ferrous and precious metals as well as the iron mines. It would have to take in the employment of miners and peasants as well as the activities of the entrepreneurs. The question regarding the extraction of salt and glass manufacture also have a tie to the metal industry (see Agricola, *De Re Metallica*, Book 12).

In the 15th century, the Upper Palatinate had a special position in the iron industry; it had been developed here early. There were favourable natural conditions; and moreover, a qualified working class arose in Nuremberg and in other parts of Upper Germany. Necessary technics were developed, and the class of entrepreneurs was in the hands of the laity. Commerce between the Upper Palatinate and Pegnitz was operated by the carters and the shippers in the 16th century; this amounted to 27.5% of the entire working population of the Upper Palatinate. Many Upper Palatinate manual labourers worked for the Nuremberg operation. The hammer and smelting works [*Hammer—und Hüttenwerke*] grew, as we have seen, in proportion to the number of products and productivity. A special relationship evolved between the Nuremberg iron trades and sheet metal production in the Upper Palatinate in the 15th century. For the production of sheet metal, *Deucheleisen* is essential, which was in the Middle Ages a byproduct of the hammer mills. Tin and steel are both products of the iron industry, and both protect metal from rust. Yet the tin (bright, shiny metal) is malleable, unlike steel. Early in the modern period there arose two kinds of sheet metal, black plate and tinplate, and only tinplate had a coating of tin, which protected the iron from rusting. The discovery of the utility of *Deucheleisen* in this connection can be traced back to the 14th century; its further industrial development occurred in the 15th century. Tin in the Fichtel mountains was under the control of Nuremberg. At this time, the number of sheet metal hammer mills [*Blechhämmer*] in the Upper Palatinate amounted to 100 enterprises.

The small trade towns were tightly bound to a strongly imprinted guild organization of iron production. In opposition to this, the Hessian district Waldschmiedbezirk was organized agriculturally. In Upper Germany the separation of smelting from mining began at the same time as the participation of the entrepreneurs from the town in the latter. The townspeople from Kolmar and Strasbourg appeared in Vogesen and the East Alps as lay entrepreneurs, and were engaged on behalf of the excavation of iron ore necessary for their own enterprises.[48] We will consider some examples regarding the size of operations and the structuration of labour in the iron industry of Upper Germany. The hammer and smelting mills were small. In a hammer mill producing for drawbar smiths [*Deuchelschmiedehammer*] in the Upper Palatinate there were employed 1 *Zerrennmeister* [master of the clay hearth], 1 master smith, 1 hewer (coal extractor), 1 *Handpreu* [helper/assistant] and 1 coal assessor [*Kohlenmesser*].

In 1432, the citizens of the entire region of Sulzbach (Upper Palatinate) received the monopoly on the exploitation of the iron ore. In 1454, the same authorities added further privileges. The townsfolk had already received the privilege of prospecting, then the privilege of freedom of assembly was granted to the hammer masters and smiths, and in 1464 they were granted further advantages, which came to the owners of the hammer works [*Hammerherren*], to the labourers as well as to the *Handpreu* and *Hauerbuben* [(child) helpers]. These privileges were continued until the Thirty Years' War. The iron mining operations and smelting industries found themselves in an economic boom from the middle of the 15th century until 1620. In the 15th century, Sulzbach had temporarily excluded Nuremberg from its great hammer works consortium [*Hammerwerksvereinigung*] and achieved superiority over Amberg. In the 15th century, the Sulzbachers had reached a depth of 35 Klaftern (74.5 meters) in the 16th century, 50 Klaftern (106.5 meters) in the iron mines. The winch was replaced by the *Pferdegöpfel*. In the year 1610 the transition to waterpower in the extractive activity [*Förderungsarbeiten*] and the work of mine drainage was accomplished.

In the 15th and 16th century, a massive increase in the production of iron occurred. The cause of this development was the expansion of the *Blähhäuser* [medieval furnace for the extraction of pig iron] and the limiting of the portion of profit share in the cost of wages in the process of production. The first reason for this increase refers to the development of the capital investment in the iron industry of Central Europe during the 15th century and later. The second reason points to the rationalization of these enterprises. The workforce in the branches of the iron industry was paid according to their qualification in production. However, the iron workers declined in social position in this period. The lowest stratum in the areas of production was formed by the smelter workers, the miners and the non-independent operation managers. The middle layer was constituted by the entrepreneurs, who were simultaneously engaged in manual labour and as capitalists, the upper stratum the landowners [*Grundherren*] and iron traders.

At the end of the 16th century, seasonal workers emerged in Sulzbach iron mining.[49] Here is the breakdown in numbers for types of seasonal workers in Table 20:

Table 20: Number and Types of Seasonal Mining Workers at the End of the 16th Century in Sulzbach.

Type of Worker	Number of Workers
Cart runners [*Karrenläufer*]	65
Manual labourers [*Handwerker*] (a)	100
Miners for digging and water drainage (b)	210
Miners hewing ore [*für das Erzhauen*]	639
Supervising managers (c)	20
Total	**1,034**

(a) Forge smiths [*Gezähschmiede*], master carpenters [*Zimmermeister*] und cartwrights to the different crafts [*Stellmacher zu den Künsten*], leather workers [*Lederarbeiter*], saddle makers [*Sattler*], and so on.
(b) Of these 100 horse boys [*Rossbuben*] at the *Göpelwerken* [machines in which the muscular strength of donkeys, horses or dogs but also of people was used to drive various works] c) Clerks and accountants [*Schrift und Rechnungsbeamte*]
(c) Secrataries and accountants [*Schrift- und Rechnungsbeamte*]
In 1489, the workforce in a hammer mill amounted to: 1 furnace master [*Ofenmeister*], 9 smith servants [*Schmiedeknechte*], 9 furnace servants [*Ofenknechte*]; together 19 men.

Struggles over wage increases played out between the wage workers and the hammer masters in the 15th century. The first conflict was in 1384, when the landowners supported the hammer masters. There were further struggles over wages in the Thüringen forest and in the Erzgebirge. In 1483, during a conflict over wages in Gießhübel in the Erzgebirge, several hundred men "burnt out the mountain and destroyed some windlasses [*Haspeln*], caissons [*Kasten*] and stamping machines [*Stempelin*]." The wages were structured in three grades: The highest wage was paid in Friesach at 30 pfennigs a day, the second grade at 22.5 pfennigs, the third at 15 pfennigs. By way of comparison, in Munich in 1450, a carpenter's apprentice earned 20 pfennigs a day, working 240 workdays, 22 florins per year. Thus, the mid-grade hammer mill workers stood somewhat better than the carpenter's journeyman on average.[50] The iron industry of the Upper Palatinate was operated in small smelters in the 16th century. The work force of a hammer works in Friesach in 1500/05 amounted to 8 men not including transportation workers, colliers and mining personnel. In the Styrian Erzberg the work force of the hammer works amounted to 3 to 5 men on average including the hammer master.

In one operation with two clay hearths [*Rennherden*], 7 men were employed: 1 master smithy and 1 hauling master with 1 assistant; in addition, 1 hewer, 1 helper and 1 master collier. With two clay hearths 84 tons of iron per day could be forged, with one, 64 tons.[51] Productivity (production of wrought iron according to labour power) was higher in enterprises with one clay hearth than in operations with two of them, to wit in a relation 106:100. If the support staff in the operation received a lower wage, then the operation with two clay hearths was more profitable. These relations continued into the 17th and 18th century.

In 1581, the work force of a smelter in Steinfels amounted to 1 hut watchman [*Hüttenkapfer*], 1 master smith [*Schmiedemeister*], 1 smitty servant [*Schmiedeknecht*], 1 helper, 1 melting master, 1 hewer, and 1 coal assessor [*Kohlenmesser*]. 7 skilled tradesmen were employed in the operation, alongside of three or four unqualified workers, who were seasonally employed. These amounted to 2 or 4 unskilled labourers and one or two child workers in the hammer mill [*Hammerbuben*]. The structuration of labour is approximately the same as in the above-mentioned case. The number of unschooled workers increased.[52]

Comparison of the numbers of wage labourers in the hammer mills of the Upper Palatinate in the 14th and 15th century points to a certain dynamic. In 1387, the number of wage workers in these operations amounted to 4 or 5, in 1406 it rose to 5 or 6; in the successive periods it increased further. According to Table 21 for one pit in the year 1595/96 the wages for different types of workers amounted to:

Table 21: Number, Type of Mine Worker, and Weekly Wages for One Pit 1595/1596

Type of Worker	Number of Workers	Weekly Wage in Gulden (approx.)
Piecework miner [*Gedinghäuer*]	26–30	1
Mountain surveyor [*Markscheider/ Bodenscheider*]	1	1
Mountaineer [*Obersteiger*]	1	3
Downstream climber [*Untersteiger*]	1	1
Counter [*Zähler*]	1	1
Total	**30–34**	**7**

In addition to these there were 20–22 shift hewers [*Schichthäuer*] during the day, and 12–15 shift hewers on the night shift. The weekly wage of the single shift hewer amounted to 28 pfennigs. For the shift hewers, all told six guldens were expended. Agricola remarks that the night shifts received a smaller remuneration. The *Gedinghäuer* [hewers contracted for measurable work not paid wages for time but for actual work accomplished] had engaged in rock work [*Gesteinarbeit*] for a piece rate according to time and measure [*Lachtern*].[53]

The iron works did not get bigger on average and the cooperatives [*Genossenschaften*] became less important. The owners of the hammer mills were entrepreneurs, who kept themselves apart from the operations. The number of wage workers rose, while the number in the labour force remained about the same. The production of iron also became more rational and economical, so that iron production as a whole rose in the 15th and 16th century in Central Europe. However, this rise was not as quick or steep as it would be in the ensuing period of high capitalism.

The entrepreneurs transformed themselves and became capitalists in the iron industry. The putting-out system expanded, the *Hammermeister* sunk in the class structure of society and became wage labourers. Medieval production of iron in the cloisters disappeared. In Styr in the 16th century, the manual labourers wrested domination from the iron entrepreneurs in the putting-out system [*Eisenverleger*] and established their own iron trading companies, to which any townsman could belong. However, those who established a company, represented the wealthy stratum in society because they could acquire their own deposits.

The developments of iron casting and of the blast furnace operation had a reciprocal influence on one another, which consisted in the transition from direct clay hearth processing to the immediate preparation of iron, in connection with the production of unrefined iron and beyond that with the process of refining. To this belonged the processes of iron casting as well in the production of unrefined iron together with the increasing use of waterpower for the iron hammer mills and the bellows in the iron works. Increasingly more complicated labour processes were tied to the rise of the blast furnace. Waterpower began to be used through the water mill to set in motion the bellows for the smelting furnaces. The benefits of the water mills and the strength of the wind from the bellows, which dominated the movement of the water wheels, could not be efficiently controlled. Experience was lacking in controlling the wind blowing into the blast furnaces. Sometimes the wind was so strong that the temperature rose and the formation of raw iron set in; the result of the uncontrolled process was not the iron bloom, but rather molten iron, which, like the slag, drained off. At first the smelter had considered the product as something spoiled, as pig iron. Thereupon it was learned that with this iron, which was melted down with an easily controlled furnace temperature from the wind, a better and more even product was produced. The consistent quality of the iron and steel was demonstrated in the improved quality of the hammer mill and smelting products. Thus, the molten iron was thereafter produced according to plan, the cast iron was transformed in a second process by melting down the unrefined iron from the wind in a hearth into malleable iron. The stronger the water wheels moved, the more force was generated by the water mill, the stronger the bellows operated, the more forcefully the fire burned and the higher the temperature of the furnace rose. From the wolf furnace and dome light or distillation fire [*Luppenfeuer*] of the previous epoch, the new blast furnace arose.[54]

The [*Luppenfeuer*] or wolf furnace was the means to refine the clumps of metal called wolf, or in Latin, lupus. The new furnaces, the heavy hammers, the water mills for the operation of the hammer mills and the buildings for smelting required greater capital investments than had previously been the case. The newer smelting system originated at the end of the 15th century, but the investment processes were limited, and the old clay hearths [*Rennfeuer*] and the wolf furnace were kept alongside the new furnace down to the 17th century.[55]

Other related techniques were developed. In the 15th century the breaking up of the ore into pieces with the hand mill was replaced by the wet crushing mill [*Naßpochwerk*]. The old hand mills had caused great losses in the tin smelting works by vaporizing the product. The *Naßpochwerk* reduced this metal loss and enabled a further crushing of the product of smelting. The production processes in the hammer and smelting mills became increasingly complicated, the mechanization of productivity, the quality and the quantity in the hammer and smelting system rose. The single crushing mill had three or four stamping machines, which were driven by water wheels. The crushing mills were repeatedly coupled and with three water wheels three crushing mills could be operated at the same time. The productivity of the wet crushing mill rose. A crushing mill with three stamping machines could crush 450 to 750 tons, with four stamping machines 650 to 1000 tons of ore in the same time period. Increasing productivity is connected with the expansion of the work force in the operation. In the smaller and medium sized operations 2 to 11 men were employed, in the larger 12 to 29. In the districts of Schlackenwald and Schönfeld (Bohemia) 30 larger preparation plants were in operation in the 16th century.[56]

The expansion of the preparation plants for tin, the expansion of the work force in the operation and the widening of capital investments are tied together in an economic and social process in the 15th and 16th century.

Developments in the iron and tin operations in the period of early capitalism provide information concerning an increased dynamic in the production of commodities and in productivity. The exploitation of the workers became more intense. The increase in capital investment, the increasing structuration of labour, the introduction of new machinery and technics in production combined to rationalize the production process of iron ore. New methods of labour meant that more and more unskilled and unqualified workers who were paid less than the earlier masters could be hired. Productivity in the operation increased, the costs of production and of labour decreased.

Agricultural and cooperative [*genossenschaftliche*] enterprises as well as the undertakings of the monks in the production of iron disappeared, the master craftsmen were transformed into wage labourers.

The working class was formed primarily into a class of wage labourers, only the wage was not entirely in the form of money wages. The subdivisions of the wage as weekly or daily and piece wages had already been introduced. The entrepreneurs are in part *Verleger*, in part *Cux* or shareholders, partners, participants. The separation between capitalists and labourers was accomplished.

The industrialists were not the large capitalists, but rather traders, merchants and bankers. Now let us turn our attention to the workers as well as to the entrepreneurs in the development of the capitalist system in modern times.

Already in antiquity, iron in its various forms such as raw iron, soft German iron [*Deucheleisen*], pick or ground iron [*Masseleisen*], horse shoe [*Hufeisen*], cast iron [*Gußeisen*], wrought iron [*Schmiedeeisen*], sheet iron [*Blecheisen*] and steel—was the most important means for the production of tools, utensils and weapons. Iron is encountered in all parts of Europe and on all continents. Thus, the period of the last +/—3000 years is the iron age in Europe. In the stone age, iron was processed from meteorites; in the iron age, on the contrary, it was produced from iron ore. Until the industrial revolution iron was smelted and processed primarily by wood and charcoal. The fuel was the same in antiquity, in the Middle Ages and in the first centuries of modern times. In the 14th, 15th, and 16th century, hard coal as fuel was known, but the use of this material for fuel was rare. Agricola and Biringuccio thoroughly investigated metals, mining, the system of smelting, and pyrotechnics in the 16th century and had little to say about hard coal. Where they did speak of the coals, as a rule they meant charcoal. Hard coal was excavated already from the 12th to 14th century in Limburg and Lüttich, afterwards in Aachen, in the Saarland and in the Ruhr region, that is in the same regions as in the period of high capitalism.[57]

The commercial use of hard coal by smiths, limeburners [*Kalkbrenner*], vitriol boilers [*Vitriolsieder*], dyers—less by beer brewers in the vicinity of the hard coal pits—occurred in the 15th century. The difficulty, that the hard coal pits like those of brown coal in Bohemia were shown only here and there to be sufficiently coal bearing, and this limited its use as fuel. Operations near locations with hard coal like Wettin, or Rothenburg an der Saale, among others had used hard coal, but in establishments with open hearths only charcoal was taken. In the 16th century it came to an increasing application of bituminous coal for salt mining, lime kilns, vitriol boilers [*Vitriolsiedereien*] and alum boiler works [*Alaunsiedehütten*].

Hard coal was already used as fuel in forging in the Middle Ages, however, the main fuels were wood and charcoal, and this remained so until the 18th century. At first, wood was fetched from the immediate surroundings of the mine, of the hammer mills and smelting works; subsequently, it was transported over long distances for the metal industry and production in the town in general. Wood as means of construction as well as fuel was indispensable. The forests surrounding the towns and the mines were felled; wood disappeared or became uneconomical on account of the costs of transportation. Hard coal was used as industrial fuel in England earlier than in Central Europe. Forests were devastated in the transition to the operation of the blast furnace. This devastation occurred more quickly in England than in Central Europe.[58]

The wolf furnace [*Stücköfen*] and the bloomery hearth [*Rennfeuer*] were the main apparatuses for smelting ore in antiquity and in the Middle Ages; they were replaced by the blast furnace [*Hochöfen*] in modern times. Malleable iron was produced immediately from the raw ore in the Middle Ages, in modern times from raw iron. At the same time freshening [*das Frischen*] was introduced, that is, the removal of carbon by the introduction of fresh air into the process of the creation of iron. Freshening was complicated and varied according to location and according to the tradition of refining and of its particular origin. Iron smelters had the open hearth, the non-ferrous and precious metal workers had the shaft furnace [*Schachtofen*]. Agricola describes the kinds of freshening with bellows and the kinds of furnaces. Freshening is closely bound up with the origin of the blast furnace.[59]

The fact that iron ore was first transformed into raw iron in modern times and thereupon made into malleable iron, points to a change in the labour process and in the relation of man to the material world. Material nature, raw iron was treated in antiquity and the Middle Ages immediately, in modern times mediately. Several intermediate stages were inserted in the process of production of malleable iron and metal working in general. In antiquity and in the Middle Ages the process of metal working was relatively simpler than the process of metal working in modern times. Labour and the instruments of labour constitute a mediation between man and nature.[60]

Social and economic movements reciprocally affect one another in the process of change. In the past, one searched for the actuality behind the appearance. We shall not partake in this search. There is no secret cause which is hidden behind the world of appearance; the world and its parts are as they are and what they are; the appearance is the form and substance of the world; and conversely: the world is not different from that which appears, in its form and substance.

The processes of movement and transformation are not unitary; some proceed formally or substantially, others follow behind. According to our observations of the history of capitalism the substantial processes are those of the liberation movement of the peasants, of the circulation of money, of the growth of the merchant class, mining, the system of smelting, shipbuilding and the printing industry. These substantial processes preceded the political and juridical form of capitalist predominance in modern bourgeois society in the transition to the capitalist system of Central Europe. The process of progression and succession is contradictory. The peasants fought for their formal and substantial freedom yet attained only formal freedom.

The struggles of the wage workers were related to the substantial conditions of the remuneration and of their conditions of labour. The peasants tried to reach the level of the wage labourer; some, but not all peasants participated in it. There are factors in history, which, like the deeds of the class of entrepreneurs, are noticeable and noteworthy. In many cases the entrepreneurs are wealthy, like Jacob Fugger; the decline of his house is thus an equally noteworthy event. However, no less noticeable is the technics of waterworks; this machinery is splendid, labour saving and expensive. We treat the various factors, the noteworthy and the inconspicuous, the physical and the mental in their reciprocal effects on one another.

The forms of labour, of the entrepreneurs and of money are complicated and move unevenly. The substantial processes of economy and society are transformed with varying rates of speed. Schumpeter saw this and presented it. Marx had correctly conceptualized the historical process in this regard; he emphasized the system only in Central Europe. He considered everything that happened in Italy, as a dawning and, moreover, as a sporadic appearance. For him, as for the others of Central European provenance, the system, the spirit or the occurrence was only actual on Central European soil; in Italy, on the contrary, it was an advance notice, a drumbeat, a harbinger of the future. Thanks to the mediation of these great thinkers, we see the world differently. The labourers, peasants, entrepreneurs, owners and masters had constructed an early capitalist system of wage labour, the circulation of money and of the credit system. Some of what they had taken up did not pan out, other elements continued forward as a foundation of high capitalism.

In Central Europe, the guild system, the system of putting-out, the *Hansa* society are transient events in capitalist development, which have been lost. Other processes were integrated into those of high capitalism. The money economy, the system of banking and credit, wage labour and the formal freedoms of capital, of the workers and of burgesses [*Bürger*], were expanded and spread across the capitalist-bourgeois world from the 15th to the 20th century.

In the 15th and 16th century one was already conscious that great changes had come to society. We have mentioned in relation to this question the opinions of the peasants, of Dürer, Biringuccio, Agricola and Vasari. Regiomontan, in the 15th, Adam Ries and Simon Stevin in the 16th century, adopted the system of arithmetic from the region of the Mediterranean; they developed it and further disseminated it. The historical consciousness in the transitional period from the Middle Ages to modern bourgeois society was not unitary. Dürer took up the historical events in an exact, factual and objective way. He knew that a discontinuity between antiquity and his own age had arrived and that the Italians played a leading role in the mediation between the antique and modern. He studied Euclid just as Regiomontan studied Archimedes in the 15th century. Regiomontan had also known of the role of the Byzantine philologist in the tradition.

The rise of the structuration of labour in mining and in smelting can be seen in the development of deep mining [*Tiefbau*] and the enlargement of the shafts and tunnels as well as in the increasing productivity and volume of the ore mines and in the production of metal in the 16th and 17th century. In different parts of Europe, in the Harz region, in Upper Germany, in Western Germany, in Austria and Hungary the production of silver, gold, copper, lead, tin and iron was expanded in terms of sales and value. The credit institutes, domestic and foreign trade as well as market and money relations of the states in Germany, in the Netherlands, Italy, France, England and Spain are closely linked with these developments. The rise in the structuration of labour is demonstrated in the increase of the categories and types of tasks in the process of labour as well as in the introduction and mastery of new approaches and skills of the labourer. The deepening of the mines and shafts and the expansion of the underground tunnels and passageways posed great problems in the process of production and distribution, which were solved in part. The introduction of new practical arts of facilitation of water and ventilation required the increasing qualification of the working class. Inventions were developed in connection with this advancement and set into operation. The collaboration of the carpenters, leather and metal workers had led, as a consequence, to the hewers in the mine producing more ore. In the 16th century fewer labourers were involved in the facilitation of weather and waterpower [*Förder—Wetter—und Wasserarbeitskräfte*] than in the 15th century. The costs of production in the realm of wages of labour did not rise in relation to revenue and productivity; in fact, wages decreased in this relation.

The classifications of the categories of qualification, such as of those of untrained and experienced miners, in addition those of the masters in the system of mining and smelting, in the smelting labour force, the forging labour force and in the skilled labour force, finally as those of the pit foreman [*Steiger*], the supervisors and controllers [*Hutmänner*]. [Der wichtigste Mann einer Grube war der Hutmann (mhd. huot-man = Wächter, Aufseher), der die Bergleute einstellte, die Arbeit zuwies und überwachte und den Lohn abrechnete. Mittelalter-Lexikon.de—trans.], and scribes [*Schreiber*], are reflected in the scale of wages. Remuneration was composed variously of daily and weekly wages, piece wages, money and wages in kind. The development of literature, of literacy, of the art of printing, of arithmetic and of image making, the expansion of the school system, of the systems of education and instruction by teachers, books, the universities, are parts of an internationalized system of training. We recall that Copernicus, Dürer, Regiomontan, Agricola among others, emigrated to Italy and returned home with the newly acquired scientific, technical and artistic training. Conversely, the Italians studied and employed the new methods of mining, of smelting, of assaying and processing metals in Central Europe. Instruction in the sciences, technics and arts in the mining industry and in the related branches of smelting and forging were further utilized and developed. The aristocrats and capitalists became rich by these means but were bankrupted when dynasties rose and fell; the working class conducted their struggles for higher wages, better working conditions and protection of life; the peasants, their struggles for liberation according to the model of the wage workers. The peasants, the hewers, forgers, carpenters, windlass or winch operators [*Häspeler*], schoolteachers, artists, physicians and mathematicians were all pulled into an exceedingly multifaceted structured labour process. The process was rich in its internal organization and in its inner and external production. The organization, that is, the structuration and division of social labour, was unitary and integrated the miners and their young, unskilled helpers [*Bergknappen und—buben*], the pit foremen [*die Steiger*] up to Dürer and Jost Amman into a common process. We can comprehend, how the structuration of the parts—like those in the wood cuts sketches of Dürer—had an impact on practical labour. He intended his *Unterweisung der Messung* with the circle and straight edge to be useful for the painter, goldsmith, architect, stonemason, joiner and the appropriate labourer. Arithmetic had exerted a comparable impact on the merchant class, which constituted a part of the labour process as well.

We have already seen how the development of training and of the qualification of labour in mining was brought to expression very early on. The small work of Rühlein von Calw appeared in the form of a dialogue between the experienced miner and his young pitman. Dürer and Rühlein von Calw had made efforts on behalf of training in common. Agricola and Adam Ries were schoolmasters as well.

The differences in wages between the simple workers and the skilled workers at the top were great, and these differences continued uninterruptedly forward down to the present day. The difference between the labour practices in the first centuries of the capitalist system and its contemporary situation lie in the collapse of the then system of guilds, of putting-out and manufacture.

1. The organization of labour and society is a process which cannot be disentangled. In Central Europe from the 15th to the 17th century, society was structured into estates and classes, from the poor agricultural and town labourers to the middle stratum to the patricians in the towns to the aristocrats and the royal court. The structuration of society and social organization were reflected in the guild system, so that the guilds and the miners' guilds behaved inflexibly and intransigently. Fugger could break through these walls, and in mining, rifts were added to the social organization. The miners were free in the Middle Ages. In modern times there were more miners [*Bergknappen*], yet not more freedom in mining. In some cases, the miners could become wealthy, for a portion of the miners were also shareholders. The shareholders of the mines, the copartners, the companies and certificate holders were interested in expanding the production of ore and metal in the spirit and meaning of capitalism. In opposition to this, the weavers' guild was interested in covering the immediate need of cloth for the social surroundings, not to raise profits. The city council in the different parts of Europe was in agreement with this and had favoured, protected and followed up on this goal. The council and the guilds came into opposition to the system of mining, insofar as they tried to maintain the estates and status quo. The attempt was temporarily crowned with success but was struck down in the period of high capitalism. The weavers' guild in Central Europe, England and elsewhere was able to prevent the introduction and employment of new labour arrangements and technics into the 18th century. Manufacture and the industrial factory destroyed in part the old putting-out system and the guilds. This conclusion can be exaggerated for domestic labour and piece wages are still known today.
2. A break with the prohibitive system of the guilds and of the council appeared. The class of wage workers and formal equality and freedom were expanded. The miners' freedom of movement hung together with the increasing social transformations of the estates. The demarcation between the estates had been loosened. The relocation of the miners and the turnover

of commodities, the circulation of money, of wage labour and the rise of market relations were tied up with one another. Furthermore, capital was not limited to a national market; from Upper Germany outward it was invested in Spain, the Netherlands and in the New World. The miners emigrated and were hired; their movement was—as was that of capital—international. Many German miners worked for the Fugger-Works in Spain.

3. The system of mining as the model for the further development of capitalist industrialization thereafter continued to advance and extended itself into the other branches of industry. We have seen how the cloth company in Iglau had been formed according to the model of the mining company.
4. The system of mining in Upper Germany, in Tirol and in the Harz was not organized into guilds. Work in the mines was constantly being transformed and restructured. New methods of labour and technics were introduced in the 15th, 16th, and 17th century. The entrepreneurs and copartners tried to acquire money, to increase profits and thereby to accumulate capital. Fugger was not alone in his orientation in this relation. The copper kings tried to acquire as much money as possible; the mine and smelter workers tried to raise their wages. The gain in the guild system of the 15th, 16th and 17th century was not primarily related to the accumulation of capital; rather it was bound up with the continuity of the guild and of the family life of the guild members. The weavers' guilds in Augsburg, Danzig, Frankfurt am Main and Cologne were not oriented to acquiring as much money as possible, as, for example, were the copper syndicates and companies, but rather wanted to maintain their families through the production of cloth and the sale of commodities and to clothe people. The guild and putting-out system had exploited the poor labourer. The social struggles of the weavers as those of the miners were multiple and passionately portrayed. The guild system and the putting-out system were efficiently conducted; however, the purpose of labour and its efficiency were different than the purpose of the mining capitalists who were rather allied with the system of high capitalism.

The miners, like their mining colleagues in the 19th and 20th century, had set themselves in opposition to the big capitalists of the 15th and 16th century. The big capitalists of the later epoch, on the contrary, continued the orientation of the earlier mine administrators and owners. The class struggles of the peasants and town guilds had shown themselves among the weavers, the cutlers, and the construction journeymen. The guilds and the workshop system were capitalist concerns, but quantitatively small and qualitatively different from the corporations and firms of the capitalist period. The mines in the 15th, 16th and 17th century were quantitatively smaller than the later ones; they had the same goal of maximization of profit, but brown coal played a smaller role in their operation and the steam engine not at all. The rationalization of the labour process in the modern sense was introduced early in the mining system and thereafter transferred to other branches of industry. This cannot be absolutely confirmed, but in general this assertion is valid.

In a similar way these relations and developments occurred in shipbuilding. The state showed an early interest in the system of mining, in the war industry and in shipbuilding, but only later in the cloth and construction guilds, and those of the gardeners, fishers, and so on. The state as capitalist appears systematically in the systems of mining and smelting, in the cannon factories, the saltpeter and gunpowder works, early as well in shipbuilding; and then it retreated in the face of the rise of big capital of the later period. Its main role in this relation was shown in the epoch of the absolute state in the 18th century.

5. The old guild and the putting-out system did not disappear, but rather formed a part of the capitalist system in the 15th century. These old forms of the entrepreneurial class still showed themselves in the 19th century, although in a weakened form. Like other human institutions, capitalism is only in part rational and rationalizable. It contains members, who do not belong together in all cases. The attempts, in early capitalism, to acquire money and to accumulate capital, were in some cases successful. We are not speaking of singular persons, but rather about the institutes and forms of organization. Still the capitalist system in Central Europe in the 15th century arose as a system perhaps a century earlier than in Italy.
6. Through the development of the acquisition of precious and non-ferrous metals and of the iron industry in Upper Germany, in the Harz, in Bohemia and Hungary, of the metal processing industry in Nuremberg, of the credit institutes in Augsburg, of the printing industry in Mainz, Frankfurt am Main, Strasbourg and elsewhere, finally of the art of shipbuilding and of the shipping companies on the coasts of the North Sea and the Baltic did capitalist industry contain contradictory elements.
7. Commerce between the branches of industry of Central Europe was systematically developed in the 15th and 16th century. Non-ferrous metal like bismuth, lead, tin, zinc and copper as well as iron from the Upper Palatinate and the Harz district was employed in the casting of type in the printing industry in Mainz, Frankfurt am Main, Nuremberg, Strasbourg, Augsburg and elsewhere. Commerce was in this relation systematically developed, expanded and intensified between the different branches of industry. The

same can be asserted about the armaments industry and the system of coinage. These characteristics of durability, of expansion, of differentiation and the linkage between the parts, point to the systematic appearance of capitalism in Central Europe in the 15th century. The majority of the population remained on the land, yet parts of the peasantry integrated themselves into the industrial enterprises. In the Harz and in the Upper Palatinate the peasants worked in support and transport service as wage labourers or as private entrepreneurs for the mines.

8. Wage labour as well as the circulation of money was extended. The peasants demanded the general right to work for wages. The spirit of parsimony and of inner-worldly asceticism of the 16th century accommodated itself to this system. It is not the cause of it, but rather an expression of an entrepreneurial aspect of it.

The capitalist system was introduced by different historical moments. The primary matter in its establishment and development is the expansion of the wage system, of the money economy, of the market and trade, the liberation of the peasants, the accumulation of capital and the origin of opposed classes of the town proletariat and of the bourgeois entrepreneurs. The various historical moments were emphasized by different authors. Marx mentioned the moments of long distance and foreign trade, of oversea voyages, of technology and of the mobility of the peasants. B. Schoenlank and O. Johannsen observed the class struggle in early capitalism.

8.1. The peasants formed an active and not a passive moment in the history of capitalism from the beginning. They moved in the direction of formal freedom and equality of the capitalist system of wages and of the liberation from serfdom and corvée.

9. The problem of the liberation of the peasants in the 19th century was raised by Zimmermann, Kriegk and Engels. We have dedicated a particular chapter in this work to their role in the formation of the capitalist system. We mention the class of entrepreneurs as well; it has been treated extensively by Ehrenberg, Strieder, Sombart, Brentano, von Below, Weber, Troeltsch, Kulischer and Schumpeter.

The capitalist system alludes to several changes of form in its history. Commercial capitalism is replaced by mercantilism, and the latter by the industrial revolution and high capitalism. It is common to divide the period into four main epochs: commercial capital, mercantilism, the industrial revolution, and high capitalism. The system of wage labour and of capital arches over the relations between town and countryside as well as between the metropolis and the colonies. The development of capitalism depends on the elaboration of the relations and processes within the peasant estate, within the estate of wage labour, among the entrepreneurs and of the state. It also depends on the relations of the classes, estates and social organs among themselves.

10. Capitalism reveals itself as a variation of the human process of reproduction of modern times and is treated as a system with different moments. It is a town event, which appears originally in the 14th and 15th century in the Ligurian, Tuscan, Adriatic and Lombard-Emilian commercial towns, and which grappled with the reciprocal relationships and contradictions between town and countryside, between peasants, proletarians and merchants as well as between the Italian entrepreneurs and their trading partners in the Near East. Capitalism expanded thereafter across the Alps into Central and Western Europe, into the Netherlands and England in the 15th and 16th century. The origin of capitalism is systematic, if considered internally, or sporadic, if looked upon from the standpoint of high and late capitalism which followed. The capitalist system in the form in which it appears early, was developed as all human matters, unevenly, unequally and haltingly. Yet it is a system with parts, regularities, differences and connections of the parts, with inner and outer relationships, oppositions, limits and centres. As a social system capitalism moves by the forms of freedom and equality and by the striving after them. In substance, capitalist relationships are not determined by justice but rather by profit, exploitation and property. The stages of the historical development of capitalism in Europe from the 15th to the 20th century was grappled with in § 9.

That which sporadically appeared earlier, was systematically developed later. From the standpoint of high capitalism, the earlier epoch of commercial capitalism appears as a sporadic attempt by merchants to acquire money, as an attempt by the proletarians to raise their wages and as an attempt by the peasants to transform themselves into wage labourers or petits-bourgeois. In this sense, however, capitalism appears as a systematic phenomenon only in the 19th and 20th century. If, however, the capitalist system is considered as a sheaf of activities, whose main theme is constituted by the relations of wage labour and capital, then the whole of modern bourgeois society is capitalist.

The historical epochs of the capitalist system are not to be understood as a step ladder or as an advance into paradise. They do not appear everywhere at the same time and in their persistence, they overlap. The appearance of capitalism in northern Italy in the 14th and 15th century and in Central Europe in the 15th and 16th century propagated itself. In this epoch some attempts at manufacture began, sometimes with success, sometimes, as with the weavers, they were repressed. Mercantilism was introduced in the 16th, 17th and 18th century, the industrial revolution in the 18th and 19th century, at first in England, thereafter in Germany, America, and so on in the transition to high capitalism. The countries and the states of capitalism in Europe are not to be considered uniform but rather variegated. Germany was not homogeneous; east of the Elbe capitalism was introduced and developed more slowly and later than in the western parts of the country; in northern Italy earlier than in the south, and so on.

These epochs are thus not mechanically to be separated from one another; customs last into the epochs of high capitalism. In the earlier epochs of the capitalist system capitalists were not as powerful as they later were, while large sectors of the economy in the countryside were not operated in the capitalist mode. Yet, in considerable parts of agriculture, in the town and in the mines the economy operated capitalistically and not in the feudal mode. Capitalism arose as a systematic phenomenon in the 15th century in Central Europe in several important industries and branches of industry.

Sporadic appearances are singular, they quickly disappear. The interweaving and linkages of the parts in several directions are lacking in the sporadic phenomena, and various conditions are missing. We will concretize these observations.

In the Middle Ages the cooperatives [*Genossenschaften*] and companies were occupied with distant trade. They went from Central Europe to the east, north, and south, and they returned with profit when they succeeded. It could also have been a single trader who made such an attempt. Thus, the merchant Marco Polo started his world-renowned journey to Asia in the 13th century. This great undertaking was singular, solitary, linked to no other commercial journey. The unparalleled commercial activity of Marco Polo can be compared with the unique mathematical activity of Fibonacci. Both were men of the 13th century, both Northern Italians—the one from Venice, the other from Pisa. Only 100 years later were their spheres of activity further developed and systematically worked by others. Then the investigation and discovery of the earth began in all directions systematically from Europe outward.[61] Constantinople was an important trading partner of the Italian cities in the first half of the 15th century, Genoa became wealthy from Byzantine trade. Conversely, in their arts, Venice and Ravenna display the influence of the Byzantine style.

Some researchers trace the systematic development of the capitalist system back to the 16th century. This century links two elements: immediacy in relation to the Reformation, to Protestantism and confessional disputes, and mediacy in relation to the beginning of the capitalist system. We have seen that different aspects of the economic life in Central Europe were driven capitalistically: mining, the printing industry, the credit institutes. Mining was closely tied to the system of credit, of coinage and of the circulation of money. The circulation of money was tightly bound up with payment for wage labour, the hewers in mining were wage labourers; the metals, as the product of mine work, were indispensable for the expansion of money wages, of market trade, the circulation of money, the system of coinage and for printing. Thus, we can see how the different branches of industry were interwoven. This occurred in the 15th century, to wit in a systematic process. It didn't happen once and for all; the system expanded rather slowly and was not introduced simultaneously in all branches of the economy. Distance trade was operated capitalistically, the weaver offered resistance, construction did not have the same rhythm of development as mining, and so on.

Forms appear and disappear; the substance of wage labour and of capital remains, as long as the capitalist system exists. The German Hansa disappeared in the old form; the great trading houses in Upper Germany were replaced by other institutes in Central Europe, these by new, freer forms of undertaking of the industrial revolution. The newer forms were freed to some extent from state intervention.

Trade was systematically linked to production. The putting-out system had loosened the ties between production and distribution in the 15th and 16th century and in part dissolved them. This loosening and dissolution was introduced into the system of mining and into the printing industry in the 15th and 16th century. At this time, the guild system had preserved the close relationship between product and the sale of the commodities produced. The hook and eye makers were, as Jost Amman recorded it, the sellers of commodities. But in other branches of industry through the development of the capitalist market, the stock exchange, wage labour and the circulation of money, the joint-stock company and in part by the putting-out system, the separation of producers from sellers, hence the separation of production from distribution was introduced if not generally accomplished.

We have taken up the question concerning the sporadic and systematic appearance of capitalist processes in Central Europe rather qualitatively and treated the quantitative side only by means of examples. But the point however is to take it up quantitatively in a systematic way.

The structuration of labour did not remain static. The economic moments of wants/needs [*Bedürfnisse.* German does not distinguish wants from needs with the single word *Bedürfnis*—trans.] and their satisfaction through the production of goods, commodities, comestible goods, cloth and habitation, tools and pathways, through means of transportation, heating and lighting, were carried forward. The increase in population by means of natural growth and the decrease of population through plagues and war are also to be included in the economic moments. The economic conditions in Central Europe improved from the 15th to the 17th century, in spite of plague, war, exploitation and oppression. The peasants had liberated themselves, the working class in the town had grown. At the end of the 17th century life became more stable and assured. Exploitation in the industrial factories presents a further problem, which was taken up only in the 19th and 20th century by the class-conscious workers' movement in a humane fashion, even though a solution could not be found. The foundation of civil rights, of the national state and of the modern political constitution in Central Europe is traced back to the second half of the 17th century.

These formal-legal and political institutions are founded on the system of wage labour and capital and constitute the substance of modern bourgeois society. These substantial arrangements are formed as a system in Central Europe in the 15th century and earlier in Italy. The organization of labour was carried on in mining and smelting, in the printing industry, in shipbuilding, in the systems of money, credit and trade as well as in other branches of industry capitalistically in the 15th century. These industries and branches of industry were in an abiding, complicated, differentiated, dynamic and interwoven intercourse with one another. The circulation of money and the credit system expanded. The peasants increasingly were transformed into wage labourers, and this transformation led to the revolution of the domestic market in Central Europe. Towns grew through the immigration of peasants and foreigners. The increase of the town population was determined primarily through the growth of the town proletariat. Poverty increased thereby, for most of these immigrants were skilful peasants in the countryside, but they were unskilled labour in the town. From their numbers the new industrial reserve army was formed. The structuration of labour in the system of mining and smelting became increasingly rational through the increase of qualified labour in the metal industry. The rise of technology in this period was based on the increasing skill of the labourers and the increasing inventive activity in the sciences, which we today call chemistry, metallurgy and geology. The developments in mathematics and physics in the 17th century should be added to this.[62] Research into the origins of the capitalist system have been ascribed by some scholars to the merchant activities of the entrepreneurs.[63] Another group of researchers linked the most curious inventions to the context of the beginning of the capitalist period.[64] Marx introduced another consideration, which was not related to technology, but rather to the accumulation of capital, sea trade and the passive physical movement of the peasants as well. These perspectives are valuable and impact our thesis. The periodization question is solved through the economic data. Modern bourgeois society arose in modern times and defines this period of world history. The primary moments in the determination of the modern period, are the liberation of the peasants, the emergence of wage labour and capital and the expansion of both, further, the predominance of capital in modern society and the formation of the working class as the class of wage labour, the oppositions between the two interests, the interest of capital and that of wage labour, and the founding of modern bourgeois society as the society of the two opposed spheres, the private and the public. The period of modernity follows the era of medieval feudalism in the history of Europe. This periodization is not related to Africa, the Islamic world, India, China, Mesoamerica or the kingdom of the Incas; there, it is a matter of other historical categories.

The history of capitalism is not the history of the entrepreneurs and of technology, but rather the relations between the labourers and the entrepreneurs, of the reciprocal relations between the two and the history of economic and social changes in these relations. Technics is a part, perhaps the most curious part, but not the whole in the process of labour. We distinguish the scientific investigation of the processes from the inspection of attractions in the landscape. We will mention some fields of research which often still appear to be open, both qualitatively as well as quantitatively. Systematic investigation of the development of the working class in Germany during the 15th to the 17th century according to the numbers in the various towns, provinces and branches of industry as well as in general is the most important problem for the future. Quantitative investigation of the founding of firms and enterprises in the towns, provinces and branches of industry and of their size and endurance constitutes the second important problem in this area. The history of the putting-out system can be treated quantitatively and qualitatively. The putting-out system was an important event of the late Middle Ages and of the first centuries of modern times. Its historians and theoreticians will teach us more about its historical importance.

We have searched out and put into context some data, which highlight the structuration and magnitude of the mining operations and those of the smelters in the 15th and 16th century. The dynamic of the structuration and magnitude of this labour process is implicitly found in the data itself. Further research into this dynamic will be given emphasis in the investigation of those operations in the following periods. Parallel to this the structuration of labour and the size of operations in the printing industry, in shipbuilding, in weaving among others should be investigated. Not just the introduction of newer technics, but also the structuration and division of labour, the training of the workers, the relations between the labourers, their education, finally the relationship of these factors to writing, arithmetic, technics, science, to the merchant class and capital are the starting points of the investigations. Only then can the effect of the new steam machinery, the iron scaffolding in construction, the iron ship and the railways, electricity and electronics can be investigated and understood.

The history of social labour is that of the structuration of labour, of training, of increasing qualification, of communication and of the redirection and transmission of the same, then that of labour practices as well as the technics of labour and their social organization. The division of labour constitutes a part of the structuration of labour, the combination, composition by communication and transmission is another aspect, and the social organization of the same is yet a further part of this historical process.

The rationalization of labour of the enterprises was developed *pari passu* with these antecedents and under these circumstances.

The capitalist system and modern bourgeois society taken together determine the form and substance of modernity. Their antecedents appear sporadically in the late Middle Ages, systematically in the modern period. We have tried to present some of the most important characteristics qualitatively. It will be the task of another, to present them quantitatively, with numbers and tables.

The confrontation of the qualitative and quantitative kinds of treatment is only a moment in the development of the system. It is equally about a process of elaboration. The operations at their start-up have a small workforce, the structuration of labour is simple in comparison to that in the high capitalist enterprise. We see how the era of early capitalism was dominated by the German Hansa, the guilds, the town council, the system of putting-out, the credit institutes of Augsburg and Antwerp. They, however, were attempts, which in the 15th to the 17th century, had set the tone for economic life, which were replaced by other forms of organization of capitalism in the mercantile and industrial period. The concept of organizational form is fitting. Only there is no direct, linear history of these forms. Some of the preceding ones disappear, newer ones come to the fore, some of the older ones surviving into the 20th century.

The enterprises of high capitalism are great, powerful and complicated, but not as durable, as the heavenly bodies. The shareholders of a pit are transformed into trade unions, the companies into joint-stock companies—the political parties of capital and of the working class are continually changing. Europe is no longer the centre of the capitalist world, neither is North America.

The periodization in history is not formally determined. In antiquity and in the Middle Ages the majority of the population consisted of labourers in the countryside and in the town; the majority of workers were unfree, either as slaves bound to the person of their masters, or serfs *glebae adscripti*, ascribed to the earth and soil. In modern times, the majority of the population belong to the working class, but these workers are free only pro forma. They enjoy the freedom of concluding a contract and of seeking employment elsewhere. Substantial freedom does not exist in actuality, only in utopia. These people are forced to work for others; only in rare cases is one free of this pressure. The theory of the form and substance is presented here in relation to the theory of freedom and of the periodization of history.

Changes of the forms in the labour process and in the formal relation of the working class to the system of state and law determine the sequence and the boundaries of the periods in the history of the antique, medieval and modern bourgeois society.

We have frequently emphasized the concept of system. A society like the German or some other is a system, because it is made up of links which are human members. The links are different and linked together in the system. The social system is abiding, and it is also ephemeral because the parts do not have a unitary but rather a divergent and contrary historical course. The human social system is equally non-uniform and contradictory, within a society as well as generally in human history. However, the society is a system by means of the connections of the oppositional and antagonistic parts. The journeymen fought immediately against the council, the peasants against their landlords, not against the distant emperor and the state. The state set itself immediately against the peasants, and state officials tried to dominate the journeymen organizations through the guilds and the council.

The big capitalists of the 15th and 16th century strove for profits and the increase of profits of money and of capital. The striving for capital and the wish to accumulate it, they had in common with the representatives of high capitalism in the 19th and 20th century. They tried to acquire money at the same time through production in the system of mining and so on, as well as in distance trade, in the credit system and in domestic trade. They exploited the workers like the high and late capitalists. Their means were limited, the turnover was originally small, profit limited in comparison to the later epochs. The labourers worked for money wages, but the industrialization of the operations, the structuration of the labour process and the qualification of the labourers were small in relation to contemporary processes. Yet the differences between the 15th and 20th century were rather quantitative than qualitative. The workers' organizations are in part old, in part new; the joint-stock company as well as the banks and the remaining credit institutes go back to earlier epochs. The class struggle of the earlier journeymen's organizations and of the newer trade unions extends across the history of the entire capitalist system. Only the forms of the journeymen's organizations were changed; the substance, that is the wage and the increase of wages, the shortening of the working day and of labour time over the entire year, the improvement of the conditions of labour, of heat and of light and the struggle for them continues to the present day.

The industrialization of high capitalism expanded, yet the difference in the system of mining and in the printing industry is not to be assessed qualitatively and substantially in comparison to them today, but rather quantitatively and formally. In other branches of industry, like in the production of cloth and in transportation, the difference is to be assessed quantitatively and qualitatively. The same relations of capital and of wage labour determine the entire capitalist epoch from the 15th to the 20th century. The formal liberation of the peasants, of wage labour and of capital, determine the aspirations of our epoch.

Developments in the history of entrepreneurship like Calvinist asceticism and frugality of the 16th century, of mercantilism of the 17th century and of cameralism of the same period, are interesting and important subdivisions in the history of capitalism. They are epoch making, yet in their impact they are limited. They disappear shortly after their florescence. The protestant spirit appears early in the history of capitalism, but it is not the cause of the new phenomenon, rather more likely the spirit reacted to the new development of the market. This history of spirit is myopic, because it is only related to the entrepreneur. The spirit of the peasantry which strove for liberation, stirred itself much earlier, and is more important. Freedom and wage labour are the moments of the early capitalist spirit of the peasants.

We have mentioned the history of the relationship between the state and the merchants. First the state discovered that the merchants could serve its interests. Later the capitalists became powerful, had their own interests and made the state officials into their servants. Now it appears that a balance has been struck between the public sphere of the state and the private sphere of the capitalists.

The transformation of part of the peasants into wage labourers, the increasing training and qualification of the working class, the rise of class consciousness and of the organizational forms of the working class and of capital are the deeply rooted moments in the history of the capitalist epoch.[65]

The development of the printing industry is bound up with the system of mining and smelting, of capital, of the training of the working class and its rising qualification, with writing, with arithmetic and with the education of the entire population. The introduction of steam machinery and of the electric industry is based on the skilled working class. Just as important as these moments in the history of European capitalism are colonialism and colonization.

Notes

1. Bermannus [Lorenz Bermann]was his friend and colleague, the bookkeeper [Hüttenschreiber] in a smelting plant —trans.

2. G. Agricola, *De Re Metallica*, Basel 1556, *Zwölf Bücher vom Berg– und Hüttenwesen*. C. Schiffner et al. (eds.), 5th edition, Düsseldorf 1978. *De Re Metallica* (mining and metallurgy), G. Fraustadt and H. Rescher (eds.) Berlin 1974. *De Re Metallica*, H. C. Hoover and L. H. Hoover (eds.), New York 1950. H. Wilsdorf and W. Quellmalz, *Bergwerke und Hüttenwesen der Agricola-Zeit*, Berlin 1971. The edition by Schiffner, *Zwölf Bücher vom Berg – und Hüttenwesen*, is complemented by Agricola's *Buch von den Lebewesen unter Tage* in the edition of E. Darmstaedter.
3. The main edition in the 20th century is by Aldo Mieli. Vannoccio Biringuccio, 1480–1539, *De la Pirotechnia*, Bari 1914ff. (Introduction, biography, text). O. Johannsen, translator: *Die zehn Bücher von der Feuerwerkskunst*, Braunschweig 1925.
4. The title of the work describes the content better than the table of contents. The complete title of the work by Lazarus Ercker reads: *Beschreibung: Allerfürnemsten Mineralischen Erzt/ unnd Berckwercksarten/ wie dieselbigen/ unnd eine jede in sonderheit/ irer natur und eigenschaft nach/ auff alle Metaln Probirt/ und im kleinen fewer sollen versucht werden/ mit erklerung etlicher fürnemen nützlichen Schmeltzwerken im grossen fewer/ auch Schaidung, Goldt/ Silber unnd andere Metalln/ Sampt einem bericht des Kupfer saigerns/ Messing brennens/ und Salpeter siedens, auch aller saltzigen Minerischen proben/ und was denen allen anhengig in fünff Bücher verfast/ Dergleichen zuvorn niemals in Druck kommen. Allen liebhabern der Fewer künste/ jungen Probirern/ unnd Berckleuten zu nutz/ mit schönen Figuren unnd abriß der instrument/ trewlich unnd fleissig an Tag geben. Durch/ Lazarus Erckern,* Prag 1574. 2nd edition Frankfurt am Main 1580, in the publishing house of Sigmund Feyerabends. P. R. Beierlein (ed.). Berlin 1960. A. G. Siscon, C. S. Smith (translator), Chicago 1951 (see images).
5. Thus, the rise into the mountain is 1%. The Tuscan ell = 0.5836 metres.
6. Biringuccio, *De la pirotechnica*.
7. A. Arendt. Bergbau, *Handwörterbuch der Staatswissenschaften*, 3rd edition, 1909. Fr. Rütten, *Bergarbeiter. Staatslexikon,* 2nd edition, 1926. H. Wiegmann, R. Specht, *Bergarbeiter, Staatslexikon*, 6th edition, 1903. H. Wilsdorf. *Bergwerke* (see above).
8. Agricola, *De Re Metallica*, 4th book, the distribution of ownership rights among the shareholders was variable, carried out according to the kind of ore and local customs. In the 16th century the iron ore pits remained either undistributed, or they were divided into two or four parts; in very rare cases did it come to further divisions. The pits containing lead, copper, bismuth, tin, and mercury on the contrary were divided into eight, sixteen or twenty-three parts, seldom more. The division of the Schneeberger silver pit went further, for the pits and even the singular tunnels were divided into 128 parts according to the memory of the fathers; of those, 126 parts of the pit or the tunnels belonged to the shareholders, one portion belonged to the state and one to the church. In Joachimsthal on the contrary, 122 shares belonged to the shareholders, one share to the state, one to the church and four to the landowners. In Agricola's time a further share was added for the poorest of the people. Only the shareholders paid an additional amount. In Joachimsthal the landowners paid nothing further, but rather supplied for their four share certificates as much wood as was necessary from their forests for the expansion of the mines, for machines, for buildings and structures and as fuel for the smelters. Thus, the number of shareholders came to 129 or more. The pit was called *Zeche* as well or symposium. The additional payments which the shareholders paid for the operation of the pit, were called symbolum. The extraction could be very high. The participants in the St. George mine in Schneeberg received for each of the 128 shares *Silberkuchen* quarterly which amounted to 1100 Rhenish gold guldens. Apian remarks in this regard: "Notice, that the entire repository is first divided into 10 shares. The shareholders received 9 of them, the tenth belongs to the authorities. The 9 are divided into

some fractions, as ½ of one ninth and ¼ of one ninth and a half quarter, a sixth. The six tenths are called by some Kukis." Cf. C. Rudolff, *Exempel vom Bergwerk*, in: J. Tropfke, *Geschichte der Elementarmathematik,* 4th edition, Vol. 1; K. Vogel et al. (eds.), Berlin 1980. The merger of the mines is bound up with the expansion of capital investment. The share certificates were variously distributed by the mergers.
The Rappolt-Great Company of 1515 had 138 shareholders:

Shareholders/Location	Number of Shareholders	Number of Share Certificates
Augsburg (merchant)	1	½
Central Germany	5	3 ¾
Clerics	5	4
Erzgebirge	5	4
Jülich (mint master)	1	1
Leipzig (merchants, manual labourers among others)	13	11 ¼
Leipzig (merchants, county princes, officials)	9	13
---	2	1
Nuremberg (merchants among others)	39	41 ½
---	8	7 ¾
Others	32	22 ½
Provincial and court nobles	5	7
Schneeberg (resource seekers, fore-men, shift masters)	8	8
Zwickau	5	4 ¼
All	**138**	**129 ½**

T. G. Werner, 'Die große Fusion der Zechen um den Rappolt von 1514.' *Mitteilungen des Vereins für Geschichte der Stadt Nürenberg*, Vol. 57, 1970. Werner reckons 129 3–4 shares. With the assembly of the collieries [*Zechen*] Agricola wrote about the division of the shares.

9. O. Gierke, *Das deutsche Genossenschaftsrecht* (1868), Vol. 1, Graz 1954, §§ 42 and 43. Leuthold, '*Knappschaft*,' Ersch and Gruber, *Enzyklopädie*, Leipzig 1885. They base themselves on G. W. Leibniz [Script. Rer. Brunsv, 1711] among others. We will concern ourselves in the following section with mining in Upper Germany.
10. J. Strieder, *Studien zur Geschichte kapitalistischer Organisationsformen*, 2nd edition, Munich 1925, Book 1, 3rd chapter.
11. According to folk etymology of the *Huntestößer* or *Karrenläufer* the carts made noises like dogs, underground.
12. For a short discussion of the word *Kunst*, please see the Translator's Foreword above.
13. Lazarus Ercker (*Beschreibung: Allerfürnemsten Erzt …*, Book II) behaved sceptically, when the philosophers or alchemists said they could transform copper into silver and silver into gold, for he, Ercker, "invoked in his books only natural and proven methods upon which everyone might

rely, and would not awaken any vain hopes." Yet he admitted in the first book that assaying is an ancient art, which, like all other *Feuerarbeiten* [pyrotechnical works] was established by the alchemists. Vannoccio Biringuccio (*De la Pirotechnia*) campaigned against alchemy, as his publisher Mieli demonstrates. Lippmann and Johannsen call attention to the fact that already in the 14th century *alchimia* was put on a level with forgery. Agricola went a step further with his practical orientation in relation to sorcery of the diving rod and believed that the serious mining man ought to avoid all these supernatural arts. Agricola returns repeatedly to the mine spirits (*De animantibus subtaneneis, Concerning the living beings underground*). He believes that there are benevolent and malevolent spirits of the mine and cites theologians and philosophers like Psellus, in order to show that these spirits have specific characteristics and properties. This orientation contradicts the pragmatic views of Agricola. Yet Agricola, Biringuccio and Ercker were all in agreement already in the 16th century that the sciences of chemistry and metallurgy were chasing after rainbows, when they believed in the transformability of metals, like the alchemists did.

14. Agricola, *De Re Metallica*, Books 3 and 6. The miner of Hans Sachs worked on Sanct Annaberg.
15. Kellenbenz, in: C. M. Cipolla, K. Borchardt (eds.), *Europäische Wirtschaftsgeschichte. 16th and 17th Century*, Stuttgart 1979.
16. H. Wilsdorf, *Bergwerke*. In Goslar at Rammelsberg, as we have seen, 400 men worked together, who lost their lives. Whether or not they had worked in one operation, was not said.
17. J. Strieder, *Studien zur Geschichte kapitalistischer Organisationsformen*, 2nd edition, Munich 1925. Book 1, Chapter 3. H. Kellenbenz, in: *Europäische Wirtschaftsgeschichte*. C. M. Cipolla, K. Borchardt (eds.), Stuttgart 1979, Chapter 3. Regarding smelting furnaces in the 16th century see Agricola, *De Re Metallica, (Saigern, Saigerofen, Garherd, Darrherd)*, Book 11. By these means, silver, copper and lead were acquired. The foundational process is the removal of silver from the black copper, through the remelting of the lead and the crushing of the black copper. Small amounts of silver were also acquired from iron ore.
18. Agricola, *De Re Metallica*, Book 8. The unskilled male labourers climbed down into the mines; the women did not do so.
19. The philological, economic-historical, scientific-historical and technical-historical works by Hoover, Schiffner, Darmststädter, Fraustadt, Prescher, Wilsdorf, Smith and Beierlein, Mieli and Johannsen have created the grounds for further research. With regard to the romanticization of the past, in particular with regard to the conception that the class struggles are only related to the capitalist period, we have already spoken. The capital relations, wage labour and class struggles were already present in the Middle Ages and in classical antiquity. Only in the pre-capitalist period did they arise sporadically, in the capitalist period systematically.
20. Grimm, *Wörterbuch*. Cf.
21. A share made over to the owner in return for his providing the mines with wood from his forest.
22. H. Wilsdorf, *Bergwerke und Hüttenanlagen*, 1971. The number of people in mining in this region in 1527 amounted to 610. The *Huntestößer* as a precursor to the *Hauer* was a *Fördermann* in mining.
23. *Der Freiberger Bergbau*. O. Wagenbreth, E. Wachtler (eds.), Leipzig 1985.
24. H. Wilsdorf, *Bergwerke und Hüttenanlagen*, 1971. The number of mining people in this region amounted to 610 in 1527. The *Huntestößer* as a preperatory stage to hewer was a transport or delivery worker [*Fördermann*] in mining.
25. Agricola, *De Re Metallica*, Book 6, Hoover (ed.).

26. It is assumed that it was Agricola's intention to compose a work concerning iron mining, yet we do not have that book.
27. Agricola, *De Re Metallica*, Book 4.
28. Agricola's 9th book, translated by C. Schiffner; 4th book, translated by E. Wandhoff.
29. *Werke und Tage* (Ἔργα καὶ ἡμέραι [Érga kaì hêmérai]) title of a poem by Hesiod—trans.
30. The lamps are supposed to be procured by the miner himself.
31. It is assumed that Agricola is himself also pictured here.
32. Biringuccio, *De la Pirotechnia,* O. Johannsen (ed.). Agricola, *De Re Metallica.* For later research see H. Hoover, L. Beck, O. Johannsen, H. Wilsdorf, R. Sprandel.
33. Agricola, *De Re Metallica,* Book 6, Hoover (ed.) K. T. Inama-Sternegg, *Deutsche Wirtschaftsgeschichte* (see above).
34. Agricola, *De Re Metallica,* Book 9, H. Kellenbenz in: *Europäische Wirtschaftsgeschichte.*Cipolla, Borchardt (eds.) op. cit.
35. Grimm, *Wörterbuch.* Agricola, *De Re Metallica,* Book 7, *Künste als Instrumente im Probierwesen.*
36. Agricola, *De Re Metallica,* Books 9–12. Grimm, *Wörterbuch.*
37. Agricola, *De Re Metallica,* Books 6, 8, 9. With regard to the dangers of bad weather in the pits he had previously commented. The danger was increased by the depths which were reached in the 16th century.
38. H. Kellenbenz, in: Cipolla and Borchardt. Ibid. *Über die Geschichte der Technik.*
39. Rülein von Calw, *Ein Nützlich Bergbüchlein,*in 1500, 1527, an so on. Agricola, *De Re Metallica,* Books 1 and 6 and passim.
40. L. Brentano, (*Die Anfänge des modernen Kapitalismus,* Munich 1916) signalled the philanthropic activity of the Fuggers; M. Weber (*Die Protestantische Ethik* 1929, Tübingen 1969) agreed with him. F. M. Feldhaus (*Die Maschine,* 1954, p. 274) pointed to the reverse side of this activity. An earlier edition of the *Bergbüchleins* is known. (see above).
41. Johannasen, *Geschichte des Eisens.*
42. R. Sprandel, *Eisengewerbe.* The list of wage labourers originates from the poem *Ferraria* by Nicolas Bourbon, 1518.
43. Johannsen, Sprandel, Kulischer, Kellenbenz, op. cit.
44. O. Johannsen, *Geschichte des Eisens,* 3rd edition, Düsseldorf, 1953.
45. J. Kulischer, *Allgemeine Wirtschaftsgeschichte,* Vol. II, 1958, Section 3, chapter 9.
46. O. Johannsen, *Geschichte des Eisens,* 3rd edition, Düsseldorf 1953, p. 170ff.
47. Johannsen, ibid., p. 90. For the history of extraction and smelting of gold, silver and copper at this time cf. P. Arnold and W. Quellmelz, *Sächsische Thüringische Bergbaugepräge,* Leipzig 1978. They stood in favor of this for they developed the capitalist trade union prior to 1300 in the Saxon silver mines. This assertion was related to the sporadic appearance of capitalist relations in the 13th or 14th century.
48. R. Sprandel, *Das Eisengewerbe in Mittelalter,* Stuttgart 1968.
49. H. Wilsdorf and W. Quellmalz, *Bergwerke und Hüttenanlagen der Agricola-Zeit,* Berlin 1971, p. 484.
50. R. Sprandel, loc. cit.
51. O. Johannsen, *Die Geschichte des Eisens,* 3rd edition, Düsseldorf 1954.
52. H. Wilsdorf and Quellenmalz, op. cit.
53. Agricola, *De Re Metallica,* Book 6. H. Wilsdorf, *Bergwerke und Hüttenanlagen,* 1971. In addition, there were *Pferdeknecht, Wasserheber, Bergschmiede* and possibly also *Karrenläufer,* altogether 70–100 workers in the work force of a pit. [A Lachter was a unit of measure of length which

often expressed depth of mine shafts and tunnels. It was the equivalent to distance between a man's outstretched arms on both sides of the body—roughly 5–6 feet—trans.]

54. L. Beck, *Geschichte des Eisens,* Braunschweig 1884–1903., vol. II.
55. J. Kulischer, *Allgemeine Wirtschaftsgeschichte*, Vol. II.
56. H. Kellenbenz, in: C. M. Cipolla, K. Borchardt (eds.), *Europäische Wirtschaftsgeschichte. 16. und 17. Jahrhundert*, Stuttgart 1979.
57. F. M. Feldhaus, *Die Machine*, Basel 1954.
58. J.Kulischer, *Allgemeine Wirtschaftsgechichte*, Vol. II, chapter 1.2.
59. Agricola, *De Re Metallica*, Book 9. *Zu Frischfeuer, Frischstücken, Saigerherd,* Book 11. O. Johannsen, *Geschichte des Eisens*, 1953. H. Wilsdorf, *Bergwerke und Hüttenanlagen,* 1971.
60. G. W. F. Hegel had already seen this. This has to do not only with tools, but also with intellectual labour, concrete labour, the abstract instruments of labour and the concrete tools. The mediation in this process is displayed in the relation between man and external nature, namely in three ways: through the organization of labour, through the treatment of the instruments of labour and through the processing of ore. At first labour is simple through the processing of the ore and thus further organized, thereupon more complicated, through the dealings with ore, then with raw iron and finally with malleable iron. The process of mediation is not static but rather dynamic. *Das Rennen* in the production of malleable iron was predominant in the Middle Ages, refining in the early historical period of capitalism, puddling during the industrial revolution and the Bessemer process in the period of high capitalism. The art of forging by means of wrought iron [*Schweißeisens*] and of wrought steel [*Schweißstahls*] was transformed after the industrial revolution in the forging of soft iron and soft steel (Johannsen). The organization of labour became more complicated; the labourer, the mining men, transporters, the coal measurer, the puddler, the smelter, the oxidizing smelter [*Zerrenner*], the wood cutter, shipper, hammer forger, agricultural labourer, welder were structured and integrated; increasingly more intermediate stages were inserted in the production of iron and steel: beside one another and after one another and in reaction and feedback to one another. The view of Strieder who from the standpoint of the forms of organization of capitalist enterprise imputes the beginning of the capitalist period to the 15th century, finds himself in agreement with the schema from O. Johannsen. Accordingly, the new period begins in 1450, modern times in 1800, that is, with the industrial revolution and high capitalism. F. M. Feldhaus has suggested the same conception on grounds of the history of technics. These views, which are based on the history of trade of the merchant class, of investions and discoveries, are interesting and even important; they are to be taken seriously, but not as definitive. Only when they are posited in relation to the peasant movements and the process of labour and when the oppositions between the moments are analysed, can a picture of the revolution of the Middle Ages and of feudalism be introduced. The views and activities of Regiomontan, Nicolas of Cuso, Dürer, Luther, Calvin, Agricola and Copernicus caused nothing, but they belong to the picture that the objective historical moments showcase.
61. Henry Yule, Henri Cordier and Paul Pelliot conducted research in this area. Leonardo Olschki, *Marco Polos Asia*, California 1960.
62. Edgar Zilsel investigated the relationship between occupational skill and science.
63. From this point of view we have already mentioned the works of Ehrenberg, Strieder, Sombart and Kulischer, v. Below and Brentano, Weber and Schumpeter.
64. The primary researches in the area of technology in relation to early capitalism were undertaken by F. M. Feldhaus, L. Beck, O. Johannsen, R. Sprandel, H. Kellenbenz and H. Wilsdorf.
65. It would be important to investigate the connection between the merchant class and arithmetic.

Europe in the World

The transition from sporadic to systematic commerce can be shown in the local relations of the domestic market as well as in distance trade. The commerce of isolated spots, districts and localities is transformed and linked with interregional and international commerce. The transition from sporadic to systematic commerce is presented in the various branches of the economy and expands from there. The opposed relations of the system of mining, of the hammer mills and smelting system, of coinage, of the assembling of iron tools and of the metal processing industry, of the merchant class, of the printing industry, of the clock industry, of the weapons and war industry, of shipbuilding and of the art of seafaring were systematically elaborated, not only in interregional and international relations to one another, but also in the reciprocal support of the branches of industry among one another.

Instruments of credit, market relations, the exchange of commodities and the circulation of money, wage labour and the accumulation of capital are the practical means towards the transformation of isolated localities into nationally linked localities, towns and provinces. Commerce is operated on an ongoing basis in markets, in the stock markets and banks, in the representatives, subsidiaries, settlements, factories and the like. In this connection the weekly market, the annual market and so on are transformed into department stores and other durable and permanent establishments. Money, paper money, securities, mining shares, letters and stocks are spread by commerce. The rate of interest is transformed directly with increasing and decreasing risk in the investment of capital.

The question concerning the effect of the discovery of America on the beginnings of the capitalist system was put into the foreground of research in this area by F.M. Feldhaus. In lectures as well, students have again and again highlighted this same question. The answer to it is not simple, for the discovery of America is closely linked with the discovery of the sea passages to Africa and India as well as with the expansion of wage labour in the port cities of southern Europe and of the development of the arts of seafaring and shipbuilding. The sacking of Constantinople by the Turks (1454) constituted a difficulty in this respect, for the Italians in the east of the Mediterranean region still remained active at this time in trading, so that the war with the Turks did not prevent the expansion of wage labour and the further development of technics. The discovery of America (1492) had only a limited impact on the development of capitalism on the Iberian Peninsula. The beginnings of the capitalist system can already be noted in the trade across the Gulf of Leon and the Ligurian Sea, mainly between Genoa and Barcelona, and in connection with the founding of the dockyard industry in Gades (Cadiz). The dockworkers were paid a money wage in the 15th century. Thus, the Queen of Spain, Isabella "the Catholic", pawned her jewels, in order to finance the ships and the voyage of discovery by Columbus.

And thus, traces of so-called paleo-capitalism in the 15th and 16th century on the Iberian Peninsula were already present. The people of Spain and Portugal had profited but very little from their American colonies in the 16th and 17th century which they had subsequently conquered following their discoveries. Their economy in this period remained paleo-capitalist, and it persisted in this condition through the 18th and 19th century. The economic structures of these countries were not transformed by the discoveries and conquests—on the contrary, they remained bound to their previous condition. German merchants and bankers took over the precious metals which the Spaniards had transported from America and lent them further, again to the Spanish monarchs. In Cervantes' *Don Quijote*, 1605, *fucar* (=Fugger) meant: *un hombre muy rico,* a very wealthy man. The Spanish kings had lost their riches through the wars of the 16th and 17th century, could not repay their debts, and thus the great trading firms and credit institutes of Augsburg and Nuremberg went bankrupt for lack of money. This sad history, however, pertains only to the fate of single persons. The history of capitalism in general is different.

The structural processes of capitalism are related to the relations of wage labour and capital and were continually extended in Central Europe in the 15th and 16th century. This doesn't just concern the Augsburgers or the Nurembergers, but rather all the branches of industry, like mining, printing, the clock industry, the metal industry, the trading firms and shipbuilding. In opposition to these branches of the economy weaving, agriculture and construction which continue the medieval characteristics of their production practices into modern times, appear not to have been progressive, that is, reorganized on a capitalistic basis. In all branches, workers produced their commodities, they were oppressed and exploited, they received their wages, and their technics and skill were further developed. This development was accomplished quicker in Central Europe than in Italy, Spain and Portugal and it was more pronounced in Holland and England.

We recall, for example, the fact that the Russian Czar, Peter the Great, travelled to Holland in the 17th century in order to study the new shipbuilding art there. The Central Europeans, in particular the Germans, in trade and in the production of iron had the edge over the Mediterranean countries, and the Dutch and the English would take it over from the Central Europeans in the 17th and 18th century.

The discovery of America played several roles in the history of capitalism. For the Spanish and the Portuguese, who had achieved a weak development of wage labour and capital, there came a weak expansion of capitalism in the following centuries. A stronger development of wage labour and capital had led to the stronger expansion of capitalism in Germany, England and Holland. The relative weaknesses of Iberian capitalism in comparison to the German, Dutch and English had led to the exploitation of the Spaniards and the Portuguese by the Central and Northern Europeans. These Europeans had treated all the countries of the Iberian Peninsula almost as semi-colonies, while Spain and Portugal could confirm themselves as colonial powers not only in America, but rather in the regions of the Pacific and Indian Oceans as well. Thus, not only was Brazil conquered by the Portuguese, but so too were Macao, Timur, Goa, Mozambique and Angola. And the Spaniards conquered not only Mexico, Peru and other parts of North, Central and South America, but also the Philippines, and Morocco, among others. Portugal and Spain had imported precious and non-ferrous metals from Mexico and Peru, spices, cotton, wood and later sugar, coffee, rum and cocoa from the whole of their colonial domain and forwarded them on.

Colonialism and colonization exerted a reciprocal influence on one another. The great traders, merchants and bankers sent German and other miners into their Spanish operations. Colonization by European workers in the New World went a step further. Unfree labourers from Europe were established in America, later it was the slaves from Africa. The colonial powers led American Indians into slavery and peonage. The peon was a kind of peasant, who was burdened with debt; he could not move freely. Colonization was a means to further develop colonialism in America and colonialism in turn was a means to further develop colonization. The

Basques worked as shepherds along the entire Cordillera in Mexico and North America. The discovery of America by the Europeans had great significance for the first appearance of capitalism and its further expansion, if the entire continent of Europe is taken into consideration. Only its significance is to be evaluated differently. For those capitalists like the German, French, Dutch and the English, who were already on the way to the developing into commercial, mercantile, industrial capitalists, the discovery not only of America but also of the sea routes to Africa and Asia were a progressive occurrence.

In this context it's not only about the entrepreneurs but also and perhaps, above all, about the labourers, who in the town during the capitalist period were exploited more than in the Middle Ages. This increase in exploitation awakened the impression in O. Johannsen and F.M. Feldhaus, also in Johann Janssen and Vilfredo Pareto that the hour of class struggles had struck only with the beginning of capitalism. What these people asserted, is not entirely true, nor is it false. They have only exaggerated their judgment.

Capitalism as a system created more jobs as well as more mental and physical movement for the working class.

Mental activity is closely linked with bodily movement in modern times. People travel to America, Africa and Asia. They discover new sea routes and develop the new arts of seafaring and with them the instruments for measuring time. Peasants set themselves in motion, as do poets, painters, physicians, miners and mathematicians in equal measure.

The discovery of America constitutes a part of these movements. The search for money, the voracious appetite for gold—*auri sacra fames*—, the search for new jobs, the discovery of what is for the Europeans new worlds, the discovery of antiquity and their spiritual riches occur at the same time. At the same time as Columbus had discovered America, Petrarch, Dürer, Vasari, Regiomontan discovered antiquity. At this same time Pacioli, Micheal Stifel and Adam Ries took up arithmetic from India and Persia, and Regiomontan and Albrecht Dürer brought geometry from antiquity and from the Near East to Germany.

For those countries which had attained a weakly developed level of capitalism, the discovery of America did not signify any enrichment, but rather the exploitation of their country by those who had attained a more powerful economic position. Only in the 20th century was Spain able to alter this relationship.

For Central Europe the discovery of America had a deep-reaching effect on the mining industry. The sizeable development of mining in Germany, Austria, Bohemia, Moravia and Hungary did not come to a halt, but was constricted by the importation of American precious and non-ferrous metals. Only the richest mines, like, for example, in Joachimsthal, could survive in competition with Mexican gold, silver and copper. The poorer European pits containing metals were abandoned. The transition to iron mining followed in the second half of the period. The bituminous coal industry and its connection to iron and steel in a major industrial enterprise was first assembled in the period of high capitalism.

Right at the beginning of the capitalist era the importation of cotton of Mexican and later of North American provenance was of great importance for the production of cloth made of fustian, among others. The importation of new species for planting from America, like potatoes, tomatoes, corn and some types of squash, was undertaken first in the second half of the 18th century and later. Agriculture in Central Europe was fundamentally changed by the planting of potatoes, not so much by tomatoes and corn.

For the Italians corn in the form of polenta, for the Rumanians in the form of mameliga, was an important food; for the Germans on the contrary, corn was not important. Sugar cane was significant as a source of sugar, and drinks made of sugar, syrup and molasses were significant in Central Europe for trade and consumption, not for planting. Cocoa and coffee were likewise imported from America for the preparation of drinks, without exerting an effect on the agriculture of Europe, for these kinds of plants were only suitable for tropical and subtropical climatic conditions.

Persia and India had a large economic significance in the first centuries of the modern bourgeois period for the Dutch and the English, not for the Germans.

Johann Albrecht von Mandelslo and Adam Olearius published their genial descriptions of their journeys in the middle of the 17th century (J.A. Mandelslo *Morgenländische Reyse Beschreibung*. Schleswig 1658. Adam Olearius, *Moskowitische und Persische Reise*. Schleswig 1656). Both journeys were officially compelled, just as the contemporary journeys of Sir Thomas Roe from England. The journey of François Bernier to Mogulistan was not official, but the publication of his book (*Voyages, contenant la description des Etats du Grand Mogol*, 1670) was dedicated to the French minister and mercantilist Colbert. William Methold from England, Joost Schouten from Holland and many other private people published journey books in the 17th century. (See Lawrence Krader, *Die asiatische Produktionsweise*, in: *Antworten auf Bahros Herausforderung des "realen Sozialismus"* Ulf Walter (ed.) Olle und Walter, Berlin 1978, pp. 100–127; idem. *The Asiatic Mode of Production*. Assen 1976; idem. *Il despotismo orientale*. Rom. Enciclopedia della scienze sociale. 1996).

The effects of the travels of Roe, Methold, Bernier, and Schouten were closely bound up with trade. The English and the Dutch founded their East Indian Companies in the 17th century and accomplished many trade voyages. The books of Olearius and by Mandelslo are both literarily appealing, but in practice, the princes in Germany did not engage in trade with the West. A few colonies, in what is today the State of Pennsylvania, were established by the Germans in the 17th century, however, their impact on further colonization and on world trade was limited and of little significance in comparison to the Dutch, English, Spanish, Portuguese and French enterprises of this kind. It can be asserted that the discoveries in America, Africa and Asia by the Europeans had a mediated and not an immediate effect on the development of capitalism in Central Europe in the early centuries of the modern period. The Italians, Columbus and Amerigo Vespucci discovered America, however, exploitation in further relations to America took place by other countries.

A look beyond the borders of Central Europe will clearly show that the establishment of modern bourgeois society and the beginnings of the capitalist system cannot be imputed to any single country. Many countries, around the same time in Southern, Central and Western Europe, contributed to the fact that the medieval economy and society in the 15th, 16th and 17th century were substantially, although not formally pushed back. The victory of the capitalist system in the formal system of the bourgeois state and law extends across the entire era of the modern period from the 15th to the 20th century. The struggle for the formalities and the defeat of the old prerogatives took much longer and were much more complicated than the rational advance of the economic system. The victory of the new system can also not be imputed to a single historical moment. The liberation of the peasants is an essential moment in this regard, as are the training and the increasing qualification of the working class in the mastering of new machinery. A further such moment is the increase in entrepreneurial activity of the middle class.

All social classes and groups took up the struggle against the old feudal lords and the Church, only it came to pass that some wealthy people from the middle class deserted to the nobility as soon as they could buy title and landed property.

Then all the wealthy people said that the struggle against poverty was not their affair but rather that of society, the Church and the state as a whole.

The various authorities, which we have cited, give emphasis to various single factors in the transition from the old to the new system of economy and society. Weber together with Kulischer, names in this regard the Protestants, Sombart the Jews and together along with them Brentano, von Below and Schumpeter, the entrepreneurial class. What they have contributed is not false—but in each case insufficient. Regarding the treatment of the problem of transition, Marx had recommended some moments, for example, the expulsion of the peasants from the land, among others. Other moments, such as the class struggles and the movement of liberation of the peasants, on the contrary, he left out.

The transformation of feudalism, of fiefdom and of the medieval church had caused great suffering and devastation in the life of the people. The religious wars of the 15th and 16th century in Bohemia, Germany, France, the Netherlands and Spain, of the Sacco di Roma in the year 1527, the Thirty Years' War and the expulsion of the Huguenots from France were not isolated but rather reciprocally determining events. Max Weber steered attention to the Protestants in the founding process of the capitalist epoch. Protestants in the middle class led commerce in the domestic market and in foreign trade, and the Calvinists among them accumulated capital through their thrift. The middle class was not only strengthened by Calvinism in Germany but rather also by the Huguenots. The latter emigrated from their stronghold in La Rochelle and in Nantes in Western France to settle in England, the Netherlands and Germany. They advanced qualified labour in the textile industry, in the metal processing industry, in the merchant class and in commerce, in the working class as well as in the middle class. The nobles among the Huguenots had joined the German nobility. France lost much through its politics, and capitalism in the 17th century was not driven by the men of state after the expulsion of the Huguenots, but rather was guided by them. This double-sided activity in the French economy had drawn to it the attempt from the side of such men of state as Colbert to engage the merchants in service to the interests of the state.

From the side of the state and statesmen this attempt found its expression in mercantilism. The weaknesses in the development of capitalism in France during the 16th and 17th century, resulting from the expulsion of the Huguenots, were damaging—loss of trained labourers, particularly in the textile enterprises and in the metal industry, and losses in the merchant class. Mercantilist politics followed in their train. Adam Smith had sharply criticized both political practices in the 18th century, yet the politics of the economy of *dirigisme* remained powerful in France.

The peasant uprisings in England in the 14th century and the civil war in the 17th century contributed much to the establishment of modern bourgeois society and of the capitalist system in that country. Both moments will not explain everything, but they played a large role in the development of the capitalist economy and of bourgeois politics. To this is to be added the activities of the German mine manager (Anglice Barmaster), the resettlement of a branch of the French Huguenots, the admittance of the Jews by Oliver Cromwell and the great wave of colonization and colonialism in North America, India, the West Indies and elsewhere. All these factors, together with the wealth in iron and hard coal, with the training of the working class and technical developments, led to the Industrial Revolution of the 18th and to high capitalism in the 19th century.

Capitalism was established by the total activities of the peasants, the town working class and the entrepreneurs. These activities were carried out not through the common consciousness, but rather separated in the various social classes in the different countries. Thus, one cannot speak of a unitary revolution but rather of several waves of activity independent of one another. The linking of the aspirations for wage labour, for capital, for freedom and equality was taken up sporadically in the 15th and 16th century, systematically as capitalistic activities, as wage labour and accumulation of capital in the 18th, 19th and 20th century.

The connections between districts and localities as well as between industries and their branches were strengthened with increasing intercourse in modern times through the spread of literacy and of the art of printing and through the unification of the universal legal system. It is here that the social and economic foundations for the system of the nation states of modern bourgeois society are to be found.

The economy raised its productivity, the sum of products, the wealth of society and the variety of that which was produced.

The capitalist system did not solve the problem of poverty but treated it in two ways. First, poverty is recognized as a social problem, and civil society as a whole, not the Church on its own, is challenged to solve it. Second, and primarily the problem of poverty in bourgeois society was parried by pushing it, sweeping it first and foremost into the deprived areas of the town and into the colonies.

Since the epochs of the colonial victories and of high capitalism from the 18th to the early 20th century the Europeans arrogantly over-estimated their position in the human world. Yet, this was not always the case. In antiquity, the Celts, Germans, Slavs and other peoples of Europe were considered by scholars in the Eastern Mediterranean as primitive, so to speak. They were unable to read or write. In the early Middle Ages, this rough assessment had not essentially improved. Only in the late Middle Ages with the increase in commerce, and to some extent of production and the money economy as well could this situation be changed. In the interim, the Islamic powers broadened their capacities and finally overtaxed them.

When the Europeans had retreated after the defeats in the Crusades, the Muslim conquerors surrendered the Iberian Peninsula, Sicily and large parts of the Balkan region. Yet military-political superiority in this case was insufficient. In Spain, the Islamic epoch in architecture, in art and in science was resplendent in world history, the impact of European culture on the Near East in the Crusades was, on the contrary, really meager. By means of this comparison the judgment can be made how low Europe stood in art and science and as a world power to the beginning of the modern period.

The mathematical sciences in their history had a close tie to the merchant class, to labour in the workshop as well as to statecraft, for instance in the collection of taxes and in the art of war. Dürer applied geometry to sculpting and the architecture of the fortress, Leonardo da Vinci to the same and to water canals. We do not follow the historical course of these great events further, but rather sketch developments in mathematics in connection with economic and cultural history. European mathematics was at first dependent on the mathematics in the Near East. Leonardo da Pisa (also called Fibonacci or Bignolli) had made business trips to Egypt, Syria and Algeria, where he had learned the Indo-Arabian numerals and written and disseminated the books *Liber abbacci* (1202) and *Liber quadratorum* (1225). They were not books, in our sense, but rather in the medieval one. He also published his *Practica Geometricae* and a book on mathematics, which he entitled *Flos*. In these books he employed equations and solutions with unknowns to the calculation of debts with negative solutions, that is negative numbers. He also mastered the quadratic as well as some diophantine equations. His mode of treatment is traced back to the methodology of al-Khwarizmi, to that of the Hebrew *Misnat ha-Middot* and further to the work in Sanskrit of Brahma gupta and Aryabhata. This mathematical tradition was concerned with questions regarding the calendar, with the movement of the sun and the moon in relation to the reckoning of space and time and with the beginnings of algebra and algorisms (see Al-Khwarizmi, above). Terminology and calculation were in this mathematical tradition rhetorically executed; concrete questions were solved; pure mathematical notation was not yet developed. Al-Khwarizmi's main questions are related in one book to the distribution of inheritances. The astronomical tables were continued by him.

Leonardo da Pisa had further developed those kinds of mathematical treatment and their results; his accomplishments were recognized by the city of Pisa with a sum of 20 pounds annually and sundry emoluments. In mathematics and in the history of the merchant class he remained, however, a singular phenomenon. He had no immediate successor, and practices in mathematics, in the merchant class and in statecraft of the 13th and 14th century were not essentially changed through his great knowledge and contributions, let alone developed. Master Dardi of Pisa was active at this time (1344).

Only in the 15th century, through the Florentine Masters, Master Benedetto, Master Biaggio and Master Antonio Mazzinghi, did it come to a stirring development in arithmetical practice, not, however, in the theories.

Great progress in this connection was made by Luca Pacioli. His work was printed in a book, *Summa arithmetica, geometria, proportioni e proportionalita* in Venice in 1494; it was crowned with great success and appeared in the Italian language with algebraic notation. The work is mainly related to general rules, which were useful not only for the mathematicians, but also for merchants and working people, astronomers, state chancelleries, and so on. He calculated with roots as well as with quadratic and cubic equations and with unknowns. He had access to the classical Greek and to the Western mathematicians.

It can be asserted, that in contrast to Fibonacci, the impact of Pacioli was closely related to his surroundings. Shortly thereafter, Scipione del Ferro, Tartaglia, Cardano, Ferrari, Bombelli among others came to solutions of the cubic and biquadratic equations in the course of the 16th century. Modern notation was further developed by M. Stiefel, Chr. Rudolff among others, and all of these works were also published in Italy and Germany, so that they appeared as books in the modern sense.

The focal point of this sketch does not rest on the relationship of talented mathematicians, astronomers, merchants and master workers to one another, but rather on the changes and developments in the European economy and society from the 13th century, the time of Fibonacci to the 15th century, the time of Pacioli. Only in the 15th century were the Italians, the Germans and other European peoples of the North and West in the position to understand the new mathematical practices, to apply them to economic practice, to comprehend them abstractly to a certain extent and to develop them further.

The art of printing was widespread at that time in Central and Upper Germany, in Upper Italy and in the Netherlands; commerce, production in mining and in the metal industry, in trade and in the merchant class, education and literacy, science and the art of arithmetic and the fine arts and productivity, in general, grew. Further, circles in northern and southern Europe expanded and deepened their relations quantitatively as well as qualitatively through increasing traffic in the economic and in the intellectual realm. The impact of these developments in economic life, in the arts and sciences are concretized at the end of the 20th century through the desire of the European powers to be recognized as great powers were in the past. Out of irrational grounds reason comes forth.[1]

The shareholders in mining were mostly workers and members of the middle class simultaneously, thus mediators between the process of production and distribution and the authorities. The council was the mediator between the town and authorities as well as between the guild system and town life. Many landowners and aristocrats were active as mediators in this regard, and the authorities in Saxony had inserted themselves on the side of the distributors regarding the new methods in cloth production.

The roles of individuals, whether progressive or reactionary, are complicated and always difficult to measure. Nevertheless, the progression of capitalism and of bourgeois society can first sporadically, and thereafter systematically, be judged objectively. Originally its representatives, such as Dürer, were satisfied with this advance and optimistic with respect to its future, but at the end of the beginning period Goethe hinted at other paths for humanity than those which his epoch was following.

Capitalism is founded on wage labour and on the appropriation of capital, capital investment and capital accumulation. The same laws of wage labour and capital are valid for the beginning period of capitalism as they are for the present. Capitalists, wage labourers and capital as well as their laws were there in classical antiquity and in the Middle Ages, but not the system and not to the same extent of wage labour and capital as in the capitalist period. Capitalism, modern bourgeois society, the epoch of modernity, which cover one another and fall together, began in the middle of the 15th century in Europe north of the Alps. Capitalism did not arise as a social and economic system and era like a living being or as a divine figure at one time and in one place. Rather it arose as a cultural system at several locations and over a long period of time and out of the relations and contexts of many peoples, towns and natural conditions. The first steps on the road to capitalism were made in the towns of northern Italy, in Venice, Florence, Pisa, Lucca and in Genoa in the 13th to the 15th century. Commerce, banks and production in this archeo-capitalist period were small in their extent; they were operated by the nobility of the medieval kind, like for example, the Duke of Milan, and were guarded by the Church. Money was lent, instruments of credit were brought out, and the lending rate was fixed, but the Church preached against usury. In traffic with the Near East the northern Italians served as mediators at the time. It was here that the important preconditions for the beginnings of capitalism were developed.

For the starting point of the capitalist era, the towns of northern Italy were important in another sense. People of the modern era, like Jacob Fugger, Regiomontan, Albrecht Dürer, Copernicus, Agricola, went there to work and to learn. What followed from this was the expansion, the qualitative reforming and the systematization of the processes of commerce and production, of wage labour and capital in northern Europe.

The beginnings of capitalism are to be traced back to the mutually supporting activities in the different branches of industry, especially in mining, in the processing of metal in the towns, in seafaring, in the printing industry, and in the practices of merchandizing and finance. With some exceptions—to them is reckoned primarily sea travel in the region of the Mediterranean—the operations of commerce, banking, ore, metal, printing and transportation of the early capitalist period were led by private undertakings.

The beginnings of capitalism as a system in Europe on both sides of the Alps are thus to be sought in the cities of northern Italy, Upper Germany, the Netherlands and England, in the mines in the Upper Palatinate and in the Harz region, in the towns of the printing industry, Mainz and Strasbourg. In this connection it is not about the mercantile and financial undertakings alone. Customarily the history of capitalism is divided into two main epochs, the first of which was designated the epoch of mercantile capitalism down to the 18th century, the following period was that of industrial capitalism. For this attempt at periodization the industrialization of capitalism in the closing years of the 18th and the early years of the 19th century are supposed to be decisive. There was a quantitative difference between the two epochs and we fundamentally agree with this periodization, yet on another ground. We understand that the pivotal element of the transition from the Middle Ages to modern times is the work of mining in the 15th century, which belongs not to the commercial branch but rather to the industrial branch of the economic system. The work of mining is linked with coinage, with money and the circulation of money, the printing industry, with armories and with sea travel. The organization of factories, the division of labour, the steady introduction of new inventions in mining machinery, the buying and selling of mining shares are rather more quantitatively than qualitatively to be distinguished from those in the enterprises of the following epoch in the history of capitalism.

Considered from the cultural-historical standpoint, the capitalist epoch is earth-shaking. The exploitation of the workers is intensified; by contrast the working class was freed from the feudal yoke. The peasants and most of the labourers in the town are to be considered unfree in the Middle Ages. In the modern period labour was expanded. The rights of the wage labourer as a class are related to the freedom and equality of contract and the freedom of movement. Only in the capitalist period did the workers secure these rights for themselves. In classical antiquity and in the Middle Ages the labourers were mainly slaves, serfs, or they were bound in some other way. For the freedom of the working class then, in capitalism, the freedoms of mining served as an example and as a general template. Hereafter the peasants asserted their freedom. The mining works were driven by wage labour and capital at that time.

The processing of metal in the workshops is distinguished in the magnitude of the operations from those in the epoch of high capitalism. In both cases the organization of labour was rationalized; in one workshop various products were produced. Thus, the tinsmiths created not only clasps, but rather also bric-a-brac of brass or simple tin. The bric-a-brac again is not only a plaything, and therefore the work of the great lexicographers Matthias Lexer and Moriz Heyne is to be supplemented here. Lexer (Grimm, *Deutsches Wörterbuch,* XI/I) writes (here concisely presented): "brica-a-brac [*Tand*]: idle talk, also a negligible plaything." However, the bric-a-brac was for the merchants everywhere in Europe indispensable. With it, they added, subtracted and kept their books. This is the meaning of the sentence: *Nürnberger Tand geht durch alle Land* [brica-a-brac from Nuremberg goes through every country]—for the calculation or arithmetic pennies [*Rechenpfennige*] and the bric-a-brac are one and the same.

The ore from the local mining works, its transport into the nearby towns and the processing of metal there did not alone create the foundation for capitalism, but the presence of natural materials, of labour power and labour tradition and of capital was of fundamental significance for its formation.

No less significant was the wood, which was derived from the northern European virgin forest; technics was based on wood in early capitalism. Machinery in mining, in the construction of houses and workshops, ships and carriages, were based on wood; fire for the processing of metal, for the kitchen and heating was made from wood. The virgin forest and the ore of northern Europe served as the material foundation of modern bourgeois society. Cloth was woven out of wool and linen. Cotton was imported from the East; it was increasingly used in the production of clothes made of fustian, a stuff made of cotton and linen.

The great difference between the forerunners of capitalism in the late Middle Ages and the capitalism in the 15th century is to be sought in the extent of economic activity in modern times in contrast to the same in the previous period. The presence and extent of money and of the circulation of money, of the economic enterprises and the discoveries of the bourgeois period have their source in the organization and spread of wage labour and capital. The new industries of printing and seafaring were introduced, the new organization of labour and the division of labour were further developed, and the arable land and the towns were extended. Ore and virgin forest disappeared.

Note

1. Fibonacci and Pacioli, see: J. Tropfke, *Geschichte der Elementarmathematik*. B.L. v.d. Waerden, *A History of Algebra*, 1985.

Capitalism and Developed Culture

The beginning of the bourgeois epoch is characterized by a great intellectual activity in art, natural science and mathematics. This is veiled by the words Renaissance, *Rinascimento*, and so on. Rather, in intellectual activity as well as in social and economic life, the peoples of northern Europe grew into a developed culture in the capitalist period. The opposite side of this developmental process consists in the fact that in the capitalist period it was asked how much everything costs: the natural material, the commodity, human life. Every being, inorganic and living, is measured according to its quantitative value.

In the whole of world history, developed culture is determined by three processes: first by the establishment of the big cities, second by the establishment of the state and third, by the introduction of writing into the colloquial language of the people. Measured by these determinations, modern bourgeois society in northern Europe counts as a developed culture. The Middle Ages presents itself as the period of transition to the developed culture in Europe in the capitalist period. The medieval states of northern Europe were small in relation to the numbers in the population, and the extent of their activities was limited in relation to those in the cities of the East; the system of state was weak through the contradictions of its centripetal and centrifugal tendencies, and writing in the colloquial languages first experienced its hours of birth. In antiquity there was no developed culture in the European region at all. When Marco Polo reported on the cities in the Orient, his audience laughed at his remarks and called the world traveller *Marco Millions*. They believed that he exaggerated everything, and they could not understand that there were such large cities in the world. In Europe the largest city in 1550 was Naples with a population of 210,000 inhabitants; there was no city of this size in northern Europe. The medieval state of northern Europe was unusual in comparison to that in ancient China, in Persia, Rome, Byzantium as well as in comparison to the state of modern times on account of the above-mentioned contradictions. The large cities, the unified and centralized state power and writing in the indigenous languages of northern Europe, developed only in modern bourgeois society. The result of this process is—for the first time in the history of northern Europe—the origin of a culture characterized by the features mentioned, whose foundation, the systematization and expansion of capital and of wage labour, has been outlined here.

From the Social Contract to the Concept of Society in the Capitalist Period

Society—Latin *societas*—can also be considered as a cooperative [*Genossenschaft*]. Among other things, society had functioned as an association of merchants. These men of commerce were in part travelling comrades on commercial journeys, yet their undertakings were in no way in common: the number of enterprises corresponded to the number of merchants—from Roman times to the beginnings of the capitalist period. The associated persons thus formed a corporation neither in the classical nor in the modern sense of the word; they had no common liability, and after the commercial journey, the company was normally dissolved without remainder. Profit and loss were to the account of the individual merchant, for the group had no common capital. Property was present; however, it was only maintained and imputed to the singular individual. The travelling companions shared danger and bread hence they were *cum pane*—compagnons, company, *compañeros*, *Kumpel*; they reciprocally protected one another on the journey, and they established rules against internal and external thievery. The society of the *Social Contract* (in the 17th and 18th century till Rousseau and Kant) had little in common with the society or company as a commercial enterprise or commercial company. Yet, the society or company was conceived of in the sense of an association for the distribution of bread and for the sociality of the fellow travellers, for the defense of the group as well as for the maintenance of internal peace; they offered themselves as a model of social life in the capitalist period. This society was conceived of as an association of individualities, hence as a minimum of social life. Society in this historical process manifests two developmental lines: the one, which leads to the company with limited liability (GmbH, Ltd.), the other, as the by-product of *societas* in the sense of a commercial or trading company, to the general concept of society. The social contract has fallen away.

Bibliography

Translator's Note: References preceded by an * indicate translator's bibliographic additions to the text.

Abel, W. *Geschichte des deutschen Bauernstandes*, 2. Aufl., Stuttgart 1974.

———. *Handbuch der deutschen Wirtschafts- und Sozialgeschichte,* Bd. 1, 1971, Kapitel 13, 20.

———. *Agrarkrisen und Agrarkonjunktur in Mitteleuropa vom 13. bis zum 19. Jahrhundert* (1935), 3. Aufl., Hamburg 1978.

———. *Geschichte der deutschen Landwirtschaft*, 3. Aufl., Stuttgart 1978.

D'Addio, M. *L'Idea del contratto sociale dai sofisti alla riforma e il 'De Principatu' di Mario Salamonio*, 1954.

Agricola, G. *De Bello adversus Turcam*, Basel 1528 (In German: *Oration, Anrede und Vormannunge... wider den Türcken*. L. Berman translator, Nürnberg 1530).

———. *De Re Metallica (Zwölf Bücher vom Berg—und Hüttenwesen)*, Basel 1556 (posthum).

Alberti, L. B. *De Re Aedificatoria (Von der Baukunst)* 1 450 vollendet und 1 485 posthum gedruckt.

Arendt. A. Bergbau, *Handwörterbuch der Staatswissenschaften*, 3. Aufl., Fischer Verlag Jena 1909.

Aristoteles. *Nikomachische Ethik*, Buch V.

———. *Physik.*

———. *Poetik.*

———. *Politik* I.

Arnold, P. u. W. Quellmolz. *Sächsisch-Thüringische Bergbaugepräge*, VEB Dt. Verlag für Grundstoffindustrie Leipzig 1978.

Baldwin, J. W. 'The medieval theories of the just price.' *Transactions of the American Philosophical Society*, N.F., Vol. 49., Part 4., 1959.

Bath, B. H. Slicher v. In: *Cambridge Economic History of Europe*, Bd. 5., Cambridge University Press Cambridge 1977.

Battisti, C. & G. Alessio. *Dizionario etimologico italiano*, Barbèra Florenz 1951.

Baumann, J. J. *Die Lehren von Raum, Zeit und Mathematik*, 1. Bd. Reimer Berlin 1868. Minerva Frankfurt am Main 1981.

Bechtel, H. *Wirtschaftsgeschichte Deutschlands*, Vol. 1, Georg Callway München 1952.

Beck, L. *Geschichte des Eisens*, Friedrich Viehweg und Sohn Braunschweig 1884–1903, Bd. II.

Below, G. von. *Probleme der Wirtschaftsgeschichte*, Mohr Tübingen 1926.

Biringuccio, V. De la Pirotechnia, Bari; 0. Johannsen, Obers.: *Die zehn Bucher van der Feuerwerkskunst*, Viehweg Verlag Braunschweig 1925.

Blum, R. *Der Proceß Fust gegen Gutenberg*, Harrassowtiz Wiesbaden 1954.

Boas, M. 'The Establishment of the Mechanical Philosophy,' *Osiris*, Bd. 10., 1952.

Borkenau, F. 'Zur Soziologie des mechanistischen Weltbildes,' *Zeitschrift für Sozialforschung*, Jahrgang I, 1932.

———. *Der Übergang vom feudalen zum bürgerlichen Weltbild*, Felix Alcan Paris 1934, Repr. Wissenschaftliche Buchgesellschaft Darmstadt 1971.

Botero, G. *Delle Cause della Grandezza delle Città*, 1596.

Braudel, F. *Civilisation matérielle, économie et capitalisme, XVe-XVlll^e^ siècle*, Armand Colin Paris 1979 (dt. *Sozialgeschichte des 15—18. Jahrhunderts*, 3 Bde., Kindler München 1985/86).

Brentano, L. *Die Anfänge des modernen Kapitalismus*, Verlag der K. B. Akademie der Wissenschaften in Kommission des G. Franz'schen Verlags München 1916.

Brunner, O. Das "ganze Haus" und die alteuropäische „Ökonomik", in *Neue Wege der Verfassungs— und Sozialgeschichte*, 2. Aufl., Vandenhoeck u. Ruprecht Göttingen, 1968.

Brunschwygk, H. *Liber de arte destillandi de simplicibus* (*Das Buch der rechten Kunst zu distilieren die eintzigen Ding*) 1497.

———. *Chirurgie*, 1500.

———. *Liber pestilentiolis de venenis epidimie* (*Das Buch der Vergift der Pestilenz*), 1500.

Bücher, K. *Die Bevölkerung von Frankfurt Main im XIV. und XV. Jahrhundert*, Laupp Tübingen 1886.

Cassirer, E. *Individuum und Kosmos in der Philosophie der Renaissance*, B.G. Taubner Leipzig und Berlin 1927.

Cipolla, C. M. *Before the Industrial Revolution. European Society and Economy 1000–1700*, Methuen London 1976.

———. *Clocks and Culture*, Norton New York 1978.

Clapham, M. In: C. Singer et al. (Hrsg.), *A History of Technology*, Bd. III, Oxford University Press Oxford 1958.

Dantzig, T. *Number*, 4th ed., The Free Press New York 1954.

Darwin, Ch. *The Origin of Species*, John Murray London 1859.

Daumas, M. *Histoire générale des techniques*, Bd. I, Introduction, Presses Universitaires de France Paris 1962.

Davis, J. P. *Corporations* (1905), New York 1961.

del Mante, G. *Mechanicorum liber* in 1577.

Deloney, T. *The Story of John Winchcombe, Commonly Called Jack of Newbury*, 1597.

Depping, S. *Les juifs au moyen age*, Knapen fils Paris 1834.

Dietrichs, K. *Die Buchdruckpresse*, Mainz 1930.

Dijksterhuis, E. J. *Die Mechanisierung des Weltbildes*, Springer Berlin 1983.

Dobb, M. *Studies in the Development of Capitalism*, Routledge, London 1975 (dt. *Entwicklung des Kapitalismus vom Spätmittelalter bis zur Gegenwart*, 1979).

Dollinger, P. *Die Hanse*, 3. Aufl., Kroener Alfred Gmbh Stuttgart 1981.

Duhem, P. *L'évolution de la mécanique*, A. Hermann Paris 1905.

Dürer, A. *Unterweisung der Messung mit dem Zirkel und Richtscheit in Linien, Ebenen und ganzen Korporen*, Nürnberg 1525.

———. *Etliche Unterricht zu Befestigung der Städte, Schloss und Flechen*, Nürnberg 1527.

Ehrenberg, R. *Das Zeitalter der Fugger*, Gustav Fischer Jena 1896, Bd. 1.

Elkar, R. S. 'Umrisse einer Geschichte der Gesellenwanderungen,' in: R. S. Elkar (ed.), *Neuzeit*, O. Schwartz Göttingen 1983.

Ellul, J. *La technique ou l'enjeu du siècle*, A. Colin Paris 1954.

———. *Le système technicien*, Calmann-Lévy Paris 1977.

Endres, R. Einwohnerzahl und Bevölkerungsstruktur Nürnbergs im 15./16. Jahrhundert. *Mitteilungen des Vereins für Geschichte der Stadt Nürnberg*, Bd. 57, 1970.

Engels, F. *Der deutsche Bauernkrieg* (1850), 3. Aufl., 1875.

Ercker, L. *Beschreibung: Allerfürnemsten Mineralischen Erzt/ unnd Berckwercksarten/ wie dieselbigen/ unnd eine jede in sonderheit/ irer natur und eigenschafft noch/ auff alle Metaln Probirt/ und im kleinen fewer sollen versucht werden/ mit erklerung etlicher fürnehmen nützlichen Schmeltzwerken im grossen fewer/ auch Schaidung, Goldt/ Silber unnd andere Metalln/ Sampt einem bericht des Kupfer saigerns/ Messing brennens/ unnd Salpeter siedens, auch aller saltzigen Minerischen proben/ und was denen allen anhengig in fünff Bücher verfast/ Dergleichen zuvorn niemals in Druck kommen. Allen liebhabern der Fewer künste/ jungen Probirern/ unnd Bercklеuten zu nutz/ mit schönen Figuren unnd abriß der Instrument/ trewlich unnd fleissig an Tag geben. Durch/ Lazarus Erckern*, Prag 1574. 2. Aufl., Frankfurt Main 1580, in Verlegung Sigmund Feyerabends. P. R. Beierlein (Hrsg.), Berlin 1960.

Eulenberg, F. 'Berufs—und Gewerbestatistik Heidelbergs im 16. Jahrhundert,' *Zeitschrift für die Geschichte des Oberrheins*, N.F. Bd. 11, 1896.

Fechner, G. T. *Über die physikalische und philosophische Atomenlehre*, 2. Aufl., Leipzig 1864.

Feldhaus, F. M. *Die Technik*, Athenaion Potsdam 1931.

———. *Der Weg in die Technik*, Seemann Leipzig 1935.

———. *Die Maschine im Leben der Völker*, Birkhäuser Basel 1954.

———. *Die Technik der Antike und des Mittelalters*, Repr. Olms 1971.

Feuerbach, L. *Das Wesen des Christenthums*, 1841.

Flinn, M. W. & D. Stoker. *The History of the British Coal Industry*. Vol. 2, 1700–1830. Oxford University Press Oxford 1985.

Forbes, R. J. *Man the Maker*, Abelard Schumann London 1958.

Franck, S. *Deutsche Chronik*, 1538.

Franz, G. *Der Dreißigjährige Krieg und das deutsche Volk*, 3. Aufl., G. Fischer Stuttgart 1961.

———. *Quellen zur Geschichte des Bouernkrieges*, Munchen 1963. *Der deutsche Bauernkrieg*, 10. Aufl., Darmstadt 1975.

———. *Geschichte des deutschen Bauernstandes*, 2. Aufl., Stuttgart 1976.

Furger, F. *Zum Verlagssystem als Organisationsform des Frühkapitalismus im Textilgewerbe*, H. Kohlhammer Stuttgart 1927.

Gierke, O. *Political Theories of the Middle Ages*, translated with an Introduction by Frederic William Maitland, Cambridge, Cambridge University Press 1900.

———. *Das deutsche Genossenschaftsrecht*, 4 Bde. (repr.) Akademische Druck und Verlagsanstalt Graz 1954.

———. *Die Genossenschaftstheorie und die deutsche Rechtsprechung* (1887), Graz 1963.

Goldstein, H. *Klassische Mechanik*, 8. Aufl. Wissenschaftliche Buchgesellschft Darmstadt 1985.

Goltz, T. von der. *Geschichte der deutschen Landwirtschaft* Verlag Cotta Stuttgart 1902, Scientia-Verlag Aalen 1963.

Grammateus. *Buchhaltung durch Zornal (Kaufmannsbuch) Kaps (Warenbuch) und Schuldbuch*, 1549.

Grimm. *Wörterbuch*.

Grossmann, H. *Handwörterbuch der Staatswissenschaften*. J. Conrad et al. (Hrsg.), 3. Aufl., Gustav Fischer Jena1911 (Stichwort Gemeinheitsteilung). Ebd. W. Lexis, (Stichwort Abbau).

———. 'Die gesellschaftlichen Grundlagen der mechanistischen Philosophie und die Manufaktur,' *Zeitschrift für Sozialforschung*, Jahrgang V, 1935.

Grotius, H. *De Jure Belli ac Pacis* (*Vom Recht des Krieges und des Friedens*) 1625.

Habermas, J. *Technik und Wissenschaft als "Ideologie"*, Suhrkamp Frankfurt am Main 1968.

Haguenauer, S. *Das justum pretium bei Thomas Aquinas*, Kohlhammer Stuttgart 1931.

Hasemann, J. G. in: *Ersch und Gruber, Encyklopädie*, Brockhaus Leipzig 1853.

Haussherr, H. *Wirtschaftsgeschichte der Neuzeit vom Ende des 14. bis zur Höhe des 19. Jahrhunderts*, 4. Aufl., Böhlau Köln 1970.

Hegel, G. W. F. *Die Verfassung Deutschlands*, 1802.

———. *Rechtsphilosophie*, 1821.

———. *Enzyklopädie der Philosophischen Wissenschaften*, 1830, 3. Teil.

———. *Vorlesungen über die Philosophie der Geschichte*, Sämtliche Werke, 11. Band, Stuttgart 1949.

———. *Vorlesungen über die Philosophie der Weltgeschichte*, J. Hoffmeister (Hrsg.), Bd. 4, Hamburg 1968.

Hegel, K. *Städte und Gilden der germanischen Völker im Mittelalter*, Bd. 2, Duncker und Humblot Leipzig 1891.

Helleiner, K. In: *Cambridge Economic History of Europe*, 5.4., Cambridge University Press Cambridge 1967.

Helmont, J. B. van. *Annals of Science*, Bd. I, 1938.

Hesse, M. B. [*Über die Korpuskular-Theorie*] *Forces and Fields*, Greenwood Westport 1970.

Hicks, J. *A Theory of Economic History*, Oxford University Press Oxford 1973.

Hintze, O. *Kalvinismus und Staatsräson in Brandenburg, Gesammelte Abhandlungen* 3. 1943.

Hobbes, T. *Leviathan*, 1651.

Hübinger, P. E. (ed.). *Zur Bedeutung und Rolle des Islam*, Wissenschaftliche Buchgesellschaft Darmstadt, 1968.

Ifrah, G. *Universalgeschichte der Zahlen*, 2. Aufl., Campus Verlag Frankfurt am Main 1978.

Inoma-Sternegg, K. T. v. 'Bevölkerung,' in Conrad et al. (eds.) *Handwörterbuch der Staatswissenschaften* 3. Auflage Fischer Verlag Jena 1909.

———. *Deutsche Wirtschaftsgeschichte*, Duncker und Humblot Leipzig Bd. 3, 1. 1899.

Irsigler, F. 'Zur Problematik der Gilde—und Zunftterminologie,' 15772-Artikeltext—35787-1-10-20140819.pdf.

Janssen, J. *Geschichte des deutschen Volkes seit dem Ausgang des Mittelalters*, 19. Aufl., Bd. 1, Herder Freiburg.

Johannsen, O. *Geschichte des Eisens*, 3. Aufl., Verlag Stahleisen Düsseldorf 1953.

Kant, I. *Metaphysische Anfangsgründe der Naturwissenschaft*, 1786.

———. *Kritik der reinen Vernunft*, 1. Aufl., 1781.

Kapp, E. *Grundlinien einer Philosophie der Technik. Zur Entstehungsgeschichte der Cultur* Georg Westermann Braunschweig 1877, VDI-Verlag Düsseldorf 1978, Einleitung: H.-M. Sass.

Kaps, A. *Deutsche Schriftkunst*, Verlag der Kunst Dresden 1955.

Karlgren, B. *Analytic Dictionary of Chinese and Sino-Japanese*, P. Geuthner Paris 1923.

Kaser, M. *Das römische Privatrecht*, 2. Aufl., C. H. Beck München 1971.

Kaulla, R. „Die Lehre vom gerechten Preis". *Zeitschrift für die gesamte Staatswissenschaft*, 1904.

———. *Die geschichtliche Entwicklung der modernen Werttheorien* (1906), Topos Vaduz 1977, 2. Teil.

Kellenbenz, H. u R. Walter. In: *Handbuch der Europäischen Wirtschafts- und Sozialgeschichte*, W. Fischer (Hrsg.), Klett-Cotta Stuttgart 1986.

Kellenbenz, H. 'Nürnberger Handel um 1540.' *Mitteilungen des Vereins für Geschichte der Stadt Nürnberg*, Bd. 50, 1960.

Kennedy, Paul. *Rise and Fall of the Great Powers. Economic change and Military Conflict from 1500 to 2000*, Random House New York 1988.

Kluge, F. u. W. Mitzka. *Etymologisches Wörterbuch der deutschen Sprache*, 20. Aufl., de Greuter Berlin 1967.

Knapp, G. *Landarbeiter in Freiheit und Knechtschaft*, Duncker und Humblot Leipzig 1909.

Kobuch M. u. E. Müller (Hrsg.). *Der deutsche Bauernkrieg*, Weimar 1975. Aus den Staatsarchiven in Dresden und Weimar.

Koehler, L. u. W. Baumgartner. *Lexikon in Veteris Testamenti*, Brill Leiden 1958.

Krader, L. 'Ecology of Central Asian Pastoralism,' in: *Southwestern Journal of Anthropology*, Bd. 11, 1955.

*———. *Peoples of Central Asia*, Indiana University Press Bloomington 1963.

*———. *Anthropology and Early Law*, Basic Books New York 1966.

*———. 'Pastoralism' in: *International Encyclopaedia of the Social Sciences*. David Sills ed. New York 1968.

*———. *The Formation of the State*, Prentice-Hall Englewood Cliffs 1968.

———. *The Ethnological Notebooks of Karl Marx*, Van Gorcum Assen 1972.

———. *The Asiatic Mode of Production*, Van Gorcum Assen 1975.

———. *Dialectic of Civil Society*, Van Gorcum Assen 1976.

———. *A Treatise of Social Labor*. Van Gorcum Assen 1979.

*———. *Labor and Value*, C. Levitt (ed.) Peter Lang New York 2003.

*———. *Noetics: The Science of Thinking and Knowing*. C. Levitt (ed.) Peter Lang New York 2010.

Kriegk, L. G. *Frankfurter Bürgerzwiste im Mittelalter*, Sauerländer Frankfurt am Main 1862.

Kuchenbuch, L. (ed.), *Feudalismus-Materialien zur Theorie und Geschichte*, Ullstein Frankfurt am Main 1977.

Kulischer, J. *Allgemeine Wirtschaftsgeschichte*, Bd. I, II 1928, 2. Aufl., R. Oldenbourg München, 1958.

Landes, D. *Revolution in Time*, Harvard University Press Cambridge 1983.

Lasswitz, K. *Geschichte der Atomistik vom Mittelalter bis Newton*. Voss Hamburg und Leipzig 1890, Olms Verlag Hildesheim 1984.

Lautink-Ferguson, A. *Nature*, Bd. 330, 1987.

Leibniz, G. W. *Script. rer. Brunsv*. 1711.

Leonardo da Pisa *Liber abaci*, 1202.

Leuthold. 'Knappschaft.' *Ersch und Gruber, Encyklopadie*, Brockhaus Leipzig 1885.

*Levine, D. & K. Wrightson. *Whickham. An Industrial Society in the Pre-Industrial World*, Oxford University Press Oxford 1991.

*Levitt, C. 1978. 'L. Krader's Research on the Asiatic Mode of Production,' *Critique of Anthropology*, No. 11, 1978, pp. 39–56.

———. 'Dialectica y Sociedad Civil, primera parte,' *comunicación e informática*, Mexico, Vol. 2, no. 8, 1981 agosto, pp. 3–14.

———. 'Dialectica y Sociedad Civil, segunda parte,' *comunicación e informática*, Mexico, Vol. 2, no. 9, septiembre, pp. 3–14.

———. 'Dialectica y Sociedad Civil, primera parte,' *comunicación e informática*, Mexico, Vol. 2, no. 10, octubre, pp. 35–46.

*Levitt, C. & S. Sander (eds.). *Beyond the Juxtaposition of Nature and Culture*, Peter Lang New York 2017.

Lexis, W. *Handwörterbuch der Staatswissenschaften*. J. Conrad et al (Hrsg.), 3. Aufl., Gustav Fischer Jena 1911.

Lloyd, H. A. 'Mechanical Timekeepers.' In C. Singer et al. (Hrsg.), *A History of Technology*, Bd. 3, Oxford University Press Oxford 1957.

Luther, M. Von Kaufhandlung und Wucher, 1534.

Lütge, F. *Deutsche Sozial-und Wirtschaftsgeschichte*, 3. Aufl., Springer Berlin Heidelberg New York 1966.

———. *Geschichte der deutschen Agrarverfassung*, 2. Aufl., Ulmer Stuttgart 1976.

Mach, E. Die Mechanik in ihrer Entwicklung historisch-kritisch dargestellt, Brockhaus Leipzig 1883; 1976.

Machiavelli, N. *Il Principe*, 1532.

Maddalena A. De. In: *Europäische Wirtschaftsgeschichte*, Bd. 2, C. M. Cipolla, K. Borchardt (Hrsg.), Ficher Stuttgart 1979.

Maier, A. *Die Mechanisierung des Weltbildes*, Springer Berlin 1983.

Mantoux, P. *La révolution industrielle*, Paris: Société de librairie et d'édition Paris 1905, Paris 1973.

Marx, K. Briefwechsel mit F. Lassalle, 16. Januar 1861; mit F. Engels, 18. Juli 1862. Vgl. L. Krader, *The Ethnological Notebooks of Karl Marx*, Assen 1974. (dt. *Die ethnologischen Exzerpthefte von Karl Marx*, Suhrkamp 1976).

———. *Das Kapital*, Bde. I, III, Karl Marx/Friedrich Engels, Gesamtausgabe (MEGA), Berlin 1976.

———. *Zur Kritik der politischen* Ökonomie, Karl Marx/Friedrich Engels Gesamtausgabe (MEGA) II, Berlin 1976.

———. *Formen vorkapitalistischer Produktion*, H. P. Harstick (Hrsg.), Campus Frankfurt am Main 1977.

———. *Grundrisse der Kritik der politischen Ökonomie*. MEGA II, 1.2, Berlin 1981.

———. *Manuskript 1861–1863, Zur Kritik der politischen Ökonomie*, MEGA II, 3.6, Berlin 1982.

Maurice, K. *Die deutsche Räderuhr*, C.H. Beck München 1976.

Mendels, F. "'Proto-industrialization': the first phase of the industrialization process", *Journal of Economic History*, 31, 1971, 241–261.

Menninger, K. *Zahlwort und Ziffer*, 3. Aufl., Vandenhoeck und Ruprecht Göttingen 1979.

Mols, R. In: C. M. Cipolla (Hrsg.), *Wirtschaftsgeschichte Europas*, Bd. 2, Fischer Stuttgart 1979.

Mommsen, T. *Römische Geschichte*, 6. Aufl., Bd. l, 3. Buch, Kap. 12, Berlin 1874.

Mumford, L. *Technics and Civilization*, Harcourt Brace New York 1934.

———. *The Culture of Cities*, Harvest New York 1970.

Newton, Sir Isaac. *Mathematische Prinzipien der Naturlehre* (1686). J. P. Wolters (Hrsg.), Berlin 1872.

*Ogilvie, S. (ed.). *Germany: A New Social and Economic History. Vol. 2, 1630–1800*, Arnold London 1996.

*Ogilvie, S. & R. Overy, (eds.). *Germany: A New Social and Economic History. Vol. 3, Since 1800*, Arnold London 1996.

Olschki, L. *Marco Polo's Asia*, University of California Press Berkeley 1960.

Panofsky, E. *Albrecht Dürer*, 4. Aufl., Princeton University Press Princeton 1955 (dt. München 1977).

Pareto, V. *Trattato di sociologia generale*, 2. Aufl., Barbèra Florenz 1923.

Pirenne, H. *Mahomet et Charlemagne*, Alcan Paris 1937.

Pokorny, J. *Indogermanisches etymologisches Wörterbuch*, Francke Bern München 1959.

Preuss, H. *Die Entstehung des deutschen Städtewesens*, B. G. Teubner Leipzig 1906.

Ramelli, C. A. *Le Diverse et Artificiose Machine*, 1588. (*Schatzkammer Mechanischer Künste des … Herrn Augustini de Ramelli*, 1620).

Reininghaus, W. *Die Entstehung der Gesellengilden im Spätmittelalter*, Steiner Wiesbaden 1981.

———. 'Die Migration der Handwerkergesellen in der Zeit der Entstehung ihrer Gilden' (14. Bis 15. Jahrhundert), *Vierteljahrschrift für Sozial- und Wirtschaftsgeschichte* 68. Bd., H. 1 (1981), pp. 1–21.

———. „Das ‚ganze Haus' und die Gesellengilden," in R. S. Elkar (ed.) *Deutsches Handwerk in Spätmittelalter und früher Neuzeit*, Schwartz Göttingen 1983.

Reti, L. *The Unknown Leonardo*, McGraw Hill New York 1974.

Ries, A. *Rechenbüchlein uf den Linien mit Rechenpfenigen und Ein neu geordnet Visierbuch*, 1515.

———. *Mit Kreiden oder Schreibfedern durch die Zifferzahl zu rechnen*, 1520.

———. *Rechenbuch auf Linien und Ziffern*, Frankfurt am Main 1574.

Roscher, W. *Geschichte der Nationol-Oekonomik in Deutschland*, R. Oldenbourg München 1874.

Rossi, P. *Il filosofi e le Macchine*, Feltrinelli Milano 1962.

Rousseau, J. J. *Discourse on the Origins of Inequality among Men*, 1754.

Rudolff, C. *Künstliche Rechnung mit der Ziffer und mit den Zahlpfennigen*, Wien 1526.

———. 'Exempel vom Bergwerk,' in: Johannes Tropfke, *Geschichte der Elementarmathematik*, 4. Aufl. Bd. 1; K. Vogel et al. (Hrsg.), de Gruyter Berlin 1980.

Ruppel, A. *Johann Gutenberg*, 2. Aufl., Verlag Gebr. Mann Berlin 1947.

Rühlein von Calw. *Ein nützlich Bergbüchlein*, um 1500, 1527.

Rütten, Fr. 'Bergarbeiter'. *Staatslexikon*, 2. Aufl., Herder Verlag Freiburg 1926.

Sachs, H. u. J. Amman. *Eigentliche Beschreibung aller Stande auf Erden*. Verlegung Sigmund Feyerabends, Frankfurt am Main 1568.

Salamonio, M. S., *De Principotu*, 1544.

Sambursky, S. *Physical Thought*, Pica Press New York 1975.

*Sander, S., C. Levitt, & N. McLaughlin. "Beyond Fields, Networks, and Fame: Lawrence Krader as an 'Outsider' Intellectual". *Journal of the History of the Behavioral Sciences*, 53(2), 155–175 Spring 2017.

Santorio. *De medicina statica* 1614.

Schanz, G. 'Kolonisation und Industrie in Franken,' in „Bayrische Wirtschafts- und Verwaltungsstudien", Erlangen 1884.

Schelsky, H. *Der Mensch in der wissenschaftlichen Zivilisation*, Westdeutscher Verlag Köln-Opladen 1961.

Schirmer, A. *Wörterbuch der deutschen kaufmännischen Sprache*, Karl J. Trübner Strassburg 1911.

Schlumbohm, J. "'Proto-industrialization' as a research strategy and a historical period—a balance sheet", in Sheilagh C. Ogilvie and Markus Cerman, (eds.) *European Proto-Industrialization*, Cambridge University Press Cambridge 1996, 12–22.

Schmidt-Wiegand, R. *Die Bezeichnungen Zunft und Gilde in ihrem historischen und wortgeographischen Zusammenhang*. https://doi.org/10.11588/vuf.1985.0.15771.

Schmoller, G. *Jahrbuch für Gesetzgebung, Verwaltung und Volkswirtschaft im Deutschen Reich*, Vols. 14–17, Duncker und Humblot Leipzig 1890–1893.

Schoenlank, B. *Soziale Kämpfe vor dreihundert Jahren*, 2. Aufl., Duncker und Humblot Leipzig 1907.

Schoenlank, B. & G. Schonz. „Gesellenverbände". *Handwörterbuch der Staatswissenschaften*, 3. Aufl., J. Conrad et al. (ed.), Gustav Fischer Jena 1909.

Schopper, H. *Panoplia mechanicarum aut sedentarium,* Frankfurt am Main 1568.

———. *De Omnibus illiberalibus sive mechanicis artibus*, Frankfurt am Main 1574.

*Schorkowitz, D. (Hg.). *Ethnohistorische Wege und Lehrjahre eines Philosophen: Festschrift für Lawrence Krader zum 75. Geburtstag*. Peter Lang, Frankfurt am Main, 1995.

Schönberg, G. *Zur wirtschaftlichen Bedeutung des deutschen Zunftwesens im Mittelalter*. Ernst Siegried Mittler und Sohn Berlin 1868.

Schreiber, E. *Die volkswirtschaftlichen Anschauungen der Scholastik*, Jena 1913.

Schreittmann, C. Probierbüchlin. *Frembde und subtile Kunst, vormals im Truck nie gesehen, von Woge und Gewicht/ auch von aller handt Proben/ auff Ertz, Golt, Silber und andere Metall etc. Nützlich und gut allen denen so mit subtilen Künsten der Bergwerck umgehen*. Frankfurt am Mayn bei Christian Egenolffs seligen Erben, in Veregung Doct. Adami Loniceri, Doct. Johannis Cnipii Andronici Secundi und Pauli Steinmeyers 1578.

Schumpeter, J. A. *History of Economic Analysis*, Oxford University Press New York 1954 (dt. *Geschichte der ökonomischen Analyse*, Göttingen 1965).

Schwarz, M. *Copia und Abschrift ab und von Matheus Schwarzen eigne Handschrift, was das Buchhalten sei. Die Musterbuchhandlung mit Beispielen dem Fugger-Geschäft in Venedig entnommen*, 1516–1550.

*Scribner, B. (ed.). *Germany A New Social and Economic History*. Vol. 1, 1450–1630. Arnold London 1996.

Simmel, G. *Philosophie des Geldes*, Duncker und Humblot München Leipzig 1930.

Singer, C. *From Magic to Science*, Dover New York 1958.

———. *A Short History of Scientific Ideas*, Oxford University Press Oxford 1982.

Slicher v. Bath, B. H. In *Cambridge Economic History of Europe*, Vol. 5, Cambridge University Press Cambridge 1977.

Smith, A. *Wealth of Nations*, 1776.

Smith, C. S. 'A Sixteenth-Century Decimal System of Weights,' *Isis*, Bd. 46, 1955.

Sohm, R., L. Mitteis, & L. Menger. *Institutionen. Geschichte und System des römischen Privatrechts*, Duncker und Humblot Berlin 1930.

Sombart, W. *Das Europäische Wirtschaftsleben im Zeitalter des Frühkapitalismus vornehmlich im 16., 17. und 18. Jahrhundert*, Duncker und Humblot Berlin (1902) 1969.

———. *Der Moderne Kapitalismus*, Bd. 1, 1. Halbbd. Dunker und Humblot München und Leipzig 1921.

———. *Die Juden und das Wirtschaftsleben*, Dunker und Humblot Berlin 1911.

Sonnemann, R. *Geschichte der Technik*, Vorwort Leipzig 1978.

Sprandel, R. *Das Eisengewerbe im Mittelalter*, Anton Hiersemann Stuttgart 1968.

———. In: H. Aubin, W. Zorn (Hrsg.), *Handbuch der deutschen Wirtschafts-und Sozialgeschichte*, Union Verlag Stuttgart 1971.

Steinberg, S. H. *500 Years of Printing*, 3rd ed., Pelican London 1974.

Stevin, S. *De Thiende (Das Zehnte)*, 1595 in den Niederlanden.

Stieda, W. *Jahrbücher für Nationalökonomie und Statistik*, Bd. 8, Gustav Fischer Jena 1867.

———. *Zur Entstehung des deutschen Zunftwesens*, Jena 1877. Conrad et al. (Hrsg.) 'Das Zunftwesen.' *Handwörterbuch der Staatswissenschaften*, 3. Aufl., Duncker und Humblot Jena 1911.

Stifel, M. (Stiefel). *Die Coss Christoph Rudolphs mit schönen Exempeln gebessert*, Königsberg 1553/54.

———. *Deutsche Arithmetica inhaltend die Haussrechnung, die deutsche Coss*, Nürnberg 1545.

Strauss, G. *Nürnberg in the Sixteenth Century*, John Wiley Hoboken 1966.

Strieder, J. *Studien zur Geschichte kapitalistischer Organisationsformen*, 2. Aufl., Duncker und Humblot München Leipzig 1925.

Sweezy, P. M. In: R. H. Hilton (eds.), *The Transition from Feudalism to Capitalism*, 2. Aufl., New Left Books London 1976 (dt. Frankfurt 1984).

Swetz, F. J. *Capitalism & Arithmetic. Including the text of the Treviso Arithmetic of 1478*, D. E. Smith transl. Open Court Chicago 1987.

Tait, H. *Clocks and Watches*, British Museum London 1983.

Thompson, E. P. *The Making of the English Working Class*, Pelican London 1968.

———. *Poverty of Theory*, Merlin Press London 1978.

Troeltsch, E. *Die Kulturbedeutung des Calvinismus*, KGA 8, 150 1910.

———. *Der Historismus und seine Probleme*, Kap. III, § 6 C, J.C.B. Mohr Tübingen 1922.

———. *Aufsätze zur Geistesgeschichte und Religionssoziologie*, III, §§ 4–5, J.C.B. Mohr Tübingen 1925.

Tropfke, J. *Geschichte der Elementarmathematik*, 4. Aufl., Bd. 1, K. Vogel et al. (Hrsg.), Berlin 1980.

Usher, A. P. 'Machines and Mechanism,' in: C. Singer et al., *A History of Technology*, Bd. 3, Oxford University Press Oxford 1957.

Vasari, G. *Le Vite de' più Eccelenti Pittori, Scultori e Architettori* (1550). 2. Aufl., 1568.

Vogel, K. 'Fibonacci,' *Dictionary of Scientific Biography* Charles Scribner New York 1980.

Waerden, B. L. v.d. *A History of Algebra*, Springer Verlag Berlin Heidelberg 1985.

Wagenbreth, O. u. E. Wachtler (eds.). *Der Freiberger Bergbau*, Springer Spektrum Leipzig 1985.

Wagner, U. *Das Bamburger Rechenbuch von 1483*. E. Schröder (ed.) Akademie Verlag Berlin 1988.

Weber, M. *Gesammelte Aufsätze zur Religionssoziologie*, Bd. II, 2. Aufl., J.C.B. Mohr Tübingen 1922.

———. *Die protestantische Ethik II*, J. Winckelmann (Hrsg.), Hamburg 1972.

———. *Wirtschaft und Gesellschaft*, 5. Aufl. V. § II, J.C.B. Mohr Tübingen, 1972.

———. *Wirtschaftsgeschichte*, Duncker und Humblot Berlin 1981.

Weitnauer, A. *Venezianischer Handel der Fugger, nach der Musterbuchhandlung des Mattaeus Schwarz*, München Leipzig 1931.

Werner, T. G. 'Die große Fusion der Zechen um den Rappolt von 1514.' *Mitteilungen des Vereins für Geschichte der Stadt Nürnberg*, Bd. 57, 1970.

Wiegmann, H. & R. Specht. 'Bergarbeiter.' *Staatslexikon*, 6th ed. Herder Verlag Freiburg 1957.

Wilsdorf, H. u. W. Quellmalz. *Bergwerke und Huttenwesen der Agricola-Zeit*, VEB Verlag der deutschen Wissenschaften Berlin 1971.

Wis, M. *Ricerchi sopra gli italianismi nella lengua tedesca*, Societa' ne'ofilolofica Helsinki 1955.

Wittfogel, K. A. *Oriental Despotism: A Comparative Study of Total Power*, Yale University Press New Haven 1957.

*Wrigley, E. A. *Energy and the English Industrial Revolution*, Cambridge University Press Cambridge 2010.

Zimmermann, W. *Allgemeine Geschichte des großen Bauernkrieges*, 1841–1843, F.H. Köhler Stuttgart.

Illustrations

Der Bauwr

Ich aber bin von art ein Bauwr/
Mein Arbeit wirt mir schwer und sauwr/
Ich muß Ackern/Gern und Egn/
Schneyden/Mehen/Heuwen dargegn/
Holzen und einführn Hew und Treyd/
Gült vu Steuwr macht mir viel hertzleid
Trinck Wasser und iß grobes Brot/
Wie denn der Herr Adam gebot.

The Peasant

I am a peasant of sorts/
My labour is getting hard and sour/
I have to plough, reap, and harrow/
Cutting, mowing, and make hay/
Chopping wood and bringing in hay and straw/
Money and taxes cause me much heartache
Drink water and eat coarse bread/
As the Lord ordered Adam to do.

Der Müller

Wer Korn und Weitz zu malen hat/
Der bring mirs in die Mül herab/
Denn schütt ichs zwischen den Mühlstein
Und Mal es sauber rein und klein/
Die Kleyen gib ich treuwlich zu/
Hirsch, Erbeiß ich auch neuwen thu/
Dergleich thu ich auch Stockfisch bleuwn/
Würtz stoß ich auch mit ganzen treuwen.

The Miller

Who has grain and wheat to grind/
Should bring it down to me in the mill
For when I dump it into the millstone
And grind it neatly pure und small/
I faithfully add the bran/
Deer, peas I do also take/

Likewise, do I do with dried cod/
I also ground up spices with all my faith.

Der Bierbreuwer

Aus Gersten sied ich gutes Bier/
Feißt und Süß/ auch bitter monier/
In ein Breuwkessel weit und groß/
Darein ich denn den Hopffen stoß/
Laß den in Brennten külen baß/
Damit füll ich darnach die Faß
Wol gebunden und wol gebicht/
Denn giert er und ist zugericht.

The Beer Brewer

From barley I boil good beer/
Portly and sweet, also of bitter manner/
In a brewing kettle wide and large/
That is where I pound the hops/

I let the burning cool down well/
With it I fill the barrels
Well-bound and well-sealed/
Then it ferments and is well made.

Der Buchbinder

Ich bind allerley Bücher ein/
Geistlich und Weltlich/ groß und klein/
In Perment oder Bretter nur
Und beschlags mit guter Clausur
Und Spangen/ und stempff die zur zier/
Ich sie auch im anfang planier/
Etlich vergüld ich auff dem schnitt/
Da verdien ich viel geldes mit.

The Book Binder

I bind all sorts of books/
Spiritual and secular, large and small/

In parchment or in boards alone
And seal it with good book covers
And clasps that I stamp for decoration/
I level it from the start/
Many I gild the spine/
For I make a lot of money doing that.

Der Kauffman

Ich aber bin ein Handelsmann/
Hab mancherley Wahren bey mir stan/
Würtz/Arlas/Thuch/Wolln vu Flachß.
Sammat/Seiden/Honig und Wachß/
And ander Wahr hie ungennant/
Die führ ich eyn und aus dem Land/
Mit grosser sorg und gfehrlichkeit
Wann mich auch offt das unglück reit.

The Merchant

But I am a merchant
I have a lot of goods on hand
Spices, woven fabrics from Arlas, cloth, wool and flax
Velvet, silk, honey and wax
And other goods not mentioned
That I import and export
With great care and risk
Even when misfortune often comes my way.

Der Krämer

Ich bin ein Krämer langejar/
Kompt/ und kaufft hie mancherley Wahr/
Als Brüch/Pfaffen und Schlötterlein/
Item/Würtz/Zucker und Brentn Wein/
Spiegel/Schelln/ Käm/ nadl vu Harbat/
Keckkuchn/Nestel und Brillen gnannt/
Die Krämerey mancherley Wahrn/

Erfand lieber Pater vor jarn.

The Shopkeeper

I've been a shopkeeper for a long time/
Come and buy all kinds of goods here/
Such as knickers, pipes and little rattles
As well as spices, sugar and brandy/
Mirrors, Combs, needles and herbal tea/
Bundtcake, belt loops and straps and so-called glasses/
The grocery store has many goods/
Established by dear Forefathers many years ago.

Quelle: Deutsche Fotothek

Der Bergknapp

Ich treib alles Ertz Knappenwerck/
Im Thal und auff Sanct Annen Berg/
Mit den Steigern/Knappen und Bubn
In Stollen/ Schacht und den Erzgrubn/

Mit graben/zimmern/boltzn und bauwn/
Mit eynfahren/brechen und hauwn/
Wird ich fündig und Silber bring/
So ist der Bergherr guter ding.

The Miner

I work at mining all kinds of ore
In the valley and on Saint Annenberg
With climbers, miners and laboring youth
In tunnels and shaft and the pits of ore
With digging, carpentry, bolting and building
With driving in, breaking and hewing
I strike a bonanza and bring the silver
That way the mine owner is in good spirits.

Der Beutler

Hierher zu mir wer kauffen wil/

Hie find ir gmachter arbeit viel/
Hirschn, Semich, Egrisch un Preussisch/
Cöllsch, Schaffen, Kelbren un Reusisch/
Manns wetschger gemacht allerhandt/
Auch Händtschuch mancher art genannt/
Darzu Frauwen Beutel wolgschaffn/
Auch für Beuwrlin, Münch un Pfaffen.

The Bag-Maker

Come here to me who wants to buy
Here you find many designed pieces
Made of deerskin, chamois leather, Egrian
Prussian and Cologne leather
Made of sheep- and calf leather as well as Russian leather
Various bags and purses for men
Also cloves of various kinds
And as well beautiful women's bags
And for farmers, monks and priests.
Translator's note

chamois leather = a very soft and washable leather, produced by fat tanning
Egrian = leather from Eger (German: Erlau), a city in the Northeastern part of Hungary
Russian leather = a leather that receives a specific scent through a special tanning process, produced in Russia
Wetschger = medieval term for a purse with a snap closure or for a travel bag (coat sack)

Dürer. Unterweisung.

Welicher ein victoria auf richten wolt darumb das er die aufrürischen baurn uberwundern het der möchte sich eins solichen gezeugs darzu gebrauchen. – das dryt büchlein.

Dürer. Briefing.

Whoever wants to erect a victory column for having overcome the rebellious peasants may make use of such a thing. – The third booklet.

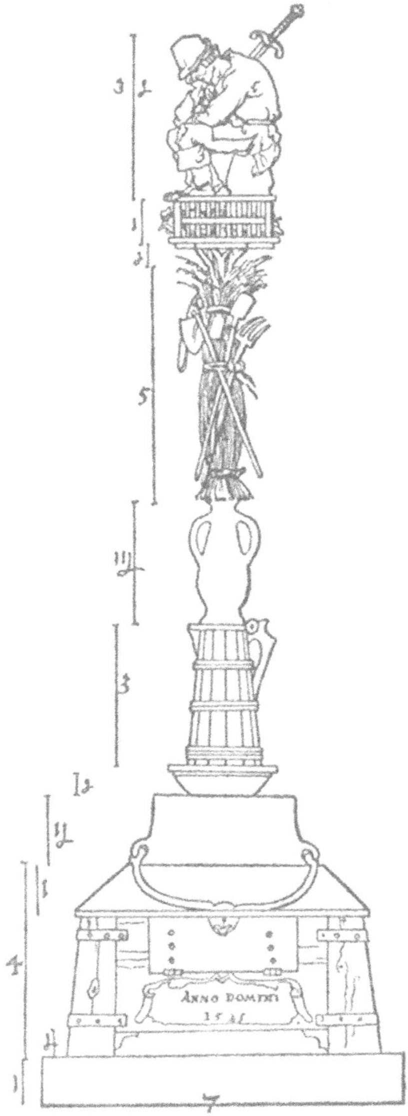

10.

Albrecht Dürer: Ritter, Tod und Teufel, 1513
Albrecht Dürer: Knight, Death and Devil, 1513

Albrecht Dürer: Melencolia I, 1514

Gregor Reisch. Margarita Philosophica.
(Die Philosophische Perle.) Freiburg 1503, 1. Aufl.
Dieselbe Vorstellung des Wettbewerbs zwischen den beiden Rechensystemen wie bei Adam Ries. Das Rechnen mit Ziffern oder indo-arabischen Zahlen immer links, mit dem Rechenbrett und Rechenpfennigen auf Linien und Spatien immer rechts. Der Typus Arithmeticae auf der Baustrophedon- (Βους, griechisch Ochs) Schreibweise, nach der Art, wie die Ochsen beim Pflügen sich wenden (Pape); dieselbe Schreibweise trifft den Namen von Boetius und Pythagoras auf dem

Titelblatt von Reisch. Man suchte nach dem mythischen Erfinder, hier Boetius, des Rechensystems mit der Feder, und Pythagoras mit Linien und Spatien, die an die Geometrie erinnern. Ähnliche Erfinder aus der Mythologie befinden sich bei Agricola und Hans Sachs (s. unten). Oben links bei Köbel ein Brett mit den indo-arabischen Zahlen.

Gregor Reisch. Margarita Philosophica.
(The Philosophical Pearl.) Freiburg 1503. 1st edition

The same presentation of the contest between the two systems of calculation as in Adam Ries. Calculating with numerals of Indo-Arabic numbers always left, with the abacus and calculating pennies on lines and spaces always right. The type of arithmetic on the baustrophedon writing style (Βους, English ox), in the way oxen turn when ploughing (Pape). The same notation corresponds to the names of Boetius and Pythagoras on the title page of Reisch. One is trying to find the mythical inventor, here Boetius, of the system of calculation with the feather pen, and Pythagoras with lines and spaces, which call to mind geometry. Similar inventors from mythology are found in Agricola and Hans Sachs. (see below). Above left in Köbel a board with Indo-Arabic numbers.

Jakob Köbels Rechenbuch 1544

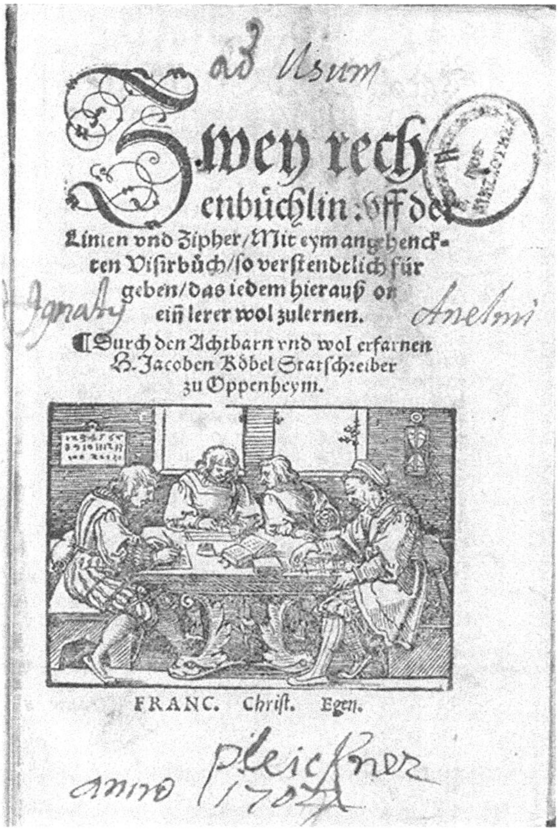
Zwey rech
enbüchlin: vff der
Linien vnd Zipher/ Mit eym angehenck-
ten Visirbůch/ so verstendtlich für
geben/ das iedem hierauß on
eyn lerer wol zulernen.
Durch den Achtbarn vnd wol erfarnen
H. Jacoben Köbel Statschreiber
zu Oppenheym.
FRANC. Christ. Egen.

Das Probierbüchlein von Rülein von Calw um 1500
The Little Assaying Book by Rülein von Calw around 1500

Probier büch-
lein/auff Gold/Silber/kupffer/
und Bley/Auch allerlay Metall
wie man die zů nutz arbayten vñ
Probieren soll.
Allē Müntzmaystern/Wardeyn/Golt
werckern/Bercklewten/ vñ kauffleütē
der Metall zů nutz mit grossem fleyß zů
samen gebracht.

Abb. 19
Förderung auf Saumtieren mittels Lutten, in Schubkarren, in zweirädrigen Karren und um Wagen.
Pferde mit Saumsätteln A. Eine Sturzrolle, geneigt an den Felsen gestellt B. Die zugehörigen Bretter C. Der Karren mit einem Rade D. Der zweirädrige Karren E. Baumstämme F. Der Wagen G. Das Erz wird vom Wagen abgeladen H. Die Riegel I. Der Steiger, der die Anzahl Wagen am Kerbholz verzeichnet K. Die Behälter, in die die Erze zur Verteilung geworfen werden.

Das sechßt bůch cxxxiij

Die erdt oder geschub der gsteinen / werffendt die knaben oder menner mitt den schäufflen in die geuäß / oder werffendts mitt den henden hinein / dahär sie
m die

Mining on pack animals by means of piping, in push cars, in two wheeled carts and in wagons.

Horses with pack saddles A. A support roller, sloping against a rock B. The boards that belong to it C. Cars with one wheel D. The two-wheeled cars E. Tree trunks F. The wagon G. The ore is unloaded from the wagon H. Locking bars I. The climber, who lists the number of wagons at the notched counting stick. K. the tanks into which the ore is thrown for distribution.

Abb. 48
Bellows driven by manpower, by treadle and horse and by horse on a horse-gin. The first described machine A. The worker who squeezes the bellows by treading B. The bellows without mouthpieces. C. The opening through which the heavy weather or air is expelled D. The lutes E. The tunnel F. The second machine described G. The wooden drum H. Their levels I. The perimeter fence K. The round hole in the drum L. The pole M. The third machine described N. The stationary wave O. Its gear wheel P. The horizontal wave Q. Its gearbox.

Das Klauben der Erze. Männer- und Frauenarbeit
Picking out the ore: Man´s work, woman´s work

Abb. 2
Das Scheiden geschmeidiger Erze

Eine Stufe Erz A. Der Quetscher B. Der eiserne Meißel C. Der Stock D. Die Schere
Image 2.
Separating of soft ore
A level of ore A. The crusher B. The iron chisel C. The stick D. The shears

Index

www.ingramcontent.com/pod-product-compliance
Ingram Content Group UK Ltd.
Pitfield, Milton Keynes, MK11 3LW, UK
UKHW020838290926
15470UKWH00004B/1424

9 781433 172106